PRAISE FOR

LEARNING SCIENCE

Learning Science is an ambitious field that now has an ambitious book. Robert S. Feldman has brought together a stunning array of authors who describe an equally stunning array of topics, problems, methods, and perspectives—all aimed at shining light on those important moments when productive learning occurs. When Magellan's crew first sailed around the globe they learned firsthand that it's a really big world out there. Similarly, Feldman has circumnavigated what is currently a varied and exciting world that, in his words, currently "lacks agreed upon boundaries, theoretical approaches, and research methodologies." That's all the more reason to explore it. This book brings us some of the best of that world, currently tied together by the editor's and authors' creative commitments to develop a science of learning.

—Donald J. Foss, PhD,
Department of Psychology, University of Houston and
author of *Your Complete Guide to College Success*

Some fields, like medicine, change their practice quickly. No one would want to treat their illnesses with patent medicines from a century ago. But the wheels of education grind slowly, and much of what schools do today closely resembles what they did a century ago. Unfortunately, many of the changes they make are not even positive. Have you tried to help your children on, or even tried to make sense of, their Common Core math homework? A large part of the problem is that the science of learning has been so utterly divorced from educational practice. Robert Feldman's book presents contributions by many of the leading experts in learning science. These experts describe not only the innovations and the theories behind them, but also, concretely how to apply these innovations in educational practice. Anyone who cares about learning and seeing students learn in ways that reflect the science of the 21st century rather than of times in the distant past will want to read this book.

—Robert J. Sternberg, PhD,
Professor of Human Development, Cornell University

LEARNING SCIENCE

Theory, Research, & Practice

EDITED BY
ROBERT S. FELDMAN

McGraw Hill

New York Chicago San Francisco Athens London Madrid
Mexico City Milan New Delhi Singapore Sydney Toronto

1 2 3 4 5 6 7 8 9 BNG 24 23 22 21 20 19

ISBN 978-1-260-45799-5
MHID 1-260-45799-0

e-ISBN 978-1-260-45800-8
e-MHID 1-260-45800-8

CONTENTS

PART III

FROM THEORY AND RESEARCH TO EDUCATIONAL PRACTICE

CONTRIBUTORS

Russell Almond, Florida State University
Juliana Ma. Alexandra L. Andres, University of Pennsylvania
Ryan Baker, University of Pennsylvania
Zhiqiang Cai, Central China Normal University and University of Memphis
Britte Haugan Cheng, Menlo Education Research
Courtney B. (Wong) Chin, Sesame Workshop
Mutlu Cukurova, UCL Knowledge Lab, University College London
Chris Dede, Harvard Graduate School of Education
Susan Fuhrman, Teachers College, Columbia University
Arthur C. Graesser, University of Memphis
Tina Grotzer, Harvard Graduate School of Education
Neil T. Heffernan, Worcester Polytechnic Institute
Xiangen Hu, Central China Normal University and University of Memphis
Tanya Joosten, University of Wisconsin—Milwaukee
Amy Kamarainen, Harvard Graduate School of Education
Fengfeng Ke, Florida State University
Jennifer A. Kotler, Sesame Workshop
Richard C. Larson, Massachusetts Institute of Technology
Xi Lu, Florida State University
Rose Luckin, UCL Knowledge Lab, University College London
Shari Metcalf, Harvard Graduate School of Education
M. Elizabeth Murray, Massachusetts Institute of Technology
Jaclyn L. Ocumpaugh, University of Pennsylvania
Andrew Olney, Central China Normal University and University of Memphis
Korinn S. Ostrow, Worcester Polytechnic Institute
Seyedahmad Rahimi, Florida State University
Valerie Shute, Florida State University
Ginny Smith, Florida State University
Rosemarie T. Truglio, Sesame Workshop
Melina R. Uncapher, University of California, San Francisco

PREFACE

This is an exciting moment in the development of learning science, an increasingly influential, cross-disciplinary field that focuses on the scientific principles that underlie learning, teaching, and educational practice. Spanning the disciplines of psychology, data science, cognitive science, sociology, anthropology, and other fields that touch on education, it brings a unique approach to the urgent issue of how we can best educate students in the 21st century.

Using data analytics, adaptive technologies, and other research tools and techniques, and bringing to bear the perspectives and methodologies of their particular disciplines, learning scientists share the goal of maximizing student success. Learning science thus represents a unique combination of theory, research, and practice that holds the promise of improving educational outcomes and driving social policy. In short, learning science is increasingly recognized as a field that is uniquely positioned to solve our most pressing educational issues.

The work of the authors in this volume represents the most contemporary approaches and perspectives on learning science. Taking a variety of approaches, the contributors consider the ways in which learning science can impact our understanding of the factors that underlie learning and teaching. Moreover, they provide examples of how a deeper understanding of learning science can improve the practice of education.

The authors have sought to show the links between their own research, its theoretical underpinnings, and the applications that can be drawn from their work. In addition, each of the chapters ends with the authors' prognostications of where the field of learning science is heading.

This book is divided into three parts. Part I grounds the volume with an overview of the theoretical and philosophical foundations of learning science. In Chapter 1, Graesser looks at what he calls intelligent agents, which virtually adapt to the behavior and psychological states of learners. He argues that the use of such intelligent agents, using natural language, allows for truly deep learning.

Addressing the limitations of traditional theoretical conceptions and measures of intelligence, in Chapter 2, Luckin and Cukurova use multimodal learning analytics to illustrate how a combination of cognitive and social factors need to be taken into account as we address what we mean by intelligence. In two compelling case studies, they show the importance of collaborative problem solving in widening our understanding of what is seen as intelligent behavior.

In Chapter 3, Joosten focuses on issues relating to philosophy of science. By looking at the development of the social sciences as sciences, she offers insights into the underpinnings of the evolution of learning science.

In Chapter 4, Hu, Cai, and Olney elucidate a sophisticated mathematical framework, Semantic Representation and Analysis (SRA). Using SRA, they illustrate the development of conversation-based intelligent learning environments to drive student performance.

Part II of the book explores novel and promising perspectives on learning science. For example, in Chapter 5, Baker, Ocumpaugh, and Andres discuss a sophisticated and well-validated methodology for collecting real-time measures of classroom behavior. Employing a cross-cultural lens to demonstrate the applicability of their work across diverse cultures, they have developed a way to measure student engagement and affect.

In a wide-ranging chapter (Chapter 6), Uncapher and Cheng introduce the discipline of learning engineering, in which the principles of learning science are used to create solutions to persistent educational challenges. Drawing on the findings from such diverse fields as medicine and neuroscience, the authors illustrate the value of multidisciplinary approaches.

Part II ends with Fuhrman's chapter (Chapter 7), which examines the implications of learning sciences for schools and colleges of education. She critically analyzes the state of teacher education today and how advances in learning science require new and innovative approaches to teacher training.

Part III focuses on the direct applications of learning science to educational practice. In Chapter 8, Ostrow and Heffernan describe a robust and well-validated online learning platform, ASSISTments, that provides students with immediate feedback and teachers with actionable assessments. They comprehensively delineate the issues involved in creating and validating programs that offer online teaching and teacher support.

Chapter 9 describes work being done by Dede, Grotzer, Kamarainen, and Metcalf on immersive technologies. They describe research in which students work together to solve real-world problems through immersion in virtual environments, resulting in increased understanding of complex STEM principles and producing higher student motivation.

Larson and Murray discuss the development of over 200 interactive video lessons in Chapter 10. Focusing on the STEM fields, the lessons developed under the BLOSSOMS rubric, which has been used around the world, facilitate project-based learning that triggers critical thinking.

In Chapter 11, Kotler, Chin, and Truglio illustrate how the theoretical richness of learning science plays out in a very applied setting: the development of television programming for children. Drawing on a variety of theoretical perspectives, they show how the impact of learning science extends far beyond the classroom.

Finally, Chapter 12, by Shute, Ke, Almond, Rahimi, Smith, and Lu, provides considerable insight into the challenges of developing a game, *Physics Playground*, that is compelling to learners and also brings about significant learning, while at the same time providing significant assessment capabilities. The authors brilliantly address these issues, and they illustrate the tremendous care required in constructing effective games.

LESSONS LEARNED

Several larger lessons, and a few predictions, can be drawn from the work described in these chapters. Among the most significant takeaways:

- ***Learning science is not yet a unified discipline.*** The blessing, and the curse, of learning science today is that it is far from a unified discipline. It lacks agreed-upon boundaries, theoretical approaches, and research methodologies. This messiness is an advantage in that it allows researchers and theoreticians free rein to draw upon multiple disciplines and approaches. On the other hand, the wild-west nature of learning science today may slow progress as scientists are impeded in their efforts to build upon prior work in an orderly fashion. Still, as the chapters in this volume illustrate, the lack of unity can lead to a creative climate in which important advances can be envisioned (for an excellent example, see Uncapher and Cheng's Chapter 6).

- ***Learning science needs a clear, agreed-upon vocabulary.*** Related to the fact that learning science is not a unified discipline is the lack of clarity even in describing the field. One example is the question of whether we should be discussing "learning science" or "learning sciences." Careful readers of this volume will note that some chapters speak of "learning science" (as in this Preface), while other chapters append the *s* to the term. It may seem like a trivial point, but nomenclature matters, driving the field in subtle, yet important, ways. We need to come to some agreement on terminology.

- ***Work in learning science focuses disproportionately on STEM disciplines.*** As illustrated by the chapters in this volume (e.g., Chapter 12 by Shute et al. and Chapter 9 by Dede et al.), great effort has been focused on applying learning science to STEM disciplines. That's understandable: arguably the greatest need is to educate the next generation in math and the sciences. (At least those are the disciplines in which students often have the greatest obvious needs, and traditional teaching techniques have been least effective.) Furthermore, as Fuhrman points out in Chapter 7, the developers of learning science–based innovations are largely housed in STEM-related fields. This is a limitation of the kinds of educational solutions being developed today, and it is clear that for learning science to advance, we need to extend the range of approaches to additional disciplinary areas such as in the humanities, foreign languages, and the social sciences.

- ***The proliferation of learning science degree programs will accelerate the development of the field.*** Already, many major universities have developed programs in learning science, and it seems likely that additional programs will be established. This increase in formal degree programs undoubtedly will hasten progress in learning science as new generations of scholars devote themselves to the field.

- ***Learning science, which has focused largely on cognitive factors in education, will broaden to encompass social-emotional and affective factors.*** As the Graesser (Chapter 1), Luckin and Cukurova (Chapter 2), and Baker, Ocumpaugh, and Andres (Chapter 5) chapters illustrate, social-emotional and affective factors can have as significant an effect on educational success as cognitive variables. In order for learning science to develop, the field will need to take noncognitive factors into account more systematically.

- ***Adaptive technologies and artificial intelligence hold great promise.*** Throughout this volume, research using adaptive technologies, driven by artificial intelligence algorithms, has yielded significant advances in promoting student success. It is hard to envision how this trend will not increase. As the proliferation of adaptive technologies increases, it will raise not only pedagogical issues in terms of the role of teachers and technology, but also philosophical issues regarding the nature of intelligence and what it means to be human.

- ***Advances in our understanding of learning science need to be translated into teacher training.*** The average curriculum provided to prospective teachers during their training contains precious little instruction in learning science, as Fuhrman points out in Chapter 7. Making the leap from the lab to the classroom is a critical step that learning scientists need to facilitate. Armed with formidable information derived on their students' performance, teachers need to be able to incorporate the data into their teaching (as shown in the wonderful examples provided by Ostrow and Heffernan in Chapter 8). How we motivate teachers to make use of the data provided by learning science, and how they can do it effectively, are crucial questions learning scientists have yet to fully come to grips with.

As these issues illustrate, learning science is experiencing some growing pains as it evolves into a full-fledged, sophisticated science. Still, it is a time full of promise for solving what is undoubtedly one of the critical issues of our time: how do we most effectively educate students to reach their full potential?

How incredibly exciting to be on the cusp of a new era in education. Although the quest to develop a viable science of learning is in some ways just beginning, the potential of learning science seems boundless.

Robert S. Feldman
Amherst, Massachusetts

ACKNOWLEDGMENTS

Many of the chapters in this volume were written by members of the McGraw-Hill Learning Science Advisory Board. I am grateful to McGraw-Hill for supporting the publication of this book and for encouraging the development of the discipline of learning science. In addition, much of the work reported in individual chapters was supported by various federal, state, and foundation-based grants. They are acknowledged in the individual chapters. Finally, I am grateful to each of the chapter authors. They have given generously of their time in producing interesting and groundbreaking chapters, and their work serves both as a model for future investigation and to advance the field in significant ways.

ABOUT THE EDITOR

Robert S. Feldman is professor of psychological and brain sciences, and senior advisor to the chancellor, at the University of Massachusetts Amherst. His interests include the social psychology of education and the promotion of student success. He is a fellow of the American Association for the Advancement of Science, the American Psychological Association, and the American Psychological Society, and he serves as chair of the McGraw-Hill Learning Science Advisory Board.

PART I

Foundations of Learning Science

CHAPTER 1

Learning Science Principles and Technologies with Agents That Promote Deep Learning

Arthur C. Graesser
University of Memphis

ABSTRACT

This chapter describes some attempts to promote deep learning through principles of learning science and technologies with computer agents. Learning environments with conversational agents have been developed to serve as substitutes for human tutors, teachers, peers, and students. The agents can be programmed to apply learning science principles systematically at varying degrees of computational sophistication. The most rudimentary agents deliver instruction, tell the learners what to do next, and interact with other agents to model ideal behavior, strategies, reflections, and social interactions. Intelligent agents are adaptive to the learners' actions, verbal contributions, emotions, and other psychological states. For example, AutoTutor helps students learn by holding a dialogue in natural language or staging a three-way *trialogue* that has two agents interacting with the student. These agent-based systems have often facilitated deep learning more than conventional learning environments on a variety of subject matters and skills, including science, technology, engineering, mathematics, research methods, metacognition, and reading comprehension. This chapter describes some agent-based learning environments that have been developed to improve deep learning in reading comprehension, use of hypermedia, conversational interaction, instructional games, academic arguments, and collaborative problem solving.

A contrast is frequently made between shallow and deep knowledge, although the boundary between them is fuzzy rather than crisp (Bransford, Brown, & Cocking, 2000; Chi, 2009; Graesser, 2015; Hattie & Donoghue, 2016; Millis, Long, Magliano, & Wiemer, 2019). Shallow knowledge of a subject matter includes recognition of key terms, their features, simple definitions, and routine skills and procedures to complete specific tasks. Deep knowledge is achieved to the extent that learners comprehend difficult technical material, construct mental models of systems, solve problems, justify claims with evidence and logical arguments, identify inaccurate information, resolve contradictions, quantify ideas precisely, and build artifacts. It is much more difficult to acquire deep knowledge than shallow knowledge. Consequently, people settle for shallow knowledge on a topic unless deep knowledge is needed in schools, employment, or attempts to overcome obstacles in achieving important goals in life.

Shallow knowledge is not sufficient for an increasing number of tasks in the 21st century. Citizens are now faced with complex technologies, social systems, and subject matters that require deeper knowledge (Levy & Murnane, 2006; National Research Council [NRC], 2012). Deep knowledge and reasoning skills are necessary for individuals who desire higher-paying jobs (Autor, Levy, & Murnane, 2003; Carnevale & Smith, 2013) whereas the routine tasks are increasingly being replaced by automated technologies (Elliot, 2017).

There are two broad approaches to meeting these demands for deeper knowledge among citizens. One approach is to increase deep learning in individuals through education and training in schools and the workforce. This chapter describes how this can be accomplished through digital technologies that implement principles of learning and instruction that have been identified in the learning sciences. A second approach is to train the citizens how to better participate in collaborative problem solving so that groups can collectively master and implement deep knowledge. Collaborative cognition is becoming increasingly prevalent as societies involve multiple stakeholders and become more dependent on deep knowledge for solutions to difficult problems (Fiore, 2008; Hall et al., 2018). Collaborative problem solving is being targeted for training and assessment because it is critical to efficiency, effectiveness, and innovation in the modern global economy (Fiore, Graesser, & Greiff, 2018; Graesser, Fiore et al., 2018; OECD, 2013). Technology once again will play an important role in the collaborative processes. As digital computers, machines, and communication media are introduced in greater numbers in both the workplace and home environments, there has been a decrease in routine manual or analytical tasks performed by humans, an increase in tasks performed by computers, and an increase in alternative types of collaborative communication platforms.

This chapter describes a number of technologies that have been developed to promote deep learning and collaboration. These technologies are guided by principles of learning and instruction that are supported by research and theory in the learning sciences, as opposed to traditional approaches that have evolved over the history of education. The next section differentiates learning science from the traditional approaches that have fortified educational practice for many decades, centuries, or even millennia. A number of the science-based principles of learning and instruction are identified, as well as their status in existing educational systems. The subsequent section identifies some technologies that implement these principles. The primary focus will be on those that promote deep learning through conversational pedagogical agents ("agents" for short). Learning environments with agents have been developed to serve as substitutes for humans who range in expertise from novices to experts. Agents can guide the interaction with the learner, instruct the learner what to do next, and interact with other agents to model ideal behavior, strategies, reflections, and social interactions (Graesser, Li, & Forsyth, 2014; Johnson & Lester, 2016).

PRINCIPLES OF LEARNING AND INSTRUCTION IN THE LEARNING SCIENCES

Questions periodically surface as to what motivated the emergence of the learning sciences. What is the field of the learning sciences? How is it any different from the fields of education, educational psychology, cognitive psychology, and cognitive science? Why was there a need to create it? What are its principles, models, and theories of learning and instruction?

In the recent *International Handbook of the Learning Sciences* (Fischer, Hmelo-Silver, Goldman, & Reimann, 2018), there is a short history of the learning sciences that identifies four distinctive features that differentiate learning sciences from other fields with missions to improve learning (Hoadley, 2018). Compared to other fields, the learning sciences are empirical, interdisciplinary, contextualized, and action oriented. The *empirical* work has a broad set of methodologies: observation of learning practices in authentic environments, laboratory studies to test theoretical claims, the tracking of behavior and thought with automated technologies, design experiments that change during the course of data collection, randomized control trials with data collected and analyzed by independent parties, and computer modeling of learning mechanisms. The broad set of methodologies reflects the *interdisciplinary* scope of the enterprise. Dozens of fields could potentially fall under the umbrella of the learning sciences, but the main disciplines are education, psychology, communication, sociology, anthropology, philosophy, information science, and computer science. Learning scientists are sensitive to learning being *contextualized* in a particular physical and sociocultural setting and population of learners (see also National Academy of Sciences, Engineering, and Medicine [NASEM], 2018). Contextual specificness makes it more difficult, but not impossible, to generalize and transfer successful instructional interventions to new settings and populations. A detailed analysis of context is needed to make informed predictions on generalization and transfer of results. Learning sciences are more *action oriented* with the desire not only to study, but also to inventively create environments for learning. These created environments sometimes involve humans, sometimes technology, and most often human-technology hybrids of instruction. It is the technology-based interventions that are of most interest in this chapter.

Learning sciences have played a major role integrating fields that have very different traditions, theories, and paradigms of learning. Figure 1.1 displays some of the paradigms within the fields of psychology, education, machine learning, and computer learning environments. For each field there is a list of popular paradigms (phenomena, models, theories, methodologies) that have captured the attention of researchers and practitioners over the decades. It is beyond the scope of this chapter to define these paradigms, but it is important to make two points. First, these paradigms were isolated within the fields to the point where researchers were in different departments, published in different journals, and presented results in different professional conferences. Second, there was the need to integrate contributions and methodologies from the different fields in order to build more sophisticated theories and applications of learning. Learning sciences have been a major player in facilitating this integration.

Principles of learning and instruction have periodically been proposed by a number of research communities and professional organizations in the learning sciences. Some examples include the seven cognitive principles in the Institute of Education Sciences (Pashler et al., 2007), the 25 principles proposed by a community of researchers in the Association of Psychological Sciences and American Psychological Association (Graesser, Halpern, & Hakel, 2008), and the principles articulated in numerous reports by

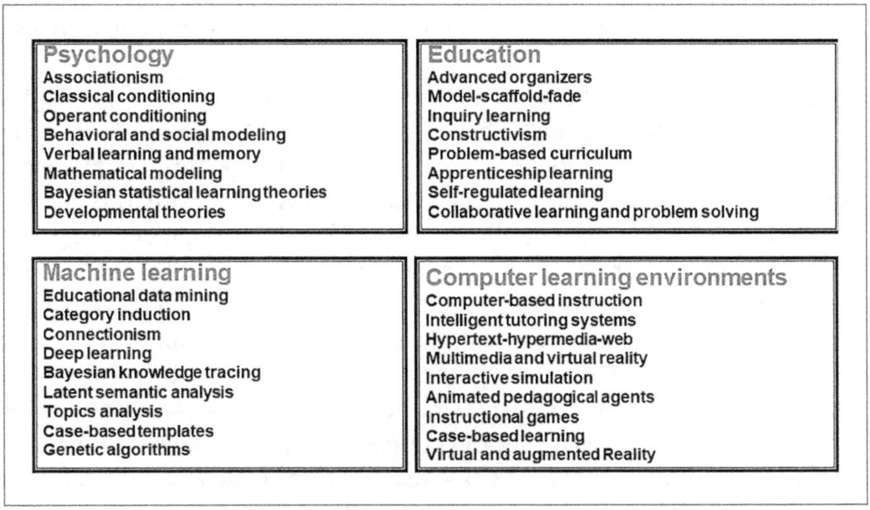

FIGURE 1.1 The landscape of learning traditions, theories, and paradigms.

the Department of Defense (www.gifttutoring.org; Sottilare, Graesser, Hu, & Goldberg, 2014). For example, an Institute of Education Science (IES) report identified the following seven cognitive principles of learning and instruction as being supported by scientific research with a sufficient amount of replication and generality (Pashler et al., 2007):

1. Space learning over time.
2. Interleave worked example solutions with problem-solving exercises.
3. Combine graphics with verbal descriptions.
4. Connect and integrate abstract and concrete representations of concepts.
5. Use quizzing to promote learning.
6. Help students manage study.
7. Ask deep explanatory questions.

The report included a research section that presented the empirical findings that supported the above principles and a practice guide that gives instructors explicit instruction on how to implement the principles in classroom teaching. This was an attempt to scale up scientific research to educational practice.

Do classroom teachers implement these seven learning principles in their classroom teaching? There are reasons to be doubtful. A study commissioned by the National Council on Teacher Quality (Pomerance, Greenberg, & Walsh, 2016) investigated whether the above IES principles of learning were included in the professional development programs in colleges of education. There was an analysis of 48 textbooks and 48 teacher education programs in the United States. The seven principles of learning were tracked in these resources with the exception of principle 6, "helping students manage study." According to the report, there was not a single textbook that covered the six principles, and no book covered more than two principles. Regarding the coursework, most programs prepared candidates for only a single strategy and one third none at all. This report supports the conclusion that the science of learning has not had much of an impact on teacher education and practice. This is one potential problem to point to when schools fail.

There are multiple reasons why the scientific principles of learning and instruction are not integrated with the mainstream educational settings. Some of the principles would be too difficult to integrate in a classroom setting. For example, it would surely be impractical for teachers to orchestrate a complex schedule of sequentially spaced materials to be learned over time. Teachers may not know that there are quick and easy ways to implement the spaced practice principle, such as using cumulative tests that encourage students to restudy materials over the months of a course. Another reason is that the teachers use more sophisticated pedagogical methods that are possibly superior to the IES principles of learning. If so, the superior principles need to be articulated, tested, validated, and compared to the IES principles. A very plausible reason the principles are not part of the professional development curriculum is that teachers simply have not been exposed to them. The learning sciences can play an important role in building bridges between science and educational practice.

It is informative to note that the IES principles of learning and instruction have successfully been incorporated in digital technologies. The IES (Pashler et al., 2007) report identifies the computer implementations that have implemented particular principles and shown gains in learning. Technology can play an important role in scaling up the scientific principles in educational practice both by helping students learn and by training teachers. Teachers can also critique available learning technologies and participate in building systems that implement their vision of successful instruction. Technology can play a central role in bridging science to educational practice (NASEM, 2018).

It is important to have a wise selection of technologies for a particular subject matter, context, and population. The second edition of *How People Learn* (National Academy of Sciences, Engineering, and Medicine, 2018, pp. 165–166) identifies some of the *affordances* of learning technologies to help guide these selections.

1. ***Interactivity.*** The technology systematically responds to the actions of the learner.

2. ***Adaptivity.*** The technology presents information that is contingent on the behavior, knowledge, or characteristics of the learner.

3. ***Feedback.*** The technology gives the learners information about the quality of their performance and how it could improve.

4. ***Choice.*** The technology gives learners options on what to learn and how to regulate their own learning.

5. ***Nonlinear access.*** The technology allows the learner to select or receive learning activities in an order that deviates from a set order.

6. ***Linked representations.*** The technology provides quick connections between representations for a topic that emphasizes different conceptual viewpoints, media, and pedagogical strategies.

7. ***Open-ended learner input.*** The technology allows learners to express themselves through natural language, drawing pictures, and other forms of open-ended communication.

8. ***Communication with other people.*** The learner communicates with one or more people or agents.

All learning technology artifacts can be analyzed from the perspectives of their affordances and whether they are suitably aligned with the subject matter and depth of mastery. Consider reading books and listening to lectures, the predominant forms of learning in the United States. Reading books and listening to lectures have few if any of these affordances but are perfectly fine, and probably even efficient, for the transmission of shallow knowledge. Books and lectures are appropriate to inspire, entertain, and expose learners to new topics, but not to help the learner acquire deep knowledge. However, the affordances listed above are needed for the mastery of deep knowledge (Chi, 2009). This has been illustrated in experiments with college students on difficult STEM topics, such as physics, computer literacy, and scientific reasoning, in tests that require reasoning and acquisition of mental models (Graesser, 2016; VanLehn et al., 2007). In these studies, students are randomly assigned during training to three conditions: (A) interacting with an intelligent tutoring system (such as AutoTutor, as described later) that had many of the eight affordances, (B) reading a textbook for an amount of time that is approximately equivalent to condition A, and (C) doing nothing. Learning gains on a test that taps deeper knowledge showed the following results: A > B = C. Therefore, the intelligent tutoring system had advantages in acquiring deep knowledge over reading, and reading was equivalent to doing nothing. Reading is quite suitable for acquiring shallow knowledge, but not deep knowledge for difficult material. It may be argued that the equivalence of reading text to doing nothing may be attributed to low engagement and motivation by the reader to dive deeply into the material. That is a reasonable argument, but it also raises the question of why many, if not most readers do not have a deep metacognitive standard of comprehension (Millis et al., 2019; van den Broek, Bohn-Gettler, Kendeou, Carlson, & White, 2011).

During the last 25 years my colleagues and I in the Institute for Intelligent Systems at the University of Memphis have investigated how deep knowledge is acquired through a number of technologies with the above affordances. Most of these technologies, such as AutoTutor, have computer agents that have conversational interactions with the learner. For example, Figure 1.2 is a screenshot of the AutoTutor system that targets adults with low literacy skills (Graesser, Greenberg, Olney, & Lovett, 2019). Readers can try out this system by accessing read.autotutor.org on the Internet. The system has two animated talking-head agents. The teacher agent is on the left, and the student agent is on the right at the top. The learner reads a text that is presented and answers a multiple-choice question. The teacher agent then gives feedback, and the peer student agent can compete with the learner or ask for help. We call this three-way conversation a *trialogue*. The next section documents highlights of our journey in finding ways to improve deep learning through various technologies, particularly those with agents.

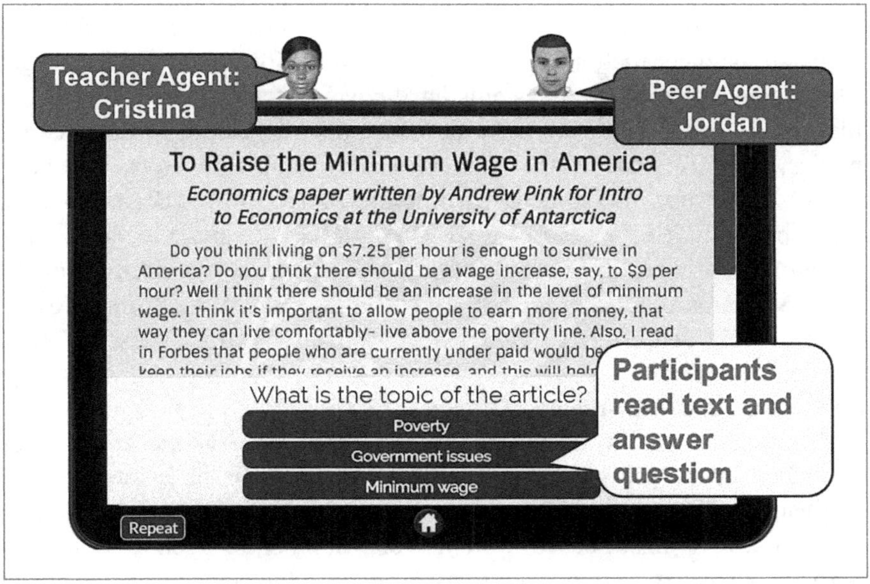

FIGURE 1.2 This is an example screenshot of the AutoTutor system that targets adult literacy (Graesser, Greenberg, Olney, & Lovett, 2019).

TECHNOLOGIES DESIGNED TO IMPROVE THE ACQUISITION OF DEEP KNOWLEDGE

Prior to the industrial revolution, learning occurred through an apprenticeship framework with conversations between the learner and a master, mentor, or tutor (Collins & Halverson, 2009). Print has become mainstream since the invention of the printing press, whereas lectures became mainstream in schools and industrial settings for optimizing efficiency of information dissemination (i.e., reception from the maximum number of people at the minimum amount of instructor effort). However, learning through conversational interaction in one-on-one tutoring has a number of advantages in improving learning over reading text and listening to lectures (Cohen, Kulik, & Kulik, 1982; Graesser, Rus, & Hu, 2017; VanLehn, 2011).

Computer agents can simulate speech, gestures, body movements, and facial expressions in ways similar to people. Agent-based systems have sometimes facilitated deep learning more than conventional learning environments and have proliferated over the last decade (Johnson & Lester, 2016). *AutoTutor* and its descendants (Graesser, 2016; Nye, Graesser,

& Hu, 2014) have successfully helped college students learn a number of skills and subject matters by holding a conversation in natural language. These conversation-based systems have covered topics such as computer literacy, physics, biology, scientific reasoning, research ethics, mathematics, and electronics. Other examples of systems with agents that have successfully improved student learning are *Betty's Brain* (Biswas, Jeong, Kinnebrew, Sulcer, & Roscoe, 2010), *iDRIVE* (Craig, Gholson, Brittingham, Williams, & Shubeck, 2012), *iSTART* (Jackson & McNamara, 2013; McNamara, O'Reilly, Best, & Ozuru, 2006), *Crystal Island* (Rowe, Shores, Mott, & Lester, 2011), *My Science Tutor* (Ward, Coles, Bolaños, Buchenroth-Martin, Svirsky, & Weston, 2013), and *Tactical Language and Culture System* (Johnson & Valente, 2009).

The agent-based systems have implemented most of the affordances described in the previous section. All of the systems have interactivity, feedback, and communication with agents; all eight of the affordances exist in several agent-based systems. The number of agents interacting with the learner is an important consideration in the design of agent-based systems. In a *dialogue*, a single agent interacts with a single human, as in the case of the original AutoTutor. In a *trialogue*, there is a three-party conversation among two computer agents and a human student. The two agents take on different roles, but often serve as tutors and peers of the student. There are alternative trialogue designs that address different pedagogical goals and levels of student achievement (Graesser, Li, & Forsyth, 2014; Graesser, Forsyth, & Lehman, 2017). For example, students can observe two agents interacting so that the student can model the actions and thoughts of an ideal agent. Agents can argue with each other over issues and ask what the human student thinks about the argument. A tutor agent can pit a human student against a peer agent in a game scenario in order to enhance motivation. It is also possible for a single agent to communicate with a small group of students, as in the case of AutoMentor, which was designed to facilitate group learning and problem solving (Morgan, Keshtkar, Graesser, & Shaffer, 2013).

One way to convey the power of these learning environments with agents is through examples. It is important to acknowledge, however, that some have been unsuccessful and others have not been fully evaluated with a full suite of rigorous assessments. An ideal convincing evaluation would have a set of highly respected outcome measures (to satisfy the psychometricians), automated online measures that track to learning processes in rich detail (to satisfy the educational data miners and those interested in fidelity of implementation), random assignment of participants to experimental versus comparison conditions (to satisfy the experimental psychologists in search of causal claims), an independent team of researchers to collect, analyze, and report the data analyses (to satisfy objective independent assessment), and a large sample of participants, instructors, and settings (to satisfy statisticians and those worried about replication and generality of findings). It is extremely expensive to satisfy all of these constraints that would be needed to pass muster in, for example, What Works Clearinghouse (https://ies.ed.gov/ncee/wwc/). Agent-based environments have not been fully evaluated in meeting the highest bar of validation because the new technology is at an early scientific phase of exploring different agent configurations and testing their feasibility. Rigorous evaluation will occur when it makes sense to take that step.

Agents to Help Readers of Text

Instructors typically assign texts for students to read in courses with the hope that the students will vigorously study the texts at a deep level, engage in reasoning, and generate important inferences. In the last section we presented an evidence-based argument that deep knowledge does not get constructed through reading but rather through a number of affordances provided by technology. Perhaps agents can interact with readers and help them improve reading at deeper levels.

One could imagine agents tracking the process of a learner's reading and giving feedback when they detect that the student is not reading optimally. We know that text is more difficult to read when it has rare words, abstract ideas, complex syntax, cohesion gaps, and technical content (Graesser & McNamara, 2011). They would presumably slow down on the difficult content and speed up on the easy content. However, readers are not particularly accurate on how well they comprehend technical text. Comprehension calibration research has revealed that college students' judgments on how well they understand expository text has only a 0.2 to 0.3 correlation with objective comprehension scores on the text (Dunlosky & Lipko, 2007; Maki, 1998). Extremely shallow readers have a word-based metacognitive standard of comprehension; they view a text as comprehended if they can recognize the words in the text. Readers with a sentence-level standard of comprehension are satisfied if they can understand individual sentences, but not necessarily the broader discourse messages. Deeper readers adopt a coherence-based standard of comprehension and identify coherence gaps and inconsistences among ideas (van den Broek et al., 2011; Zwaan & Radvansky, 1998). The deepest readers adopt a critical stance that is sensitive to the text genre (e.g., fiction, persuasion, informational), the expertise of the author, inaccurate information, and contradictions in claims between multiple texts (Bräten, Britt, Strømsø, & Rouet, 2011; Rapp & Braasch, 2014). This level of depth is extremely important in the 21st century because of the dramatically increasing number of documents available to the public on the Internet and social media that are not edited for accuracy of facts and claims.

Agents could play a role in alerting students when they are not adjusting their reading times to dimensions of text difficulty. One simple way to do that is to compare their natural reading time distributions as they read digital resources (i.e., click to advance the current screen of information) and compare that to metrics of text difficulty. To what extent do the reading times, measured as millisecond per syllable, match the text difficulty versus deviate from text difficulty? Unskilled readers have a decoupling between text difficulty and their allocation of reading time (Mills, Graesser, Risko, & D'Mello, 2017); extremely short times indicate they are not sufficiently engaged in the text, whereas extremely slow times are signals their minds may be wandering. Studies have confirmed that the extremely slow times are diagnostic of minds wandering on irrelevant ideas, as measured by eye tracking patterns and probes to readers on whether they are concentrating on the reading materials versus extraneous ideas (D'Mello, 2019). The reading time measures of decoupling could be applied to different levels of language and discourse and provide a profile of decoupling as a function of the various levels. Fortunately, automated measures of text difficulty have been developed that scale text difficulty on multiple levels of language and discourse (Graesser, McNamara, Cai, Conley, Li, & Pennebaker, 2014; McNamara, Graesser, McCarthy, & Cai, 2014; Sheehan, Kostin, Napolitano, & Flor, 2014). These measures can be used to generate such a profile of reading time decoupling. When a decoupling is detected, an agent could provide messages and guidance to repair potential deficits at specific levels, such as: "Take more time on sentences with complex syntax," "Sometimes there are contradictions in the text that need to be resolved," "Do you know why the author is sometimes not making sense?" or "Do you know who is writing this editorial and why?"

The above agent-based system has not yet been developed, but other agent-based systems have been developed to train readers how to comprehend text at deeper levels (Crossley & McNamara, 2016; Graesser, Greenberg, Olney, & Lovett, 2019). One notable reading comprehension trainer with multiple agents is iSTART (Interactive Strategy Training for Active Reading and Thinking, McNamara, O'Reilly, Best, & Ozuru, 2006; Jackson & McNamara, 2013). Readers think aloud and generate explanations while reading texts. The natural language of these open-ended reader responses is automatically analyzed by iSTART and provides data to guide the adaptive interactions with the agents that give the reader feedback and qualitative information to help them improve their explanations and comprehension strategies. Empirical research on iSTART has confirmed that the system improves subject matter comprehension.

Strategic Exploration of Hypertext and Hypermedia

One conceivable approach to acquiring deep knowledge is to grant learners the freedom to explore information sources on their own rather than being constrained by texts and lectures that are delivered in a linear order. Unfortunately, the vast majority of children and adults do not have well-developed metacognitive knowledge and strategies for self-regulated learning, so the mechanisms of self-regulated learning need to be better understood (Winne, 2005). Researchers have designed and tested agent-based systems, such as *MetaTutor* (Azevedo, Moos, Johnson, Chauncey, 2010), to train students how to acquire self-regulated learning strategies in hypertext and hypermedia environments. The results of this research support the conclusion that it takes many hours of interactive training on different subject matters to acquire self-regulation skills. It is not something that can be taught in a 1- to 2-hour session and expect benefits on transfer topics.

A self-regulated learner who desires deep knowledge would be guided by relevant deep questions that require reasoning, such as why, how, so what, what if, what if not, and so forth, but not the shallow factual questions such as who, what, when, and where (Graesser, Ozuru, & Sullins, 2009). Unfortunately, the vast majority of questions asked by students, classroom teachers, and tutors tend to be shallow rather than deep (Graesser & Person, 1994). Students rarely see good models of deep questioning so it is unsurprising that deep inquiry is rarely exhibited when students are given freedom to explore on their own. Training students to ask good questions does improve comprehension (Rosenshine, Meister, & Chapman, 1996), but this training is infrequent in most classrooms and tutoring practices. Therefore, an agent-based system called *iDRIVE (Instruction with Deep-level Reasoning questions In Vicarious Environments)* was developed to model deep reasoning questions by having two agents enact dialogues while learning science material (Craig, Gholson, Brittingham, Williams, & Shubeck, 2012). That is, a student agent asks a series of deep questions about the STEM content (such as physics, biology, or computer literacy), and the teacher agent immediately answers each question. Approximately 30 deep questions per hour are asked by an agent in this iDRIVE learning environment. This is approximately 5 times the relative frequency of deep questions asked in tutoring environments and 10 times the frequency of questions asked by teachers in classrooms (Graesser & Person, 1994); a typical student asks only 0.11 questions per hour in a classroom, and only a small percentage of their questions are deep. iDRIVE delivers many trials of good question asking and explanation-oriented answers, which are known to improve deep learning (Chi, 2009; Pashler et al., 2007; Rosenshine et al., 1996). The iDRIVE environment significantly increases the frequency of good questions and memory performance on transfer subject matters (Craig et al., 2012).

There are limitations of iDRIVE with the respect to the affordances described earlier. iDRIVE does have vestiges of the interactivity and communication affordances, but not the other six affordances that digital environments can potentially provide. The students learn in iDRIVE by vicariously observing the two agents interacting, so they are not actively constructing information. Active construction of information is an important affordance for deep learning according to Chi's (2009) *ICAP* model (interactive, constructive, active, passive). iDRIVE has entirely passive affordances for learning. This is sometimes suitable at an introductory stage of learning a subject matter, when the student cannot actively construct much information, but this is not suitable for intermediate and advanced stages of learning.

Point & Query (P&Q) is a different approach to training questioning skills for hypermedia environments (Graesser, Langston, & Baggett, 1993) and intelligent tutoring systems (Graesser, Hu et al., 2018). Students are exposed to a variety of questions as they explored the hypermedia pages. Whenever they click on a hot spot on a screen, a list of questions appears; students click the question of their choice, and then an answer appears. The questions vary on being shallow or deep. Graesser, Langston, and Baggett (1993) analyzed the frequency and percentage questions that were shallow versus deep in a study where students explored a hypermedia environment on woodwind instruments. As expected, the frequency of questions per hour was quite high in the P&Q environment, over 100 times the rate of student questions in classrooms and 10 times the rate of student questions in human tutoring. Moreover, the vast majority of questions were shallow unless students were given an explicit goal to acquire deep knowledge (e.g., write an essay on designing an instrument with a deep pure tone). Students are not prone to tread in deeper waters unless they are prompted by external events, such as a class assignment or the need to overcome an obstacle in a person's life that requires deep learning.

The final example of an agent-based system in a hypermedia environment is the *SEEK (Source, Evidence, Explanation, and Knowledge) Web Tutor* (Graesser, Wiley, Goldman, O'Reilly, Jeon, & McDaniel, 2007). This system was designed to train critical thinking about science topics by evaluating the truth and relevance of information, the quality of information sources, the plausibility of causal systems, and the implications of evidence (Braasch, Rouet, Vivert, & Britt, 2012; Bråten et al., 2011; Goldman, Braasch, Wiley, Graesser, & Brodowinska, 2012; Wiley, Goldman, Graesser, Sanchez, Ash, & Hemmerich, 2009). A deep understanding is needed to construct causal reasoning, integrate components in complex systems, and construct logical justifications of claims. This is difficult to achieve without sufficient prior domain knowledge and reasoning skills (Kendeou & van den Broek, 2007). However, a major start is for the learner to acquire a strategy of taking a *critical stance,* essentially being a skeptic about the information and the source (i.e., author, writer, speaker, creator) of the information.

SEEK Web Tutor (Graesser et al., 2007) attempted to improve college students' critical stance while they explored hypermedia web pages on the topic of plate tectonics. Some websites provided reliable information (e.g., National Aeronautics and Space Administration, Scientific American), whereas others were erroneous accounts of earthquakes and volcanoes that attributed these to the stars, the moon, and oil drilling. The students' goal in the experiments was to search the web for the purpose of writing an essay on what caused the eruption of the Mount St. Helens volcano in 1980.

SEEK Web Tutor took a direct approach to training students on critical stance by using three digital facilities with different instruction methods. The first was a *Hint* button on the Google search engine page that contained suggestions on how a student can strategically search and read a set of websites. This page approximated Google, with accessible titles and URLs for reliable and unreliable websites. When a student clicked the Hint button, spoken messages gave reminders of the goal of the task and suggestions on what to do next. The second facility was a pop-up *Rating and Justification* that asked students to evaluate the expected reliability of the information in a site. This facility appeared after the students first viewed a particular website for 20 seconds. The student rated the reliability of the information and typed in a verbal justification of the rating. The third facility was a pop-up *Journal* with five questions about the reliability of the site that the learner had just visited. These questions addressed some of the core aspects of critical stance: *Who authored this site? How trustworthy is it? What explanation do they offer for the cause of volcanic eruptions? What support do they offer for this explanation? Is this information useful to you? If so, how will you use it?* The pop-up Journal was launched whenever the student left one of the websites and required the student to think about each of the five core aspects of critical stance. The student gave a rating for each question and typed in a verbal justification.

The expectation was that the three digital facilities would improve students' critical stance by didactic training and application of the principles to the exemplar websites. We conducted an experiment that compared this Tutor condition with a Navigation condition that had no training on critical stance. College students explored the websites for approximately one hour with the goal of writing an essay on the causes of the eruption of Mount St. Helens. Students were assessed on critical stance by over a dozen measures, including an essay on the causes of a volcano. Unfortunately, the results were quite disappointing. An hour of intense training on critical stance via SEEK Web Tutor had little impact on college students when compared to the Navigation comparison condition. Only one measure showed any benefit from the SEEK: There was an increase in expressions in the essay with language about causal explanations (such as *cause* and *explanation*). SEEK did not improve learners' ability to detect reliable versus unreliable information sources during training, the amount of study time they allocated to reliable versus unreliable sites, their judgments of the truth/falsity of 30 statements about plate tectonics after the training was completed, and the articulation of core ideas about plate tectonics in the essays. SEEK Web Tutor essentially failed when confined to a one hour experiment. In contrast, another intervention with human trainers (that took more time) was moderately successful (Wiley et al., 2009).

One general conclusion from this disappointing result, as well as the studies on self-regulated learning discussed earlier, is that it takes many hours of an intervention in order to show appreciable improvements in these complex strategies and deep knowledge. There needs to be a large number of cases and contexts to apply critical thinking. Improving the quality of the intervention and associated materials may significantly reduce the time, but the application of the strategies to different cases and contexts will take time. An intervention that takes several days, weeks, or months would attract the interest of learning scientists who are attempting to understand, improve, and assess deep knowledge. The value of the 1- to 2-hour experiment is not in the ballpark.

Conversational Dialogue

As discussed earlier, one-on-one conversational dialogue between the learner and tutor (or mentor or master) is how learning occurred for many millennia and has shown advantages over reading and classroom lectures. AutoTutor (Graesser, 2016; Nye, Graesser, & Hu, 2014) was developed to simulate the discourse and pedagogical strategies of tutors and thereby help students learn by holding a conversation in natural language. AutoTutor adds on the interactive, constructive, and active learning components of Chi's ICAP model (2009), which is particularly suited to deep knowledge. In addition to interactivity and communication, it implements the affordances of adaptivity, feedback, and open-ended learner input. Some of the AutoTutor systems also add on the affordances of choice, nonlinear access, and linked representations.

How does AutoTutor simulate the tutorial dialogue of tutors? In addition to didactic instruction, AutoTutor presents problems to solve and difficult questions to answer that require reasoning and that cover a handful of sentence-like ideas (e.g., semantic propositions, claims, main clauses) in an ideal response. The human and agents co-construct a solution by multiple conversational turns. It may take a dozen to a hundred conversational turns back and forth to solve a problem or answer a difficult question. A systematic conversational mechanism called *expectation and misconception-tailored (EMT)* dialogue is implemented to cover the ideal answer to the main question or problem to solve. A list of *expectations* (anticipated good answers, steps in a procedure) and a list of anticipated *misconceptions* (bad answers, incorrect beliefs, errors, bugs) is associated with each task. As the students articulate their answers over multiple conversational turns, the contents of their contributions are compared with the expectations and misconceptions. Students rarely articulate a complete answer in the first conversational turn, but rather their answers are spread out over many turns as the tutor generates hints and other conversational moves to enable the students to express their knowledge. The students' answers within each turn are typically short (one to two speech acts on average), vague, ungrammatical, and not semantically well formed.

AutoTutor compares the students' content to expectations and misconceptions through pattern matching processes with semantic evaluation mechanisms that incorporate research in computational linguistics. Examples of AutoTutor conversations can be found in venues on the Internet (autotutor.org, read.autotutor.org).

Listed below are tutor dialogue moves that frequently occur in the EMT dialogues in AutoTutor and in most human tutoring sessions.

Main question or problem. This is a challenging question or problem that the tutor is trying to help the student answer.

Short feedback. The feedback to a student's previous contribution is either *positive* ("yes," "correct," head nod), *negative* ("no," "almost," head shake, long pause, frown), or *neutral* ("uh huh," "okay").

Pumps. The tutor gives nondirective pumps ("Anything else?" "Tell me more.") to say more or to take some action.

Hints. The tutor gives hints to get the students to do the talking or take action, but directs the students along some conceptual path. The hints vary from generic statements or questions ("What about X?" "Why?") to speech acts that nudge the student toward a particular answer.

Prompts. The tutor asks a leading question to get the student to articulate a particular word or phrase. Sometimes students say very little, so these prompts are needed to get the student to say something specific.

Prompt completions. The tutor expresses the correct completion of a prompt.

Assertions. The tutor expresses a fact or state of affairs.

Summaries. The tutor gives a recap of the answer to the main question or solution to the problem.

Mini-lectures. The tutor expresses didactic content on a particular topic.

Corrections. The tutor corrects an error or misconception of the student.

Answers. The tutor answers a question asked by the student.

Rather than simply lecturing to the student, the tutor provides scaffolding for the student to articulate the expectations through a number of dialogue moves. AutoTutor provides a cycle of *pump → hint → prompt → assertion* for each expectation until the expectation is covered. As the student and tutor express information over many turns, the list of expectations is eventually covered and the main task is completed. The student may articulate misconceptions during the multiturn tutorial dialogue. When the student content has a high match to a misconception, AutoTutor acknowledges the error and provides correct information.

AutoTutor has shown learning gains of approximately 0.80 standard deviations compared with reading a textbook for an equivalent amount of time (Graesser, 2016). Approximately a dozen measures of learning have been collected in these assessments, including multiple-choice questions, essay quality when students attempt to answer challenging questions, a cloze task that has students fill in missing words of texts that articulate explanatory reasoning on the subject matter, and performance on tasks that require problem solving. AutoTutor is most impressive for increasing learning gains on measures of deep rather than shallow knowledge.

One version of AutoTutor scaffolded learner actions in addition to verbal contributions of the students (Graesser, Chipman, Haynes, & Olney, 2005). AutoTutor 3-D had the conversational tutor interact with a simulation on Newtonian physics problems. An example main question is, *When a car without headrests on the seats is struck from behind, the passengers often suffer neck injuries. Why do passengers suffer neck injuries?* The students are encouraged to manipulate values of variables (such as the mass, speed, and direction of vehicles) and to see what happens when collisions occur in a 3-D world. The interactive simulation is a resource to help them answer the question verbally and to correct their answers when AutoTutor suggests they have misconceptions. Therefore, this version of AutoTutor had linked representations, choice, and nonlinear access to the material in addition to the other affordances.

Ideally, the students would spontaneously enact the vary-one-thing-at-a-time (VOTAT) strategy in which values of one variable are changed while other variables are held constant (Greiff, Wüstenberg, Holt, Goldhammer, & Funke, 2013; Klahr, 2000; Lorch, Lorch, Calderhead, Dunlap, Hodell, & Freer, 2010). VOTAT requires multiple runs of the simulation with systematic changes of the values and variables in order to construct a deep analysis of the system. The disappointing news is most students ran the simulation on a problem only once or twice, if at all, rather than enacting the VOTAT strategy. None of the students assessed the impact of two variables on a third variable. Strategies of control over variables in these interactive simulations require training and do not come naturally (see Lorch et al., 2010). The AutoTutor agent could play a role in providing this training, but that unfortunately has not yet been implemented and tested.

Instructional Games

Perhaps deep knowledge can be acquired in highly motivating learning environments, such as games (O'Neil, Baker, & Perez, 2016). The game would present challenging problems on difficult topics that are selected near the horizon of what the student can handle (not too easy and not too difficult). One could imagine a student spending hundreds of hours seeking solutions to problems that few have solved, or exploring optimal trade-offs between two or more factors in a simulation. Nearly everyone has stories about being absorbed in a *flow* experience in a game, with intense concentration to the point where time and fatigue disappear (Csikszentmihályi, 1990). Games have been developed to support instruction through many genres, such as facts in *Jeopardy*, collaboration in *Dungeons & Dragons*, or psychomotor skills in first-person shooter games with virtual reality (Ritterfeld, Cody, & Vorderer, 2009). Some instructional games have had multiple agents to target deeper levels of knowledge and have produced learning gains, such as *iSTART-Motivationally Enhanced* for reading comprehension (Jackson & McNamara, 2013), *Crystal Island* for biology (Rowe et al., 2011), and *Operation ARIES! (Acquiring Research Investigative and Evaluative Skills)* for scientific reasoning (Millis, Forsyth, Wallace, Graesser, & Timmins, 2017).

Meta-analyses have reported the impact of various game features on learning and motivation (Clark, Tanner-Smith, & Killingsworth, 2014; Wouters, van Nimwegen, van Oostendorp, & van der Spek, 2013). These analyses have documented both successes and failures in improving learning and motivation. Unfortunately, it has been extremely difficult to design games to promote the acquisition of deep knowledge. Available evidence suggests that games are much more suitable for shallow knowledge than deep knowledge (Graesser, Hu, Nye, & Sottilare, 2016). Deep learning takes considerable effort to achieve, so it is prone to be frustrating (Baker, D'Mello, Rodrigo, & Graesser, 2010) and viewed as work rather than play (Lepper & Henderlong, 2000). Games are pursued for pleasurable experiences that allow players to escape from the real world, so many players are skeptical of games that have too many connections to the practical world.

Agent Disagreements and Cognitive Disequilibrium

A promising approach to stimulate deep learning is to plant contradictions and information that clashes with prior knowledge to the point of the learner experiencing cognitive disequilibrium. Cognitive disequilibrium occurs when people face obstacles to goals, interruptions, contradictions, incongruities, anomalies, impasses, uncertainty, and salient contrasts (Festinger, 1957; Piaget, 1952). Cognitive conflicts can provoke information-seeking behavior, which engages the learner in inquiry, reasoning, and deep learning.

Agent-based learning environments have been designed to stage contradictions and debates, thereby inducing cognitive disequilibrium (D'Mello, Lehman, Pekrun, & Graesser, 2014). These studies had tutor and peer agents engage with the student in conversational trialogues while critiquing research studies in psychology, biology, and chemistry. Most of the research studies had one or more flaws with respect to scientific methodology. For example, one case study described a new pill that purportedly helps people lose weight, but the sample size was small and there was no control group. During the course of the three-way conversation, the agents periodically expressed false information and contradictions. In a *True-True* control condition, the tutor agent expressed a correct assertion and the peer agent agreed with the tutor. In the *True-False* condition, the tutor expressed a correct assertion but the peer agent disagreed by expressing an incorrect assertion; in the *False-True* condition the peer agent provided the correct assertion and the tutor agent disagreed. In the *False-False* condition, the two agents agreed on an incorrect assertion. During the course of the trialogue conversation, the agents periodically asked students for their views (e.g., "Do you agree that the control group in this study was flawed?"). The students' responses were coded on correctness and also the vacillation in making decisions when asked a question multiple times throughout a conversation. There were also measures of confusion, which was defined as occurring if both (a) the student manifested vacillation or incorrectness in his or her decisions when asked by the agents and (b) the student either reported being confused when asked or the computer automatically detected confusion through technologies that tracked multiple communication channels (i.e., discourse interaction, facial expressions, and body posture, D'Mello & Graesser, 2010).

The correctness and confusion scores confirmed that the cognitive disequilibrium that resulted from contradictions and false information had an impact on deep learning. Contradictions and confusion resulted in more learning at deep levels of mastery, as reflected in a delayed test on scientific reasoning. Contradictions in the False-True condition (and sometimes the True-False condition) produced higher performance than the True-True condition on multiple-choice questions that tapped deeper levels of comprehension and identification of flaws on far-transfer research studies in a delayed test. The data also suggested that the experience of confusion played a mediating, moderating, or causal role in the learning gains. That is, the experience of confusion, a signal of thinking, played an important role in the deep learning (D'Mello et al., 2014). Another intriguing result is that the False-False condition did not engender much confusion or benefits for deep learning. The students generally accepted what the tutor and student agents expressed when they agreed, even if the claims were false. This outcome is compatible with models that predict that it takes a large amount of world knowledge before students can detect what they do not know (Miyake & Norman, 1979) and detect false information (Rapp & Braasch, 2014).

Collaborative Problem Solving

Much of the planning, problem solving, and decision making in the modern world is performed by teams because many problems are so difficult that it takes a group of experts with different perspectives and talents to converge on good solutions (Hall et al., 2018). Collaborative problem solving (CPS) has recently received substantial attention for training and assessment in recognition of the complexity of the problems to be solved in today's world (Fiore et al., 2018; Fiore et al., 2017; Graesser, Fiore et al., 2018; Hesse, Care, Buder, Sassenberg, & Griffin, 2015; OECD, 2013). Teams are not always successful in solving problems, of course. The success of a team can be threatened by team members who are loafing, uncooperative, unskilled, or forming counterproductive alliances, whereas these problems can be mitigated by a strong leader who draws out different perspectives, helps negotiate conflicts, assigns roles, and promotes team communication (Salas, Cooke, & Rosen, 2008).

Individual team members are particularly important when there is interdependency among team members and no one individual can solve the problem alone. Collaborative problem solving in problems with interdependency is different from collaborative learning (Hmelo-Silver, 2004; Slavin, 2017) or collaborative decision making (Hastie & Kameda, 2005) where team members learn or make decisions on their own in the context of group activities. When the problem is difficult to solve in CPS, each team member must step up and handle the assigned task because the group will fail without the contribution of each team member. The acquisition of deep knowledge is necessary to fulfill each role on the team for difficult problems because a team member cannot loaf and expect others to fill in without the team knowing it. Deep knowledge is also needed to take the initiative to compensate for a social loafer and quickly patch the deficit. Simply put, CPS has affordances for encouraging deep learning.

Agents have been used in CPS assessment at the international level in the Programme for International Student Assessment (PISA) in the 2015 international survey of student skills and knowledge (OECD, 2013, 2017). Over 500,000 15-year-old students from 52 countries completed the PISA CPS assessment in addition to assessments of mathematics, science, and literacy. Conversational agents were used in the PISA CPS assessment. A single student interacted with one to three computer agents in each problem rather than interacting with other human students. The PISA assessment revealed that only 8% of students throughout the globe performed at the highest level of proficiency, whereas 29% of students scored at the lowest levels (OECD, 2017). The results strongly suggested that students need training to improve their CPS proficiency. Females had substantially higher CPS proficiencies than males, whereas males showed a modest advantage in individual problem solving in a previous PISA assessment in 2012. The cultural and ethnic diversity of team members in schools was found to predict CPS proficiencies positively rather than negatively after statistically controlling for socioeconomic status. Participation in group school activities, such as band, plays, sports, newspapers, and volunteer service activities, were found to be training grounds for developing CPS skills.

The finding that students have considerable room to improve in CPS proficiency is perhaps not surprising because students are not directly trained on such skills in their schooling. Researchers have argued a need to find ways to improve CPS training in schools and the workforce (Care, Scoular, & Griffin, 2016; Fiore et al., 2018; Gilbert et al., 2018). Agents could perhaps play a role in training students how to improve CPS skills. However, a teacher or mentor agent would need to be adaptive to the actions and language of the students on the team. Students theoretically learn best when they actively contribute, receive feedback on their contributions, are exposed to multiple perspectives on the problem, and coordinate progress among team members in solving the problem. A simple agent might be of some help with rules on what to say on the basis of a shallow analysis of the group conversation. For example, consider the following rules:

1. If the team is saying pretty much the same thing over and over, then the agent says, "So what's new?" or "Can we move on?"

2. If a particular team member is loafing, the agent says, "What do you think, Harry?"

3. If a particular team member is dominating the conversation excessively, the agent says, "I wonder what other people think about this?"

However, a more sophisticated analysis of natural language in group conversation is needed to analyze the student contributions by applying recent advances in automated semantic and discourse analyses (Dowell, Nixon, & Graesser, in press; Mu, Stegmann, Mayfield, Rosé, & Fischer, 2012; Rus, Lintean, Banjade, Niraula, & Stefanescu, 2013; Shaffer, 2017). A sophisticated automated analysis of the natural language among the conversational turns is an important step, but it does not solve the critical next step, namely what the teacher, tutor, or mentor agent would say under particular states of content and conversation. Natural language generation is a difficult nut to crack in the field of computational linguistics (Jurafsky & Martin, 2009). The best that can be accomplished at this point in the science is to have a mechanism that selects particular canned speech acts from a set of alternatives, depending on the automated interpretations of CPS exchanges.

CLOSING COMMENTS

This chapter has identified some computer technologies with agents that attempt to promote deep learning. The agents help learners as they read text, search hypermedia, participate in conversations, play games, engage in debate, and collaboratively solve problems. This hardly exhausts the arena in having agents facilitate deep learning. Agent-based learning environments also have been developed to improve writing, scientific inquiry, and guidance on career counseling and lifelong learning, all of which are known to improve the acquisition of deep knowledge.

At this point in the science, researchers are sorting out which subject matters, materials, discourse strategies, and learner characteristics account for successful versus unsuccessful applications of agent-based learning environments. When is it desirable to have one or two versus three or more computer agents? What subject materials and strategies do or do not benefit from the agent-based applications? What learner profile benefits most from the agents? What sort of adaptivity in agent conversation enhances learning? What is the role of motivation and emotions in successful agent environments? How do learners perceive the agents initially versus after an hour, a week, a month, or a year? The quality of computer agents has been increasing over the years and particularly during the last decade. The paradigm of developing conversational agents is destined to have a vibrant future in the learning sciences.

More generally, the learning sciences are needed to solve some of the major challenges in helping individuals achieve deeper learning of subject matters and skills. The existing educational system is well engineered to promote shallow learning but not deeper learning. A more nuanced science of learning is needed to help students achieve deeper learning of academic subject matters and for citizens to understand financial literacy, health issues, political systems, differences between truth and fiction, and so on. How can that be accomplished? Two points merit emphasis to close this chapter.

First, the report *How People Learn II* (NASEM, 2018) emphasizes the uniqueness of individual learners in their background knowledge, culture, and contexts of learning. Such differences are particularly salient for deeper learning. It is easy to orchestrate a classroom of dozens of students to respond to simple questions with short answers that tap simple facts and can be answered in a word or two within a few seconds. Classroom clickers are perfectly fine for that; the teacher can coordinate the students with a sequence of episodes with an IRE template: The teacher *initiates* a question, the student *responds*, and the teacher *evaluates* the student's response (yes, no, maybe). However, the IRE template does not scale up for deeper learning. Each learner has a unique mindset, reasoning trajectory, and pacing of understanding that cannot be coordinated by the teacher in a classroom. Thus, learning needs to be personalized in the learning sciences. That personalization does not mean that each student learns in isolation because social collaboration is essential for the acquisition of deeper knowledge in today's complex world. The journey of acquiring deeper knowledge involves a portfolio of personal exploration of subject matters as well as participation in diverse learning teams and communities. The learning sciences need to find ways for educational settings to provide these opportunities.

Second, technology will play an important role in supporting deep learning for individual learners. The technologies will need to include an assortment of adaptive intelligent tutoring, unconstrained digital environments that allow self-regulated learning, virtual and augmented realities, and systems that facilitate collaborative learning, problem solving, and projects. Moreover, these technologies need to be designed by interdisciplinary teams that include social scientists who insist on incorporating scientific principles of learning—not just those in software development or business. Deep learning will show disappointing outcomes in learning environments that are designed without the interdisciplinary scope of the learning sciences.

REFERENCES

Autor, D., Levy, F., & Murnane, R. J. (2003). The skill content of recent technological change: An empirical exploration. *Quarterly Journal of Economics, 118*, 1279–1334.

Azevedo, R., Moos, D., Johnson, A., & Chauncey, A. (2010). Measuring cognitive and metacognitive regulatory processes used during hypermedia learning: Issues and challenges. *Educational Psychologist, 45*, 210–223.

Baker, R. S., D'Mello, S. K., Rodrigo, M. T., & Graesser, A. C. (2010). Better to be frustrated than bored: The incidence, persistence, and impact of learners' cognitive-affective states during interactions with three different computer-based learning environments. *International Journal of Human-Computer Studies, 68*, 223–241.

Biswas, G., Jeong, H., Kinnebrew, J., Sulcer, B., & Roscoe, R. (2010). Measuring self-regulated learning skills through social interactions in a teachable agent environment. *Research and Practice in Technology-Enhanced Learning, 5*, 123–152.

Braasch, J., Rouet, J.-F., Vivert, N., & Britt, M. (2012). Readers' use of source information in text comprehension. *Memory & Cognition, 40*, 450–465.

Bräten, I., Britt, M. A., Strømsø, H. I., & Rouet, J-F. (2011).The role of epistemic beliefs in the comprehension of multiple expository texts: Toward an integrated model. *Educational Psychologist, 46*, 48–70.

Care, E., Scoular, C., & Griffin, P. (2016). Assessment of collaborative problem solving in education environments. *Applied Measurement in Education, 29*(4), 250–264.

Carnevale, A. P. & Smith, N. (2013). Workplace basics: The skills employees need and employers want. *Human Resource Development International, 16*, 491–501.

Chi, M. T. H. (2009). Active-constructive-interactive: A conceptual framework for differentiating learning activities. *Topics in Cognitive Science, 1*, 73–105.

Clark, D., Tanner-Smith, E., & Killingsworth, S. (2014). *Digital games, design and learning: A systematic review and meta-Analysis.* Menlo Park, CA: SRI International.

Collins, A., & Halverson, R. (2009). *Rethinking education in the age of technology: The digital revolution and schooling in America.* New York: Teachers College Press.

Cohen, P. A., Kulik, J. A., & Kulik, C. C. (1982). Educational outcomes of tutoring: A meta-analysis of findings. *American Educational Research Journal, 19*, 237–248.

Craig, S. D., Gholson, B., Brittingham, J. K., Williams, J. L., & Shubeck, K. (2012). Promoting vicarious learning of physics using deep questions with explanations. *Computers & Education, 58*, 1042–1048.

Crossley, S. A., & McNamara, D. S. (Eds.). (2016). *Adaptive educational technologies for literacy instruction.* New York: Taylor & Francis Routledge.

Csikszentmihályi, M. (1990). *Flow: The psychology of optimal experience.* Harper & Row.

D'Mello, S. (2019). What do we think about when we learn? In K. Millis, D. L. Long, J. P. Magliano, & K. Wiemer (Eds.). *Deep comprehension: Multi-disciplinary approaches to understanding, enhancing, and measuring comprehension* (pp. 52–67). New York: Routledge.

D'Mello, S., & Graesser, A. C. (2010). Multimodal semi-automated affect detection from conversational cues, gross body language, and facial features. *User Modeling and User-Adapted Interaction, 20*, 147–187.

D'Mello, S., Lehman, S., Pekrun, R., & Graesser, A. (2014). Confusion can be beneficial for learning. *Learning and Instruction, 29*, 153–170.

Dowell, N. M. , Nixon, T., & Graesser, A. C. (in press). Group communication analysis: A computational linguistics approach for detecting sociocognitive roles in multi-party interactions. *Behavior Research Methods.*

Dunlosky, J., & Lipko, A. (2007). Metacomprehension: A brief history and how to improve its accuracy. *Current Directions in Psychological Science, 16*, 228–232.

Elliot, S. (2017). *Computers and the future of skill demand.* Paris, FR: OECD.

Festinger, L. (1957). *A theory of cognitive dissonance.* Stanford, CA: Stanford University Press.

Fiore, S. M. (2008). Interdisciplinarity as teamwork: How the science of teams can inform team science. *Small Group Research, 39*(3), 251–277.

Fiore, S. M., Graesser, A. C., & Greiff, S. (2018, June). Collaborative problem solving education for the 21st century workforce. *Nature Human Behavior,* 1–3.

Fiore, S. M., Graesser, A., Greiff, S., Griffin, P., Gong, B., Kyllonen, P., . . . von Davier, A. A. (2017). *Collaborative problem solving: Considerations for the National Assessment of Educational Progress.* Alexandria, VA: National Center for Education Statistics.

Fischer, F., Hmelo-Silver, C. E., Goldman, S. R., & Reimann, R. (Eds.). (2018). *International handbook of the learning sciences.* New York: Routledge.

Gilbert, S., Slavina, A., Sinatra, A. M., Bonner, D., Johnston, J., Holub, J., MacAllister, A., Dorneich, M., & Winer, E. (2018). Creating a team tutor using GIFT. *International Journal for Artificial Intelligence in Education, 28*, 286–313.

Goldman, S. R., Braasch, J. L. G., Wiley, J., Graesser, A. C., & Brodowinska, K. (2012). Comprehending and learning from Internet sources: Processing patterns of better and poorer learners. *Reading Research Quarterly, 47*, 356–381.

Graesser, A. C. (2015). Deeper learning with advances in discourse science and technology. *Policy Insights from Behavioral and Brain Sciences, 2*, 42–50.

Graesser, A. C. (2016). Conversations with AutoTutor help students learn. *International Journal of Artificial Intelligence in Education, 26*, 124–132.

Graesser, A. C., Chipman, P., Haynes, B. C., & Olney, A. (2005). AutoTutor: An intelligent tutoring system with mixed-initiative dialogue. *IEEE Transactions in Education, 48*, 612–618.

Graesser, A. C., Fiore, S. M., Greiff, S., Andrews-Todd, J., Foltz, P. W., & Hesse, F. W. (2018). Advancing the science of collaborative problem solving. *Psychological Science in the Public Interest.*

Graesser, A. C., Forsyth, C., & Lehman, B. (2017). Two heads are better than one: Learning from agents in conversational trialogues. *Teachers College Record, 119*, 1–20.

Graesser, A. C., Greenberg, D., Olney, A. M., & Lovett, M. W. (2019). Educational technologies that support reading comprehension for adults who have low literacy skills. In D. Perin (Ed), *Wiley adult literacy handbook.* New York: Wiley.

Graesser, A. C., Halpern, D. F., & Hakel, M. (2008). *25 principles of learning.* Washington, DC: Task Force on Lifelong Learning at Work and at Home. Retrieved October 19, 2018, from https://louisville.edu/ideastoaction/-/files/featured/halpern/25-principles.pdf

Graesser, A. C., Hu, X., Nye, B., & Sottilare, R. (2016). Intelligent tutoring systems, serious games, and the Generalized Intelligent Framework for Tutoring (GIFT). In H. F. O'Neil, E. L. Baker, & R. S. Perez (Eds.), *Using games and simulation for teaching and assessment* (pp. 58–79). Abingdon, Oxon, UK: Routledge.

Graesser, A. C., Hu, X., Nye, B. D., VanLehn, K., Kumar, R., Heffernan, C., Heffernan, N., Woolf, B., Olney, A. M., Rus, V., Andraskik, F., Pavlik, P., Cai, Z., Wetzel, J., Morgan, B., Hampton, A. J., Lippert, A. M., Wang, L., Cheng, Q., Vinsen, J. E., Kelly, C. N., McGlown, C., Majmudar, C. A., Morshed, B., & Baer, W. (2018). ElectronixTutor: An intelligent tutoring system with multiple learning resources. *International Journal of STEM Education, 5*(15), 1–21.

Graesser, A. C., Langston, M. C., & Baggett, W. B. (1993). Exploring information about concepts by asking questions. In G. V. Nakamura, R. M. Taraban, & D. Medin (Eds.), *The psychology of learning and motivation: Vol. 29. Categorization by humans and machines* (pp. 411–436). Orlando, FL: Academic Press.

Graesser, A. C., Li, H., & Forsyth, C. (2014). Learning by communicating in natural language with conversational agents. *Current Directions in Psychological Science, 23*, 374–380.

Graesser, A. C., & McNamara, D. S. (2011). Computational analyses of multilevel discourse comprehension. *Topics in Cognitive Science, 3*, 371–398.

Graesser, A. C., McNamara, D. S., Cai, Z., Conley, M., Li, H., & Pennebaker, J. (2014). Coh-Metrix measures text characteristics at multiple levels of language and discourse. *Elementary School Journal, 115*, 210–229.

Graesser, A., Ozuru, Y., & Sullins, J. (2009). What is a good question? In M. G. McKeown & L. Kucan (Eds.), *Threads of coherence in research on the development of reading ability* (pp. 112–141). New York: Guilford.

Graesser, A. C., & Person, N. K. (1994). Question asking during tutoring. *American Educational Research Journal, 31*, 104–137.

Graesser, A. C., Rus, V., & Hu, X. (2017). Instruction based on tutoring. In R. E. Mayer and P. A. Alexander (Eds.), *Handbook of research on learning and instruction* (pp. 460–482). New York: Routledge.

Graesser, A. C., Wiley, J., Goldman, S. R., O'Reilly, T., Jeon, M., & McDaniel, B. (2007). SEEK Web tutor: Fostering a critical stance while exploring the causes of volcanic eruption. *Metacognition and Learning, 2*, 89–105.

Greiff, S., Wüstenberg, S., Holt, D. V., Goldhammer, F., & Funke, J. (2013). Computer-based assessment of complex problem solving: Concept, implementation, and application. *Educational Technology Research and Development, 61*, 407–421.

Hall, K. L., Vogel, A. L., Huang, G. C., Serrano, K. J., Rice, E. L., Tsakraklides, S. P., & Fiore, S. M. (2018). The science of team science: A review of the empirical evidence and research gaps on collaboration in science. *American Psychologist, 73*(4), 532–548.

Hastie, R., & Kameda, T. (2005). The robust beauty of majority rules in group decisions. *Psychological Review, 112*, 494–508.

Hattie, J. A. C., & Donoghue, G. M. (2016). Learning strategies: A synthesis and conceptual model. *Nature Partner Journal: Science of Learning, 1*, 1–13.

Hesse, F., Care, E., Buder, J., Sassenberg, K., & Griffin, P. (2015). A framework for teachable collaborative problem solving skills. In P. Griffin and E. Care (Eds.), *Assessment and teaching of 21st century skills* (pp. 37–55). Heidelberg, GA: Springer.

Hmelo-Silver, C. E. (2004). Problem-based learning: What and how do students learn? *Educational Psychology Review, 16*(3), 235–266.

Hoadley, C. (2018). A short history of the learning sciences. In F. Fischer, C. E. Hmelo-Silver, S. R. Goldman, and P. Reimann (Eds.), *International handbook of the learning sciences* (pp. 11–23). New York: Routledge.

Jackson, G. T., & McNamara, D. S. (2013). Motivation and performance in a game-based intelligent tutoring system. *Journal of Educational Psychology, 105*, 1036–1049.

Johnson, W. L., & Lester, J. C. (2016). Face-to-face interaction with pedagogical agents, Twenty years later. *International Journal of Artificial Intelligence in Education, 26*(1), 25–36.

Johnson, L. W., & Valente, A. (2009). Tactical language and culture training systems: Using artificial intelligence to teach foreign languages and cultures. *AI Magazine, 30*, 72–83.

Jurafsky, D., & Martin, J. (2009). *Speech and language processing* (2nd ed.). New Jersey: Prentice-Hall.

Kendeou, P., & van den Broek, P. (2007). The effects of prior knowledge and text structure on comprehension processes during reading of scientific texts. *Memory & Cognition, 35*, 1567–1577.

Klahr, D. (2000). *Exploring science: The cognition and development of discovery processes.* Cambridge, MA: MIT Press.

Lepper, M. R., & Henderlong, J. (2000). Turning "play" into "work" and "work" into "play": 25 years of research on intrinsic versus extrinsic motivation. In C. Sansone & J. M. Harackiewicz (Eds.), *Intrinsic and extrinsic motivation: The search for optimal motivation and performance* (pp. 257–307). San Diego, CA: Academic Press.

Levy, F. & Murnane, R. J. (2006). Why the changing American economy calls for 21st century learning: Answers to educators' questions. *New Directions for Youth Development, 110*, 53–62.

Lorch, Jr., R. F., Lorch, E. P., Calderhead, W. J., Dunlap, E. E., Hodell, E. C., & Freer, B. D. (2010). Learning the control of variables strategy in higher and lower achieving classrooms: Contributions of explicit instruction and experimentation. *Journal of Educational Psychology, 102*(1), 90–101.

Maki, R. H. (1998). Test predictions over text material. In D. J. Hacker, J. Dunlosky, & A. C. Graesser (Eds.), *Metacognition in educational theory and practice* (pp. 117–144). Mahwah, NJ: Erlbaum.

McNamara, D. S., Graesser, A. C., McCarthy, P. M., & Cai, Z. (2014). *Automated evaluation of text and discourse with Coh-Metrix.* Cambridge, MA: Cambridge University Press.

McNamara, D. S., O'Reilly, T., Best, R., & Ozuru, Y. (2006). Improving adolescent students' reading comprehension with iSTART. *Journal of Educational Computing Research, 34*, 147–171.

Millis, K., Forsyth, C., Wallace, P., Graesser, A. C., & Timmins, G. (2017). The impact of game-like features on learning from an intelligent tutoring system. *Technology, Knowledge, and Learning, 22*, 1–22.

Millis, K., Long, D. L., Magliano, J. P., & Wiemer, K. (Eds.). (2019). *Deep comprehension: Multi-disciplinary approaches to understanding, enhancing, and measuring comprehension.* New York: Routledge.

Mills, C., Graesser, A. C., Risko, E. F., & D'Mello, S. K. (2017). Cognitive coupling during reading. *Journal of Experimental Psychology: General, 146*, 872–883.

Miyake, N., & Norman, D. A. (1979). To ask a question one must know enough to know what is not known. *Journal of Verbal Learning and Verbal Behavior, 18*, 357–364.

Morgan, B., Keshtkar, F., Graesser, A., & Shaffer, D. W. (2013). Automating the mentor in a serious game: A discourse analysis using finite state machines. In C. Stephanidis (Ed.), *Human Computer Interaction International 2013, Vol. 374* (pp. 591–595). Berlin: Springer.

Mu, J., Stegmann, K., Mayfield, E., Rosé, C., & Fischer, F. (2012). The ACODEA framework: Developing segmentation and classification schemes for fully automatic analysis of online discussions. *International Journal of Computer-Supported Collaborative Learning, 7*, 285–305.

National Academy of Sciences, Engineering, and Medicine (2018). *How People Learn II: Learners, contexts, and cultures.* Washington, DC: National Academies Press.

National Research Council. (2012). *Improving adult literacy instruction: Options for practice and research.* Washington, DC: National Academies Press.

Nye, B. D., Graesser, A. C., & Hu, X. (2014). AutoTutor and family: A review of 17 years of natural language tutoring. *International Journal of Artificial Intelligence in Education, 24*(4), 427–469.

OECD. (2013). PISA 2015 collaborative problem solving framework. Paris: France: OECD. Retrieved from http://www.oecd.org/pisa/pisaproducts/Draft%20PISA%202015%20Collaborative%20Problem%20Solving%20Framework%20.pdf

OECD. (2017). *PISA 2015 Results (Volume V): Collaborative Problem Solving.* Paris: OECD Publishing.

O'Neil, H. F., Baker, E. L., & Perez, R. (Eds.). (2016). *Using games and simulation for teaching and assessment.* Abingdon, Oxon, UK: Routledge.

Pashler, H., Bain, P., Bottge, B., Graesser, A. C., Koedinger, K., McDaniel, M., & Metcalf, J. (2007). *Organizing instruction and study to improve student learning: A practice guide* (NCER 2007–2004). Washington, DC: Institute of Education Sciences.

Piaget, J. (1952). *The origins of intelligence.* New York: International University Press.

Pomerance, L., Greenberg, J., & Walsh, K. (2016). *Learning about learning: What every teacher needs to know.* Washington, DC: National Council on Teacher Quality.

Rapp, D. N., & Braasch, J. L. G. (Eds). (2014). *Processing inaccurate information.* Cambridge, MA: MIT Press.

Ritterfeld, U., Cody, M., & Vorderer, P. (Eds.). (2009). *Serious games: Mechanisms and effects.* New York and London: Routledge, Taylor & Francis.

Rosenshine, B., Meister, C., & Chapman, S. (1996). Teaching students to generate questions: A review of the intervention studies. *Review of Educational Research, 66*, 181–221.

Rowe, J. P., Shores, L. R., Mott, B. W., & Lester, J. C. (2011). Integrating learning, problem solving, and engagement in narrative-centered learning environments. *International Journal of Artificial Intelligence in Education, 21*, 115–133.

Rus, V., Lintean, M. C., Banjade, R., Niraula, N. B., & Stefanescu, D. (2013). SEMILAR: The Semantic Similarity Toolkit. In ACL (Conference System Demonstrations) (pp. 163–168).

Salas, E., Cooke, N. J., & Rosen, M. A. (2008). On teams, teamwork, and team performance: Discoveries and developments. *Human Factors, 50*(3), 540–547.

Shaffer, D. W. (2017). *Quantitative ethnography.* Madison, WI: Cathcart Press.

Sheehan, K. M., Kostin, I., Napolitano, D. & Flor, M. (2014). The TextEvaluator Tool: Helping teachers and test developers select texts for use in instruction and assessment. *Elementary School Journal, 115*(2), 184–209.

Slavin, R. E. (2017). Instruction based on cooperative learning. In R. E. Mayer and P. A. Alexander (Eds.), *Handbook of research on learning and instruction* (pp. 388–404). New York: Routledge.

Sottilare, R., Graesser, A. C., Hu, X., & Goldberg, B. (Eds.). (2014). *Design recommendations for intelligent tutoring systems: instructional management* (Vol.2). Orlando, FL: Army Research Laboratory.

van den Broek, P., Bohn-Gettler, C., Kendeou, P., Carlson, S., & White, M. J. (2011). When a reader meets a text: The role of standards of coherence in reading comprehension. In M. T. McCrudden, J. Magliano, & G. Schraw (Eds.), *Relevance instructions and goal-focusing in text learning* (pp. 123–140). Greenwich, CT: Information Age Publishing.

VanLehn, K. (2011). The relative effectiveness of human tutoring, intelligent tutoring systems and other tutoring systems. *Educational Psychologist, 46*, 197–221.
VanLehn, K., Graesser, A. C., Jackson, G. T., Jordan, P., Olney, A., & Rose, C. P. (2007). When are tutorial dialogues more effective than reading? *Cognitive Science, 31*, 3–62.
Ward, W., Cole, R., Bolaños, D., Buchenroth-Martin, C., Svirsky, E., & Weston, T. (2013). My science tutor: A conversational multimedia virtual tutor. *Journal of Educational Psychology, 105*, 1115–1125.
Wiley, J., Goldman, S. R., Graesser, A. C., Sanchez, C. A., Ash, I. K., & Hemmerich, J. A. (2009). Source evaluation, comprehension, and learning in Internet science inquiry tasks. *American Educational Research Journal, 46*, 1060–1106.
Winne, P. (2005). A perspective on state-of-the-art research on self-regulated learning. Instructional Science, *33*, 559–565.
Wouters, P., van Nimwegen, C., van Oostendorp, H., & van der Spek, E. D. (2013). A meta-analysis of the cognitive and motivational effects of serious games. *Journal of Educational Psychology, 105*, 249–265.
Zwaan, R. A., & Radvansky, G. A. (1998). Situation models in language comprehension and memory. *Psychological Bulletin, 123*, 162–185.

ABOUT THE AUTHOR

Arthur C. Graesser is a professor in the Department of Psychology and the Institute of Intelligent Systems at the University of Memphis. His research is in discourse processing, comprehension, learning sciences, problem solving, and automated technologies that help individuals learn subject matters through conversation, such as AutoTutor.

ACKNOWLEDGMENTS

The research was supported by the National Science Foundation (0325428, 633918, 0834847, 0918409, 1108845, 1443068), the Institute of Education Sciences (R305B07460, R305B070349, R305A080594, R305C120001), and the Office of Naval Research (N00014-00-1-0600, N00014-12-C-0643; N00014-16-C-3027). Any opinions, findings, and conclusions or recommendations expressed in this material are those of the author and do not necessarily reflect the views of these funding sources.

CHAPTER 2

Learning Sciences Beyond Cognition: Exploring Student Interactions in Collaborative Problem Solving

Professor Rose Luckin and Dr. Mutlu Cukurova

UCL Knowledge Lab, University College London

ABSTRACT

The meaning and measurement of intelligence remain open to question. Standardized definitions and tests that focus on purely cognitive aspects of intelligence can make intelligence sound like something we either have or do not have at any particular moment in time. However, intelligence beyond purely cognitive aspects is not static and changes over time; it is not an all-or-nothing concept. In this chapter, we argue that complex activities such as collaborative problem solving (CPS) require multiple dimensions of intelligence and they should be acknowledged as dynamic combinations of skills, abilities, and knowledge. Therefore, when they are explored as a process rather than a means to reach certain cognitive learning outcomes, they should be evaluated with suitably wide-ranging approaches beyond standardized cognitive assessments. Investigations of these dynamic processes require approaches that can provide insights into processes across multiple social planes (individual, group, classroom), multiple resources (people, tools), and multiple spaces (physical, digital, hybrid). Hence, they would benefit from a multimodal approach. Here, we discuss multimodal learning analytics as one potential example of such an approach to investigate CPS. We also present our results from two case studies investigating student interactions with their contexts and with each other during CPS processes to interpret group differences beyond cognition. We conclude the chapter with some suggestions for practice and current challenges against the more prevalent use of multimodal analytics in the learning sciences.

INTRODUCTION

In a radio show discussing his life, the eminent neuroscientist Henry Marsh reflected on his voluntary work in Ukraine and commented that to be a good neuroscientist, or indeed medic of any kind, you have to care deeply about your patients, you have to be compassionate. Clearly, you do need strong emotions and sophisticated emotional intelligence to be a good neuroscientist. And so it is with learning and teaching. Learning is the holy grail of success, and it is about a great deal more than cognitive processing—it is a whole body and mind initiative (Luckin, 2018). The learning sciences have produced a great deal of research about how and when we are best able to learn, to apply our knowledge, to synthesize what we know in order to solve problems, to communicate, to make decisions, to think, and to integrate our experiences in the world with this process of synthesized cognitive knowledge construction.

Today, as educators and as learners, we are faced with many challenges. For example, we have an increasingly automated and AI augmented world in which children will experience a very different life to that of their parents (Siraj, 2017). We must prepare for the much-anticipated upheaval through ensuring that our education and training is tuned to the new demands of the workplace and society (Tucker, 2017). We must chart a course through a potentially bumpy landscape (Walsh, 2017). Fundamental to success in this endeavor will be putting the findings of the learning sciences to work in the way that we design our intelligent technologies to support our intelligent human teachers and learners.

For example, the learning sciences have demonstrated that collaborative problem solving (CPS) can be an extremely effective means of learning (Luckin, Baines, Cukurova, & Holmes, 2017). But it is not an easy pedagogy for educators to adopt, and its positive outcomes for learning are not always consistent (Slavin, 2014). The current understanding of CPS as a generic skill acknowledges it as a complex skill set (Scoular, Care, & Hesse, 2017); as "a bundle of skills, knowledge and abilities that are required to deal effectively with complex and dynamic non-routine situations in different domains" (Funke, Fischer, & Holt, 2018). We argue that educational technologies designed to make meaning through multiple modalities can help both educators and learners to achieve better results when using CPS. And that multimodal learning analytics (MMLA) is a valuable example in this respect. MMLA can provide insights into learning processes that happen across multiple contexts between people, devices, and resources, both physical and digital, and can reflect learners' progress in terms of their synthesized integrative knowledge construction beyond the purely cognitive.

In this chapter we discuss, all too briefly, the richness of human learning, understanding, engagement, curiosity, motivation, and knowledge construction. We consider this discussion within the frame of human intelligence. We reflect the manner in which the learning sciences can help us to expand our framework for describing human intelligence beyond the merely cognitive processing of information. We discuss evidence from work investigating student activity in CPS situations beyond cognition and its potential value to learning scientists. Building upon these investigations, we explore the potential of MMLA to help us track the richness of human intelligence as it develops beyond the routine cognitive processes that are often the subject of learning and its assessment.

HUMAN INTELLIGENCE

The term *intelligence* is broad and embraces a number of concepts pertaining to knowledge, ability, reasoning, and cognition. Its meaning has been discussed since Socrates' time, fueling many academic discussions, such as those arising from Spearman's (1904) *g factor* in which intelligence reflects a broad mental capacity, Gardner's (2011) multiple types of intelligence distributed across a number of areas including both abstract and concrete thought and practice, and Sternberg's (1985) triarchic theory, which argues that analytic skills should also be incorporated into such a model and that context is significant. The significance of context is also a feature in recent studies in evolutionary biology that suggest the social and environmental context is key to the effective development of intelligence (see for example, Laland et al., 2014; Clark, 2015).

Not only is the meaning of intelligence contested, but the way that intelligence could and should be measured has also been the subject of much research, including the Simon-Binet IQ test (1905), designed to determine which children might need additional help at school, the less culturally specific Wechsler Scales (1939), the Bayley Scales of Infant Development (1969), and the less U.S.-centric British Ability Scales (1979). The meaning and measurement of intelligence remain open to question, and interest in their study has been renewed by the advent of AI applied at scale. The nature of the connection between intelligence and education is also increasingly challenged (Roth et al., 2015), with discussions exacerbated by the increasing role of AI in the workplace and the accompanying demands for changes to education, training, and assessment (Luckin, 2018). In parallel, there are calls for AI to be developed to be more "human-centered" to reflect "the depth that characterizes" human intelligence (Fei-Fei, 2018).

However, definitions and tests can make intelligence sound like something we either have or don't have at any particular moment in time, but intelligence is not static, it is something that changes over time. An early alternative conceptualization of intelligence that opposed its commonly promulgated static nature was offered by Lev Vygotsky (1980). His evaluation of human activity was that it is much more than the external performance celebrated by the behaviorist thinkers who were prevalent at the time of Vygotsky's research, such as Thorndike (1911), Watson (1926), and Skinner (1957). Vygotsky proposed that children's development was the result of their interactions with other people, which formed the building blocks for the psychological processes through which the intellect of that child was constructed.

Human Intelligence and Social Interaction

Vygotsky's work introduced a developmental approach in which the higher psychological processes, such as creative imagination and rational thinking, are specific to humans and cannot be explained in the same fashion as the elementary processes that we share with other animals. The key difference is the social, interpersonal activity that is essential to advanced human thinking and the foundation of our human intelligence. These advanced human thinking processes evolved as we learned to use gesture and spoken or written language to communicate with each other, to work together collaboratively, and to think beyond our physical interactions in the world: to think and talk abstractly.

In this sense, to conceptualize intelligence and progress in purely cognitive terms is to ignore the social history of an individual's interactions. This narrow conceptualization gives too much weight to individual psychological processes, biological maturation, or genetic inheritance, and it misses the important embodied, emotional, and social human perspective. In order to bring in arguments for the dynamic nature of intelligence and its broader conceptualizations beyond cognition, let us start from the dynamic nature of our knowledge and understanding about the world and about knowledge itself, or in other words, epistemic cognition.

LOOKING BEYOND COGNITION

Knowledge is concerned with our relationship to the world. As our world constantly changes and evolves so must we in our probing and evaluating of our own relationship to that world. We must constantly test what it means for us to know something about the world, to make sense of the world, and to construct our personal and communal knowledge of the world, both as an abstraction and as an observable, experiential reality. Through this probing and evaluating we can come to "know" something about the world.

Epistemic Cognition

However, more important than knowing something is our ability to understand what knowledge is, and where it comes from. This is our *epistemic cognition*, and we must nurture it in ourselves and in people we educate. The term *epistemic cognition* is a generic term that refers to people's understanding about the nature of knowledge; it implies some level of reflection on our part upon our thinking about knowledge.

Learning scientists have grappled with the issue of epistemic cognition across the areas of psychology and education, as well as philosophy. A seminal piece of work conducted by William Perry (1968) with Harvard undergraduate students outlined nine different positions that people could adopt toward the nature of knowledge, ranging from: naive understanding (knowledge is derived from authority) to a sophisticated understanding (knowledge is self-constructed, context relative, and evidence informed). This and later research (Hofer & Pintrich, 1997) demonstrate that most people have a fairly naive, unsophisticated personal epistemology. We also know that epistemic cognition varies when people engage in different subject areas, that it is not coherent, and that it varies between contexts. Based on decades of research on epistemic cognition and its related concepts such as epistemological beliefs, reflective judgment, ways of knowing, epistemological reflection, and personal epistemology, there is little evidence that we are the consistent, rational humans that we might like to think that we are. Yet, most of the rationalization in our thinking happens retrospectively. We lack sophistication and are inconsistent and incoherent in our beliefs, our knowledge, and our certainty about how and what we know. However, we do have the capacity to be sophisticated. For example, we are easily able to interact effectively across a wide range of contextual changes. We can use this *contextual intelligence* to help us to refine and enhance our knowledge construction and synthesis. With the right support, we can increase the sophistication of our understanding and our epistemic cognition. Humans are also capable of developing a rich understanding of themselves as thinkers: a knowledge of their own knowledge and thinking; a knowledge about how they are feeling; a knowledge of their personal context. This self-knowledge takes us beyond cognition, to meta levels of cognition and emotions.

Metacognition

Cognition is the process through which we develop our knowledge and understanding of the world. It encompasses both our experiential and our algorithmic minds (Kahneman, 2011). Effective cognition requires that we engage our attention, memory, problem solving, and evaluative abilities. Our fascination with our ability to know and regulate our own thinking—our *metacognition*—dates back to Aristotle and has grown into a substantial area of study in the learning sciences. Countless empirical studies have shown that metacognition is a key component of the way that successful people operate in the world. As a concept, metacognition has undergone much refinement. Its complexity is summarized well in a book by Pina Tarricone (2011), who has produced an excellent 20-page taxonomy of metacognition. However, despite the size of the subject, the term *metacognition* can be broadly defined as *our knowledge and control of our own cognitive processes.* Early researchers like Flavell (1979) differentiated between our knowledge of our cognitive processes and the processes that we use to monitor and regulate these cognitive processes. The latter include the executive functions of planning, mental resource allocation, monitoring, checking, and error detection and correction, for example.

Sophisticated metacognition, with good self-regulation skills, helps people to fulfill their potential. Many scholars have explored the relationship between metacognition and our intellectual performance. Jerome Bruner (1996), for example, described the way in which our metacognitive awareness can increase processes such as attention, problem solving, and intelligence. Scholars such as Marzano (1998) have demonstrated that our metacognitive skills and abilities can increase the learning outcomes that we measure in our education systems, particularly those that relate to problem solving. Goos and her colleagues (Goos, Galbraith, & Renshaw, 2002) have given us the evidence that successful students are continually evaluating, planning, and regulating their progress, thus helping them to learn and to increase their deep level processing. We also know that the development of executive metacognitive processes is associated with enhanced cognitive performance. However, as Kornell (2009, p. 12) puts it so succinctly, a person's metacognition is not a case of "turning an inward eye on their memories and somehow analyzing them directly." To believe that reflection in and of itself is sufficient for metacognition is to fail to appreciate the sophistication of our metacognitive processing. We need to appreciate the complexity of our metacognitive skills, and we need to appreciate that they are highly interconnected to other elements of our human intelligence.

Emotional Intelligence (Meta-Emotions)

As one might expect, there are a substantial number of theories about how our emotions impact upon if, when, and how we learn. For example, in the 1980s, Ortony and his colleagues (Ortony, Clore, & Collins, 1988) came up with a theory that has been popular with researchers in the learning sciences. Ortony's team saw emotions in purely cognitive terms, as functions determined by someone's goals and attitudes. This assumes, of course, that the achievement of a goal is something that is important to us, which is oversimplistic. On the other hand, much recent research into the relationship between our emotions and our learning has focused on motivation.

Motivation is the way that our emotions drive our actions to increase our knowledge and understanding of the world. When we talk about motivation, are we referring to some physiological process that influences our desire to behave in a particular way, or are we merely referring to the reasons why we do something (Bergin, Ford, & Hess, 1993; Ryan & Deci, 2000)? There are theories that can help us answer both these questions. In an epic piece of research at the start of the 21st century, Pintrich (2000) attempted to integrate the research about motivation to learn. His work incorporates a range of theories and identifies three core integrated components of motivation to learn:

1. The *expectancy component*, which is concerned with our beliefs about our ability to complete a learning action. Investigations into this expectancy component can be broadly subdivided into our belief about the extent to which we have control over the outcomes of a learning action and its environment, and beliefs about how effective we are likely to be if we attempt to complete the proposed learning action.

2. The *value component*, which refers to our beliefs about the value of the learning action under consideration. It reflects our perceptions of the importance of the learning action that will be influenced by our personal interest in the learning action and our perceptions of its utility for the future.

3. The *affective component*, which accounts for our emotional or affective reactions to the learning action in question. This is particularly complex. It is not the case that being in a positive motivational state will necessarily increase our inclination to complete a particular learning action.

The goal orientation component of Pintrich's value component has typically been defined in terms of two broad orientations, although this conceptualization varies (see, for example, Ames, 1992; Boekaerts, 2003; Dweck & Leggett, 1988): an orientation toward increasing competence (mastery orientation); or an orientation toward increasing performance relative to others (performance orientation). Within the performance orientation there is a further differentiation between our approach toward achieving high performance or our avoidance of low performance. An approach performance orientation has been linked to high achievement and learning, whereas an avoidance performance orientation has been linked to low learning outcomes (see, for example, Harackiewicz, Barron, & Elliot, 1998). Interestingly, our orientation toward a goal impacts on our social attitudes too. Mastery-oriented learners have been demonstrated to be more likely to be supportive in collaborative interactions with peers and more likely to engage in *creative risk-taking* (Damon & Phelps, 1989).

The extent to which we adopt an orientation is not fixed and can be manipulated by contextual and dispositional factors (Harris, Yuill, & Luckin, 2008). There is also a close connection between motivation and metacognition. The two are interweaved, each having a bidirectional impact on the other, and they are closely related to the concept of self-efficacy.

Perceived Self-Efficacy

In 1982, Stanford Professor Albert Bandura (1982) wrote in the *American Psychologist* journal that: "perceived self-efficacy is concerned with judgements of how well one can execute courses of action required to deal with prospective situations." (p 201). In this article, he provided evidence that *higher levels of perceived self-efficacy were related to higher levels of intellectual performance*. He observed that people avoided activities if they believed they were not capable of coping with them, but performed with confidence tasks they believed they were capable of coping with. This means that the development of our perceived self-efficacy is extremely important.

Perceived self-efficacy is not a concept whose importance is limited to students. Teachers' perceptions of their own self-efficacy are also important. Teachers' perceptions of self-efficacy have been shown to influence their instructional practices, enthusiasm, commitment, and teaching. Positive and accurate perceptions of self-efficacy in teachers have also been related to higher levels of student achievement and student motivation (Skaalvik & Skaalvik, 2007; Woolfolk Hoy & Burke Spero, 2005; Wolters & Daugherty, 2007; Klassen, Tze, Betts, & Gordon, 2009).

It is important to emphasize that the constructs described should be considered as interconnected rather than isolated. For instance, perceived self-efficacy combines elements of both metacognition and motivation, and the three concepts are inextricably bound together. The notion of self-efficacy is also related to metacognition, and in particular to metacognitive control. Self-efficacy, however, varies depending on the task. Moreover, our perceived self-efficacy also draws on our epistemic cognition in important ways. An accurate perceived self-efficacy requires an accurate evidence-based judgement about our knowledge and understanding. We need to know our ability to succeed in a specific situation and to accomplish tasks both alone and with others for our perceived self-efficacy to be accurate. To make judgements from the evidence about our knowledge and understanding, we need to recognize what good evidence is and we need to know how to make judgements. These facilities all relate to our epistemic cognition.

LEARNING FROM THE LEARNING SCIENCES

We have laid out some of the discussion with regard to the breadth of features that we need to be concerned with when trying to develop a broad conceptualization of intelligence. This chapter is not an exhaustive introduction to these concepts; however, it should be clear by now that human intelligence and learning are much broader than purely cognitive considerations. We now turn our attention to a pedagogical approach that we feel exemplifies how we can develop learners' intelligence, including and beyond their cognitive abilities: collaborative problem solving

(CPS)—in particular, CPS as a generic skill to collaboratively solve open-ended design problems that emerge during practice-based learning activities. Such activities are an essential part of STEM education and have long been argued to help foster the skills we require of young people across subject domains (Funke, Fischer, & Holt, 2018).

CPS brings together individual problem solving and the social collaborative process of more than one learner working together. For the purposes of this chapter, we define CPS as *the process of two or more persons working together as equals with mutual interactions to solve a problem*, a definition that is informed by the OECD (2015), who define CPS competency as: "the capacity of an individual to effectively engage in a process whereby two or more agents attempt to solve a problem by sharing the understanding and effort required to come to a solution and pooling their knowledge, skills and efforts to reach that solution." It should be noted that the OECD approach to CPS was developed for individual assessment purposes, and it therefore only considers CPS from an individual capacity perspective. It doesn't take different perspectives of groups and communities into account in the design and investigation of CPS processes (Dillenbourg & Jermann, 2007). By keeping the definition broad, our intention is to be able to accommodate constructs that relate to group perspectives such as equality or mutuality of contributions in the process. OECD's approach also doesn't take CPS as a tuition approach (Cukurova, Avramides, Spikol, Luckin, & Mavrikis, 2016), yet CPS can also be used in educational settings as a pedagogical approach to improve student skills.

Collaborative learning approaches broadly, and CPS more specifically, can produce positive effects on *pupil achievement*, as measured with a wide range of metrics across different studies, *including standardized attainment tasks* (Johnson & Johnson, 2002). It has also been shown to promote *positive attitudes to schooling* and to improve the *social climate* within classrooms (Kyndt, Raes, Lismont, Timmers, Cascallar, & Dochy, 2013). The OECD identifies three dimensions for CPS: context, task, and process. These three dimensions help us to unpack the concept of CPS:

1. *Context* can also be described as the *circumstances* of the problem being solved collaboratively. Context consists of the resources that are available to learners to support their collaborative learning activity (Luckin, 2010). The context of the problem relates to a wide range of elements including the content focus of the task, how it relates to other aspects of the curriculum area, and the resources associated with doing the task (see Cukurova, Luckin, & Baines, 2018 for an overview).

2. *Task*, which for CPS can be thought of as a set of features that represent a gap or crossroads where the way forward to solve the problem is to an extent unknown and must be *generated* and/or *co-constructed* by two or more participants. CPS might be as much about identifying a possible solution as about enacting the solution. An important element for ensuring collaboration takes place is to ensure that the task encourages members to be mutually interdependent. This can be achieved through the task design or via other means, such as rewards and/or group roles.

3. The *process* of CPS, which requires the combination or the interrelation of social and cognitive processes. Ideally interaction and joint problem solving will center on a number of parallel cognitive activities, such as understanding the problem situation, clarifying subgoals, and reflecting on assumptions.

In a similar manner to the features of human intelligence discussed in the initial sections of this chapter, CPS is a multidimensional construct and requires a multilevel understanding of CPS as a complex generic skill set. This common framing permits us to use the study of CPS as a window through which to study aspects of human intelligence beyond cognition. Evaluation of the CPS process itself, rather than its particular outcomes, requires approaches that the current standardized testing strategies and psychometrics cannot provide. It is argued by Blikstein and Worsley (2016) that this problem is common to the process evaluations of all kinds of constructive approaches, such as problem-based learning, project-based learning, or experiential learning, in which the ultimate purpose is to improve complex developmental processes rather than content acquisition. It could potentially be argued that most of such constructivist pedagogies consider human intelligence beyond cognition, in a way that is similar to the position taken in this chapter. However, interpretations of such dynamic processes is problematic. One particular problem is the collection of short interval times series of high quality data on these processes (Molenaar, 2004), which require the application of novel measurement approaches to such idiographic processes (Hofman, Jansen, de Mooij, Stevenson, & van der Maas, 2018). We argue here that taking a multimodal approach can have the potential to provide such data to investigate multidimensional aspects of human intelligence involved in constructivist pedagogies (see Figure 2.1 for the connection between intelligence, CPS, and MMLA). We address the need for a multimodal approach to evaluate and support complex human intelligence features in CPS processes. In this way, we aim to exemplify the approach that is needed in learning sciences research more generally.

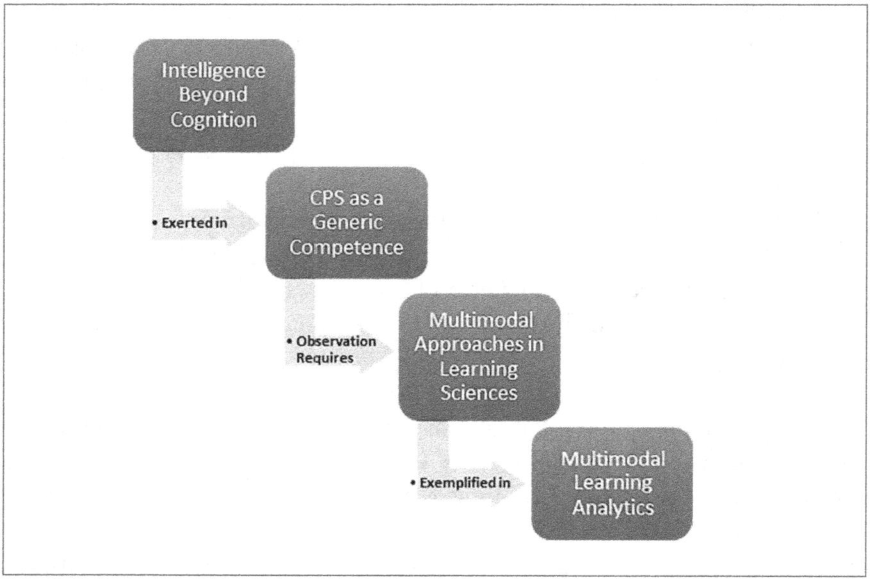

FIGURE 2.1 Connection between intelligence, CPS, and MMLA.

MULTIMODAL LEARNING ANALYTICS AS AN OPPORTUNITY TO MOVE BEYOND COGNITION IN CPS PROCESSES

As we discussed earlier, human intelligence is not limited to cognitive processes. CPS exemplifies the complex and dynamic nonroutine situations in which learners frequently operate. Learning is also not constrained to a specific physical space (e.g., the classroom) or a digital environment (e.g., an institutional learning management system or a specific digital learning tool). It happens in situ, where the learner is (Sharples & Roschelle, 2010). And it happens as a continuous process. The inherently blended nature of learning settings and the process-based nature of CPS make it essential to move beyond measurements that rely solely on a single data source (e.g., grades, questionnaires, or essays) or that focus only on the interactions that occur between learners and a specific system without considering the context of such interactions.

Multimodal learning analytics (MMLA) aims to address some of these issues. It leverages the increasingly widespread availability of sensors and high-frequency data collection technologies to provide insights into learning processes that happen across multiple settings, between a range of people, devices, and resources (both physical and digital), which are often hard to model and orchestrate (Scherer, Worsley, & Morency, 2012; Martinez-Maldonado, Dimitriadis, Martinez-Monés, Kay, & Yacef, 2013; Worsley, Chiluiza, Grafsgaard, & Ochoa, 2015; Prieto, Sharma, Dillenbourg, & Rodríguez-Triana, 2016; Ochoa, Worsley, Weibel, & Oviatt, 2016; Spikol, Ruffaldi, Dabisias, & Cukurova, 2018). Some MMLA researchers embrace the complexity of learning as an activity and attempt to identify the best modalities to track in order to capture the learning processes and to investigate the analytics for feedback (Cukurova, Luckin, Millán, & Mavrikis, 2018). By contrast, other researchers favor a bottom-up approach where the focus is on combining existing data with machine learning and AI techniques to offer a number of solutions to ubiquitous learning (Di Mitri, Schneider, Specht, & Drachsler, 2018).

Both the approaches discussed here have distinguishing features, but they are driven by different epistemological values, and they are both valuable to the advancement of the field (Cukurova, 2018; 2019). In addition, both approaches share the common aim of deploying learning analytics innovations that can be used across diverse authentic learning environments to interpret and support some of the learning processes beyond cognition. They aim to capture more of the complex human intelligence involved in dynamic processes such as CPS. MMLA researchers can now perform text, speech, handwriting, sketch, gesture, affective, neurophysical, or eye gaze analyses (Ochoa, 2017; Giannakos, Sharma, Pappas, Kostakos, & Velloso, 2019). Based on such analyses MMLA can yield novel opportunities that can generate distinctive information about what happens when students are engaged in dynamic processes such as CPS (Cukurova, Luckin, Millán, Mavrikis, & Spikol, 2017, Spikol et al., 2018). This information can subsequently be used to automate the support and continuous evaluation of student learning (Martinez-Maldonado, Kay, Yacef, & Schwendimann, 2012).

In the remaining sections of this chapter, we present two empirical case studies, each of which presents a different approach to the collection and analysis of data about learners involved in CPS process. The research goal of both of the empirical studies reported through these two case studies is to capture and understand more about the human learning processes, beyond cognition, that are involved in CPS. Our aim is to devise appropriate support for learners and teachers based on this analysis. In particular, our aim is to understand what data might constitute evidence about learners' progress, and how we can collect and analyze this evidence with a view to future automation or semiautomation of the process to produce useful feedback to students and/or teachers.

It is important to note that these case studies are not necessarily MMLA studies as they do not get into the potential automated analyses of the types of data collected. However, they present the prerequisite stage for any theoretically grounded MMLA approach. The first case study considers the thorny problem of learning context and its relationships to CPS performance. The second case study provides a much more fine-grained analysis of observable learner actions in an attempt to identify which of these actions might be both amenable to automation and informative about learner progress.

CASE STUDY 1: THE EDUCATION HACKATHON

Methodology

Our methodology reflects the three dimensions of CPS discussed earlier: context, task and process. We therefore discuss each of these CPS dimensions in turn:

Context

We use the Ecology of Resources (EoR) model and framework. The EoR can be used to analyze data from teaching and learning interactions and to design scaffolding interventions (Luckin, 2010). The EoR is based upon a particular definition of the term *context* in which learners are conceptualized as being exposed to "a single context that is their lived experience of the world; a 'phenomenological gestalt' " (Manovich, 2006). Context is a reflection of the interactions that learners have experienced with multiple people, artifacts, and environments. These interactions create partial descriptions of the world that act as the hooks for interactions in which action and meaning are built; in this sense, meaning is distributed amongst these interactions and interactors (Luckin, 2010)

The EoR model perceives the world as being composed of resources that are available to a learner for interaction and learning. These resources can be considered as falling into one of four categories: (1) *knowledge and skills:* these resources are the subject of learning; (2) *tools*: the books, pens and paper, technology with which a learner can interact; (3) *people:* who know more about the knowledge or skill to be learned than the learner does, and (4) *environment:* the location and surrounding with which the learner interacts, for example, a school classroom, a virtual world, or a place of work. The analysis of contextualized learning through CPS requires the identification, analysis, and interpretation of the relationships between the different types of resource with which learners interact. The EoR model has an associated design and analysis framework that offers a structured process for analysis and/or design that is iterative and has three phases, each of which has several steps:

> **Phase 1**: Create an EoR Model by identifying the resource components of the EoR of the learners being studied.
>
> **Phase 2**: Identify the relationships within and between the resources identified in Phase 1.
>
> **Phase 3**: Develop the Scaffolds and Adjustments to support learning.

For the purposes of the data analysis at the heart of this chapter, only phases 1 and 2 are needed. A full account of the framework can be found in Luckin (2010).

Task

A CPS task can be thought of as a set of features that represent a crossroads where the way forward to solve the problem is not fully known and must be generated and/or co-constructed by two or more participants. The task at the heart of the empirical study reported here was part of a larger engagement conducted over a four-month period. Students were initially engaged in a workshop where they were introduced to the idea of a "Smart City" and asked to work in pairs and to think about and discuss the sorts of problems that technology might be used to address in such an environment. Secondly, students were tasked to identify ideas that they would like to design and build as part of a smart city. A facilitator helped students to work together with these ideas and to refine the pool of ideas down to three potential projects that students would like to complete: (1) a glove that controlled home devices, (2) a mobile robot to help the blind with navigation, and (3) a coin reward system that gave credit to students who collected coins on school premises. The students were then set the problem of building a prototype for each of these ideas during a 2-day education hack. Students worked in three teams, with adult facilitators.

Process

As discussed earlier in the chapter, the process of CPS combines social and cognitive skills, abilities, and knowledge. These are instantiated for the purposes of this case study in the relationships between the resources with the EoR analysis. However, the identification of a relationship, for example a social relationship between two learners, is insufficient in and of itself. We therefore use the work of Michelene Chi (2009) to categorize the processes of CPS identified through the EoR framework. Chi (2009) provides a framework with four types of student engagement in learning: *Passive* engagement: students appear to be paying attention; *Active* engagement: students are doing something with instructional materials; *Constructive* engagement: students generate some information beyond what was presented to them; and *Interactive* engagement: students engage through dialogue. The significant contribution of this framework is that it defines cognitive engagement in terms of observable activities displayed by students during learning. By doing so, it moves beyond cognition toward social and interaction space. Chi (2011) argues that students are more likely to reflect a certain level of engagement as a function of the overt activities they display. We combined the context concepts of the EoR framework with the process concepts of Chi et al. to produce the analysis framework illustrated in Table 2.1, which we used to code the interaction data collected in the study we report here.

Participants

The participatory design-based study was conducted with 18 secondary school students aged 14–15 years. The students had little experience of computer science, but had done some programming in Python. None of the students had previous experience with the technology or activity used for this study.

Data Collection and Analysis

A range of data sources were collected during the hack event. These included: over 10 hours of video (two sources for each group of learners, one video of the group and one video of the laptop screen where

TABLE 2.1 The EoR-Chi Framework for Analysis

CODE NO.	CODE NAME	DEFINITION
0	Non-available	The resource exists within the learner's context, but is not in the learner's service.
1	Available	The resource is in the context of the learner, yet the learner is not engaged with it.
2	Passive	The resource is in the context and the learner pays attention to it.
3	Active	The learner pays attention to the resource, and physically interacts with the resource.
4	Constructive	The learner pays attention to the resource, physically interacts with the resource, and generates knowledge for themselves.
5	Interactive	The learner pays attention to the resource, physically interacts with the resource, and generates knowledge for themselves and helps others generate knowledge.

programming activity took place), observer notes, audio recordings, artifacts, interviews, presentations, and photos. In this chapter, we focus on the video data and in particular upon the interactions of individual learners within their CPS group. Two researchers coded the video of each group according to the EoR framework and the EoR-Chi framework to identify the resources available and in use by the learners. The coding was completed from the perspective of each individual learner in each of the groups. The relationships between the resources and between the learner and the resources was identified and recorded as changes over time. Resource use was recorded at 30-second intervals. The two researchers discussed all disagreements and reached a consensus.

Results

Phase 1 of the EoR analysis identified the resources that were used by the learners as they developed their prototypes. This analysis illustrates that whilst all learners had a very similar range of resources available to them, their use of these resources was distinctly different both within and across groups. In total, across all student groups the most popular resource was the adult helpers. This was in preference to peers, which is perhaps a little surprising given the collaborative nature of the activity. The second most popular resource was paper, used to plan and communicate between group members. This is also somewhat surprising given the technical nature of the task. However, the emphasis on design in the task may account for the heavy paper use.

In a comparison of the total resources used by all groups of learners over the same 1-hour period of the hack event, there were clear differences between the groups. For example, the group developing the glove prototype made greater use of the adult resources available and of the technology. They also interacted with the prototype. By comparison, the Coin group used each other and made heavy use of paper and instructions. They used the prototype components, but had no prototype to interact with at this time.

Phase 2 of the EoR analysis identifies the relationships between the different resources in a learner's ecology. We focus on individual learners as our unit of analysis for this phase of the analysis. This focus enables us to explore the relationships between resources at a finer level of detail.

Similarly, in a comparison between two learners from the Coin project group, we identified that the chronology of resources used by each learner over an hour period in the middle of the first day of the hack event were quite different. As an overview, Learner 2 (L2) interacted with learners L3, L4, and L5 as individuals more often than L1, and throughout the analysis period. L1's interactions with other learners were limited to working together with all other learners as a group and with the laptop. L2 also made use of the non-people resources much more widely than L1 and interacted with a particular resource for longer periods of time than L1.

Looking more closely at this data illustrates the resources that were actively in use by each learner at the same time, indicating a relationship between these resources with respect to that learner. These periods of active engagement are marked differently between L1 and L2, who were working as part of the same group: L1 started active engagement with multiple resources 15 minutes into the session and engaged actively with multiple resources for a total of 30% of the session. By contrast, L2 started actively interacting with multiple resources much earlier, in the fifth minute, and interacted in this way for 50% of the session. The individual differences between learners was reflected across all three groups. Table 2.2 illustrates the amount of time during which all learners were actively interacting with more than one type of resource and the time at which this activity started.

A closer investigation of the resources that L1 and L2 actively worked with demonstrates more clearly an interesting aspect of their resource use. The problem-solving activity required of learners during this study was

TABLE 2.2 Activity with More Than One Resource Across the Groups

NAME OF GROUP	MEAN AVERAGE TIME A LEARNER WAS ACTIVE WITH MORE THAN ONE RESOURCE	MEAN AVERAGE START FOR BEING ACTIVE WITH MORE THAN ONE RESOURCE
Glove Group	33 minutes (range 31:32)	Minute 2 (range 0:5).
Robot Group	26 minutes (range 26:26)	Minute 8 (range 0:16)
Coin Group	16 minutes (range 0:30)	Minute 9 (range 2:15)

a practical design and construction task, and required learners to interact with the tools provided to them, such as the Arduino technology, pens, and paper. Figure 2.2 (see next page) illustrates that L2 interacts with more resources and in more combinations than L1. In addition, there are 19 occasions (covering almost 32% of the session time) when L2 synchronously evidences social interactions with fellow learners and physical interactions with the design and construction tools. By comparison, L1 combines peer social interaction with design and construction tool interaction on only 9 occasions, which is 15% of the session and less than half the time spent by L2 on synchronous social and physical interactivity. The upward pointing arrows along the bottom of Figure 2.2 indicate the times when this social and physical tool activity took place.

The final part of this results section presents the findings from the analysis using the EoR-Chi framework, which enabled us to probe learners' activity with resources in greater depth. In particular we focus our attention on the interactions between learners and resources that are coded as EoR-Chi 4: The learner pays attention to the resource, physically interacts with the resource, and generates knowledge for themselves; and EoR-Chi 5: The learner pays attention to the resource, physically interacts with the resource, and generates knowledge for themselves and helps others generate knowledge. Initially we consider the EoR-Chi analysis for the learners whose activity is illustrated in Figure 2.2. We then consider findings across all learners and compare the result with the evaluations of the same sessions provided by an independent expert.

The EoR-Chi analysis for L1 and L2 reveals that there is only 1 minute, which is less than 2% of the hour-long session in which L1 interacts at EoR-Chi levels 4 or 5, both socially with other learners and physically with the tools required for the problem-solving activity. This suggests that L1 engages in little CPS activity in this particular hour-long session of the hack event. By contrast, L2 interacts at EoR-Chi levels 4 or 5 both socially with other learners and physically with the tools required for the problem-solving activity for 23 minutes (38%) of the session.

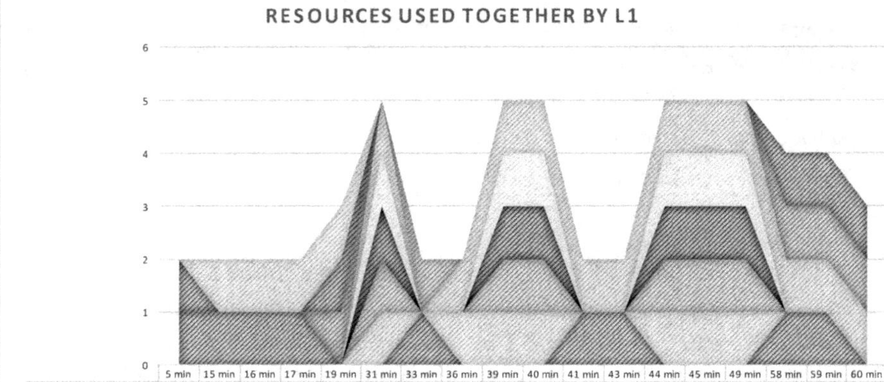

	5 min	15 min	16 min	17 min	19 min	31 min	33 min	36 min	39 min	40 min	41 min	43 min	44 min	45 min	49 min	58 min	59 min	60 min
Box Prototype							1											
Arduino board		1	1	1	1													
Coins	1				1											1	1	1
Coin Recognition Tool					1											1	1	1
Laptop-arduino software						1		1	1	1	1	1	1	1	1	1	1	1
L5						1			1	1			1	1	1			
L4						1			1	1			1	1	1			
L3						1			1	1			1	1	1			
L2						1		1	1	1			1	1	1			
Adult helper 2 (black top)	1	1	1	1			1				1	1				1	1	

FIGURE 2.2 Resources used together with L1 and L2.

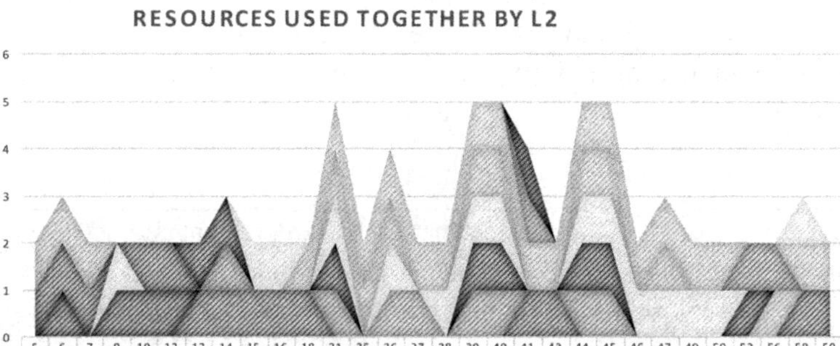

	5 min	6 min	7 min	9 min	10 min	12 min	13 min	14 min	15 min	16 min	18 min	31 min	35 min	36 min	37 min
Pen	1	1	1												
Arduino board									1	1					
Coins							1	1							
Coin Recognition Tool								1							
Laptop-arduino software											1	1	1	1	1
Drawing Paper	1	1	1		1	1									
Class teacher															
L5												1	1	1	
L4				1								1		1	
L3		1		1	1	1						1			
L1												1		1	1
Adult helper 4 (light green)															
Adult helper 2 (black top)							1	1	1	1	1				

	38 min	39 min	40 min	41 min	43 min	44 min	45 min	46 min	47 min	49 min	50 min	53 min	56 min	58 min	59 min
Pen															
Arduino board														1	
Coins				1											
Coin Recognition Tool				1											
Laptop-arduino software	1	1	1	1	1	1	1	1	1	1	1			1	1
Drawing Paper															
Class teacher												1	1		
L5		1	1			1	1		1						
L4	1	1	1			1	1	1	1	1	1				
L3		1	1			1	1					1			
L1		1	1			1	1								
Adult helper 4 (light green)													1		
Adult helper 2 (black top)				1	1									1	1

We present results for all learners across a later session in the hack event in Tables 2.3 and 2.4. The results illustrated in these tables indicate greater evidence of activity that could be considered as evidence of CPS activity.

TABLE 2.3 The % of the Session That Each Learner Spent Interacting with Constructive or Interactive Engagement with a Resource

	ROBOT GROUP	COIN GROUP	GLOVE GROUP
L1	63	66	95
L2	72	72	97
L3	45	57	92
L4	32	72	97
L5	43	71	88
Average	51	68	94

Table 2.3 shows the variance across all learners in the observable evidence of CPS, which ranges from 31.67% of the session for L4 in the Robot group to 96.67% for L2 in the Glove group. It also illustrates the range of Constructive and Interactive activity across the groups and shows both the variance between groups and the high levels of activity amongst the members of the Glove project group, who were active at EoR-Chi levels 4 or 5 for 93.67% of the session.

To verify the validity of the EoR-Chi video analysis we sought independent verification. An expert research professor from another university who had not previously been involved in our study data collection or analysis provided this verification. We asked her to watch our video data of the three groups who took part in the hack event as illustrated in Table 2.3 and identify the times during the learners' interactions when in her judgment there was evidence that the group was engaged in CPS process. Table 2.4 illustrates her judgment across all groups.

Tables 2.3 and 2.4 represent the same session of the hack event, and it is interesting to note that the coding using the EoR-Chi framework to identify signifiers of observable CPS ranks the groups in the same order as the independent expert. The EoR-Chi framework is more conservative than the independent expert, who rates activity of the learners as being consistent with CPS more frequently. The data concerning the Robot group is at particular variance between the EoR-Chi analysis and the human expert. The possible explanation for this may lie in the fact that the Robot group members were unable to develop their own prototype from scratch, because the task was simply too far in advance of their skill levels. The adult helper therefore introduced a ready-made robot to the session. The coders using the EoR-Chi framework coded the students' interactions with this ready-made robot as interactions with the prototype; the independent expert didn't consider students' interactions with this ready-made robot as constructive interactions. Closer investigation of the data suggests that it is likely that this difference of opinion is responsible for almost all of the variance in the CPS evaluations between the EoR-Chi framework and the independent expert. It is however important to recognize the significance of such a disagreement, because a successful automated MMLA system for CPS would need to be able to cope with such differences in judgment about the status of a resource.

TABLE 2.4 The % of the Session That an Independent Expert Rated as Consistent with CPS

	%
Robot Group	18
Coin Group	47
Glove Group	95

Case Study 1 presents the results of our investigation of secondary school students' CPS process as part of a 2-day hack event. A prerequisite to the design of MMLA for CPS is the assessment of CPS learning activity. This assessment demands an analytical methodology that can identify the observable signifiers of CPS with regard to students' interactions with resources. The data underlying these observable signifiers must also be amenable to automatic capture through MMLA.

The EoR-Chi analytical framework brings together the useful concepts of *educational context* and *constructive and interactive engagement.* Our results using this framework show that both individual students and groups of students present different patterns of engagement with the human and tool resources around them during the CPS task. We argue that these differences between the groups and individual students' use of resources may indicate their different degree of engagement with the CPS process. The external verification reported in this case study indicates a possible correlation between expert human assessment of CPS processes and assessment of CPS through identification of students' constructive or interactive engagement with the resources available to them.

The data used for the EoR framework requires identification of the resources that each learner interacts with during a learning session. This is an interesting computer vision challenge, but can potentially be overcome with currently existing software and tools (e.g., Babenko, Yang, & Belongie, 2009; Kalal, Mikolajczyk, & Matas, 2012). The addition of the extra evaluations in the creation of the EoR-Chi framework require identification of interactions that differentiate between learner activity beyond observable physical interaction to the identification of evidence of knowledge generation. To the best of our knowledge, this fine-grained differentiation of behaviors concerning knowledge generation is not amenable to automated capture yet, and it requires human intervention. Future research must be conducted to evaluate the extent to which (1) the identification of knowledge generation is essential to the assessment of CPS, and (2) the identification of knowledge generation can be achieved via observable signifiers that can be automatically captured with MMLA. Furthermore, it is clear from our results that certain constellations of resources are preferable to individual learners. Further exploration of these constellations is required to gauge the relationship between CPS processes and particular resource constellations in learning activities.

CASE STUDY 2: PRACTICE-BASED ACTIVITY WITH SCHOOL-AGED LEARNERS

In Case Study 2, we present an empirical study through which we explored the CPS process in six groups of three students (aged 11–12 years) while they were working on a practice-based design activity. The main goal of this study was to investigate observable differences between student behaviors during CPS. These differences can be used to automate the identification and support of behaviors that lead to effective CPS processes beyond cognition. First, we describe the context of our experiment (participants, tasks, and environment), and then we present the results and analysis of the data collected. We finish with a discussion of these results and the presentation of some final conclusions.

The overarching research aim to identify observable behavior differences of students' CPS processes was shaped into two research questions:

1. What are the observable differences between groups in terms of the amount of time spent in different CPS competencies?

2. What are the observable differences between groups in terms of nonverbal indexes of students' physical interactivity?

Participants

The participants were 18 secondary school students in the first year of their secondary education (aged 11–12 years) from a girls-only secondary school in the United Kingdom. All students were recruited from a computer science class. We obtained written consent from both students and their parents/guardians in line with our institution's ethics procedures.

Learning Activity

Students were set the task of building a working prototype of an interactive toy using an Arduino-based physical computing kit, called TALKOO, that was created as part of an EU-funded project (www.pelars.eu). The TALKOO kit comprises hardware modules, a visual IDE, and prototyping material (Katterfeldt, Cukurova, Spikol, & Cuartielles, 2018). Sensor and actuator modules are pluggable and do not require soldering, and no prior knowledge of electronics is needed. The components have the ability to "talk" back to the visual IDE and to a learning analytics system. The students were also provided with craft materials (colored paper, paper cups, wooden sticks, glitter, glue, etc.) with which to create their working prototypes in combination with the physical computing kit.

Sessions

The study involved two sessions that were run 2 days apart. Session 1 took place in the school's IT (information technology) lab, during school hours, and involved the entire class of 18 students. The session lasted for 1 hour and 20 minutes, during which students worked with a TALKOO kit in pairs or groups of three. The purpose of Session 1 was for students to familiarize themselves with the physical computing kit through a number of predefined activities that exemplified the function of specific components (RGB light, temperature sensor, and potentiometer) and logic functions (if statement, mapping function, and switch function). A researcher, who was assisted by three colleagues and the class teacher, ran Session 1.

Session 2 took place at the university and involved 18 students from the same class as Session 1. The participants were arranged into six groups of three students, and each group was identified by a different color. The students were grouped by their teacher based on her knowledge of their skills and knowledge—her aim was to create balanced groupings. The session lasted about 4 hours and involved:

(a) A refresher session, during which students worked through predefined activities that exemplified the functions of TALKOO components and logic functions (as in Session 1)—30 minutes

(b) An open-ended activity to build an interactive toy—2 hours

(c) A brief activity to demonstrate the function of a motor—15 minutes

(d) An open-ended activity to build an artifact using a motor—1 hour

Activities (a) and (c) were led by a researcher, who demonstrated how to connect and program the components. During activities (b) and (d) students worked independently, but each group was supported by an adult, who assisted the students with troubleshooting the TALKOO kit and debugging the visual programming.

Data Collection

We used a range of different data sources to answer our research questions. The first source targeted the first research question and took the form of human-collected observation data. The collection of this observation data was structured by a theoretical framework developed through previous empirical work, the PELARS CPS framework (Cukurova et al., 2016). This framework was informed by the OECD's CPS assessment and encompassed three collaboration competencies (establishing and maintaining shared understanding, taking appropriate actions to solve the problem, establishing and maintaining group organization) and six problem-solving competencies (identifying facts, representing and formulating knowledge, generating hypotheses, planning and executing, identifying knowledge and skill deficiencies, monitoring-reflecting-applying). The framework has been used to develop an observation protocol and mobile application that runs on phones, tablets, and laptops. The interface to this system is illustrated in Figure 2.3. During the study reported here, human evaluators used this mobile tool to code student behaviors in real time while students were working on a design problem.

In addition to the human observation data, we also collected video recordings of all of the empirical sessions. This data source targets research question 2. The data we discuss in this chapter focuses on Session 2 described in the "Sessions" section above, as the purpose of Session 1 was to familiarize students with the TALKOO kit. During activities (b) and (d), each group was observed by an adult, who used the mobile application to code the instances of collaboration and problem solving, as defined by the protocol in the PELARS CPS framework. In order to ensure a high kappa between different coders, all coders were trained in a daylong, hands-on workshop about the CPS competencies and the observation tool. In parallel, the groups were video recorded. We analyzed the video data using two dimensions that can also be automatically collected with MMLA (Spikol et al., 2018):

(a) Students' hand positions, which can be used to represent their physical engagement with objects;

(b) Students' face directions, which might indicate their degree of involvement in the activity (depending on whether they are looking at the manipulated objects, at other students in their group, or at something outside the activity being carried out).

Classroom Teacher and Facilitators' Judgment of Groups' CPS

The classroom teachers and facilitators involved in the practice-based activity were asked to use their expertise and experiences as teachers to judge each group's collaborative solving competence. This was done in order to create an independent variable to categorize the differences between groups of students. They were all asked to watch the video recordings of the six group sessions and to independently rank groups as high, medium, and low competence CPS groups. Then, teachers and facilitators were brought together to discuss their individual judgments. In their individual judgments of the CPS competency of the groups, there were only discrepancies for two groups. Discussion between teachers and facilitators was used to agree a final competency value for these two groups. Table 2.5 shows the results of this expert evaluation of groups' CPS levels.

TABLE 2.5 Teachers' Judgments of Groups' CPS Levels

THE COLOR CODE OF THE GROUP	TEACHERS' JUDGMENT OF CPS COMPETENCY LEVEL
Green	Low
Red	High
Purple	Medium
Blue	Medium
Yellow	High
Black	Low

Results, Identifying Observable Differences in the Amount of Time Spent by Student Groups on Different CPS Competencies

In this section, we present the analysis and results for research question 1. As mentioned previously, human researcher observers recorded and graded the different stages of student interaction during the learning activity. This information was collected in a tablet, using a mobile observation tool designed to code the CPS competencies. As shown in Figure 2.3, the mobile tool interface reflects the analysis framework with the three key dimensions for collaboration represented as columns and the six key dimensions of problem-solving competency represented as rows. The human observers watched student activity and used the tool to mark the critical incidents that related to the dimensions of collaboration and problem solving as they occurred. The tool also recorded the exact date and time each dimension was marked by the human observer.

The data collected with this observation tool was used to compute the values of the following research variables:

1. T_{PS} (G, C_i) = Percentage of time each group G spent in each competence level C_i (relative to *problem-solving* CPS), where G = {Red, Green, Purple, Blue, Yellow, Black} and $i = 1, 2, 3, 4, 5, 6$.

2. T_{CL} (G, C_i) = Percentage of time each group G spent in each competence level C_i (relative to *collaboration* CPS), where G = {Red, Green, Purple, Blue, Yellow, Black} and $i = 1, 2, 3$.

We anticipated that the human observation data would provide valuable information about the students' CPS processes. The results of the data analysis indicate differences between the groups in terms of the amount of

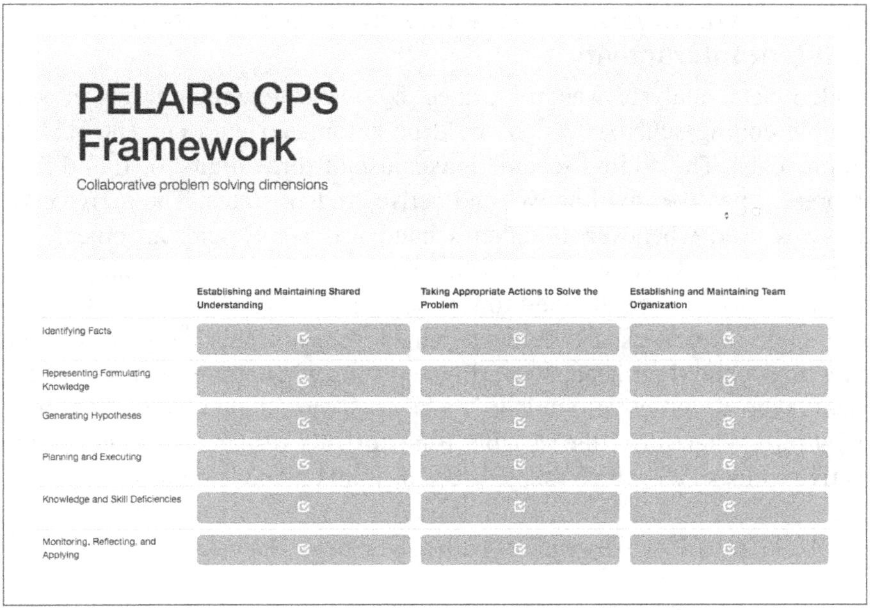

FIGURE 2.3 Screenshot of the coding tool used by observers.

time each group spent on the different activities involved in collaboration and problem solving.

The Red and Yellow groups (which were identified as high competence CPS groups by their teachers) showed a more balanced segregation of different problem-solving behaviors: they spent their time fairly equally on the different dimensions. By contrast, the other groups show unbalanced segregation of time spent in different CPS competencies. It appears that Green and Black groups (which were identified as low competence CPS groups by their teachers) spent most of their time on identifying knowledge and skill deficiencies. They spent very little or no time on some of the important stages of problem solving, such as representing and formulating knowledge, generating hypotheses, and planning and executing. These behaviors might therefore be indicative of a less effective CPS pattern. The data from the Red and Yellow groups also evidences that they spent similar shares of time on different aspects of collaboration. The Green and Purple groups, by comparison, present a greater difference in terms of the amount of time spent on the different aspects of collaboration. It appears that groups who had been evaluated as low CPS by human experts spent very little time on establishing and maintaining team organization, compared to other groups.

Results, Observable Differences in Nonverbal Indexes of Student Interactivity

Video data analysis was performed by two researchers using a very simple coding scheme, which could be automated with current MMLA approaches. The coding scheme makes use of three digits, 0, 1, and 2, to represent passive, semi-active, and active student states. The active code (2) was used whenever a student's hand was active with an object; the semi-active code (1) was used when students were not physically active but their heads were directed toward a peer who was active; and the passive code (0) was used if students hands were not physically active with any object and their heads were directed somewhere other than any of the peers who were active. Students' behaviors were coded using 10-second windows. Therefore, the variable used for this research question is the activity index AC, which takes values 0, 1, and 2 and is defined as:

AC (S, G, t) = Activity code of student S of group G at time t,

S = {1, 2, 3}; G = {Red, Green, Purple, Blue, Yellow, Black} and t = {10, 20, . . .}.

Two coders applied this coding scheme to all groups' video data using the 10-second window, to validate the coding. This procedure was used as a way of testing the reliability of the coding system generated. Where there was disagreement, the researchers discussed the data and agreed on a revised coding accordingly. We first investigated whether the perceived degree of physical activity showed any differences. To this end, we defined new research variables:

N(G, i) = Percentage of i states in group G, where i = 1, 2, 3 and G = {Red, Green, Purple, Blue, Yellow, Black}.

The results illustrate that the percentage of active states (2) was similar across all six groups and ranged from 46.4% (Black) to 66.4% (Yellow). It was interesting to observe that the two groups with the highest percentage of active codes (2) were also the two groups rated by human experts as having the highest CPS competency. Similarly, the two groups with the lowest percentage of active codes (2) were rated by human experts as less competent in CPS. However, the results were not consistent across all groups. For example, the other group rated by our experts as having low CPS competency had the second highest percentage of active codes (2), and the other group rated as being high CPS competency had the second lowest percentage of active codes (2). This result suggests that the crude measure of the percentage of active states may not be a good indicator for differentiating the CPS processes in a group (i.e., individual students' activity with objects may not be contributing to CPS processes overall). However, we also considered if students' passive codes (0) might be a predictor. The Red and Yellow groups had the lowest percentages of passive codes (0). By contrast, the Green and Black groups had the highest percentages of passive codes (0). This result is surprising because the most researched and tracked indicators in learning analytics research are often related to what students are doing. This case study's results suggest observing what students *are not doing* might be also informative.

We also wanted to analyze whether there were any patterns in the data that could be providing information about the degree of activity for each individual student. To this end, we defined a new research variable:

> Nj(G, *i*) = Percentage of *i* states for student j in group G, where *j* = 1, 2, 3; *i* = 1, 2, 3, 4, 5, 6, and G = {Red, Green, Purple, Blue, Yellow, Black}.

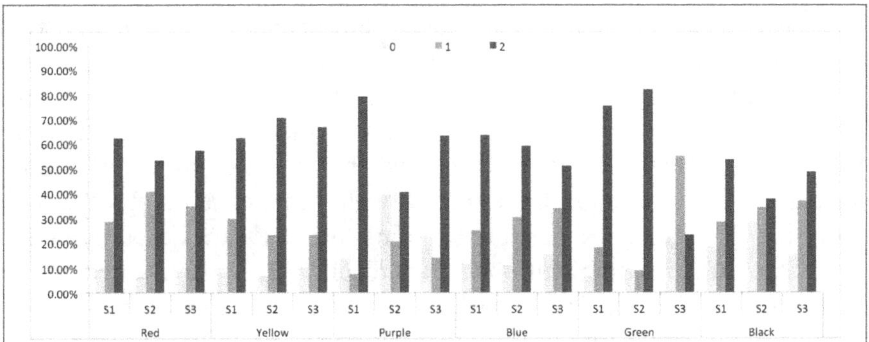

FIGURE 2.4 Percentage of individual student's number of passive 0, semi-active 1, and active 2 codes.

Figure 2.4 presents the values obtained for these new variables. It illustrates that the individual students in the Red and Yellow groups get similar values for all the codes. The rest of the groups, by contrast, illustrate bigger differences between the students' individual contributions. In the Red group, all three partners show a similar degree of involvement in the activity, ranging from 53% to 62%.

However, in the Green group there is a bigger difference in the degree of involvement (from 23% for S_3 to 82% for S_2). Clearly, in the Red and Yellow groups all members were contributing to the task in similarly active ways, while in the other two groups students' physical interactions were more passive and varied more.

DISCUSSION

In this chapter, we have discussed the richly varied repertoire that is human intelligence, a repertoire that extends way beyond cognition. We have also presented several methods for identifying differences between the ways in which different groups of learners take part in CPS. We show that learning from these differences in observable behaviors can be informed by research from the learning sciences, such as the ICAP framework (Chi, 2009), Ecology of Resources (Luckin, 2010), and PELARS framework (Cukurova et al., 2016). We have also illustrated methods of analysis that could potentially be automated with MMLA technologies to generate insights into the learning processes involved in CPS beyond the frequently studied cognitive aspects (Spikol et al., 2018).

The richness of human intelligent behavior can only be understood through a wide range of evidence, and MMLA systems provide one way to capture and analyze such evidence. The results of the case studies presented in this chapter support the suggestion that there is a relationship between a group's CPS competence and that group's observable behavior patterns. This relationship requires further investigation at scale with more robust evaluations. However, the initial results are encouraging for those interested in using multimodal approaches in learning sciences such as MMLA, as they can inform how we can collect, analyze, and automate the process of providing useful feedback about the CPS process to students and/or teachers.

Various approaches to the design and use of technology to interpret the behavior patterns investigated in this chapter are possible. For instance, the first case study investigates students' interactions with their context and provides information on the relationship between these interactions and their CPS processes. Computer vision systems that can identify and track students and resources in a learning environment can provide measures of students' interactions with their surroundings and use this information to provide valuable insights into the CPS processes of students. The second case study provides a much more fine-grained analysis of observable learner actions in CPS during practice-based learning. In this case, while some of the features can be automatically detected, such as the students' nonverbal interactions studied here (e.g., Cukurova et al., 2018; Spikol, Ruffaldi, Landolfi, & Cukurova, 2017; Spikol et al., 2018; Healion, Russell, Cukurova, & Spikol, 2017), other features require human interpretations that can be supported and augmented with MMLA support—the CPS competences of collaboration and problem solving that we collected though research observers, for example.

The emerging field of MMLA provides examples of how data science can help researchers in the learning sciences to overcome obstacles that arise when conducting investigations into learning processes in situ. The richness and complexity of human intelligence can only be interpreted, evidenced, and supported with rich, multimodal data. Data produced through the use of digital technologies are large in volume, even for single learners. They are heterogeneous, too, because they stem from different devices (e.g., keyboard, mouse, video camera), are of different kinds (e.g., actions in an online problem-solving environment, answers to online quizzes, or learners' gaze when studying a simulation), and/or of different time scales (e.g., single testing instance or continuous sampling). We argue that such large-volume, heterogeneous, and, more importantly, complex data can potentially help us to shed light on human intelligence beyond cognition in a holistic manner. However, so far, most research in the learning sciences considers large-volume data in the form of sampling data from thousands of learners at one point in time. Through the analysis of multimodal, large amounts of data, collected in situ to investigate the process of CPS with two case studies, our aim has been to exemplify a potential approach that should be taken in learning sciences research more generally.

CONCLUDING COMMENTS

The research reported here has been conducted with small sample sizes and an explorative approach. Any conclusions we draw about how to support students in their CPS processes should therefore be approached with caution. Our case studies indicate that students' interactions with both human and nonhuman resources in situ must be supported if they are to be constructive and interactive in their nature. Moreover, learners also need to be supported to avoid spending most of their time on particular aspects of problem solving, such as the identification of knowledge and skill deficiencies. Learners must be supported to progress into the other equally important aspects of problem solving. Results similar to those reported here have also been found for engineering students working on design problems (Noel et al., 2018). Finally, students should be supported to achieve effective equality and synchrony in terms of their contributions to the CPS task at hand.

Perhaps more important than identifying these implications for supporting students' learning through CPS, the potential of multimodal approaches should be realized in the learning sciences. These approaches hold the promise for overcoming some of the major limitations of past research on learning processes and human intelligence. The ability to analyze data about learning processes at a fine-grained temporal level allows for investigating the mechanisms of learning across sequences of learning opportunities (e.g., Gerjets, Walter, Rosenstiel, Bogdan, & Zander, 2014). It also provides the potential to link evidence about learners' sequences of learning opportunities to the development of a range of elements of human intelligence (e.g., Milligan & Griffin, 2016).

It should, of course, be noted that these techniques are still being developed and they do not come without their challenges. It is worth emphasizing that understanding theories and empirical findings from the learning sciences challenges the field of learning analytics to conduct further research to advance our understanding. For instance, in order to investigate the comprehensive representations of learning processes theorized in the learning sciences (see context interactions in Case Study 1 and nonverbal student interactions in Case Study 2), it is necessary to take multiple types of data into account (Spikol, Prieto, et al., 2017) which in turn increases the accuracy of models built (Giannakos et al., 2019; Cukurova, Kent, & Luckin, 2019). However, the collection, organization, and analysis of such heterogeneous data poses significant research challenges.

For instance, the identification of some of the collaborative learning processes that happen in practice-based learning and that have been identified in the literature, such as equality, mutuality, or individual accountability of student interactions (Cukurova et al., 2018) requires data collection from students' body movement and face recognition. Researchers might need to identify individual students and their manipulation of learning objects, for example. Data collection on these features poses significant research challenges that can only be overcome with further advances in AI and data science research.

Similarly, the identification of the rich intra-individual variation in the complex learning processes of CPS requires the study of these processes at the level of the individual (Molenaar, 2004). And the collection of short-interval time series of high quality data about CPS processes can only be achieved with further advancement in learning analytics research (Hofman et al., 2018).

Thirdly, the integration of heterogeneous big data is a significant research challenge (e.g., Schneider, Di Mitri, Limbu, & Drachsler, 2018). Although data from a depth camera (average 25 frames per second) and a microphone to track specific aspects of the communication of a learner (average 44,100 of volume values per second) can provide invaluable insights into learning processes, integrating and making sense of these different streams of data in order to support learning is a significant challenge for data sciences (Schneider et al., 2018). In terms of data analysis, learners' process data from different behavioral traces do not carry much semantic information when considered individually. They are however predictive of knowledge states when big data sets are processed. They also pose significant research challenges for data sciences (see Dillenbourg, 2016, for an overview).

Lastly, the accuracy and transfer of models from one population to another remains a challenging problem in the field of data science and requires substantial additional research effort (e.g., Daxenberger, Csanadi, Ghanem, Kollar, & Gurevych, 2018).

The challenges outlined here are significant. They do however also offer opportunities to illustrate the reciprocal nature of the relationship between learning sciences research and multimodal approaches to studying educational technologies when human intelligence is considered as a multidimensional construct that is strongly related to most of the generic skills of constructivist pedagogies. And when human intelligence is studied accordingly, this has the potential to lead to advancements in various fields that are relevant to, but distinct from each other.

REFERENCES

Ames, C. (1992). Classrooms: Goals, structures, and student motivation. *Journal of Educational Psychology, 84*(3), 261.

Babenko, B., Yang, M. H., & Belongie, S. (2009). Visual tracking with online multiple instance learning. In 2009 IEEE conference on computer vision and pattern recognition (pp. 983–990).

Bergin, D. A., Ford, M. E., & Hess, R. D. (1993). Patterns of motivation and social behavior associated with microcomputer use of young children. *Journal of Educational Psychology, 85*(3), 437.

Blikstein, P., & Worsley, M. (2016). Multimodal learning analytics and education data mining: Using computational technologies to measure complex learning tasks. *Journal of Learning Analytics, 3*(2), 220–238. doi:http://dx.doi.org/10.18608/jla.2016.32.11

Boekaerts, M. (2003). *Towards a model that integrates motivation, affect and learning* (Vol. 173, No. 189, pp. 173–189). British Psychological Society.

Bruner, J. S. (1996). *The culture of education.* Harvard University Press.

Chi, M. T. (2009). Active-constructive-interactive: A conceptual framework for differentiating learning activities. *Topics in cognitive science, 1*(1), 73–105.

Chi, M. T. (2011). Theoretical perspectives, methodological approaches, and trends in the study of expertise. In *Expertise in mathematics instruction* (pp. 17–39). Boston, MA: Springer.

Clark, P. (2015, March). Elementary school science and math tests as a driver for AI: take the aristo challenge!. In *Twenty-Seventh IAAI Conference.*

Cukurova, M. (2018). A syllogism for designing collaborative learning technologies in the age of AI and multimodal data. In *European Conference on Technology Enhanced Learning* (pp. 291–296). Springer, Cham.

Cukurova, M. (2019). Learning analytics as AI extenders in education: Multimodal machine learning versus multimodal learning analytics. In *Proceedings of the Artificial Intelligence and Adaptive Education Conference* (pp. 1–3).

Cukurova, M., Kent, C., & Luckin, R. (2019). Artificial intelligence and multimodal data in the service of human decision-making: A case study in debate tutoring. *British Journal of Educational Technology*, 50*(4),* 1–22.

Cukurova, M., Avramides, K., Spikol, D., Luckin, R., & Mavrikis, M. (2016). An analysis framework for collaborative problem solving in practice-based learning activities: a mixed-method approach. *Proceedings of the International Conference on Learning Analytics & Knowledge* (pp. 84–88). Edinburgh, UK: ACM.

Luckin, R., & Cukurova, M. (2019). Designing educational technologies in the age of AI: A learning sciences-driven approach. *British Journal of Educational Technology, 50*(4), 301-324.

Cukurova, M., Luckin, R., & Baines, E. (2018). The significance of context for the emergence and implementation of research evidence: the case of collaborative problem-solving. *Oxford Review of Education, 44*(3), 322–337.

Cukurova, M., Luckin, R., Millán, E., & Mavrikis, M. (2018). The NISPI framework: Analysing collaborative problem-solving from students' physical interactions. *Computers & Education, 116*, 93–109.

Cukurova, M., Luckin, R., Millán, E., Mavrikis, M., & Spikol, D. (2017). Diagnosing collaboration in practice-based learning: Equality and intra-individual variability of physical interactivity. In *European Conference on Technology Enhanced Learning* (pp. 30–42). Springer, Cham.

Damon, W., & Phelps, E. (1989). Critical distinctions among three approaches to peer education. *International Journal of Educational Research, 13*(1), 9–19. doi:http://dx.doi.org/10.1016/0883-0355(89)90013-X

Daxenberger, J., Csanadi, A., Ghanem, C., Kollar, I., & Gurevych, I. (2018). Domain-specific aspects of scientific reasoning and argumentation: insights from automatic coding. In *Scientific reasoning and argumentation* (pp. 44–65). Routledge.

Di Mitri, D., Schneider, J., Specht, M., & Drachsler, H. (2018). From signals to knowledge: A conceptual model for multimodal learning analytics. *Journal of Computer Assisted Learning, 34*(4), 338–349. http://doi.org/10.1111/jcal.12288

Dillenbourg, P., & Jermann, P. (2007). Designing integrative scripts. In F. Fischer, I. Kollar, H. Mandl, & J. M. Haake (Eds.), *Scripting computer-supported collaborative learning: cognitive, computational and educational perspectives* (pp. 275–301). Boston, MA: Springer US.

Dillenbourg, P. (2016). The evolution of research on digital education. *International Journal of Artificial Intelligence in Education, 26*, 544–560.

Dweck, C. S., & Leggett, E. L. (1988). A social-cognitive approach to motivation and personality. *Psychological Review, 95*(2), 256.

Flavell, J. H. (1979). Metacognition and cognitive monitoring: A new area of cognitive–developmental inquiry. *American Psychologist, 34*(10), 906.

Fei-Fei, L. (2018). How artificial intelligence is edging its way into our lives. Retrieved from https://www.nytimes.com/2018/02/12/technology/artificial-intelligence-new-work-summit.html

Funke, J., Fischer, A., & Holt, D. V. (2018). Competencies for complexity: Problem solving in the twenty-first century. In E. Care, P. Griffin, & M. Wilson (Eds.), *Assessment and teaching of 21st century skills: research and applications* (pp. 41–53). Dordrecht: Springer.

Gardner, H. (2011). *Frames of mind: The theory of multiple intelligences*. Hachette UK.

Gerjets, P., Walter, C., Rosenstiel, W., Bogdan, M., & Zander, T. O. (2014). Cognitive state monitoring and the design of adaptive instruction in digital environments: Lessons learned from cognitive workload assessment using a passive brain-computer interface approach. *Frontiers in Neuroscience, 8*, 385.

Giannakos, M. N., Sharma, K., Pappas, I. O., Kostakos, V., & Velloso, E. (2019). Multimodal data as a means to understand the learning experience. *International Journal of Information Management, 48*, 108–119.

Goos, M., Galbraith, P., & Renshaw, P. (2002). Socially mediated metacognition: Creating collaborative zones of proximal development in small group problem solving. *Educational Studies in Mathematics, 49*(2), 193–223.

Harackiewicz, J. M., Barron, K. E., & Elliot, A. J. (1998). Rethinking achievement goals: When are they adaptive for college students and why?. *Educational Psychologist, 33*(1), 1–21.

Harris, A., Yuill, N., & Luckin, R. (2008). The influence of context-specific and dispositional achievement goals on children's paired collaborative interaction. *British Journal of Educational Psychology, 78*(3), 355–374.

Healion, D., Russell, S., Cukurova, M., & Spikol, D. (2017, March). Tracing physical movement during practice-based learning through multimodal learning analytics. In *Proceedings of the Seventh International Learning Analytics & Knowledge Conference* (pp. 588–589). ACM.

Hofer, B. K., & Pintrich, P. R. (1997). The development of epistemological theories: Beliefs about knowledge and knowing and their relation to learning. *Review of Educational Research, 67*(1), 88–140.

Hofman, A. D., Jansen, B. R., de Mooij, S. M., Stevenson, C. E., & van der Maas, H. L. (2018). A solution to the measurement problem in the idiographic approach using computer adaptive practicing. *Journal of Intelligence, 6*(1), 14.

Hoy, A. W., & Spero, R. B. (2005). Changes in teacher efficacy during the early years of teaching: A comparison of four measures. *Teaching and Teacher Education, 21*(4), 343–356.

Johnson, D. W., & Johnson, R. T. (2002) Learning together and alone: Overview and meta-analysis. *Asia Pacific Journal of Education, 22*, 95–105.

Kahneman, D. (2011). *Thinking, fast and slow.* Farrar, Straus and Giroux.

Kalal, Z., Mikolajczyk, K., & Matas, J. (2012, July). Tracking-learning-detection. *IEEE Transactions on Pattern Analysis and Machine Intelligence, 34*(7):1409–1422.

Katterfeldt, E., Cukurova, M., Spikol, D., & Cuartielles, D. (2018). Physical computing with plug-and-play toolkits: Key recommendations for collaborative learning implementations. *International Journal of Child-Computer Interaction*, 1–23. https://www.sciencedirect.com/science/article/pii/S2212868917300351

Klassen, R. M., Tze, V. M., Betts, S. M., & Gordon, K. A. (2011). Teacher efficacy research 1998–2009: Signs of progress or unfulfilled promise?. *Educational Psychology Review, 23*(1), 21–43.

Kornell, N. (2009). Metacognition in humans and animals. *Current Directions in Psychological Science, 18*(1), 11–15.

Kyndt, E., Raes, E., Lismont, B., Timmers, F., Cascallar, E., & Dochy, F. (2013). A meta-analysis of the effects of face-to-face cooperative learning: Do recent students verify or falsify earlier findings? *Educational Research Review, 10*, 133–149.

Laland, K., Uller, T., Feldman, M., Sterelny, K., Müller, G. B., Moczek, A., . . . & Futuyma, D. J. (2014). Does evolutionary theory need a rethink? *Nature News, 514*(7521), 161. https://www.nature.com/articles/514161a

Luckin, R. (2010). *Re-designing learning contexts: technology-rich, learner-centred ecologies*. London: Routledge.

Luckin, R. (2018). *Machine learning and human intelligence: The future of education for the 21st century*. UCL IOE Press. UCL Institute of Education.

Luckin, R., Baines, E., Cukurova, M., & Holmes, W. (2017). Solved! Making the case for collaborative problem-solving. UK: NESTA.

Manovich, L. (2006). The poetics of augmented space. *Visual Communication, 5*(2), 219–240.

Martinez-Maldonado, R., Dimitriadis, Y., Martinez-Monés, A., Kay, J., & Yacef, K. (2013). Capturing and analyzing verbal and physical collaborative learning interactions at an enriched interactive tabletop. *International Journal of Computer-Supported Collaborative Learning, 8*(4), 455–485.

Martinez-Maldonado, R. M., Kay, J., Yacef, K., & Schwendimann, B. (2012). An interactive teacher's dashboard for monitoring groups in a multi-tabletop learning environment. In *International Conference on Intelligent Tutoring Systems* (pp. 482–492). Berlin, Heidelberg: Springer.

Marzano, R. J. (1998). A theory-based meta-analysis of research on instruction. Office of Educational Research and Improvement, US Department of Education.

Milligan, S. K., & Griffin, P. (2016). Understanding learning and learning design in MOOCs: A measurement-based interpretation. *Journal of Learning Analytics, 3*(2), 88–115.

Molenaar, P. C. M. (2004). A manifesto on psychology as idiographic science: Bringing the person back into scientific psychology, this time forever. *Measurement, 2*, 201–218.

Noel, R., Riquelme, F., Mac Lean, R., Merino, E., Cechinel, C., Barcelos, T. S., . . . & Munoz, R. (2018). Exploring collaborative writing of user stories with multimodal learning analytics: A case study on a software engineering course. *IEEE Access*. doi:10.1109/ACCESS.2018.2876801

Ochoa, X. (2017). Multimodal learning analytics. In. C. Lang, G. Siemens, A. Wise, & D. Gašević (Eds.), *Handbook of learning analytics* (pp. 129–141). Society for Learning Analytics Research (SoLAR).

Ochoa, X., Worsley, M., Weibel, N., & Oviatt, S. (2016, April). Multimodal learning analytics data challenges. In *Proceedings of the Sixth International Conference on Learning Analytics & Knowledge* (pp. 498–499). ACM.

OECD. (2015). Draft collaborative problem solving framework. Retrieved from http://www.oecd.org/pisa/pisaproducts/DraftPISA2015CollaborativeProblemSolvingFramework.pdf

Ortony, A., Clore, G., & Collins, A. (1988). *The cognitive structure of emotions.* New York: Cambridge University Press.

Perry Jr., W. G. (1968). Patterns of development in thought and values of students in a liberal arts college: A validation of a scheme. Final report.

Pintrich, P. R. (2000). Multiple goals, multiple pathways: The role of goal orientation in learning and achievement. *Journal of Educational Psychology, 92*(3), 544.

Prieto, L. P., Sharma, K., Dillenbourg, P., & Rodríguez-Triana, M. J. (2016, April). Teaching analytics: towards automatic extraction of orchestration graphs using wearable sensors. In *Proceedings of the Sixth International Conference on Learning Analytics & Knowledge* (pp. 148–157). ACM.

Ryan, R. M., & Deci, E. L. (2000). Intrinsic and extrinsic motivations: Classic definitions and new directions. *Contemporary Educational Psychology, 25*(1), 54–67.

Scherer, S., Worsley, M., & Morency, L. P. (2012, October). 1st international workshop on multimodal learning analytics. In *Proceedings of the 14th ACM International Conference on Multimodal Interaction* (pp. 609–610). ACM.

Schneider, J., Di Mitri, D., Limbu, B., & Drachsler, H. (2018). Multimodal learning hub: A tool for capturing customizable multimodal learning experiences. In *European Conference on Technology Enhanced Learning* (pp. 45–58). Springer, Cham.

Scoular, C., Care, E., & Hesse, F. (2017). Designs for operationalizing collaborative problem solving for automated assessment. *Journal of Educational Measurement, 54*(1), 12–35.

Sharples, M., & Roschelle, J. (2010). Guest editorial: Special section on mobile and ubiquitous technologies for learning. *IEEE Transactions on Learning Technologies, 3*(1), 4–6.

Siraj, I. (2017). Nurturing 21st century skills in early childhood education and care: the way forward. In L. Loble, T. Creenaline, & J. Hayes (Eds.), *Future frontiers: Education for an AI world* (pp. 141–153). Australia: Melbourne University Press & NSW Department of Education.

Skaalvik, E. M., & Skaalvik, S. (2007). Dimensions of teacher self-efficacy and relations with strain factors, perceived collective teacher efficacy, and teacher burnout. *Journal of Educational Psychology, 99*(3), 611.

Skinner, B. F. (1957). *Verbal behavior.* New York: Appleton-Century-Crofts.

Slavin, R. E. (2014). Cooperative learning and academic achievement: Why does groupwork work? *Anales de Psicología/Annals of Psychology, 30*, 785–791. https://doi.org/10.6018/analesps.30.3.201201

Spearman, C. (1904). "General intelligence," objectively determined and measured. *The American Journal of Psychology, 15*(2), 201–292.

Spikol, D., Prieto, L. P., Rodríguez-Triana, M. J., Worsley, M., Ochoa, X., Cukurova, M., . . . & Ringtved, U. L. (2017, March). Current and future multimodal learning analytics data challenges. In *Proceedings of the Seventh International Learning Analytics & Knowledge Conference* (pp. 518–519). ACM.

Spikol, D., Ruffaldi, E., Dabisias, G., & Cukurova, M. (2018). Supervised machine learning in multimodal learning analytics for estimating success in project-based learning. *Journal of Computer Assisted Learning, 34*(4), 366–377. doi.org/10.1111/jcal.12263

Spikol, D., Ruffaldi, E., Landolfi, L., & Cukurova, M. (2017, July). Estimation of success in collaborative learning based on multimodal learning analytics features. In *2017 IEEE 17th International Conference on Advanced Learning Technologies (ICALT)* (pp. 269–273). IEEE.

Sternberg, R. J. (1985). *Beyond IQ: A triarchic theory of human intelligence.* CUP Archive.

Tarricone, P. (2011). *The taxonomy of metacognition.* Psychology Press.

Thorndike, E. L. (1911). *Animal intelligence: Experimental studies.* Macmillan, 1911.
Tucker, M. (2017). Education for a digital future: the challenge. In L. Loble, T. Creenaline, & J. Hayes (Eds.), *Future frontiers: Education for an AI world* (pp. 21–38). Australia: Melbourne University Press & NSW Department of Education.
Vygotsky, L. S. (1980). *Mind in society: The development of higher psychological processes.* Harvard University Press.
Walsh, T. (2017). *Android dreams: The past, present and future of artificial intelligence.* UK: Hurst Publishers.
Watson, J. B. (1926). Behaviourism: A psychology based on reflex-action. *Philosophy, 1*(4), 454–466.
Wolters, C. A., & Daugherty, S. G. (2007). Goal structures and teachers' sense of efficacy: Their relation and association to teaching experience and academic level. *Journal of Educational Psychology, 99*(1), 181.
Worsley, M., Chiluiza, K., Grafsgaard, J. F., & Ochoa, X. (2015, November). 2015 Multimodal Learning and Analytics Grand Challenge. In *Proceedings of the 2015 ACM on International Conference on Multimodal Interaction* (pp. 525–529). ACM.

ABOUT THE AUTHORS

Professor Rosemary Luckin is a University College London professor whose research involves blending theories from the learning sciences with techniques from artificial intelligence (AI). She is author of *Machine Learning and Human Intelligence: The Future of Education in the 21st Century* and director of EDUCATE: a London hub for educational technology start-ups.

Dr. Mutlu Cukurova is a lecturer of digital technologies in education at University College London. His research broadly addresses the pressing social-educational challenge of preparing people for a future that will require a great deal more than the routine cognitive skills prized by many education systems. Currently, he investigates the potential of emerging technologyies such as artificial intelligence and learning analytics to continuously evaluate and support human development.

CHAPTER 3

Learning Science Research Through a Social Scientific Lens

Tanya Joosten
University of Wisconsin—Milwaukee

ABSTRACT

Science is more than proving hypotheses; it is about navigating messy and complex organizational and psychological structures to further knowledge and understand the world we live and learn in. In this chapter, I approach the field of learning science through a social science lens, taking a historical look at key social science frameworks and paradigm changes and how the modern definition of learning science situates within them. Further, I discuss the case of the National Research Center for Distance Education and Technological Advancements (DETA), and how it provides a representative illustration of the intersection between learning science and social science in online, blended, and technologically enhanced research. The chapter closes with a closer look at the paradigmatic bridges that initiatives like DETA can help build within a learning ecosystem.

Once upon a time, it was believed that there were two sciences in the world, physical and social sciences, yet "[t]oday we live in the age of science" (Lincoln & Guba, 1985, p. 7). Historically, there were two dominant sciences, the physical or natural sciences, sometimes referred to as hard sciences, and the later evolution of the so-called "softer," or social sciences. This dichotomous categorization eases one's perception of the world and science. It provides a nonmessy, black or white, solid differentiation between two sciences. However, as clinically as it may be approached, behind the scenes science is messy. Some argue that there are additional disciplinary sciences, such as normal and applied sciences, yet others argue that those are not sciences as science is historically defined as knowing the world empirically. What is and isn't science is still debated, especially in a time when claims of new sciences are manifest. In the past several decades, numerous academic and disciplinary sciences have emerged, such as learning science, the focus of this book. Intriguingly, there are no longer two sciences but many sciences.

As a social scientist who has conducted empirical research on human communication and technology, including in the contexts of education, I was perplexed at my recent exposure to the terminology of learning science. At several points, I have even been referred to as a learning scientist. In my graduate programs, this was not an area of scholarship to which I was exposed, nor had I encountered it previously in my research, teaching, or practice. In fact, it seems that learning science has evolved along similar timelines as digital learning and following similar patterns. So, I asked myself, what is learning science? Is it new jargon in educational technology? A community of like-minded individuals putting forth a coherent agenda as to how to study learning? An emerging instructional program in university schools of education to better inform K–12 education? Or maybe a subacademic discipline in education? For instance, with the rise of communication in the mid-20th century, Berlo (1960) described that universities became interested in communication as a field and "initiated a 'communication' department or college to administer the new kind of interdisciplinary approach . . . again others have simply put the new label on existing departments and traditional ways of doing things" (p. 4). Drawing parallels to the emergence of communication as a discipline, learning science posits itself as an interdisciplinary science that is a combination of social sciences and applied sciences focusing on cognitive and social processes (see Sawyer, 2014). Thus, if historical patterns are to be believed, the need for interdisciplinary ways of knowing seems to lead to the emergence of new areas of study in academia.

In a space where social scientists study learning, it is important to understand learning science from a social scientific lens, and how the two sciences can or do inform each other. Beyond our phenomenon of interest, physical or social, our understanding of who we are as researchers and scholars or our view of knowledge and reality tends to stem from our paradigmatic stances, metatheories and theories, and methodologies. Therefore, to understand learning science from the perspective of a social scientist, one must understand how social science informs learning science and where learning science situates itself within and departs from the social scientist frame of reference.

What is learning science? Sawyer (2014) stated that "[t]he learning sciences is an interdisciplinary field that studies teaching and learning" (p. 1), which is a pretty general statement on learning science. It is important to note the distinction in that it is not just the study of learning but of teaching and learning. He defined the research setting of learning scientists as "not only the formal learning of school classrooms, but also the informal learning that takes place at home, on the job, and among peers. The goal of the learning sciences is to better understand the cognitive and social processes that result in the most effective learning and to use this knowledge to redesign classrooms and other learning environments so that people learn more deeply and more effectively" (p. 1). More recently, in an analysis of learning science graduate programs, Sommerhoff, Szameitat, Vogel, Chernikova, Loderer, and Fischer (2018) described it as "target[ing] the analysis and facilitation of real-world learning in formal and informal contexts. Learning activities and processes are considered crucial and are typically captured through the analysis of cognition, metacognition, and dialog. To facilitate learning activities, the design of learning environments is seen as fundamental. Technology is key for supporting and scaffolding individuals and groups to engage in productive learning activities" (p. 320). Nathan and Sawyer (2014) also highlight the importance of design principles in the study of learning science, "[t]he learning sciences (LS) studies the design and implementation of effective learning environments, in addition to the basic scientific research on learning" (p. 21). Thus, learning science is informed by multiple disciplines including social and applied sciences with a focus on informal and formal leaning contexts. The goal is to understand the cognitive and social factors that influence learning to inform the design and redesign of learning activities and environments.

The first part of this chapter provides a foundation of understanding how learning science is situated within the social sciences by examining paradigm changes, specifically the positivist and antipositivist paradigmatic shifts in the social sciences. I examine these two predominant paradigms and paradigmatic shifts within the social sciences. I also discuss changes in the view of processes in the social sciences as a result of or attributing to these paradigm shifts. Changes in both paradigm and process in the social sciences align with the same shifts seen in learning science, and I present a discussion of these parallels to close part one. Part two of the chapter specifically illustrates an intersection of learning science and an example of a national social scientific research agenda in online, blended, and technologically enhanced education in postsecondary institutions at the National Research Center for Distance Education and Technological Advancements (DETA) by identifying a paradigmatic bridge, theory-informed framework of inquiry, mixed methodological approaches, and implications for practice.

PARADIGMATIC CHANGES

Social science consists of various paradigms traditionally focusing on the objective and the subjective. More recently, new paradigms have arisen that are viewed as critical paradigms (e.g., critical, postmodern). Paradigms are scientists' view of the world. These paradigms each include metatheoretical assumptions about the nature of the social sciences, nature of the social world, and how it should be investigated. Further, paradigm defines a scientist's role and frame of reference (Burrell & Morgan, 1979/1988). For instance, young to the field or emerging social scientists discover a paradigmatic stance about the world that is in line with their view of the world in their studies, and this position guides their inquiry throughout their career or at least some part of it. Lincoln and Guba (1985) described paradigms as "a systematic set of beliefs, together with their accompanying methods . . . [that] represent a distillation of what we *think* about the world. . . . Our actions in the world, including actions that we take as inquirers, cannot occur without reference to those paradigms." So "while paradigms are thus enabling, they are also constraining" (p. 15). They referred to Patton's (1978) definition as "a world view, a general perspective, a way of breaking down the complexity of the real world . . . deeply embedded in the socialization of adherents and practitioners . . . tell[ing] them what's important . . . also normative, telling the practitioner what to do without the necessity of long existential or epistemological consideration" (p. 203; Lincoln & Guba, 1985, p. 15). Kuhn (1996) viewed paradigms as more of models that "spring particular coherent traditions of scientific research" from achievements and examples including "law, theory, application, and instrumentation" (p. 10). For instance, many early efforts in science were to identify laws that influenced the behavior of organisms or humans. Not only do paradigms guide scientists' view of the world and inquiry, the achievements of scientists can produce a revolution or new paradigms. The influence of paradigms on social science is quite evident and is an important foundation for understanding the emergence of learning science.

People have different ways they view the world. Some individuals may be looking to tinker with and iterate upon situations to improve outcomes. For instance, some examples include questions like: What can be changed in a class or course that will improve student outcomes? What intervention or interventions can be implemented to change behavior, such as to improve student content retention or persistence at the course or degree level? Others may be driven by deeply understanding one situation or event and the webs of significance around the event. Why does one student or group of students have such a hard time comprehending certain material? What about the learning environment is hindering or helping the student? Moreover, individual educators and researchers can consider how they view the world or how they view teaching and learning. Are educators experts or sages on the stage who transmit knowledge to students, or do they create scaffolded experiences that assist students in creating knowledge? These questions and more can help people start to consider their paradigmatic stance regarding the study of learning.

Notably, Burrell and Morgan (1979/1988) devised what they called a tool for the analysis of social theory, an analytic scheme, or a heuristic device when they developed a model of paradigms. These paradigms of social theory allow scholars to develop their own distinctive analysis of social theories. Moreover, paradigms provide scholars a frame of reference in which to view others' scholarship and understand others' view of the world. There are different iterations of social science paradigms (e.g., Deetz, 1996), yet every iteration usually consists of a positivist or objective paradigm and an antipositivist or subjective paradigm. The revolution or shift from positivist to antipositivist is not only pertinent in understanding social science, but it is the crux to understanding the emergence of learning science. This revolution is often referred to as a paradigm shift. Although the dichotomy is an overly simplistic view of science, it can clarify emerging perspectives over the last half century.

Positivism and Behaviorism

Traditionally, the bulk of theory and research in the social sciences and the study of learning has centered in the more objective, which many felt was a narrow range of theoretical possibilities but was dominant in the field of social science. The objective paradigm was greatly informed by theory and research relevant in the physical or natural sciences, and in return, the social sciences were immensely influenced by the objective approach to understanding the world through observations already used in the natural sciences. Traditional or objectivistic approaches search for universal laws and are viewed as scientific or "normal science" as Kuhn (1996) referred to them. This traditional approach was often described as positivist where scientists search for laws and regulation, seek to explain and predict, and search for regularities and causal relationships between elements. Positivist paradigms have dominated the natural sciences with their experimental research designs and focus on verifying and falsifying hypotheses. There were also similar approaches to science in education research through hypothesis testing and experimental design (e.g., Lindquist, 1940).

Behaviorism, pertinent because of its influence in learning sciences, is seen as objectivism in the functionalist paradigm. Functionalism falls within the positivist epistemology with the belief that knowledge can be gained through careful and objective observation of a phenomenon, and that systems are composed of variables that are causally interrelated. Burrell and Morgan (1979/1988) described behaviorism as the boundary of this paradigm due to the adhesion to the models and methods of the natural sciences where human beings are treated as machines or biological organisms, and social structures are seen as physical structures that influence human behavior. Also, they discussed Skinner's (1953) work as a behaviorist as the "archetype of positivism" (p. 103). Behaviorism consists of causal theories of behavior where investigations focus on relationships of stimulus and response and use experimental methods as used in the natural sciences. It holds the belief that individuals' behavior is controlled by their environment and responds to conditions to which they are subjected or that they are a product of their environment. It is positivism in the way it attempts to uncover universal laws and regulations and is deterministic.

Many scholars today still hold behaviorist values. Subsets of researchers still think of the study of learning as one that requires objective observation of learners or instructors to understand, although most understand that complete objectivism is impossible in real-life contexts such as education. For instance, some researchers consider what variables can influence student learning or other outcomes or question how certain variables are related to or have a causal relationship with student outcomes. Or, what intervention or stimulus can be introduced to influence student outcomes. Although paradigms have shifted, there are still studies conducted from this more objective paradigmatic stance.

The focus on these approaches became an ongoing debate with new and emerging approaches. For instance, Demerath and Peterson (1967) addressed the "functionalist controversy" (p. 3) in their work. They included work from other disciplines, such as anthropology, and noted the troublesome distinction between theory and empirical analysis. Also, they posited the question whether societies could even be viewed as systems, including wondering what the logical and substantive differences were in level of analysis from the individual to the society. Social science was evolving to question the traditional paradigm. Kuhn (1996) described emerging approaches as searching for explanation and understanding of the social world rather than searching for laws to predict. The evolution of more subjective approaches to the social sciences brought about philosophical debates and problems of ontology and epistemology, in particular when examining problems of order and conflict. Burrell and Morgan (1979/1988) went as far to call them "rival intellectual traditions" and described that *positivist* "has become more of a derogatory epithet than a useful descriptive concept" (p. 5). The paradigms are not only different philosophically, they are different in methodological nature. As Burrell and Morgan (1979/1988) mentioned, the differences will provide an inclination to social scientists toward different methodologies. Specifically, "how does one attempt to obtain knowledge about the social world" (p. 2). In part, this is driven by whether you are searching to provide order or to understand conflict. In practical terms, sometimes our questions are not about objective views or observations to understand relationships between variables, but our questions are simply to understand one phenomenon or to describe one event with great richness within a social context.

Antipositivism and Naturalist Inquiry

The antipositivism movement focused on the subjective influencing their perceptions and methodologies. Lincoln and Guba (1985) described this movement as a result of an old paradigm that could not deal with or explain new facts. "Normal science in the Kuhnian sense is becoming more and more difficulty to sustain" (p. 7). As discussed by Burrell and Morgan (1979/1988), antipositivists believed that the social world was relative and must be understood from the view of the individuals who are directly involved in the activities that are being studied by scientists while rejecting the belief in observation, which some link back to Plato (see Demerath & Peterson, 1967). Their assumptions included that the scientists must occupy the frame of reference and participate in the action, they must understand from the inside, and that science cannot generate objective knowledge of any kind. Subjective methodological approaches tended to forgo a focus on observation through experiments, but focus more on a "phenomenological, ethnomethodological, and action frame of reference" (p. 8). Moreover, Patton (2008) stated that the "alternative to the dominant quantitative/experimental paradigm was derived from the tradition of anthropological field studies and undergirded by the philosophical tenets of phenomenology and constructivism. Using in-depth, open-ended interviewing and direct observation, the alternative paradigm relies on qualitative data, naturalistic inquiry, and detailed description derived from close contact with people in the setting under study" (p. 425). More specifically, Lincoln and Guba (1985) chronicled the role of the investigator in this research, referencing a definition from Willems and Rausch (1969) where this type of inquiry must consider the degree to which the investigator imposes units upon behavior studies and their influence upon the antecedent conditions. Mackenzie and House (1978) described these experimentally designed studies: "[m]any scientists conduct 'experiments' . . . such exercises often employ elaborate controls on antecedent conditions and imposition of units" (p. 11). Measurement requirements can limit behaviors that are captured because they are determined prior to the study and imposed in data collection in artificial settings, whereas "[n]aturalistic observations are often explorations into a phenomenon" (Mackenzie & House, 1978, p. 12). The inquirer should not include imposed units, but those units should develop naturally. Interestingly, grounded theory had just been introduced by Glaser and Strauss (1967). Some describe grounded theory as the "qualitative revolution" (Denzin & Lincoln, 1994, p. ix). Glaser and Strauss (1967) reported their discovery of grounded theory and shared a strategy for the discovery of this theory through qualitative methods in social research. Their efforts were in response to their questioning whether logically deduced theories would advance sociology noting the lack of confirmation of theories and creation of new theories. Many believed this to be a critical point in social science history where we moved beyond experimental and quantitative studies to create knowledge.

The interpretive paradigm, as it is generally called, was a paradigmatic shift from the positivist paradigm or "normal" science, as it was called by many. However, as Lincoln and Guba (1985) noted, this new alternative paradigm had many names, such as naturalistic, postpositivism, ethnographic, phenomenological, subjective, case study, qualitative, hermeneutic, and humanistic. The new paradigm had a different view of the world and the role of research and the researcher. Burrell and Morgan (1979/1988) described that interpretive sociology was "attempting to understand and explain the social world primarily from the point of view of the actors directly involved in the social process" (p. 227). The focus moved to understand the subjective experiences of the individuals, the ways in which social reality is meaningfully constructed and sustained, and the social context. Rather than research being conducted from observations of actions, knowledge is constructed through the subjective experience, viewing social reality as emergent and studied through manners other than that of natural science. Burrell and Morgan referred to the parallelism in Kuhn's (1970) view of science: "Scientific knowledge here is in essence socially constructed and socially sustained; its significance and meaning can only be understood within its immediate social context" (p. 255). Kuhn (1996) discussed the shift of paradigms: "After the discovery had been assimilated, scientists were able to account for a wider range of natural phenomena or to account with greater precision for some of those previously known. But that gain was achieved only by discarding some previously standard beliefs or procedures and, simultaneously, by replacing those components of the previous paradigm with others" (p. 66).

Today, the interpretive paradigm is a common way to examine the world, especially in the study of learning. Here, researchers may participate actively in the phenomenon being researched and hold the belief that the social world is understood from those directly involved in teaching and learning. They implement qualitative methodologies with a focus on interaction and context rather than measuring individual behavior with predetermined measurement instruments in a control condition where they attempt to control for differences of student demographics and the environment.

Paradigmatic Interrogation and Evolution

Just as social scientists were questioning traditional paradigms for research and some were shifting to an interpretive paradigm, education researchers were questioning these positivist paradigms for the study of learning. There was a shift in paradigms due to the change in how researchers and practitioners viewed the process of learning. The traditional paradigm was unable to account for the new conception of the process of learning that was emerging. When an area of scholarship begins to change its view of a process, it can change the view of the world requiring an alternate way of knowing and methodologies to understand and examine the phenomenon of interest.

Behaviorism was the historically predominant approach to understanding the learning process and many cognitive and social phenomena in the early 20th century, as examined by social scientists. Behaviorism and the study of learning focuses on individuals and their change in behavior. If an individual has learned, there will be an observed change in her or his behavior. For instance, Greeno and Engestrom (2014) described behaviorism as an area of study of behaviors of individual organisms. Stahl, Koschmann, and Suther (2014) illustrated the history of the study of learning by describing it as something that is wholly an individual phenomenon and happens when there is a change in behavior, which is the behavioristic perspective. Additionally, several authors have discussed behaviorism as it relates to learning and its similarity to cognitivism as it relates to learning science. Specifically, there may be change in an individual's behavior, but there may also be a change in an individual's mental models or structures. Both focus on the individual level. As Greeno and Engestrom (2014) described, cognitivism studies mental process and structures within an individual's mind, similar to a behaviorist perspective since they are looking for change at the level of the individual. Similarly, Stahl, Koschmann, and Suther (2014) described that learning is "something that happens to individuals . . . whether a change in behavior (as in behaviorism) or a change in unobservable mental entities (as in cognitivism)" (p. 489) referencing Koschmann's (2002) earlier work examining Dewey's critique of Thorndike behaviorism. Moreover, they described Thorndike (1912), whose work was positivistic and behavioristic, as the founder of the traditional educational approach.

Thorndike was one of the first scholars to develop theories and methods for understanding learning, and his work is important to the study of both social and learning sciences. Although his work was the traditional approach to understanding learning, it became methodologically confining to researchers and theorists. Thorndike's work was experimentally designed to mirror natural scientific approaches, and his methods and theories built upon Pavlov's (1897/1902) physiological examination of animals resulting in the idea of classical conditioning with principles founded in the exploration of a stimulus and response relationship. Thorndike (1913) published *The Psychology of Learning*, in which he discussed the rewarding of desirable connections in his illustration of the laws of learning in animals and humans. The laws and rules approaches are traditional approaches to building theory from a positivist paradigm and testing through experimental methods. As he describes, "[p]sychology laws and educational rules for the learning process are among the elementary principles taught to beginners" (p. 20). Skinner (1953) expanded this behaviorist approach studying, again, human behavior with the use of experimental methods. As Burrell and Morgan (1979/1988) described, Skinner's work did not directly inform the social sciences, but it did inspire behavioral theories that were principled in universal laws where social or environmental influences were discounted. Moreover, the research design was focused on individual-level factors within controlled environments, which many learning scientists felt were limiting to the study of learning, and new research designs were needed.

Many philosophers, scientists, and practitioners questioned this traditional view of learning, which led to an evolution in their paradigmatic stance in the study of learning. Learning science, in part, developed due to the interrogation of traditional views on learning and the measurement thereof. In discussing the challenges of behaviorism and cognitivism and the established epistemological traditions, Stahl, Koschmann, and Suther (2014) illustrated that "[c]ontemporary philosophy has called these traditions into question . . . rebelled against the view of learning as an inaccessible event during which knowledge is inscribed in an individual mind. They aspired to construct a new view of learning and knowing" (p. 489). For instance, Sawyer (2014) in his discussion of how learning happens from a learning science lens described the behaviorist assumption of learning as "children enter school with empty minds, and the role of the school is to fill up those minds with knowledge" (p. 9), yet he claims that "students don't enter the classroom as empty vessels; they enter the classroom with half-informed ideas and misconceptions about how the world works" (p. 9). Also, there was a movement to develop theory and methodologies beyond individual factors in controlled environments. Greeno and Engestrom (2014) described that learning science is distinguished from the field of cognitive psychology in that the unit of analysis is two or more people and activity systems and asserted that these expanded levels of analyses beyond the individual are common among learning scientists. Sawyer (2014) stated that "[i]n the late 1980s, researchers in these fields who were studying learning realized that they needed to develop new scientific approaches that went beyond what their own disciplines could offer and to collaborate with other disciplines" (p. 1).

Learning science was a shift in the research of education, teaching, and learning to an interpretive paradigm that viewed the world more subjectively and explored new methodological approaches in doing so. The traditional disciplinary confines of the positivist paradigm were not adequate in solving the problems that were presented to inquirers of how humans learn. Sommerhoff et al. (2018) reported that the learning sciences involve multiple disciplines and investing and supporting learning in real-world contexts and naturalistic settings. Learning science resulted from a paradigmatic change to an interpretive paradigm, which many areas of the social sciences experienced as well. This shift revealed the development of new theories and methods to understand learning and other social phenomena. Also, as in other fields, the phenomena of interest focused on the role of human and technology interactions and the setting or context within which these interactions occur. Specially, learning scientists became interested in understanding and improving learning in real-world contexts.

CHANGE IN PROCESS

The rise in learning sciences was not only a result of the changing paradigm and resistance to behaviorism and cognitivism and their associated views of learning, it was also a rejection of instructionism or an instructionist view of learning. There was an evolution in paradigm as well as in the understanding of the process of learning or how humans learn. Learning was no longer considered a linear process of filling students with knowledge. Papert (1993) described instructionism as "a more ideological or programmatic level as expressing the belief that the route to better learning must be the improvement of instruction" (p. 139), whereas Sawyer (2014) asserted that instructionism was deeply flawed and that the focus needed to be on how students learn and learn deeply rather than purely focusing on instruction. Moreover, he stated that instructionism was ill-suited in preparing students in today's society and economy but was focused on better preparing students for an industrialized economy. The instructionistic learner is described as a vessel or a clean slate, essentially a passive receiver of knowledge and skills (facts and procedures) delivered through one-way instruction similar to a vase being filled with water. Behaviorism, cognitivism, and instructionism are positivist and objectivist views; however, learning science developed because of the consensus that these were not appropriate for studying human learning and improving learning. Students have prior knowledge, and learning environments play an important role in student learning beyond the instruction itself. Although research is still informed by these approaches, research designs and phenomena of interest have greatly expanded to enhance the field's ability to better understand learning and create environments to improve learning.

Learning science is theoretically driven by constructivism and situated cognition. Learning science focuses not only on the cognitive, but on social processes as well. Learning science was a reaction to the limitations of behaviorist and instructionist approaches and of objective and experimental research design and methodologies. Scholars believed the focus needed to be more on interaction illustrated in new theoretical standpoints. As Sawyer (2014) detailed, "knowledge is not just a static mental structure inside the learner's head; instead, knowing is a process that involves the person, the tools and other people in the environment, and the activities in which that knowledge is being applied" in his description of situated activity. "This situativity perspective moves us beyond a transmission and acquisition concept of learning" (p. 6). Therefore, learning science's theoretical stance situated within theories of cognition and constructivism, including social constructivism, provides an opportunity to explore social interaction in relation to learning since both place emphasis on the understanding of learning as mediated by or grounded within social interaction.

Many areas of study saw similar movements from transmission models to more interactive models. While education and learning scientists started to understand the importance of interaction and other social variables, and a need to move from transmission models, other fields moved to more interactive models as well. For instance, early interdisciplinary communication models developed by Shannon (1948), Shannon and Weaver (1949), and Berlo (1960) were transmission models and were linear and unidirectional. Berlo (1960) even described the learning process in the behaviorist stimulus-and-response frame of reference, presenting a model of learning as well, noting similarities in communication and learning processes, claiming, "[i]n large part, we can translate one of these process models into the other" (p. 99). Barnlund (1970) and Fisher (1978) later presented more interactive or transactional models that viewed communication as being sent and received simultaneously with an emphasis on feedback loops to account for weaknesses in traditional one-way transmission models. Fisher (1978) references the work of Mead, Goffman, and Dewey in presenting a new interactional perspective stemming from sociology's symbolic interaction, which is similar to the progression of learning science. Communication models were evolving in recognizing that all individuals come with knowledge and experiences that influence their perception and interpretation of the messages they receive, as do the noise and channel associated with learning (including technology mediated). Communication happens within a social system over time. The social sciences became less about generalizable observations that create a model and more about identifying the complexities of the process. Paralleled learning and communication processes were evolving beyond transmission models to account for variables to better understand how humans create meaning. Learning became viewed as more of an active social process.

The move to more constructivist approaches of learning that focus on interaction were due to the influence of Vygotsky, Piaget, and Dewey in the learning sciences and education in general. These influencers brought a new focus on activity, interaction, conversation, experience, scaffolding, reflection, and collaboration. Dewey (1933), a philosopher, argued that the mind is lively with activity and is "alert to react with interpretation" (p. 28) rather than an empty vessel to be filled. He asserted that learning happens through experience and not through knowledge transmission of texts nor teachers. Learning is a process. Dewey (1933) and Piaget (1953) believed that teachers and students are both senders and receivers. Piaget (1953) also referred to similar ideas that Berlo (1960) presented as to problems with perception and interpretation of messages. Moreover, instructors develop an environment for student learning and continually evaluate student progress (giving feedback) and coach students. Piaget took a more constructivist view and focused on the individual, while Vygotsky (1978) used an active theory approach that focused on social interaction (social constructivism). Also, Vygotsky (1978) believed that key factors in learning were in activity and play, social interaction and co-construction of knowledge, scaffolding (guidance, interaction to support the learner), group learning, and the instructor's active participation. Nathan and Sawyer (2014) declared that "[c]onstructivism has been broadly influential in education and forms one of the core elements of learning sciences approaches" (p. 25). This includes the work of Piaget, constructivism, and Vygotsky, social constructivism. Sawyer (2014) noted that Vygotsky was a foundational theorist since he believed that all knowledge began as visible social interaction that is gradually internalized by the learner to form thought similar to how communication and other social sciences believe meaning is formed.

Social sciences and the positivistic behaviorist approach guided the majority of early work on understanding learning using experimental methodologies and observations of stimulus and response effects or causality influences by the work of physical or natural scientists. Social scientists in the 20th century realized that this approach to knowing was restrictive and new approaches to theorizing and methodologies for studying phenomenon needed to be explored. Interpretive or naturalistic theorizing and methods of inquiry were being explored, and a new paradigm was evolving. Moreover, the models of understanding communication and learning were moving from transmission models to focus on reciprocal interactions between individuals, the influence of the individual's existing knowledge and experiences in perception and interpretation, the influence of social and cultural systems and contexts, and the continuation of process and influence of temporality on process. Similarly, scholars of learning science felt the same challenges in the traditional view of learning and methodological approaches. Learning scientists wanted to create space for new thinking about the process of learning with a purpose to improve learning environments and create opportunities for deeper learning from a paradigmatic stance that provide opportunities in the interpretive and naturalistic.

EXTERNAL INFLUENCES

There were two important factors that influenced social science resulting in changes in view of process and view of the world: (1) economy and (2) technology.

Berlo (1960) noted that changes in industry resulted in changes in how we work, needs of employees, and needs for individual skills. We needed to examine social organizations, economic relations, and cultural values. Sawyer (2014) described that "in the 1970s, economists were shifting from an industrial economy to a knowledge economy . . . traditional schools . . . were designed for a vanishing world" (p. 727). Schools were no longer needed in order to provide workers for an industrial economy, but were instead producing workers for an emerging knowledge economy. These continuous economic changes influence sciences in that world economics bring to light new things to study as well as how they are studied. These changes influence our phenomena of interest, methodologies, and theories as well as highlighting emerging paradigms and paradigm shifts.

Technology also alters and expands one's view of the world, reveals new questions to be answered, and presents implications for science applications to advance practice. In their discussion of social-technical systems theory, Burrell and Morgan (1979/1988) reported that technology developments influencing the work of employees in the 1950s led to "the study of the organisation as a whole, and move[d] away from the equilibrium model to one based upon an organismic analogy" (p. 147). Berlo (1960) noted that "[t]he technological revolution in communication has created or developed a greater need for competence in communication" (p. 4). Technology changes influence the way we think about how we interact with each other, how we work, and how our reality and societies evolve. In looking at historical patterns, educational technology emerges as a primary driver in the learning science movement. Sawyer (2014) discussed the rise of computer-assisted instruction, artificial intelligence, intelligent tutoring systems, and computer-supported collaborative learning as well as the challenges in implementing these technologies into the classroom effectively. There was a need to identify how learning environments could be designed and what teaching methods could foster successful implementation of technology outside of a lab where current methodologies were limited (e.g., experiential) and new methodologies (e.g., qualitative methods, such as interaction analysis) needed to be explored to help address the real-life classroom challenges.

METHODOLOGICAL OPPORTUNITIES

There were limitations to experimentally designed lab studies. Learning science researchers looked for new methodologies to better understand real-life contexts of how individuals learn and how learning environments should be designed to enhance their learning. Packer and Maddox (2016) explained that "[t]he learning sciences (LS) has become an influential approach within educational research. Its popularity has come in part from the maxim that it has taken the study of learning out of the laboratory and into real-world settings" (p. 126). This methodological relocation did not completely desert experimentally or quasi-experimentally designed studies as there is still a substantial amount of research conducted in this area. Learning scientists looked to new methodologies, in particular qualitative methodologies or forms of natural inquiry, as opportunities to answer new questions that could not be answered through experimental designs, such as to advance innovations in methodological approaches, position research as subjective rather than objective, or perform studies in real-life contexts. Sawyer (2014) described the methods used by learning scientists as being more qualitative, such as anthropological (e.g., collection of video data) as well as other forms of analysis, such as conversational, interaction, and observational as well as quantifiable coding. Others reported design-based research as the dominant methodological approach. For instance, Sommerhoff et al. (2018) asserted that design-based research is the primary methodological approach across disciplines and graduate programs. For instance, they state that "among research methods, design-based research (DBR), discourse and dialog analyses, and basic statistics stand out. Results show substantial differences between programs, yet programs focusing on DBR show the greatest similarity regarding the other concepts and methods they teach" (p. 320). Bell, Hoadley, and Linn (2013) noted that "[d]esign-based research studies draw on the full range of social science research methods to improve design for instruction and advance the understanding of learning" (p. 73).

Learning science uses data science methodologies as well. Many statistical methods in data science are used also in the traditionally social sciences (e.g., linear regression), highlighting important methodological overlaps, yet there is greater use of mathematics and emerging predictive modeling techniques. Educational data science is of great importance to learning science in regard to technology aspects as well as the history of learning science. Learning science has particular interest in individuals learning with technology, while data science informs the gathering of data and analysis of data from technology systems.

AN EXAMPLE: A SOCIAL SCIENTIFIC APPROACH TO THE STUDY OF ONLINE LEARNING AND THE RELATIONSHIP WITH LEARNING SCIENCE

For the second part of this chapter, I will focus on an example. A predominantly social scientific representative of The National Research Center for Distance Education and Technological Advancements (DETA) has developed an agenda to identify key factors that influence student learning in distance education, in particular online, blended, and tech-enhanced courses and programs, including competency-based education. DETA examines teaching and learning mediated by technology in formal higher education settings. Although many learning science efforts in education are focused primarily on both formal and informal settings in K–12 education rather than on postsecondary education, there are learning science efforts in higher education as well, and learning science can inform postsecondary education. Also, research in higher education can inform learning science. Additionally, when related to technology, it appears that learning science is not particularly interested in differences in mode, rather, interest is focused on phenomena surrounding cognitive- and computer science–based approaches to artificial intelligence, such as intelligent tutoring systems, or surrounding education data science, such as data mining from learning technology applications and learning analytics. Also, learning science from a social constructivist view is particularly interested in technologies that facilitate collaboration, such as computer-supported collaborative learning, virtual worlds, and mobile learning. DETA has examined similar phenomena, but again, from a social scientific lens.

Paradigmatic Bridges

DETA studies are situated within multiple paradigms, but predominantly a postpositivist and interpretive paradigm using mixed methodologies when possible with the distinct goal of improving student learning, including improving design of the learning environment as well as larger organizational and systemic processes by understanding social variables that influence the learning process. Previously, I described the evolution of a new paradigm that allowed for opportunities in the social sciences and the learning sciences, a new view of the world and approaches to theories and methodologies. Beyond the explanation of the evolution process, this dichotomy does little to advance current research efforts. Deetz (1996) called it "[the] boring and misleading subject-objective problem" (p. 193). Miller (2000) highlighted the idea that many scholars may find themselves straddling the division between paradigms or conducting research under the assumption of different paradigms on a by-project basis and promoted more "jumping and straddling among paradigms" (p. 48). Therefore, I posit that research that can take advantage of the assumptions of multiple paradigms will be most beneficial in improving practice. Furthermore, social research is seldom positivistic as the flaws in pragmatic ontology are well disputed. Instead, postpositivism has emerged as a leading paradigm. Miller (2005) noted that "[b]y the 1960s, positivism was almost dead and new views of the philosophy of science ascended" (p, 36). She described postpositivism as positivism with moderation where postpositivism is consistent with social constructionist views, ontologically, in that there is a focus on the patterned nature of the social construction process and predictable effects.

DETA's paradigmatic stance often straddles or bridges paradigms, while considering the degree of knowing about a phenomenon of interest and the importance of replication and triangulation of data and findings emphasizing mixed methodological approaches. For some DETA projects, the previous literature or work in practice has led to a potential relationship or hypothesis that can be tested to help improve practices. For instance, one project examined the relationship of the online course design and its influence on student outcomes. By capturing students' perceptions across institutions of how their university, for-credit online course was designed through a student survey and examination of the relationships between student outcomes (e.g., learning, satisfaction, academic achievement), multivariate statistical results provided generalizable recommendations to faculty and instructional designers on how to best design courses to improve student outcomes. Through the ability to straddle paradigms, DETA research bridges scholarship and application. This is similar to learning science's work in activity systems (see Greeno & Engestrom, 2014). It should be mentioned that data was not only collected from students through surveys, but also through student information systems to capture outcome measures and examine demographic effects. With advances in technology, scholars studying learning have the opportunity to investigate data from multiple sources.

In addition to the quantitative portion of this study, qualitative methodologies were used to complement and confirm quantitative findings. Open-ended questions were included on the predominantly Likert-based survey asking students to describe an experience that influenced their success. Often the qualitative findings do confirm the quantitative findings, yet the richness of the qualitative results from using a grounded approach to analysis of the text data more often leads to surfacing further results that can influence practice and enhance our understanding of student attitudes about online education and the impact those attitudes have on learning and learning design. Qualitative methodologies are often used at DETA to replicate quantitative findings, provide more robust descriptions of phenomena, and develop new measures and instrumentation, as described in the next example. Learning science researchers are less interested in conducting more traditional observational studies to show statistical influence on student outcome variables, yet in online learning and in higher education, there is a focus to improve student outcomes leading to support for these approaches. Learning science has an imperative to improve education for students, therefore, improving student outcomes should be a priority.

While some DETA projects look like the one described above, in others there is very little or no phenomenological research, much less is there an operationalization of variables or instrumentation yet developed to measures or form hypotheses about relationships. What there is, however, is exploration. For instance, another DETA project explored academic success coaches in competency-based education (CBE). Very little research existed that could help one form a hypothesis about coaching practices and the influence on student outcomes. To get there required an exploratory study to better understand who coaches were, their past and current experiences, and how coaches felt they influence student success. Through qualitative techniques of interviewing and an interviewing schedule, data from coaches across the country was collected and analyzed. Again, the study bridged paradigms, since it was not targeted at understanding one coach or one coaching program at an institution and providing a thick description or identifying the webs of significance. Rather, the researchers gathered this information and data from multiple individuals from several institutions to provide a deep narrative as to who these coaches were and to provide generalizations that would inform the field of CBE's understanding of coaching practice. The study's aim was to improve coaching practice by implementing recommendations for practices that could influence student success and to advance research by providing findings that could be used in developing instrumentation to measure students' perceptions of coaching practice to be linked to student outcome variables. These are just two examples of how DETA work straddles ontological and methodological paradigms to build and share rich, applicable research.

Framework of Inquiry (FOI): Metatheories

Social theories can be advantageous when studying student learning in education. DETA uses several metatheories and theories to inform its research agenda to identify key factors that influence student learning and highlight the importance of individual agents and agency as well as structural and cultural influences. One of the challenges with the objective/subjective paradigmatic dichotomy is that it limits us from understanding the interplay between rules and the influence of human action upon structure. It tends to limit studies in focusing on either the micro or the macro with little thought on the interplay between them or the large system within which education occurs.

DETA created a framework of inquiry (FOI) to guide its own research and that of its partners (see Joosten & Reddy, 2015). At a national summit, numerous experts in distance education identified an extensive listing of variables and their importance, which then informed the FOI. The framework provides the capacity to understand the relationship between and among the phases as well as the interrelatedness between individual behaviors and structure. Developed using grounded theoretical methods, the DETA FOI takes a systems approach highlighting a three-phase model—input-throughput-output—of teaching and learning design in higher education with varying levels of analysis ranging from the individual student to the structural areas of inquiry, such as institutional or programmatic structures, specifically students, instructors, course, program, institutional, and societal factors. In a sense, it intended to bring attention to the fact that there are multiple levels of analysis spanning the individual to system levels, similar to the argument presented by Greeno and Engestrom's (2014) criticism of behaviorism and advocation for an expanded focus on individual changes in behavior in learning science. DETA has predominantly promoted a systems approach to studying digital education to bring greater understanding to the input-throughput-output process in online learning. The goal of using systems theory as a framework to guide inquiry was not intended to push a positivist agenda in determining the rules and laws of the system of learning or online education, but to illustrate the multiple levels of a system, consideration for the system as a whole, and emphases on the interrelatedness of the elements of educational systems and the potential effect on student learning.

Previous researchers have emphasized the relevance of using a systems approach to studying distance education and online learning (e.g., Hiltz, 1994; Moore & Kearsley, 2011). Von Bertalanffy (1968) noted that although systems are complex, general systems science is capable of providing definitions for concepts of organized systems that can be quantitatively analyzed and is better than functionalist theory because it takes maintenance and change into account. It can be a useful tool that provides models to be used in and transferred to different fields, which is pertinent because of the interdisciplinary nature of research in distance education. Using a systems approach provides researchers and practitioners in distance education with a common framework to guide inquiry into these complex systems and phenomena of interest. Also, von Bertalanffy described the application of a system's approach to social systems, as higher education can be positioned as a social system, describing it as having the ability for system analysis to focus on relations and potentially provide "an amount of explanation and even prediction" (p. 195) while also providing "definite answers and practical advice" (p. 196). Researchers and practitioners are interrelated themselves in that the work of one will inform the work of the other, and/or the roles of researcher and practitioner may both be filled by the same individual. The relationship may appear as a loop linking research to practice in a cyclical manner or as a transactional process with continuous change and transformation. Both researcher and practitioner are situated within the system that they are examining to provide explanation and prediction to improve practice.

This metatheoretical approach to studying online learning is appropriate as a framework because it moves beyond a black box model that focuses only on input (usually mode) and outputs, but focuses on throughput or process variables that can affect student outcomes as well. The three phases provide a predictive direction of relationships examined. For instance, one study at DETA examines students' interactions with content, the instructor, and their peers within the course with student outcome variables. This allows the findings to influence the design and delivery of courses to positively influence student success rather than simply treating courses as a black box and comparing online to face-to-face courses to determine if online courses are as effective as face-to-face or on-campus courses. The key is not in mode comparison, but understanding the process, what is happening in the course. Also, viewing higher education as a system with varying levels of analysis from micro, agent levels (e.g., the student), to macro, structural levels (e.g., the institution), helps illustrate the hierarchical ordering of the system. The framework provides the capacity to understand the relationship between and among the phases as well as the interrelatedness between individual behaviors and structure. Importantly, the three-phase model illustrates that inputs are imported into a system to sustain that system, each bringing characteristics that will influence throughputs. In addition, throughputs are processes that will yield an outcome whereas outputs are system returns to the environment that might also possibly return to the system. Although originally developed for the natural sciences, the applicability and utility in distance education research is conspicuous and well documented (see DETA Research Toolkit).

Importantly, other theories such as structuration theory, adaptive structuration theory, social presence theory, group development theories, decision-making theories, media richness theory, academic and social involvement theory, and engagement theory have informed the research agenda and efforts, in particular research design and instrumentation development.

Moving Forward

There is ample opportunity to expand the world's knowledge of student learning. As the paradigmatic shift opened the way for advancements in social science and the emergence of learning science, the most valuable research will be research informed by traditional social theories and transdisciplinary philosophies that bridge paradigms. These efforts will create new theories and methodological approaches that integrate and transcend discipline-specific approaches to studying learning considering the micro and macro influences surrounding learning and associated phenomena. Developing theory appears scarce over the past few decades, yet theoretical development is of the upmost importance to provide a foundation to emerging studies in teaching and learning. Research designs will focus on addressing problems of practice and providing results that will inform practice. This research to practice to research cyclical process is crucial to improve our education systems in particular as we have rapid cycles of implementations of new technologies, pedagogical innovation, and instructional design and engineering. As a natural progression of practice-informed research design, the phenomena of interest will move beyond the individual level of analysis of behavior and typical outcomes to understanding multiple levels and phases of organisms that influence and are influenced by the process of learning. The implications for research informing practice and research designed to solve questions of practice are vital.

Advances in the variables measures and relationships between variables will occur due to the transdisciplinary nature of the research. Outcomes examined will transcend typical academic achievement or performance measures of quizzes, examinations, and grades to include more robust measures of learning effectiveness. Additional forms of behavioral and attitudinal measures will be captured and included into multivariate statistical methods. Student level data and interaction data can be gathered to capture structure level artifacts that can be better designed to improve student outcomes. Moreover, due to advancements in technology and associated data storage and retrieval systems, more data are available to enhance the understanding of multiple factors that can influence student learning. Technological advancements increase researchers' ability to gather meaningful data and help them move beyond traditional experimentally designed research methods. Yet, caution should be taken in letting the data drive the hypotheses. Hypotheses and approaches to the study of the data to understand learning should remain informed by social and education theory and philosophy.

Importantly, as we implement new learning resources and technologies, researching their effectiveness is important, yet advancing our research designs beyond experimental design for efficacy is paramount. Research on learning must move away from treating randomized control trials and experimental research designs as the gold standard, since, for the most part, they limit knowledge creation, as has been reported for decades. This is not to say that there is not room for this type of research, but with the advancement in data collection techniques and storage as well as statistical techniques, greater knowledge creation is available. Advanced statistical multivariate analysis offers new approaches to understanding effectiveness that are as good as if not better than experimental design when examining social and cognitive phenomena. Also, treatment versus control conditions or randomized control conditions can be accounted for in these analyses without withholding a potential treatment that could improve learning for a group of students for the sake of efficacy, which has ethical challenges. Advancement in informed federal policy in the area of methodological preference for funding is needed. Additionally, quantitative-based research designs need to integrate qualitative methods for mixed methodological perspectives. The richness of the data and webs of significant qualitative data can validate quantitative findings, assist in developing new measures and instrumentation, or reveal missed voices from important stakeholders, specifically students, but also importantly faculty and staff. Beyond the approach to determining effectiveness and its associated methodology, the scope and focus of the research needs to be advanced to gather richer data and to provide evidence-based guidance to practice.

Although traditionally studies examining learning focused on control conditions, implementation of the innovation from multiple levels needs to be considered to identify systematic factors that influence or hinder success in order to replicate and scale the study or to diffuse the practices. Research examining effectiveness needs to focus on implementation within the course but also within the program or institution. There is an array of factors that can influence the effectiveness of a pedagogical or technological advancement. These factors need to be understood. For example, why did the advancement or innovation work, or will it work for others? Researchers not only need to determine if the innovation was effective, they need to identify what structural factors, institutional and instructional, were critical to the influence upon student success. Furthermore, research needs to move beyond the micro level of student behaviors, and methods need to be utilized that capture not only the micro level data, but structural or macro level data that influences the human behavior and interactions. Research needs to be able to uncover the process in order to improve practice or what is happening within the course, program, or institution, and the relationship between input-throughput-output needs to be explored to ensure that instructional and institutional efforts are improving students' outcomes. To truly develop a belief that the innovation is effective it needs to be replicated or scaled throughout a program, institution, and potentially, cross-institutionally. Many institutions struggle with the same problems of practice. Learning science research should provide solutions to the problems of practice that have been proven effective in differing context or in identified contexts.

Finally, a challenge and opportunity that presents itself in the goal to advance the study of learning and improve student learning is the diversity of the individuals researching learning. In digitally mediated teaching and learning particularly (though it could be said that all learning today qualifies as such), including tech-enhanced, blended, and online education, there is a lack of coherency in the approach to the science of learning or study of learning. Individuals come from an array of disciplinary backgrounds and professional experiences. Although some individuals who research learning with technology are faculty with scholarship experience in the area, many individuals, like myself, come with scholarship experience in the social sciences or other backgrounds (e.g., communication, sociology, psychology). Further, my scholarship focuses on human interaction with technology, but some faculty come from disciplines (e.g., biology) with little experience or knowledge of theory or methods to study the social or cognitive phenomena associated with student learning with technology. Other individuals have very little scholarship experience yet have professional experience in supporting faculty or students in teaching and learning with technology. These individuals include online program managers, instructional designers, technologists, and more. In moving forward, this diverse community needs to be embraced. To improve student learning and educational practice, considerations need to be made for the roles in research for all stakeholders involved. Research needs to be inclusive, particularly in the involvement of student voices in research.

REFERENCES

Barnlund, D. C. (1970). A transactional model of communication. In Sereno and Mortensen (Eds.), *Foundations of communication theory*. Harper and Row.

Bell, P., Hoadley, C. M., & Linn, M. C. (2013). Design-based research in education. In *Internet environments for science education* (pp. 101–114). Routledge.

Berlo, D. K. (1960). *The process of communication.* Holt, Rinehart and Winston.

Burrell, G., & Morgan, G. (1979/1988). *Sociological paradigms and organisational analysis: Elements of the sociology of corporate life.* Heinemann.

Deetz, S. (1996). Describing differences in approaches to organization science: Rethinking Burrell and Morgan and their legacy. *Organization Science, 7*(2), 191–207.

Demerath, N. J., & Peterson, R. A. (Eds.). (1967). *System, change, and conflict.* Free Press.

Denzin, N. K., & Lincoln, Y. S. (1994). *Handbook of qualitative research.* Sage.

Dewey, J. (1933). *How we think: A restatement of the relation of reflective thinking to the educative process.* DC Heath.

Fisher, B. A. (1978). *Perspectives on human communication.* MacMillan Publishing Company.

Glaser, B. G., & Strauss, A. (1967). *The discovery of grounded theory: Strategies for qualitative research.* Aldine Publishing Company.

Greeno, J. G., & Engestrom, Y. (2014). Learning in activity. In R. K. Sawyer (Ed.), *The Cambridge handbook of the learning sciences*, 128–149. Cambridge University Press.

Hiltz, S. R. (1994). *The virtual classroom: Learning without limits via computer networks.* Intellect Books.

Joosten, T., & Reddy, D. (2015). Distance education and technological advancements research toolkit. National Research Center for Distance Education and Technological Advancements (DETA).

Koschmann, T. (2002, January). Dewey's contribution to the foundations of CSCL research. In *Proceedings of the Conference on Computer Support for Collaborative Learning: Foundations for a CSCL Community* (pp. 17–22). International Society of the Learning Sciences.

Kuhn, T. S. (1970). *The structure of scientific revolution* (2nd ed.). University of Chicago Press.

Kuhn, T. S. (1996). *The structure of science revolutions* (3rd ed.). University of Chicago Press.

Lincoln, Y. S., & Guba, E. G. (1985). *Naturalistic inquiry.* Sage.

Lindquist, E. F. (1940). *Statistical analysis in educational research.* Houghton Mifflin Company.

Mackenzie, K. D., & House, R. (1978). Paradigm development in the social sciences: A proposed research strategy. *Academy of Management Review, 3*(1), 7–23.

Miller, K. (2000). Common ground from the post-positivist perspective. In S. R. Corman and M. S. Poole (Eds.), *Perspectives on organizational communication: Finding common ground* (pp. 46–67). New York: The Guilford Press.

Miller, K. (2005). *Communication theories: Perspectives, processes, and contexts.* McGraw Hill.

Moore, M. G., & Kearsley, G. (2011). *Distance education: A systems view of online learning.* Cengage Learning.

Nathan, M. J., & Sawyer, R. K. (2014). Foundations of the learning sciences. In R. K. Sawyer (Ed.), *The Cambridge handbook of the learning sciences*, (44–62). Cambridge University Press.

Packer, M. J., & Maddox, C. (2016). Mapping the territory of the learning sciences. In M.A. Evans, M. J. Packer, & R. K. Sawyer (Eds.), *Reflections on the learning sciences* (126-164). Cambridge University Press.

Patton, M. Q. (1978, 1986, 2008). *Utilization-focused evaluation.* Sage.

Papert, S. (1993). *The children's machine: Rethinking school in the age of the computer.* BasicBooks.

Piaget, J. (1953). *The origin of intelligence in the child.* Routledge and Kegan Paul.
Pavlov, I. P. (1897/1902). *The work of the digestive glands.* Griffin.
Sawyer, R. K. (2014). Introduction: The new science of learning. In R. K. Sawyer (Ed.), *The Cambridge handbook of the learning sciences*, 1–19. Cambridge University Press.
Shannon, C. E. (1948). A mathematical theory of communication. *Bell system technical journal, 27*(3), 379–423.
Shannon, C. E., & Weaver, W. (1949). *The mathematical theory of communication.* University of Illinois Press.
Skinner, B. F. (1953). *Science and human behavior.* Macmillan.
Sommerhoff, D., Szameitat, A., Vogel, F., Chernikova, O., Loderer, K., & Fischer, F. (2018). What do we teach when we teach the learning sciences? A document analysis of 75 graduate programs. *Journal of the Learning Sciences, 27*(2), 319–351.
Stahl, G., Koschmann, T., & Suthers, D. (2014). Computer-supported collaborative learning. In R. K. Sawyer (Ed.), *The Cambridge handbook of the learning sciences*, 479–500. Cambridge University Press.
Thorndike, E. L. (1912). *Education, a first book.* Macmillan.
Thorndike, E. L. (1913). *The psychology of learning* (Vol. 2). Teachers College, Columbia University.
Willems, E. P., & Rausch, L. R. (1969). *Naturalistic viewpoints in psychological research.* Holt, Rinehart and Winston.
von Bertalanffy, L. (1968). *General systems theory: Foundations, development, applications.* George Braziller.
Vygotsky, L. S. (1978). Internalization of higher cognitive functions. In M. Cole, V. John-Steiner, S. Scribner, & E. Souberman (Eds. & Trans.), *Mind in society: The development of higher psychological processes* (pp. 52–57). Harvard University Press.

ABOUT THE AUTHOR

Tanya Joosten, PhD, is a senior scientist, the director of digital learning research and development, and co-PI and co-director of the National Research Center for Distance Education and Technological Advancements (DETA) at the University of Wisconsin–Milwaukee.

CHAPTER 4

Semantic Representation and Analysis (SRA) and Its Application in Conversation-Based Intelligent Tutoring Systems (CbITS)

Xiangen Hu
The University of Memphis and Central China Normal University

Zhiqiang Cai and Andrew Olney
The University of Memphis

ABSTRACT

This chapter provides an overview of semantic spaces and introduces a mathematical framework called Semantic Representation and Analysis (SRA) developed by the authors. It then demonstrates how such a framework enables efficient conversation-based learning environments, using AutoTutor as an example of conversation-based learning environments. The chapter uses an alternative model of intelligent tutoring systems and argues that SRA is most useful in knowledge representation of the domain and in enhancement of evaluation methods in conversation-based learning environments.

It has long been a dream of learning scientists to produce computerized learning environments that enable computers to teach human deep knowledge similar to skilled human tutors (du Boulay & Luckin, 2001). According to explanation-based constructivist theories of learning (Aleven & Koedinger, 2002; VanLehn, Jones, & Chi, 1992), an effective and deep learning environment needs to be able to guide the learner to generate explanations and functional procedures. To provide this kind of instruction, researchers have been trying to develop intelligent tutoring systems (ITS) that adaptively respond to the learner's actions and language inputs (Anderson, Corbett, Koedinger, & Pelletier, 1995). One of the challenging tasks in such systems is to infer what the learner knows from natural language input.

Over the last few decades, substantial research has investigated technologies such as text mining and natural language processing (NLP) to address this challenge. These technologies are the basis for producing so-called semantic spaces. A semantic space represents the semantics of language entities (words, phrases, sentences, etc.) and the similarity as distances between them (Dumais, Furnas, Landauer, Deerwester, & Harshman, 1988; Landauer, Foltz, & Laham, 1998; Riordan & Jones, 2011). Although it was originally developed for entirely different purposes such as information retrieval (IR; Furnas et al., 1988; Landauer et al., 1998), it has been used for assessment of learning, cognitive modeling, and a variety of other learning tasks (Landauer, 2003). One of the most well-known examples of a semantic space is latent semantic analysis (LSA) (Deerwester, Dumais, Furnas, Landauer, & Harshman, 1990; Landauer, 2006), and it has been used widely in advanced learning environments such as conversation-based ITS for over 20 years (Nye, Graesser, & Hu, 2014). Semantic encoding and decoding algorithms similar to LSA have been developed and applied, such as latent Dirichlet allocation (LDA; Blei, Ng, & Jordan, 2003; Hoffman, Bach, & Blei, 2010; Shams & Baraani-Dastjerdi, 2017), GloVe (Pennington, Socher, & Manning, 2014), and Word2Vec (Goldberg & Levy, 2014; Rong, 2014; Yu & Dredze, 2014). Semantic spaces have primarily been used to measure learning and to provide a cognitive model of the learner. The advances in research, development, and application of semantic spaces made this dream of learning scientists a possibility.

In this chapter, we will first provide a brief overview of semantic spaces and introduce a mathematical framework called Semantic Representation and Analysis (SRA) developed by the authors (Hu et al.,

2014). Then we will demonstrate how such a framework would enable efficient conversation-based learning environments. Our example of a conversation-based learning environment will be AutoTutor (Graesser, Dowell, & Clewley, 2017; Graesser, Hu, & Person, 2001; Nye, Graesser, & Hu, 2014; Nye, Graesser, Hu, & Cai, 2014).

SEMANTIC REPRESENTATION AND ANALYSIS (SRA)

Semantic Representation and Analysis (SRA) is a canonical class of models that was first introduced by the authors when they attempted to measure differences between different semantic encoding and decoding methods (Hu, Cai, Graesser, & Ventura, 2005). It was then used as a general framework in extracting, representing, and applying semantic analysis in a conversation-based ITS (Hu et al., 2014). SRA can be understood as a class of methods in computational linguistics (Gabrilovich & Markovitch, 2007; Landauer, McNamara, Dennis, & Kintsch, 2013) that specialized in encoding and decoding semantics from a large body of texts.

A Brief Overview of Vector-Based Semantic Models

There are two ways to categorize semantic models. When considering the original definition of *semantics*, a class of semantic models is called *distributional models* where semantic meanings of language entities are defined by the ways they have associated with other language entities (Harris, 1954; Riordan & Jones, 2011). As an intuitive example, in a distributional model, the semantic meaning of a word is defined by how the word appears in language environments (such as paragraphs) with other words in a selected body of text data. Another way to categorize semantic models is based on the resulting mathematical form of the semantic representation. *Vector-based model* is a class of semantic models in which the final semantic representation is in the form of a vector. Vector representation of the semantics of a term can be obtained by human experts. For example, the word association norms (Nelson, McEvoy, & Schreiber, 2004), in which each term is associated with a small collection of other terms, is an example of a vector-based model where the dimension of the vector is large, but each term vector only has a small number of nonzero elements. In general, vector representation can be explicit or latent with the similar computations (Hu, Cai, Wiemer-Hastings, Graesser, & McNamara, 2007).

The basic vector-based model has been used for decades in information retrieval (Salton, Wong, & Yang, 1975). In their original model, words are orthogonal, so semantic similarity judgments are too brittle to be of use in learning environments. However, the basic model was later extended by latent semantic indexing (LSI) for information retrieval (Deerwester et al., 1990). The breakthrough provided by LSI is a solution to the synonymy problem, in which multiple words can express similar meaning. In the basic vector-based model, distinct words with similar meaning are kept distinct, but LSI gives them equivalent or near equivalent meanings. LSI's solution to the synonymy problem made it attractive to a variety of researchers outside of information retrieval (Graesser et al., 2001; Hu, Cai, Franceschetti, et al., 2003; Hu, Cai, Louwerse, Olney, Penumatsa, & Graesser, 2003; Landauer et al., 1998; Olney & Cai, 2005a, 2005b; Wolfe et al., 1998).

While the meaning of words seems to be very well encoded in LSI (currently often referred to as LSA, for *latent semantic analysis*), the meaning of each dimension of an LSI space is unknown. Latent Dirichlet allocation (LDA; Blei et al., 2003) provided an acceptable solution to this. LDA assumes (1) each document in a given corpus is a mixture of a given set of topics with a probability distribution over the topics; (2) each word appears in a topic with a certain probability, and (3) each word in a given document is drawn from a topic with the given topic probability and the word probability. The topic probability distribution of each document and the word probability distribution of each word is determined by maximizing the likelihood of the given corpus. Once determined, each word has a probability value on each topic and thus gets a vector representation as weights to the given topics. What made researchers excited about LDA is that the words with the highest probabilities in each topic often form a good interpretation of the topic. In other words, researchers can often see what a topic is by looking at the words ranked at the top by probability. Once an LDA model is built (i.e., the document topic probabilities and the topic word probabilities are found), any text can be represented by a vector known as "topic proportion scores," indicating how much each known topic is contained in a text. Similar to LSI, such vector representation can be used to compute semantic similarities between texts (Cai, Li, Hu, & Graesser, 2016). Word2Vec is a more recent way of generating word vector representations. Word2Vec uses two-layer neural networks to train vectors from a given corpus. The basic idea is to position word vectors in a space so that words that share common contexts are located closely (Goldberg & Levy, 2014).

Similar to LSA (Deerwester et al., 1990; Landauer et al., 1998), most of the other methods such as LDA (Blei et al., 2003; Hoffman et al., 2010; Shams & Baraani-Dastjerdi, 2017), and Word2Vec (Goldberg & Levy, 2014; Rong, 2014; Yu & Dredze, 2014) are examples of vector space models. In the next section, we outline the steps to create vector-based semantic spaces.

The Complexity of Creating Vector-Based Semantic Models

Conceptually, representing the semantic meaning of a term in the form of vectors is intuitive, at least to those who think computationally. The goal of creating an alternative vector (mathematical) representation of the semantic of the original language entities is to make it possible for computers to compute semantic relations between the relevant language entities. There are several available computational/statistical techniques to achieve this goal. As an example, LSA uses singular value decomposition (SVD; Golub & Kahan, 1965). SVD is a technique that creates an approximation of the original word by document matrix. Other vector space models (such as LDA, Word2Vec) most often used recently are results of sophisticated statistical techniques that represent the similarity between collections of words as vectors "distance" in multidimensional space (Manning & Schütze, 1999). The process begins by collecting text into a corpus. A matrix is created from the corpus, having one row for each unique word in the corpus and one column for each document or paragraph. The cells of the matrix consist of a simple count of the number of times word *i* appeared in document *j*. Since each document only contains a small number of word types, the matrix is often highly sparse. Weightings are often applied to the cells that take into account the frequency of word *i* in document *j* and the frequency of word *i* across all documents, such that distinctive words that appear infrequently are given the most weight. Two collections of words of arbitrary size are compared by creating two vectors. Each word is associated with a row vector in the matrix, and the vector of a collection is simply the sum of all the row vectors of words in that collection. Vectors are compared geometrically by the cosine of the angle between them. This geometric interpretation is likely the reason that vector space models have become so popular: the interpretation is simple, clean, and elegant (Hu et al., 2007).

To explicitly outline the above-described process, we use the example steps of LSA to offer a taste of the complexity of the process. There are nine steps:

1. ***Selection of a domain.*** This is determined by the purpose of semantic space. For example, a semantic space may be used as a semantic engine for a tutoring system of a specific domain (Franceschetti et al., 2001; Olde, Franceschetti, Graesser, & Karnavat, 2002) or for grading essays in a given subject (Foltz, Laham, & Landauer, 1999).

2. ***Selection of corpora.*** This step involves collecting and selecting relevant texts for the given domain. For example, if the domain is physics, there is a choice of textbooks, research articles, or both.

3. ***Processing of raw material.*** It is possible that collected material contains not only text but also graphics (a bitmap of a scanned document). Even if the materials are texts, there may be strings that are tags and attributes (for example, in HTML files). This step also includes inserting a proper sentence or paragraph markers. In some cases, it is at this step that the researcher may need to decide the size of the document.

4. ***Obtain word-document frequency matrix* A.** At this step, one needs to decide the value of each entry of the matrix as a function of global weight g_i (weight of the word i) and local weight l_j (weight of the document j) and the frequency of word i in document j: f_{ij}. It usually takes the form of $(A)_{ji} = g_i l_j f_{ij}$. Notice that g_i, l_j, and f_{ij} can take different forms.

5. ***Decomposition of the word-document matrix to represent words by vectors.*** There are different ways one could process the matrix. SVD is the most popular method used, but one could use others to represent words as vectors.

6. ***Dimensional reduction.*** This is the step to determine how many dimensions are enough for a vector representation. Some scholars reported that 300 is the best for some applications (Landauer et al., 1998). However, there are cases in which higher or lower dimensions are used.

7. ***Processing of the vectors.*** This is the step to decide (1) if the first dimension of the word vector needs to be removed, and (2) if the dimensions need to be weighted (Hu, Cai, Franceschetti, et al., 2003). After the seven steps, each word is represented as an *n-dimensional* vector with *n* being a number chosen at step 7*:* There are also different ways to use the vectors to compute similarity.

8. ***Similarity computation.*** Cosine is the default similarity measure for LSA. Researchers have also suggested that other similarity measures can be used.

9. ***Use of the similarity value.*** In the case of comparing similarity values between documents, one could use the value by itself, or one could use the value and consider the size (number of words) of the document.

Other semantic spaces such as Hyperspace Analogue to Language (HAL; Burgess, 1998) and non-latent similarity (NLS) algorithm (Cai et al., 2004) are only different from LSA in some of the steps (such as step 5, for example). The first three of the above-listed steps are essential for generating any semantic spaces. To make sure a given semantic space is truly *domain-specific*, some special domain and corpora selection algorithms need to be used. For example, the so-called *seeding method* suggested by Cai et al. (2018) makes them intuitive and efficient.

The seeding method starts with a small seed corpus representing the core of a domain. By comparing with a general reference corpus, the domain keywords are extracted and each keyword is assigned a "keyness" value. With these keyness values, documents in a large corpus (e.g., Wikipedia articles) are ranked by the total sum of keyness of words in each document. Top documents are then selected into the domain-specific corpus.

In general, there are many parameters that need to be determined for any semantic space. One of the challenges is to select the best set of parameters for a given application. For example, there are possible alternatives for each of the nine steps outlined above. With so many choices at each of the steps, the resulting number of semantic spaces is combinatorial. This makes it impractical to evaluate and select an appropriate semantic space for a given application. The general framework of vector-based semantic space called semantic representation and analysis (SRA; Hu et al., 2014) was introduced to tackle the problem of semantic space evaluation and selection.

Semantic Representation and Analysis (SRA) Framework

Considering common properties of the popular vector-based semantic spaces such as LSA or LDA, a formal definition of vector-based semantic spaces was introduced in order to build a unified mathematical framework to measure differences between semantic spaces (Definition 1; Hu et al., 2005): A vector-based semantic space contains five components:

- A set of words $X_0 = \{ x_1, \ldots, x_n \}$.
- A hierarchy of layers: $X_1, \ldots, X_M$, where an element in set X_i is a finite ordered array of elements in X_{i-1}, $i = 1, \ldots, M$.
- Vector representation for elements in each of the layers.
- A measure of similarity between elements within each of the layers.
- Maps from vector representation of layer X_{i-1} to vector representation of X_i, $i = 1, \ldots, M$.

This definition can be summarized in three basic assumptions of vector-based semantic spaces (Hu et al., 2005, 2014):

- ***Hierarchical.*** Semantics of different levels of a language entity may be represented differently.
- ***Algebraic.*** The semantics of any level of language entities must be capable of being represented numerically or algebraically.
- ***Computational.*** The semantic representations of a higher-level language entity are computed as a function of semantic representations for its lower-level language entities. At the lowest level of language entities, a numerical semantic comparison measure must exist between any two items (e.g., words).

With these assumptions, especially the computational assumption, it is possible to consider any vector-based semantic space as *induced semantic structure* (ISS; Hu et al., 2005, 2014). When considering the ISS of a vector-based semantic space, a word is represented as its (numerical) semantic relation with other words in the space. For example, the semantic meaning of *life* can be expressed as nearest neighbors (Table 1 of Hu et al., 2005). Intuitively, ISS can be understood as "nearest semantic neighbors" but with several useful properties. Among them are three additional types of semantic similarity measures (*combinatorial*, *permutational*, and *quantitative*) that can be used to measure semantic similarity *between* semantic spaces (Hu et al., 2005).

Although the original goal of introducing SRA was for the purpose of evaluating the quality of semantic spaces and selecting appropriate semantic spaces from among multiple spaces produced from a different set of parameters, the ISS of SRA and the derived similarity measures made it possible for an intuitive interpretation of similarity (Hu et al., 2005) and computer implementation (Hu et al., 2014).

CONVERSATION-BASED INTELLIGENT TUTORING SYSTEMS (CBITS)

The Institute of Electrical and Electronics Engineers (IEEE) recently approved a standard committee for Adaptive Instructional Systems (AIS; P2247.1—Standard for the Classification of Adaptive Instructional Systems). This is one of the significant milestones to *advance personalized learning*, which is identified by the National Academy of Engineering as one of the grand challenges of the 21st century (http://www.engineeringchallenges.org/9127.aspx). Conversation-based intelligent tutoring systems (CbITS) is a class of AIS that are among the most studied and efficiently implemented in the last 20 years. One of the reasons for the advances is largely due to the use of NLP, especially the use of semantic encoding and decoding algorithms such as LSA (Graesser, Penumatsa, Ventura, Cai, & Hu, 2007).

AutoTutor as an Example Implementation of CbITS

To demonstrate the use of SRA in CbITS, this chapter will use a successful implementation of CbITS called AutoTutor (Graesser et al., 2004; Nye, Graesser, & Hu, 2014; Nye, Graesser, Hu, & Cai, 2014; Person et al., 2000). AutoTutor holds conversations with humans in natural language. The authors of this chapter are among those who have developed multiple versions of AutoTutor that teach critical thinking (Graesser et al., 2010; Wallace et al., 2009), computer literacy (Graesser et al., 2004; Person, 2003), physics (Graesser et al., 2003), reading (Graesser et al., 2016), and electronics (Morgan et al., 2018).

AutoTutor applications are built with the guidance of human learning principles (Graesser, Halpern, & Hakel, 2008), such as *deep questioning*, to help students learn by holding deep reasoning conversations (Graesser & Person, 1994). AutoTutor converses with learners following the expectation-misconception tailored (EMT) dialogue (Graesser et al.,

2004) pattern. An AutoTutor conversation often starts with a main question about a certain topic. The goal of the conversation is to help students construct an acceptable answer (expected answer) to the main question. Instead of telling students the answer, AutoTutor asks a sequence of questions (hints, prompts) that target specific concepts involved in the ideal answer to the main question. AutoTutor systems respond to students' natural language input, as well as other interactions, such as making a choice, arranging some objects in the learning environment, etc.

A Formal Framework of CbITS

In this section, we introduce a simple and formal (mathematical) framework of CbITS. Again, we use AutoTutor as a typical CbITS. From the perspective of this framework, we analyze AutoTutor and then show the role of SRA in AutoTutor. The formal model is based on a behavioristic account of AutoTutor. In a typical tutoring session, AutoTutor interacts with students with the following five steps: AutoTutor (1) provides a seed question, (2) gets a response from the learner, (3) evaluates the response, (4) selects the next item, and (5) delivers the item to the learner. The minimum content requirements for a functional AutoTutor implementation would be a "bag" of items. These items are in the form of questions, pumps, prompts, hints, elaborations, or summaries (Nye, Graesser, & Hu, 2014). For each item, there may be associated *elements*. For example, in AutoTutor, *prompt completions* are elements that are used to evaluate the student's responses to the prompts. In this model, items are generically defined, such that each item can have possible purposes (diagnostic, grounding, etc.) or be a question, simple feedback, elaboration, and so on. Items are also organized such that the organization can reflect the domain knowledge and teaching knowledge of the tutor. AutoTutor always starts with a main question. The interactive dialogue between AutoTutor and Learner can be simplified into a repetition of four turns:

1. AutoTutor selects an item and presents it to the student.
2. The student responds to the selected item.
3. AutoTutor evaluates the student's response.
4. AutoTutor selects the next item based on the evaluation.

Although AutoTutor always starts with a seed question, the student's response (step 3) can be a follow-up question (considered as student initiative), so AutoTutor is a typical mixed-initiative dialogue system with natural language interaction (Graesser et al., 2007). The interaction repeats until the AutoTutor selects an item that does not require a response from the student.

In the above simplification of tutor-student interaction, the knowledge of the tutor is represented by certain items and the relationship among them. The teaching tactics are also represented by certain items, their relations, and most importantly, the way the tutor selects them. In this model, the student model is indirectly represented by the evaluation of a stimulus-response pair. AutoTutor evaluates a student's input as a semantic representation vector and its relations with associated elements (such as answers corresponding to the given items such as hints or prompts). The mathematical model that goes with the above description can be explicitly formulated as the following components:

> ***Knowledge representation.*** A set $X = \{ x_1, \ldots, x_n\}$ is a set of items with an algebraic structure modeled as a subset of $X \times X$. An item may be a collection of structured elements.
>
> ***Evaluation method.*** The evaluation method uses a function that assigns a vector of numerical values to any combination of (x_i, r_i), where r_i is a generic notation for response of item x_i. The evaluation model is generically denoted as $E_n(i) = (x_i, f_n(x_i, r_i))$, AutoTutor's evaluation of student's response r_i to items x_i presented on n^{th} turn.
>
> ***Selection mechanism.*** A selection mechanism is a conditional probability distribution for any item x as the nth iteration between the tutor and the student. $P_n\{x_i\} = Pr\{x_i|E_{n-1}(i_{n-1}), \ldots, E_1(i_1)\}$.
>
> ***Delivery model.*** A delivery model specifies how any selected item x_i is presented in a given turn n. Several factors go into this model: the structure of the elements contained in the item, the frequency of how other items have been selected, and how items were presented in previous turns.

The above is a general model that may be used to describe both the outer loop and the inner loop of ITS (VanLehn, 2006). The evaluation method may be different for different ITS implementations. For CbITS such as AutoTutor, the evaluation method uses similarity measures of a domain-specific vector-based semantic model.

SRA IN CBITS

We now illustrate roles that SRA could play in CbITS and critical issues that occur when SRA is used in CbITS. We continue to use AutoTutor as an illustrative example. The basic interaction mechanism of AutoTutor is guided by EMT. EMT contains a well-organized (as knowledge representation) set of items such as expectations, pumps, prompts, hints, and elaborations. Some of the items, such as expectations, prompts, and hints, require answers so they can be used to evaluate students' input. These answers in CbITS are in the form of natural language; hence SRA can serve as their semantic answers. With the formal model of CbITS outlined in the previous section, it is obvious that SRA can be used in the first two of the four components, knowledge representation and evaluation method. For example, an expectation for an EMT in ElectronixTutor (Graesser, Hu, et al., 2017) could be:

> *In cut-off mode, the transistor works as an open switch when both the emitter and collector junctions are reverse-biased.*

Some expected answers may be typical good answers, and some of them are typical bad answers:

- ***Good Answer 1:*** *In cut-off mode, the transistor works as an open switch when both emitter and collector junctions are reverse-biased.*
- ***Bad Answer 1:*** *In cut-off mode, the transistor works as a closed switch when both emitter and collector junctions are forward-biased.*
- ***Bad Answer 2:*** *In cut-off mode, the transistor works as an amplifier.*
- ***Bad Answer 3:*** *In cut-off mode, both emitter and base junctions are reverse-biased.*

For each of the expectations, there are multiple hints and prompts. For example, this is a hint that helps students understand the expected answers:

Under what junction bias conditions will the transistor operate as an open switch in the cut-off mode?

Corresponding to this hint, there are possible good answers and bad answers.

- ***Good Answer:*** *When both emitter and collector junctions are reverse-biased.*
- ***Bad Answer 1:*** *When both emitter and collector junctions are forward-biased.*
- ***Bad Answer 2:*** *When both emitter and base junctions are reverse-biased.*

In the same way, prompts are similar to hints, but the answers are shorter. For example, this is a prompt:

Both emitter and collector junctions are biased in what direction in cut-off mode, when the transistor works as an open switch?

With very short answers:

- ***Good Answer:*** *In reverse-biased*
- ***Bad Answer:*** *In forward-biased*

In AutoTutor EMT dialogue (Graesser et al., 2004), multiple prompts and hints are associated with each expectation. It is obvious that SRA can be used to represent semantic keys for all the answers. The semantic keys on one hand are used to create relationships between these items, so SRA may help to build knowledge representation. Most importantly, it is used to compare answers with students' natural language contributions.

Requirements for SRA in CbITS

From the above example, we observe that (1) answers to expectations, hints, and prompts are in the form of natural language, and (2) good answers and bad answers only differ in *keywords*. For example, the expected answers for the hint "Under what junction bias conditions will the transistor operate as an open switch in the cut-off mode?" are "When both emitter and collector junctions are reverse-biased" (good answer) and "When both emitter and collector junctions are forward-biased" (bad answer). For most of the widely used semantic encoding and decoding methods, it is not easy to distinguish highly similar texts when large portions of the two texts are the same (Hu et al., 2007). In addition, efficient ITS applications are domain-specific, interaction between ITS and students should be context-sensitive, and most desirable, adaptive and individualized. With these requirements for an ideal CbITS, effective and efficient SRA should have additional attributes:

SRA should be domain specific. The examples of SRA we have described in this chapter are generic framework for semantic processing. Most of the widely used semantic encoding and decoding methods share the common properties. They are started with a large body of texts. The selection of the texts is the key for domain specificity. For example, a semantic representation for term *plane* in mathematics (Figure 4.1a) should be different from that in a general domain (Figure 4.1b).

The key steps for domain-specific semantic encoding are the first two steps, namely selection of a domain and selection of corpora.

SRA should be used in conjunction with other methods. Very often, typical good answers and bad answers only differ in key terms or presence or absence of negations. For example, "When both emitter and collector junctions are reverse-biased." and "When both emitter and collector junctions are forward-biased." are a good answer and a bad answer for a hint. SRA's evaluation of students' input will not be sensitive because the two answers have high levels of similarity (common texts; Hu et al., 2007). It would be easier and more efficient to use other methods such as regular expression (Thompson, 1968) for comparison.

DISCUSSION

Enabling computers to understand natural language and converse with humans has been a continuous effort for generations of scientists. From the computer therapist Eliza (Weizenbaum et al., 1966) 50 years ago to the most recent implementation of AutoTutor (Graesser et al., 2004; Nye, Graesser, & Hu, 2014), the key enabling technology is to let computers efficiently compare *similarity* between texts.

(a)

Grid | Notes

Associated Terms	Association Strength ▼	Term Weight	AT_WT	Frequency
planes	0.70881129946	0.5141379	0.36442675300063554	1
perpendicular	0.544126752666	0.4367839	0.23766580512379087	1
inversive	0.478123381579	0.8045472	0.384672827903916	1
geometry	0.437094010737	0.3317178	0.14499186363485403	1
euclidean	0.430235028546	0.4307213	0.18531139080087022	1
antipodal	0.427633662609	0.8369601	0.3579123130205949	1
parallel	0.404965252279	0.3700851	0.14987160588619894	1
intersect	0.396941504674	0.529506	0.21018290837391107	1
stereographic	0.39670863185	0.7708712	0.3058112590845677	1
axis	0.388475141929	0.3874579	0.1505177626940123	1
quadric	0.386948834816	0.7708305	0.2982719638156347	1
ultraparallel	0.361864494523	0.9033308	0.3268833433290572	1
collinear	0.359626513485	0.6988999	0.25134293431201515	1
circles	0.358867885457	0.5111023	0.18341820165320924	1
hypercycle	0.351240295914	1	0.351240295914	1
hypercycles	0.35124029248	1	0.35124029248	1
projection	0.350131680425	0.4860015	0.1701645218840706	1
points	0.338684517892	0.2866703	0.097090792349455	1
axes	0.329477690823	0.4851248	0.1598377988649697	1

(b)

Grid | Notes

Associated Terms	Association Strength ▼	Term Weight	AT_WT	Frequency
plane	1	0.46	0.46	1
planes	0.8406	0.5148	0.43274088000000005	1
pilot	0.8007	0.524	0.4195668	1
runway	0.7936	0.7294	0.57885184	1
airport	0.7791	0.5536	0.43130976	1
stewardess	0.7443	0.8353	0.62171379	1
runways	0.7177	0.7946	0.57028442	1
airplane	0.7168	0.5041	0.36133888	1
hijackeres	0.7051	1	0.7051	1
testrake	0.7051	1	0.7051	1
beiruit	0.7051	1	0.7051	1
derickson	0.7051	1	0.7051	1
cockpit	0.6935	0.6826	0.4733831	1
hijackers	0.6857	0.8821	0.60485597	1
boelcke	0.6844	0.9098	0.62266712	1
zags	0.6839	1	0.6839	1
fuselage	0.6823	0.7806	0.53260338	1
trimetric	0.6726	1	0.6726	1

FIGURE 4.1 ISS for *plane* (a) created from a large corpus of mathematics-related texts and generated using the seeding methods (Cai et al., 2018), and (b) semantic space created from a general purpose text corpus

Touchstone Applied Science Associates (TASA)

There are different ways to compute similarity between texts. The easiest and most intuitive way is to count the number of common words. The more sophisticated way is to semantically encode terms, sentences, and documents for each of the texts and then compute their semantic similarity. To apply the semantic encoding technology in learning science, there are two challenges: (1) how fast to generate a domain-specific and context-sensitive semantic representation for a given application, and (2) how to systematically evaluate quality of the semantic representation for a given application. This chapter tries to offer a solution for both challenges by introducing a general framework of semantic representation. High quality domain-specific and context sensitive semantic representation enable an effective and efficient conversation-based intelligent tutoring system (CbITS).

CbITS plays a very important role in learning science and technology. CbITS implementations are directly inspired by human tutors. The current CbITS prototypes such as AutoTutor (Graesser et al., 2004; Nye, Graesser, & Hu, 2014) are built with the guide of learning principles from cognitive psychology. They are proven effective and behaviorally similar to human tutors (VanLehn et al., 2007).

In addition to CbITS, the SRA framework may also be used in other applications and technologies in learning science. For example, it can serve as general assessment framework to assess learners' knowledge and build context-specific student models (Hu, Morrison, & Cai, 2013) or to build student models in a team tutoring environment (Hu et al., 2018).

CONCLUSIONS

Semantic encoding and decoding is one of the essential enabling technologies for conversation-based intelligent tutoring systems (CbITS). There are various ways to computationally represent the semantics of a piece of text. In this chapter we used a general framework called Semantic Representation and Analysis (SRA). The definition of SRA is general enough to capture most of the widely used semantic encoding and decoding methods used in text mining. For illustrative purposes, we used latent semantic analysis (LSA) as a typical instance of SRA to describe the process of creating domain-specific semantic representation.

In this chapter, we used AutoTutor as a typical example of CbITS. AutoTutor is an intelligent tutoring system that holds conversations with humans in natural language. To explain how SRA would be used in

CbITS, we used an alternative model of ITS and argue that SRA is most useful in *knowledge representation* of the domain and in enhancement of *evaluation methods* in CbITS. Because CbITS applications are mostly domain specific and conversational in nature (short answers with similar good or bad answers), we suggest that SRA for any CbITS be domain specific and used in conjunction with other methods.

REFERENCES

Aleven, V. A. W. M. M., & Koedinger, K. R. (2002). An effective metacognitive strategy: learning by doing and explaining with a computer-based Cognitive Tutor. *Cognitive Science*, *26*(2), 147–179.

Anderson, J. R., Corbett, A. T., Koedinger, K. R., & Pelletier, R. (1995). Cognitive tutors: Lessons learned. *Journal of the Learning Sciences*, *4*(2), 167–207.

Blei, D. M., Ng, A. Y., & Jordan, M. I. (2003, January). Latent Dirichlet Allocation. *Journal of Machine Learning Research: JMLR*, *3*, 993–1022.

Burgess, C. (1998). From simple associations to the building blocks of language: Modeling meaning in memory with the HAL model. *Behavior Research Methods, Instruments, & Computers: A Journal of the Psychonomic Society, Inc*, *30*(2), 188–198.

Cai, Z., Cheng, Q., Graesser, A. C., Shaffer, D. W., Windsor, L. C., & Hu, X. (2018). Impact of corpus size and dimensionality of LSA spaces from Wikipedia articles on AutoTutor answer evaluation. In K. E. Boyer & M. Yudelson (Eds.), *educational data mining* (pp. 127–136). Buffalo, NY: EDM Society.

Cai, Z., Li, H., Hu, X., & Graesser, A. (2016). Can word probabilities from LDA be simply added up to represent documents? In *EDM* (pp. 577–578). educationaldatamining.org

Cai, Z., McNamara, D. S., Louwerse, M., Hu, X., Rowe, M., Graesser, A. C., . . . Others. (2004). NLS: A non-latent similarity algorithm. In *Proceedings of the Annual Meeting of the Cognitive Science Society* (Vol. 26). cloudfront.escholarship.org. Retrieved from https://cloudfront.escholarship.org/dist/prd/content/qt0sc5p977/qt0sc5p977.pdf

Deerwester, S., Dumais, S. T., Furnas, G. W., Landauer, T. K., & Harshman, R. (1990). Indexing by latent semantic analysis. *Journal of the American Society for Information Science*, *41*(6), 391–407.

du Boulay, B., & Luckin, R. (2001). Modelling human teaching tactics and strategies for tutoring systems. *International Journal of Artificial Intelligence in Education*, *12*(3), 235–256.

Dumais, S. T., Furnas, G. W., Landauer, T. K., Deerwester, S., & Harshman, R. (1988). Using latent semantic analysis to improve access to textual information. In *Proceedings of the SIGCHI Conference on Human Factors in Computing Systems* (pp. 281–285). New York: ACM.

Foltz, P. W., Laham, D., & Landauer, T. K. (1999). Automated essay scoring: Applications to educational technology. In *EdMedia: World Conference on Educational Media and Technology* (pp. 939–944). Association for the Advancement of Computing in Education (AACE).

Franceschetti, D. R., Karnavat, A., Marineau, J., McCallie, G. L., Olde, B. A., Terry, B. L., & Graesser, A. C. (2001). Development of physics text corpora for latent semantic analysis. In *Proceedings of the 23rd annual conference of the cognitive science society* (pp. 297–300). Mahwah, NJ: Erlbaum.

Furnas, G. W., Deerwester, S., Dumais, S. T., Landauer, T. K., Harshman, R. A., Streeter, L. A., & Lochbaum, K. E. (1988). Information retrieval using a singular value decomposition model of latent semantic structure. In *Proceedings of the 11th Annual International ACM SIGIR Conference on Research and Development in Information Retrieval* (pp. 465–480). New York: ACM.

Gabrilovich, E., & Markovitch, S. (2007). Computing semantic relatedness using Wikipedia-based explicit semantic analysis. In *IJcAI 7,* 1606–1611). aaai.org.

Goldberg, Y., & Levy, O. (2014). *word2vec Explained: deriving Mikolov et al.'s negative-sampling word-embedding method. arXiv [*cs.CL*].* Retrieved from http://arxiv.org /abs/1402.3722

Golub, G., & Kahan, W. (1965). Calculating the singular values and pseudo-inverse of a matrix. *Journal of the Society for Industrial and Applied Mathematics Series B Numerical Analysis, 2*(2), 205–224.

Graesser, A., Britt, A., Millis, K., Wallace, P., Halpern, D., Cai, Z., . . . Forsyth, C. (2010). Critiquing media reports with flawed scientific findings: Operation ARIES! A Game with animated agents and natural language trialogues. In *intelligent tutoring systems* (pp. 327–329). Berlin, Heidelberg: Springer.

Graesser, A. C., Cai, Z., Baer, W. O., Olney, A. M., Hu, X., Reed, M., & Greenberg, D. (2016). Reading comprehension lessons in AutoTutor for the Center for the Study of Adult Literacy. *Adaptive educational technologies for literacy instruction*, 288–293.

Graesser, A. C., Dowell, N., & Clewley, D. (2017). Assessing collaborative problem solving through conversational agents. In A. A. Davier, M. Zhu, & P. C. Kyllonen (Eds.), *Innovative assessment of collaboration* (pp. 65–80). Springer International Publishing.

Graesser, A. C., Halpern, D. F., & Hakel, M. (2008). *25 principles of learning.* Washington, DC: Task Force on Lifelong Learning at Work and at Home.

Graesser, A. C., Hu, X., Nye, B. D., VanLehn, K., Kumar, R., Heffernan, C., . . . Others. (2017). ElectronixTutor: an intelligent tutoring system with multiple learning resources for electronics. *International Journal of STEM Education: Innovations and Research.*

Graesser, A. C., Hu, X., & Person, N. (2001). Teaching with the help of talking heads. In *Proceedings IEEE International Conference on Advanced Learning Technologies* (pp. 460–461).

Graesser, A. C., Jackson, G. T., Matthews, E. C., Mitchell, H. H., Olney, A., Ventura, M., . . . Others. (2003). Why/AutoTutor: A test of learning gains from a physics tutor with natural language dialog. In *Proceedings of the Annual Meeting of the Cognitive Science Society* (Vol. 25). cloudfront.escholarship.org. Retrieved from https://cloudfront.escholarship.org/dist/prd/content/qt6mj3q2v1/qt6mj3q2v1.pdf

Graesser, A. C., Lu, S., Jackson, G. T., Mitchell, H. H., Ventura, M., Olney, A., & Louwerse, M. M. (2004). AutoTutor: a tutor with dialogue in natural language. *Behavior Research Methods, Instruments, & Computers: A Journal of the Psychonomic Society, Inc, 36*(2), 180–192.

Graesser, A. C., Penumatsa, P., Ventura, M., Cai, Z., & Hu, X. (2007). Using LSA in AutoTutor: Learning through mixed initiative dialogue in natural language. *Handbook of Latent Semantic Analysis*, 243–262.

Graesser, A. C., & Person, N. K. (1994). Question asking during tutoring. *American Educational Research Journal, 31*(1), 104.

Harris, Z. S. (1954). Distributional structure. *Word & World, 10*(2–3), 146–162.

Hoffman, M., Bach, F. R., & Blei, D. M. (2010). Online learning for latent Dirichlet allocation. In J. D. Lafferty, C. K. I. Williams, J. Shawe-Taylor, R. S. Zemel, & A. Culotta (Eds.), *Advances in Neural Information Processing Systems 23* (pp. 856–864). Curran Associates, Inc.

Hu, X., Cai, Z., Franceschetti, D., Penumatsa, P., Graesser, A. C., Louwerse, M. M., & McNamara, D. S. (2003). LSA: First dimension and dimensional weighting. In

Proceedings of the Annual Meeting of the Cognitive Science Society (Vol. 25). cloudfront.escholarship.org. Retrieved from https://cloudfront.escholarship.org/dist/prd/content/qt0p3526z0/qt0p3526z0.pdf

Hu, X., Cai, Z., Graesser, A. C., & Ventura, M. (2005). Similarity between semantic spaces. In *Proceedings Of The 27th Annual Conference Of The Cognitive Science Society* (pp. 995–1000). Hillsdale, NJ: LEA.

Hu, X., Cai, Z., Louwerse, M., Olney, A., Penumatsa, P., & Graesser, A. (2003). A revised algorithm for latent semantic analysis. In *Proceedings of the 18th International Joint Conference on Artificial Intelligence* (pp. 1489–1491). San Francisco, CA: Morgan Kaufmann Publishers Inc.

Hu, X., Cai, Z., Wiemer-Hastings, P., Graesser, A. C., & McNamara, D. S. (2007). Strengths, limitations, and extensions of LSA. *The Handbook of Latent Semantic Analysis*, 401–426.

Hu, X., Dowell, N., Cai, Z., Graesser, A. C., Shi, G., Cockroft, J. L., & Shorter, P. (2018). Constructing individual conversation characteristics curves (ICCC) for interactive intelligent tutoring environments (IITE). In R. Sottilare, A. Graesser, X. Hu, and A. M. Sinatra (Ed.), *Design recommendations for intelligent tutoring systems: Volume 6—team tutoring* (Vol. 6, p. 133). US Army Research Laboratory.

Hu, X., Morrison, D. M., & Cai, Z. (2013). Conversation-based intelligent tutoring system (Vol. 1, p. 97). US Army Research Laboratory.

Hu, X., Nye, B. D., Gao, C., Huang, X., Xie, J., & Shubeck, K. (2014). Semantic representation analysis: A general framework for individualized, domain-specific and context-sensitive semantic processing. In *Foundations of augmented cognition: Advancing human performance and decision-making through adaptive systems* (pp. 35–46). Springer, Cham.

Landauer, T. K. (2003). Automatic essay assessment. *Assessment in Education: Principles, Policy & Practice, 10*(3), 295–308.

Landauer, T. K. (2006). Latent semantic analysis. In *Encyclopedia of cognitive science.* John Wiley & Sons, Ltd.

Landauer, T. K., Foltz, P. W., & Laham, D. (1998). An introduction to latent semantic analysis. *Discourse Processes, 25*(2–3), 259–284.

Landauer, T. K., McNamara, D. S., Dennis, S., & Kintsch, W. (2013). *Handbook of latent semantic analysis.* Psychology Press.

Manning, C. D., & Schütze, H. (1999). *Foundations of statistical natural language processing.* MIT Press.

Morgan, B., Hampton, A. J., Cai, Z., Tackett, A., Wang, L., Hu, X., & Graesser, A. C. (2018). ElectronixTutor integrates multiple learning resources to teach electronics on the web. In *Proceedings of the Fifth Annual ACM Conference on Learning at Scale* (pp. 33:1–33:2). New York: ACM.

Nelson, D. L., McEvoy, C. L., & Schreiber, T. A. (2004). The University of South Florida free association, rhyme, and word fragment norms. *Behavior Research Methods, Instruments, & Computers: A Journal of the Psychonomic Society, Inc, 36*(3), 402–407.

Nye, B. D., Graesser, A. C., & Hu, X. (2014). AutoTutor and family: A review of 17 years of natural language tutoring. *International Journal of Artificial Intelligence in Education, 24*(4), 427–469.

Nye, B. D., Graesser, A. C., Hu, X., & Cai, Z. (2014). AutoTutor in the cloud: A service-oriented paradigm for an interoperable natural-language ITS. *Journal of Advanced Distributed Learning Technology, 2*(6), 35–48.

Olde, B. A., Franceschetti, D. R., Graesser, A. C., & Karnavat, A. (2002). The right stuff: Do you need to sanitize your corpus when using latent semantic analysis? In *Proceedings of the Annual Meeting of the Cognitive Science Society* (Vol. 24).

cloudfront.escholarship.org. Retrieved from https://cloudfront.escholarship.org/dist/prd/content/qt56m7s0j2/qt56m7s0j2.pdf

Olney, A., & Cai, Z. (2005a). An orthonormal basis for entailment. In *FLAIRS Conference* (pp. 554–559). aaai.org.

Olney, A., & Cai, Z. (2005b). An orthonormal basis for topic segmentation in tutorial dialogue. In *Proceedings of the Conference on Human Language Technology and Empirical Methods in Natural Language Processing*: Association for Computational Linguistics.

Pennington, J., Socher, R., & Manning, C. (2014). Glove: Global vectors for word representation. In *Proceedings of the 2014 Conference on Empirical Methods in Natural Language Processing (EMNLP)* (pp. 1532–1543). aclweb.org.

Person, N. K. (2003). AutoTutor improves deep learning of computer literacy: Is it the dialog or the talking head? *Artificial Intelligence in Education: Shaping the Future of Learning Through Intelligent Technologies*, *97*, 47.

Person, N. K., Craig, C., Price, P., Hu, X., Gholson, B., & Graesser, A. C. (2000). Incorporating human-like conversational behaviors into AutoTutor. In *Proceedings of the Workshop on Achieving Human-like Behavior in the Interactive Animated Agents at the Agents 2000 Conference* (pp. 85–92).

Riordan, B., & Jones, M. N. (2011). Redundancy in perceptual and linguistic experience: Comparing feature-based and distributional models of semantic representation. *Topics in Cognitive Science*, *3*(2), 303–345.

Rong, X. (2014). *word2vec Parameter Learning Explained. arXiv [*cs.CL*]*. Retrieved from http://arxiv.org/abs/1411.2738

Salton, G., Wong, A., & Yang, C. S. (1975). A vector space model for automatic indexing. *Communications of the ACM*, *18*(11), 613–620.

Shams, M., & Baraani-Dastjerdi, A. (2017). Enriched LDA (ELDA): Combination of latent Dirichlet allocation with word co-occurrence analysis for aspect extraction. *Expert Systems with Applications*, *80*, 136–146.

Thompson, K. (1968). Programming Techniques: Regular Expression Search Algorithm. *Communications of the ACM*, *11*(6), 419–422.

VanLehn, K. (2006). The behavior of tutoring systems. *International Journal of Artificial Intelligence in Education*, *16*(3), 227–265.

VanLehn, K., Graesser, A. C., Jackson, G. T., Jordan, P., Olney, A., & Rosé, C. P. (2007). When are tutorial dialogues more effective than reading? *Cognitive Science*, *31*(1), 3–62.

VanLehn, K., Jones, R. M., & Chi, M. T. H. (1992). A model of the self-explanation effect. *Journal of the Learning Sciences*, *2*(1), 1–59.

Wallace, P. S., Graesser, A. C., Millis, K. K., Halpern, D. F., Cai, Z., Britt, M. A., . . . Wiemer, K. (2009). Operation ARIES! A computerized game for teaching scientific inquiry. In *AIED* (pp. 602–604). niu.edu.

Weizenbaum, J., et al. (1966). ELIZA—a computer program for the study of natural language communication between man and machine. *Communications of the ACM*, *9*(1), 36–45.

Wolfe, M. B. W., Schreiner, M. E., Rehder, B., Laham, D., Foltz, P. W., Kintsch, W., & Landauer, T. K. (1998). Learning from text: Matching readers and texts by latent semantic analysis. *Discourse Processes*, *25*(2–3), 309–336.

Yu, M., & Dredze, M. (2014). Improving lexical embeddings with semantic knowledge. In *Proceedings of the 52nd Annual Meeting of the Association for Computational Linguistics (Volume 2: Short Papers)* (pp. 545–550). aclweb.org.

AUTHOR INFORMATON

Xiangen Hu is a professor of psychology, adjunct professor of Electrical and Computer Engineering, Computer Sciences at the University of Memphis. He is also a professor and dean of the School of Psychology at Central China Normal University.

Zhiqiang Cai is a research assistant professor in the Institute for Intelligent Systems at the University of Memphis. His research interests are in educational system designing, development, and data analysis. He is the chief designer and developer of QUAID (quaid.cohmetrix.com), Coh-Metrix (cohmetrix.com) and AutoTutor (autotutor.org).

Andrew Olney currently serves as professor in both the Institute for Intelligent Systems and Department of Psychology at the University of Memphis. He is widely published in the fields of artificial intelligence, education, and psychology and is editor of the *Journal of Educational Data Mining.*

PART II

New Perspectives on Learning Science

CHAPTER 5

BROMP Quantitative Field Observations: A Review

Ryan S. Baker, Jaclyn L. Ocumpaugh, and Juliana Ma. Alexandra L. Andres
University of Pennsylvania

ABSTRACT

In this chapter, we discuss over a decade of research to establish the Baker Rodrigo Ocumpaugh Monitoring Protocol (BROMP) as a method for conducting rapid, high-quality, and time-synchronized quantitative field observations. We discuss work to establish standards and scalable training methods for the protocol in four countries, as well as work to develop and refine a handheld app that sped and facilitated uptake and use of the method. We then discuss the use of BROMP in research at scale, from its use in developing automated detectors of student engagement and affect, to use to study classroom pedagogy in settings from Pittsburgh to Chennai, to use in the iterative refinement of blended learning software.

The systematic observation of classroom behavior is one of the most commonly used methodologies in education research (Wilson & Reschly, 1996; Shapiro & Heick, 2004), and a variety of tools have been created to accommodate a range of research questions (see reviews in, for example, Adamson & Wachsmuth, 2014; Anderson, 1981; Fredricks & McColskey, 2012; Hops, Davis, & Longoria, 1995; Nock & Kurtz, 2005; Riley-Tillman, Kalberer, & Chafouleas, 2005; Skinner, Rhymer, & Daniel, 2000; Volpe, DiPerna, Hintze, & Shapiro, 2005). Like other systematic observation methods used in psychology (e.g., Furr & Funder, 2007), the direct observation of a classroom enables rigorous quantitative analysis, as well-designed observation protocols (e.g., Hintz, 2005) reduce rater bias (Kent, O'Leary, Diament, & Dietz, 1974) and standardize data collection (Volpe and McConaughy, 2005) in studies of student and teacher behavior.

Classroom evaluation of teachers via observation protocols is used to assess instruction (Danielson, 2011; Junker et al., 2005; Walkington & Marder, 2013; PACT Consortium, 2012; Pianta, La Paro, & Hamre, 2008), with observation protocols addressing a range of research questions, including those that evaluate the content of instruction as well as those that evaluate pedagogical activities (Institute for Research on Policy Education and Practice, 2011) and their effect on students' learning and social outcomes (Grossman, Loeb, Cohen, & Wyckoff, 2013; Hill et al., 2012; Hamre, Goffin, & Kraft-Sayre, 2009).

Many protocols attempt to capture large numbers of constructs across samples of students, focusing on overall aggregate frequencies or degrees of variables of interest. For example, the Reformed Teacher Observation Protocol (RTOP; Piburn & Sawada, 2000; Sawada et al., 2002) uses Likert scales to evaluate the degree to which the teacher is encouraging certain kinds of student behaviors (e.g., communicative practices), and the Classroom Observation Scale (COS; Waxman & Padron, 2004) records student behaviors (e.g., on task, waiting for teacher, distracted, disruptive, or other) at a classroom level, along with teacher activities. Similarly, the Classroom Observation Protocol for Undergraduate STEM (COPUS; Smith, Jones, Gilbert, & Wieman, 2013) records a set of 12 instructor behaviors and 13 student behaviors, looking at the frequency of each behavior across 2-minute intervals, and the Code for Instructional Structure and Student Academic Response (CISSAR; Stanley and Greenwood, 1981; Carta, Greenwood, Schulte, Arreaga-Mayer, & Terry, 1988) collects classroom observational data related to the classroom ecology, teacher behavior, and student behavior, sorted and categorized according to 105 individual codes in 13 categories of variables (Lee, Wehmeyer, Palmer, Soukup, & Little,

2008; Soukup, Wehmeyer, Bashinski, & Bovaird, 2007). These tools measure a variety of variables at different grain sizes and in different ways, but each is designed to collect data that can be used in both formative and summative analyses on the effect of different teacher practices on student engagement measures.

Observational protocols that focus on instructional practice generally do not log the frequency of student behavior for individual students, often for very practical reasons. It would not be feasible, for example, for a single observer to accurately report Likert scales on each student in a large classroom (e.g., the RTOP system) on an array of different measures, and introducing extra observers could quickly become a distraction that would invalidate any observations obtained. Frequency scores of very specific student behaviors (e.g., students raising their hands, a category included in COPUS) might be more manageable for a single observer, but could become unwieldy when trying to score each student for a large variety of codes, especially since there is documented bias toward identifying more extreme behaviors in aggregate classroom behavior rating scales (e.g., Christ, Riley-Tillman, Chafouleas, & Jaffery, 2011).

Observations that focus on the behavioral patterns of individual students tend to be structurally and thematically different, both because of the challenges of observing multiple students and because many of them were developed for the screening and diagnosis of potential emotional and behavioral problems (Abikoff, Gittelman-Klein, & Klein, 1977; Gadow, Sprafkin, & Nolan, 1996; Walker & Severson, 1990). These protocols tend to focus on very small numbers of students at a time. For instance, the Classroom Observation Code (COC; Abikoff et al., 1977; Abikoff, Gittelman-Klein, & Klein, 1980) and the Student Observation System (SOS; Reynolds & Kamphus, 2004) assess the classroom behaviors of students with ADHD in order to evaluate therapeutic interventions and the typicality of behavior of the diagnosed student. These studies often evaluate only a small number of students at a time (e.g., two students in COC and one individual student in SOS). The Individualized Classroom Assessment Scoring System (inCLASS; Downer et al., 2010) uses two observers to evaluate an individual preschool student's self-regulatory skills.

Other observation systems for student behavior use a scan method for sampling, where the observer watches either a student or a group of students (sometimes the whole class) and tallies the presence of behaviors of interest as they occur. Richards, Heathfield, and Jenson (2010) used a scan method to study the effect of interventions designed to increase on-task behaviors. Harrison, Riley-Tillman, and Chafouleas (2014), however, argue that while observers using scanning methods are quite able to accurately rate broad categories on the more extreme ends of engagement (e.g., disruptive or compliant behaviors), they are less likely to achieve inter-rater reliability on less extreme behaviors. This finding reflects a general consensus among methodologists that scan-based observational methods are efficient but only appropriate for "overt, readily observable behaviors" (Ostrav & Heart, 2014).

While inter-rater reliability has been established for many observation systems, it has been insufficiently studied for many other methods (i.e., the discussion in Volpe et al., 2005). Some observation systems also require a considerable amount of training. While only a few hours are required for COS training (Waxman & Padron, 2004), 10 to 15 hours are required for the BOSS protocol (Shapiro & Heick, 2004; Shapiro, 2011; Volpe, DiPerna, Hintze, & Shapiro, 2005) and over 50 hours (across a three-week period) is reported to be required for COC training, which also has a high failure rate for coder certification (Abikoff et al., 1977; Abikoff et al., 1980). The time and resources consumed by longer training periods potentially limit the degree of applicability and scale that can be achieved for a method.

The robust literature on classroom observations has provided us with considerable information that can be used to guide teacher training (Waxman & Padron, 1994) and diagnose student problems (Volpe et al., 2005), but for some time, there have been concerns that many of the observation systems have focused on categories that are convenient to code rather than those that are more connected to theoretical concerns (Ornstein, 1990; Lewis, Scott, Wehby, & Wills, 2014). While concrete categories like on/off-task behaviors can be quite important to learning (e.g., Karweit & Slavin, 1982), the need to explore student emotion and emotional supports, for example, has led to observation systems like the Classroom Assessment Scoring System (CLASS; Pianta, La Paro, & Hamre, 2008) that have expanded coding beyond more basic classifications of on/off task or compliance/disruption.

One area of particular recent interest has been affect related to student learning outcomes (Baker, D'Mello, Rodrigo, & Graesser, 2010). Prior to the work described in this chapter and related work on video coding (e.g., Graesser et al., 2006), most of the quantitative research in affective learning employed some form of retrospective survey scales, either self-report (e.g., McCroskey's, 1994, Affective Learning Scale, or ALS) or from an observer (e.g., Pianta et al.'s, 2008, CLASS). Work around a decade ago began to instead follow Schutz and Pekrun's (2007) call for more observational measures of affective states to be developed, as these may capture more fluid and dynamic characteristics of affect than can be adequately described in post hoc retrospective analyses. Systematic, direct observation of students' affective states may also provide opportunities to focus the grain size of the research to capture things that survey items may miss. For example, observational methods may help to contextualize the emotional experience (Fredricks, Blumenfeld, & Paris, 2004), rather than ascribing it as a property of the individual, as some survey question formats may lend themselves to. (This criticism of surveys is given, for instance, in Wigfield & Cambria, 2010.) What's more, observations of emotion may serve to contextualize more traditional observational measures of behavior, as they may reveal the extent to which a student's active or passive compliance with an activity reveals their engagement with the material.

Early approaches to studying affect through video coding and observation often relied upon Ekman's Facial Action Coding System (FACS; Ekman & Friesen, 1978). Researchers using FACS code a set of six basic emotions, argued to be the only emotions seen universally across human cultures (Ekman & Friesen, 1971). However, more recent research suggests that many of these basic emotions are uncommon during learning, and that other, less universal "academic" emotions are considerably more common in this context (D'Mello, Lehman, & Person, 2010). FACS has some key limitations; it requires hundreds of hours to learn (Ekman, Friesen, & Hager, 2002) and, as Furr and Funder (2007) note, even documenting the presence of a smile (a composite of several muscle units coded for in FACS) requires further interpretation, since a person may smile as the result of a variety of different emotional experiences. As such, interpreting emotions within this paradigm requires the use of a constellation of features (Planalp, 1998), a complex and time-consuming process that yields only a small number of emotions, many of which do not seem highly relevant to educational contexts.

The development of classroom observation systems that include codes for theoretically grounded affective categories could help to expand the research community's understanding of the role of emotions in learning. However, these observation systems must be carefully constructed; in addition to considering the theoretical literature on emotions in learning and engagement (e.g., Csikszentmihali, 1990; D'Mello, Picard, & Graesser, 2007), they must also be sensitive to social and cultural differences between groups of students (e.g., Fischer, Rodriguez Mosquera, Van Vianen, & Manstead, 2004; Krumhuber, Kappas, & Manstead, 2013).

And, like more traditional behavioral observation systems, observers of affective states must be aware of potential self-presentation effects and other observer effects (Wragg, 2002), particularly in cases where a student becomes sensitized to the observer's presence.

This chapter describes the development and use of a system that attempts to address these challenges, the Baker Rodrigo Ocumpaugh Monitoring Protocol (BROMP). It includes a description of BROMP's general practices and its adaptation for use in several different countries through the use of culturally sensitive training practices.

BROMP OVERVIEW AND THEORETICAL FOUNDATIONS

The Baker Rodrigo Ocumpaugh Monitoring Protocol (BROMP) was developed to address some of the limitations in prior classroom observation protocols, while also facilitating second-by-second synchronization between classroom observations and other data sources. BROMP is a method for conducting quantitative field observations (QFOs) of student behavior and affect. BROMP is mostly used in classroom settings, but it has been used in other settings as well (e.g., Baker, Ocumpaugh, Gowda, Kamarainen, & Metcalf, 2014). It was initially designed for observing students using educational software, however, BROMP has been adapted and used to study student engagement in other educational environments, such as research on elementary school students in classrooms with non-technological pedagogy (e.g., Hymavathy, Krishnamani, & Sumathi, 2014; Godwin et al., 2016).

Within BROMP, students are observed using a momentary time sampling method (Meany-Daboul, Roscoe, Bourret, & Ahearn, 2007), where students are repeatedly coded individually, in a predetermined order. This sampling method is designed to achieve a representative sample of behavior and affect among the students while reducing the tendency to focus on more extreme events. Both affect and behavior are recorded in each observation. If a student transitions between multiple affective states or behaviors within the 20-second interval, only the first affective state or behavior is coded. If two states seem to occur simultaneously, the observer is trained to code the most prominent behavior or affective state. If the behavior or affect presented by the student is outside of the coding scheme or if an observer is not sure what behavior or affect is being presented, a

"?" is used to label the event. In the past, the "?" has also been used for cases where coding is impossible (e.g., the student is out of the room), but the protocol now differentiates students who are difficult to code (e.g., their affective state is ambiguous) from those who physically cannot be coded (e.g., they have been sent to the nurse's office). If coders can make an assessment in less than 20 seconds, they do so and move on to the next student.

Observers record student affect and behavior using side glances and strategic positioning within the classroom. The frequency of observations recorded for each student is dependent on the number of students in the class. Coders consider multiple cues and environmental influences the students are exposed to (i.e., work context, actions, utterances, facial expressions, body language, and interactions with teachers or fellow students) in determining student affect and behavior (cf. Planalp, 1998).

BROMP assumes affect and behavior are at least partially orthogonal and can be coded separately. Behavior and affect are coded simultaneously but separately using a custom-built computer-assisted direct observation (CADO; Wessel, 2015) application for Android, the Human Affect Recording Tool (HART) (Ocumpaugh, Baker, & Rodrigo, 2015). HART presents coders with menus for affective or behavioral categories and automatically lists the potential categories that are currently being observed for. If required by the given research focus, HART also supports the addition of a third coding scheme for recording classroom activities, teacher actions, and interventions in the classroom.

HART helps to enforce correct use of the BROMP protocol in an automated fashion. It provides a far more precise time stamp than could possibly be manually recorded, synchronized to Internet time, while enabling observers to maintain their focus on the classroom context rather than the more mundane challenges of recording observations on paper. It also helps to reduce observer effects, as it is typically used on smaller handheld devices (e.g., smartphones rather than tablets). This minimizes the number of observations being displayed on the screen at any given time (only the info for the student currently being observed), facilitating an observer's ability to collect information discreetly. HART also improves data security, both by limiting the information displayed and by ensuring that only someone with password-protected access is ultimately able to access the information.

HART's time stamps not only make it possible to sequence observations for analysis, but also make it possible to synchronize between HART data and other data streams. For example, it is possible to correlate a specific observation of a student with exactly what that student is doing within a learning application, either at the level of log files or actual screen recordings.

Over 20 coding schemes have been developed for a variety of learning environments in order to capture categories unique to certain environments and contexts. However, most incorporate a common set of academically relevant emotions (e.g., Baker et al., 2010), including boredom, confusion, engaged concentration, frustration, and delight (most commonly studied in game contexts) along with the codes for on-task or off-task student behavior. We will discuss some of the development of these coding schemes for different learning systems and countries below.

BROMP training and certification typically takes a few hours over the course of 1 or 2 days. BROMP coders are trained and certified through a process consisting of three phases: (1) pre-field training, (2) field training, and (3) inter-rater reliability (IRR) testing. Pre-field training is often completed in one hour. In this phase, novices become familiar with the concepts that the field observations will be capturing. This is accomplished by reading the training manual, interacting with the android application, HART, and discussing the coding scheme and ambiguous examples with the trainer. Once this phase is completed, the trainee shadows an experienced coder in the field, discussing the coding process used for the observed students and practicing the use of the HART application. The field-training phase is most commonly accomplished within two or three observation sessions, lasting around 50 minutes each. The last phase of BROMP certification is the IRR testing. In this phase, the novice's ability to conduct BROMP is field-tested using a criterion-referenced agreement test to determine the novice's understanding of the process as well as the consistency of coding with that of the expert trainer (Ocumpaugh, Baker, & Rodrigo, 2015). During IRR testing, the novice and the trainer simultaneously code each student at the same time for at least 60 observations. If agreement is insufficient at the first IRR check, further field-training occurs before testing for IRR again.

In order to be certified, trainees must first satisfy the recommended inter-rater agreement value. The BROMP measures IRR using Cohen's (1960) Kappa. Kappa scales between –1 and +1 and is used to reveal how much better the level of agreement is than what might be expected due to the base rate of each affective category. BROMP certification requires trainees to achieve a Kappa of 0.6 or higher for each coding scheme (both affect and behavior).

Another key aspect of BROMP training is discussion of how to minimize observer effects (e.g., McCall, 1984), including strategies for communicating with both teachers and students, as well as techniques for the observer's positioning and movement, even in unusual classroom conditions. Observers coordinate with the teachers before the class observation begins to minimize any additional interaction throughout the sessions and to let the teachers know how to explain the observer's role to the students, if needed. During the observation session, observers are expected to avoid prolonged interaction with students without seeming threatening or interesting. Observers are recommended to maintain either a "clueless but friendly" or a "bored and disinterested" disposition (in contrast to some earlier protocols, where coders were instructed to be hostile to students to reduce student interest in interacting with them—e.g., Reyes & Fennema, 1981). While recording, observers use side glances and peripheral vision. However, if students become aware that they are being coded, the observation for the given time period is abandoned.

As McCall (1984) notes, the likelihood of observers creating effects on the data observed depends on the reactivity of the subjects, the social norms involved in the context being studied, and the degree to which the behaviors being studied are socially desirable. In our experience, US students are used to having outside observers come into classrooms to evaluate pedagogical practices, and since it is rare that these observations have any direct, salient consequences for students, the presence of BROMP coders is rarely questioned. Nevertheless, BROMP coders are also trained to minimize their presence in the classroom to remain as inconspicuous as possible, as affective states, in particular, are well known to have social functions (e.g., Fischer & Manstead, 2008) that may be influenced by self-presentation, which has made BROMP observations more challenging in some contexts than in others. (See discussion in the "BROMP Mexico" section below.)

BROMP observers are discouraged from taking on other tasks during an observation session. The observer should not, for example, provide technical or pedagogical support, as this may sensitize the student to the observer. Similarly, if complicated coding schemes are required for other classroom activities (e.g., teacher behaviors), an additional observer is generally recommended. It is possible to keep track of simple changes in classroom activity, and the ability to code a tertiary coding scheme has been added to HART for such purposes. This functionality has been used in a few studies, including work by Godwin and colleagues (2016) and DiStefano (2018) to study how disengagement varies depending on which type of classroom activity is occurring. However, any tertiary scheme that diverts the observer's attention away from the individual student being observed is likely to interfere with the BROMP coding process, which can already be difficult in a crowded classroom.

BROMP USA

The first version of BROMP was developed as part of Ryan Baker's doctoral dissertation research. BROMP was first used, in its earliest form, in February 2003 and published in Baker, Corbett, Koedinger, and Wagner (2004). It used a momentary time sampling method to compare the effect of two different types of disengaged behavior during the use of educational software. Specifically, that research compared the learning associated with off-task behavior to the learning associated with gaming the system, a behavior where students progress through educational material by exploiting properties of the software (in this case systematic guessing or repeated quick help requests from the learning software) instead of by actively engaging in learning. Researchers found that gaming the system was quite infrequent (3%) compared to other behaviors (78% for on-task solitary behavior, 4% on-task conversation, 1% for active off-task solitary behavior, 11% for off-task conversation, and 3% for inactivity), but it had a disproportionate effect on learning, correlating to poorer learning twice as strongly as off-task behavior did. Papers soon followed in which BROMP observations were used to inform the development of automated models of gaming the system (Baker, Corbett, & Koedinger, 2004) and off-task behavior (Baker, 2007). BROMP was also used to assess the effectiveness of automated interventions attempting to reduce the frequency of gaming the system (Baker et al., 2006). In this early work, involving only disengaged behavior, an inter-rater reliability of 0.84 (Cohen's Kappa) was achieved.

In these early studies, BROMP observations included only observations of behavior and were recorded using pen and paper. The first observations of BROMP involving affect were conducted in the Philippines in 2006 and are discussed in the "BROMP Philippines" section. In 2009, researchers moved from recording BROMP observations with pen and paper to using HART, discussed above. HART went through several design revisions and upgrades, primarily developed in the context of BROMP USA.

In 2012, the first BROMP manual (Ocumpaugh, Baker, & Rodrigo, 2012) was developed in the United States in conjunction with researchers in the Philippines, as part of efforts to streamline the training process.

This effort formalized the training process, increased methodological consistency between the researchers in the two countries where it was being used, and cut the US training time down from 10–15 hours across 4–5 days to 5–7 hours across 1–3 days (sometimes shorter). It was later expanded upon in a more comprehensive manual (Ocumpaugh et al., 2015), which broadened the effort to more thoroughly document the theoretical foundations underlying the observation system.

BROMP has been extensively used in the United States, where there are currently more than 50 certified coders. As these numbers have grown, BROMP-based research has expanded beyond its original use (Baker et al., 2004) in the development of automated models of student behaviors in educational software. In addition to continuing to be used to model student behaviors (e.g., Pardos et al., 2014; Jiang et al., 2018), it has now been used to develop automated models of student emotions in many types of learning systems (Baker et al., 2012; Miller et al., 2014; Baker et al., 2014; Bosch, D'Mello, Ocumpaugh, Baker, & Shute, 2016; Jiang et al., 2018; Gobert et al., 2015). These automated "detectors" are developed by synchronizing field observations to the exact behavior occurring in the learning system at the same time, using the precise time stamps provided by the HART handheld app.

In turn, the detectors built for these systems have been used to study how different patterns of affective states relate to learning outcomes, including some nontraditional long-term measures. For example, they have been used to model state standardized exam scores (e.g., Pardos et al., 2014), college attendance (San Pedro, Baker, Bowers, & Heffernan, 2013), and enrollment in STEM careers or graduate degree programs postcollege (Patikorn, Heffernan, & Baker, 2018). These detectors have also been used to conduct more basic research on the relationship between patterns of different affective states and behaviors in learning contexts (e.g., Liu et al., 2013; Karumbaiah et al., 2018; Ocumpaugh et al., 2017; Baker, Rodrigo, & Xolocotzin, 2007; Rodrigo et al., 2012; Baker et al., 2011; Botelho et al., 2018).

BROMP has also been used to conduct research in nontechnological contexts. For example, Godwin and colleagues used BROMP to study how classroom design impacts student engagement in kindergarten and elementary school classrooms (Godwin et al., 2016), and DiStefano (2018) used BROMP to study engagement in graduate-level courses. Others have used BROMP in unpublished studies to provide formative engagement measures to teachers, within a regional charter school network, and to study the affect of learners participating in informal science education programs.

BROMP Philippines

BROMP in the Philippines began in 2006 when researchers were seeking an alternative to sensor-based detection of student affect and behavior. Sensors commonly used in wealthier nations, such as galvanic skin response sensors and posture sensors, are neither readily available in the Philippines nor economically feasible options for local research. After meetings between Didith Rodrigo and Ryan Baker (the first developer of BROMP in the United States), Rodrigo's team in the Philippines started conducting data collection using a protocol inspired by Baker's work in detecting gaming behavior among students (discussed above), but extended the protocol to include a second coding scheme (simultaneously implemented) for affective states, focusing on flow (engaged concentration), confusion, frustration, boredom, neutral, delight, and surprise.

The initial version of the modified protocol was tested in a private school in Quezon City, Metro Manila, and was initially implemented by either two or three coders who observed individual students together. As part of scaling BROMP in the Philippines, a more formal certification process for new coders was adopted, requiring an inter-rater reliability (Cohen's Kappa) of 0.6 or higher—a number lower than was common in the highly straightforward coding schemes popular in many laboratory psychology studies, but much higher than the numbers seen for other affect labeling protocols such as FACS (Sayette et al., 2001).

In this early work, observations were conducted in pairs or groups of three either once per 180 seconds (Andallaza, Rodrigo, Lagud, Jimenez, & Sugay, 2012; Rodrigo & Baker, 2011; Rodrigo et al., 2012; San Pedro, Baker, & Rodrigo, 2011), and the coders observed each student within a fixed period of 20 seconds. More recent studies (Andres, Rodrigo, Baker, Paquette, Shute, & Ventura, 2015; Banawan, Rodrigo, & Andres, 2015) have moved to the American practice of having a single observer conduct the protocol, and have adjusted the observation length to fall between 5 and 8 seconds when faster labeling is feasible.

Within the Philippines, BROMP has been used for a range of analyses. Some of the first studies using BROMP in the Philippines included the first-ever study showing the long-term correlations between moment-to-moment affect and learning outcomes (Rodrigo & Baker, 2009), the second-ever study of affective dynamics (Baker, Rodrigo, & Xolocotzin, 2007), and the first-ever study comparing affect in intelligent tutors and games (Rodrigo & Baker, 2011). Later BROMP research in the Philippines examined the relationship of confusion with student-driven in-game events (Andres, Rodrigo et al., 2015), the relationship of student affect with the frequency of careless errors (San Pedro, Baker, & Rodrigo, 2014), the differences between the facial expressions, behavior, and confusion trajectories of Filipino and American learners (Tabanao & Rodrigo, 2016), the correlations of boredom and confusion with student action sequences (Andres, Rodrigo, et al., 2015), the relationship between frustration and student achievement (Banawan, Rodrigo, & Andres, 2015), the affective experiences around figuring out a challenging problem (Andres, Andres, Rodrigo, Baker, & Beck, 2015), and the development of a predictive model on wheel-spinning (Palaoag et al., 2016). All in all, BROMP has been used in the Philippines by 17 BROMP-certified coders, throughout the country (from Manila to Davao), and in well over 100 published scientific articles.

BROMP India

In 2014, India became the third country to have BROMP-certified coders. The process of seeding BROMP for India was conducted by two local researchers, in consultation with Baker, who traveled to India to participate in the process. To understand affect and behavior in India to adapt BROMP for use in India, the two Indian researchers conducted qualitative observations in multiple classrooms in government-run schools. Baker initially intended to participate in this process, but his presence was highly disruptive to these classrooms. The Indian researchers met with Baker outside the school context to develop a first-draft coding scheme and implement it within the HART phone app. They then returned to the school to practice coding together before checking for inter-rater reliability. The researchers discussed the results before returning to the classroom to try again. The two Indian coders reached acceptable inter-rater reliability on their second try, with a Kappa of 0.78 for behavior and 0.72 for affect. After this point, the two initial coders trained and certified a third coder in the following week, and then the three of them began training other coders over the following months.

One of the key goals in India was to train a large number of coders for broad use of BROMP. Therefore, efforts were made to further streamline the training process. A video was created by the American team explaining the overall process and theory behind BROMP coding. This video was shown to groups of coders, followed by an explanation of the process and question-and-answer session held locally. After this, the same certification process (of simultaneous but separate coding of the same student and the same time by a previously certified coder and a new coder, requiring Kappa over 0.6) was followed. A total of 72 people were certified in BROMP within India; 68 of them teachers or school personnel in a single large city, working with a local research center. These coders used a slightly modified version of the HART app that adjusted the interface to fit very small and inexpensive phones.

The coding scheme adopted was different in India than in the United States or Philippines, based on the different affect and behavior expressed by students in India and in the learning context. Behaviors such as gaming the system were not relevant in the Indian classrooms; instead three behaviors were coded: active participation (42.7% during last seeder inter-rater checking session), passive participation (41.1% during last seeder inter-rater checking session), and off-task (16.4% during last seeder inter-rater checking session). Boredom (34.3%), confusion (4.1%), and engaged concentration (34.3%) were seen in both India and earlier settings; other affective states were new to India, specifically disinterest (1.4%), enthusiasm (8.2%), and mild interest (17.8%). Engaged concentration was referred to as "focused" to be clearer to the coders but was considered to be the same category by the researchers. A final category, contempt, was hypothesized as a counterpart to the American practice of coding for frustration but was not seen during the seeder inter-rater checking session.

BROMP was used in India for multiple purposes. It was used to provide formative data to teachers and school leaders on individual students' engagement (Hymavathy, Krishnamani, & Sumathi, 2014). It was used to determine which students might be at risk of dropping out (Hymavathy, Krishnamani, & Sumathi, 2015), and it was used to assess whether a specific reform curriculum was more effective at engaging students than traditional classroom practice. However, the systematic and extensive use of BROMP in India has largely ceased after governmental changes and the dissolution of the scientific research center that used BROMP.

BROMP UK

BROMP was adapted for use in the United Kingdom in 2015 by researchers at the University of London, led by Manolis Mavrikis, Beate Grawemeyer, and Wayne Holmes. These researchers needed a systematic protocol to gather affective and behavioral observations of students for studies on adaptive feedback, and they used BROMP in several studies (e.g., Grawemeyer, Mavrikis, Holmes, Hansen, Loibl, & Gutiérrez-Santos, 2015a; Grawemeyer, Mavrikis, Holmes, & Gutierrez-Santos, 2015b;

Grawemeyer et al., 2016; Grawemeyer, Mavrikis, Holmes, Gutiérrez-Santos, Wiedmann, & Rummel, 2017).

Research in the United Kingdom focused on younger students (usually 8–10 years old) who were using the iTalk2Learn math tutor. In early studies (Grawemeyer et al., 2015a), inter-rater reliability (IRR) was quite good (Cohen's Kappa = 0.71), but was established using a substantially different method than implemented in other countries. In this classroom study, BROMP field-workers recorded several affective states (boredom, confusion, frustration, surprise, and flow/concentration) as well as behavioral states (off task, on task, on task conversation, on task reflection, and gaming the system). The BROMP observers' codes were then compared to codes generated by researchers who retrospectively coded both video and audio recordings of the classroom study after the fact (Grawemeyer et al., 2015a).

Later, a subset of BROMP-generated field data was also compared to automated detectors of affect (Grawemeyer et al., 2017). The automated detectors were informed by students' interactions with the iTalk2Learn software (including voice recordings of students' interactions with a help system). In this research, the reliability between BROMP observers and automated detectors of affect was more moderate (Kappa = .551), in part because the automated detectors never recognized an instance of delight (Kappa = .643 with delight excluded).

BROMP UAE

BROMP was adapted for use in the United Arab Emirates in 2018 by researchers affiliated with Alef Education, working in public schools, led by Aishah Al Yammahi, Rand Muhsen, and Guzelle Shahid. There was some consideration of adding an additional affective state of restlessness, but it was not found to be common within classrooms within the initial investigations. The commonly occurring affective states in the UAE were the frequently studied boredom, frustration, confusion, engaged concentration, and delight. A new behavioral category of distracted was also added to represent students who were multitasking while actively working within the learning system. Each of the three initial BROMP coders achieved inter-rater reliability with each other of above 0.6, for both affect and engaged/disengaged behavior. BROMP norming for Abu Dhabi was only completed immediately before publication of this article, but there are plans to use BROMP for both curricular refinement and comparison of different curricula and designs.

BROMP Mexico

As discussed in previous sections, BROMP has been successfully implemented outside of the United States in four other countries: the Philippines, India, England, and the United Arab Emirates. A team of researchers led by Genaro Rebolledo-Mendez at the Universidad Veracruzana attempted to bring BROMP to Mexico as well. Rebolledo-Mendez planned the adaptation of BROMP to Mexico during an extended visit to Baker and Ocumpaugh's laboratory in the United States. Having previously used other methods to study affect and behavior, specifically self-reports and video observation, BROMP provided an alternative that only required minimal technical setup.

In 2015, a pilot of BROMP was conducted in Veracruz, Mexico, within a public secondary school. In this study, a set of 83 students were observed while interacting with a Cognitive Tutor for middle school mathematics that had previously been studied using BROMP in the United States (e.g., Baker et al., 2004). Across several 50-minute class sessions, multiple Mexican researchers (accompanied by researchers from the United States) attempted to create a coding scheme and then reach acceptable inter-rater reliability. However, acceptable inter-rater reliability was not reached despite multiple attempts conducted by three different Mexican researchers from the same region as the students being observed.

One possible explanation is that students may have been uncomfortable displaying visible affect in the presence of the external observers and their teachers due to cultural factors not seen in the other countries where BROMP has been established. It is possible, for example, that the high power distance (the degree of hierarchical inequality that is acceptable between a superior and subordinate—in this case, the teacher and students (Bochner & Hesketh, 1994) may have contributed to this phenomenon. Some evidence against this hypothesis, however, is the success of BROMP in the Philippines, which Hofstede's (1984) research suggests has slightly higher power distance than Mexico. For example, Hofstede (1984) reports a substantial difference between Mexico and the Philippines/United States for a separate but related cultural dimension known as uncertainty avoidance, which captures the degree to which individuals are comfortable with ambiguous or uncertain situations, such as those seen in the use of a new and very different practice during learning. Hofstede and McCrae (2004) suggest that uncertainty avoidance is related to the expression or inhibition of affect, and Mesquita and Walker's (2003) research on cross-cultural differences in the regulation of emotions suggests that children with high levels of uncertainty avoidance, as is common in Mexico, may seek to avoid demonstrating undesirable behaviors or affect. These values may lead to self-presentation effects (e.g., suppressing emotions with negative valance), which could make it more difficult for outside observers to discern affective states like confusion, boredom, and frustration. The researchers noted that students seemed concerned about being evaluated on criteria that were unknown to them and as a result remained constantly aware of the researchers noting their observations. Unfortunately, evidence to disambiguate between these possible explanations is not yet available .

Whatever the reason, the first attempt at implementing BROMP in Mexico was unsuccessful. Future attempts to study BROMP in Mexico are currently in the planning stages, and researchers will study the potential hypotheses for BROMP's initial failure in future attempts to refine BROMP for use in Mexico. A protocol like BROMP cannot succeed if students are uncomfortable with the observation process. It may be possible to determine whether the difficulty in observation is due to observer effects by coding the same categories from video data rather than field observation data. It also may be possible to reduce observer effects by more clearly explaining to students that observations are for research purposes only and will not impact their grades. Overall, the process of adapting BROMP for successful use in Mexico may not solely be beneficial in terms of making BROMP available for research; it may produce broader insight into the characteristics of students in Mexico and the conditions of Mexican classrooms.

SUMMARY OF CROSS-CULTURAL DEVELOPMENT STANDARDS AND RESEARCH

The development of BROMP coding schemes for multiple countries offers the opportunity for new kinds of research on student engagement, but only if the adaption of BROMP for new cultures adheres to appropriate safeguards. In addition to adhering to strict training and inter-rater reliability checks and taking precautions to ensure that observer effects are appropriately minimized, there are two key components to developing BROMP in new cultural environments that are absolutely essential.

First, while some consistency in the content of BROMP coding schemes is important for comparative studies, it would be highly inappropriate to fully impose an American coding scheme in other contexts. Affective categories have different meanings in different contexts, and these differences need to be taken into account. For example, researchers in India who collaborated with us on the development of coding schemes for use there suggested that "frustration" would be seen as a socially embarrassing category that would be subject to considerable presentation effects, and therefore it was not included in BROMP India coding schemes. Therefore, any development of BROMP for a new cultural context must be done in consultation with researchers who are native to the culture being observed.

However, despite the need to revise coding schemes for different cultural contexts, one interesting finding is how much commonality there is across countries. Boredom and confusion show up in every country we have normed BROMP for. Engaged concentration also shows up in every country we have normed BROMP for, though an alternate term, *focused*, was preferred in India. Delight is seen in every country studied when game-based or playful contexts are considered. Frustration is seen in four of the five countries where BROMP has been normed, with the exception in India discussed in the previous paragraph. Behaviors also have a great deal of commonality between countries, with general off-task and on-task categories being common across countries, though other constructs are more prominent in some contexts than others. For example, on-task conversation with other students is relatively rarer in the Philippines than in the other countries where BROMP has been studied, and multitasking "distracted" behavior appears to be more common in the United Arab Emirates than in the other contexts studied, leading to its inclusion in UAE coding schemes but not in other countries. Still, the difference between learning contexts (e.g., games versus intelligent tutors versus teacher-led instruction) appears to be at least as important in terms of the behavior seen as the cultural context is.

Second, the judgments of nonnative researchers should not serve as the baseline in inter-rater reliability checks, even if that researcher has considerable BROMP-coding experience in his or her own culture. While there is some evidence in the literature about the universality of six basic emotions (e.g., Ekman & Friesen, 1971), there are growing concerns about these claims (e.g., Nelson & Russell, 2013; Jack, Garrod, Yu, Caldara, & Schyns, 2012; Porter & Samovar 1996; Tsai & Levenson, 1997; Matsumoto, 1991), and the affective states typically studied with BROMP are more complex than the basic emotions claimed to be universal (Ortony, Clore, & Collins, 1990). Moreover, given the holistic approach that people use to perceive and identify emotions (e.g., Planalp, 1998), it is not surprising that research shows that these perceptions are not culturally universal (e.g., Gendron, Roberson, van der Vyver, & Barre, 2014). There is also the possibility that self-presentation effects may be magnified for academic and achievement-related emotions. This is not to say that all BROMP coders must be from the same population as they are coding—indeed, at the time of this writing four people have become BROMP-certified for cultures they did not grow up in—but that the baseline for certifying BROMP coders and establishing protocols should rest on native coders. Typically, cross-cultural coding is less reliable and contains specific biases (Okur, Aslan, Alyuz, Esme, & Baker, 2018).

Meeting these conditions makes it possible to use BROMP in a valid and useful way in new contexts. Failing to meet these conditions creates significant risks of invalid inference, and researchers conducting affect coding in new contexts without meeting these standards are not using BROMP.

BROMP IN THE BROADER LEARNING SCIENCE CONTEXT

Recent decades have seen increased interest in engagement and affect among learning science researchers (Reschly & Christenson, 2012). One of the key recent trends in learning science has been increasing awareness of the value of larger-scale data, both in terms of more intensive data, more data per learner (cf. Blikstein, 2011), and data on more learners (Baker & Siemens, 2014). Traditional methods for measuring engagement and affect, such as self-report, emote-aloud, video coding, and previous generations of classroom observation protocols are limited in terms of the degree to which they can achieve both intensity and scale. BROMP makes it feasible to achieve higher intensity and scale compared to previous-generation methods for measuring engagement and affect. In addition, by facilitating the development of automated detectors of engagement and affect (e.g., Baker et al., 2012, 2014; DeFalco et al., 2018; Kai et al., 2015; Miller et al., 2014; Pardos et al., 2014; Bosch et al., 2016; Jiang et al., 2018; Gobert et al., 2015), BROMP makes it feasible to use this even more intensive and scalable method.

The value of BROMP to the broader endeavor of learning science can be seen in the broad range of research questions and problems that have become more amenable to analysis through BROMP. This is particularly true for research on affect. The majority of studies on the moment-by-moment prevalence of different affective states during learning have been conducted using BROMP. The majority of studies on affective dynamics have been conducted using BROMP. Well more than half of the studies of the relationship between moment-by-moment affect and student outcomes have involved either BROMP or automated detectors developed using BROMP. By far, the largest-scale studies on student affect have involved BROMP or automated detectors developed using BROMP (e.g., Pardos et al., 2014; Godwin et al., 2016). A large proportion of modern research on affect in the learning sciences has been made possible through BROMP.

BROMP has not been quite as dominant a method for engagement and disengagement research, but has still played a substantial role, leading to papers that have been cited, in aggregate, well over a thousand times, on phenomena ranging from studying the relationship between disengagement and learning (e.g., Baker, Corbett, Koedinger, & Wagner, 2004) to studies on the disengagement associated with different pedagogies (Mulqueeny, Kostyuk, Baker, & Ocumpaugh, 2015) to studies on the relative proportion of different forms of disengagement in different countries (Rodrigo, Baker, & Rossi, 2013).

As engagement and affect continue to be key foci of learning science research, we anticipate that methods like BROMP will continue to be an important part of research in this area. The trend in learning science is toward research methods that are scalable but with established validity, a trend in line with BROMP's advantages.

CONCLUSIONS AND ONGOING DEVELOPMENT

BROMP was originally developed for the training of automated models of student engagement among students using educational software in the United States. The protocol led to the first automated detector of gaming the system, a type of disengaged behavior that has since been shown to correlate with poorer student outcomes. Relatively quickly, in consultation with Didith Rodrigo, its use was expanded from an observation protocol used solely to code for behavior to one that included a separate coding scheme for affective states (and since then, for other classroom conditions as well). Since 2012, when it was used for the first sensor-free, automated models of students' affective states (Baker et al., 2012), BROMP has been used to develop automated detectors of engagement and affect for several learning systems (Baker et al., 2012, 2014; DeFalco et al., 2018; Kai et al.,

2015; Miller et al., 2014; Pardos et al., 2014; Bosch et al., 2016; Jiang et al., 2018; Gobert et al., 2015).

BROMP's use has expanded considerably over the last decade. Currently, BROMP has been used to study more than 20 different software systems, and there are over 150 BROMP-certified coders in the United States, the Philippines, India, the United Kingdom, and the United Arab Emirates. Done properly, there is no reason to think BROMP could not be adapted to a range of other international contexts as well, although the example of Mexico shows that doing so may sometimes present unexpected challenges.

In addition to its use in other countries, BROMP has increasingly been used in nontechnological contexts. The extension of its use, from training educational software to recognize how students behave when they are engaged (or not) to estimating the frequency of behaviors and affective states in a range of contexts, has also led to new research questions. However, there is not currently sufficient knowledge about how large samples need to be for momentary time sampling methods such as BROMP. While extremely large studies are clearly safe (e.g., Godwin et al., 2016), we do not yet know how small our samples can safely be. Further statistical work to develop power analysis for this context (e.g., Paquette et al., 2015) is needed.

Additionally, BROMP may support research into what thresholds are important for intervention during the development of affect. For example, a student may need an intervention for confusion eventually, but understanding what length of confusion or frustration is educationally desirable in a given context requires further research. Likewise, understanding the antecedents to boredom (Baker et al., 2011) is important to developing appropriate interventions (e.g., Daschmann, Goetz, & Stupnisky, 2011; Pekrun, Goetz, Daniels, Stupnisky, & Perry, 2010).

However, there is now a growing body of research showing interest in both the kinds of automated models that BROMP is used to construct (cf., D'Mello, Dieterle, & Duckworth, 2017) and in the use of BROMP for other types of classroom observations. BROMP has also influenced the development of new approaches to coding student interaction and experiences, including the Human Expert Labeling Protocol (HELP) developed by Intel (Aslan et al., 2017) and the system used by researchers at Carnegie Mellon to develop the Spatial Classroom Log Explorer (SPACLE), a system that helps to integrate analysis of different types of learning data (Holstein, McLaren, & Aleven, 2017). We look forward to seeing how this research unfolds in the coming years.

REFERENCES

Abikoff, H., Gittelman, R., & Klein, D. F. (1980). Classroom observation code for hyperactive children: A replication of validity. *Journal of Consulting and Clinical Psychology, 48*(5), 555.

Abikoff, H., Gittelman-Klein, R., & Klein, D. F. (1977). Validation of a classroom observation code for hyperactive children. *Journal of Consulting and Clinical Psychology, 45*(5), 772.

Adamson, R. M., & Wachsmuth, S. T. (2014). A review of direct observation research within the past decade in the field of emotional and behavioral disorders. *Behavioral Disorders, 39*(4), 181–189.

Andallaza, T. C. S., Rodrigo, M. M. T., Lagud, M. C. V., Jimenez, R. J. M., & Sugay, J. O. (2012). Modeling the affective states of students using an intelligent tutoring system for algebra. In *Proceedings of the Third International Workshop on Empathic Computing (IWEC 2012),* (3), 4.

Anderson, L. W. (1981). Instruction and time-on-task: A review. *Journal of Curriculum Studies, 13*(4), 289–303.

Andres, J. M. A. L., Andres, J. M. L., Rodrigo, M. M. T., Baker, R. S., & Beck, J. B. (2015). An investigation of eureka and the affective states surrounding eureka moments. In *Proceedings of the 23rd International Conference on Computers in Education.* China: Asia-Pacific Society for Computers in Education.

Andres, J. M. L., Rodrigo, M. M. T., Baker, R. S., Paquette, L., Shute, V. J., & Ventura, M. (2015, June). Analyzing student action sequences and affect while playing physics playground. In *EDM (Workshops).*

Aslan, S., Mete, S. E., Okur, E., Oktay, E., Alyuz, N., Genc, U. E., . . . & Esme, A. A. (2017). Human expert labeling process (HELP): Towards a reliable higher-order user state labeling process and tool to assess student engagement. *Educational Technology*, 53–59.

Baker, R. S. J. d. (2007) Modeling and Understanding Students' Off-Task Behavior in Intelligent Tutoring Systems. *Proceedings of ACM CHI 2007: Computer-Human Interaction*, 1059–1068.

Baker, R. S. J. d., Corbett, A. T., Koedinger, K. R., Evenson, S. E., Roll, I., Wagner, A. Z., Naim, M., Raspat, J., Baker, D. J., & Beck, J. (2006) Adapting to when students game an intelligent tutoring system. *Proceedings of the 8th International Conference on Intelligent Tutoring Systems*, 392–401.

Baker, R. S. J. d., D'Mello, S. K., Rodrigo, M. M. T., & Graesser, A. C. (2010). Better to be frustrated than bored: The incidence, persistence, and impact of learners' cognitive-affective states during interactions with three different computer-based learning environments. *International Journal of Human-Computer Studies, 68*(4), 223–241.

Baker, R. S., Corbett, A. T., Koedinger, K. R., & Wagner, A. Z. (2004). Off-task behavior in the cognitive tutor classroom: When students game the system. In *Proceedings of the SIGCHI Conference on Human Factors in Computing Systems* (pp. 383–390). ACM.

Baker, R. S., Corbett, A. T., & Koedinger, K. R. (2004). Detecting student misuse of intelligent tutoring systems. In *International Conference on Intelligent Tutoring Systems* (pp. 531–540). Berlin, Heidelberg: Springer.

Baker, R. S. J. d., Gowda, S. M., Wixon, M., Kalka, J., Wagner, A. Z., Salvi, A., Aleven, V., Kusbit, G., Ocumpaugh, J., & Rossi, L. (2012). Towards sensor-free affect detection in Cognitive Tutor algebra. *Proceedings of the 5th International Conference on Educational Data Mining*, 126–133.

Baker, R. S. J. d., Moore, G., Wagner, A., Kalka, J., Karabinos, M., Ashe, C., & Yaron, D. (2011). The dynamics between student affect and behavior occurring outside of educational software. *Proceedings of the 4th Bi-annual International Conference on Affective Computing and Intelligent Interaction.*

Baker, R. S., Ocumpaugh, J., Gowda, S. M., Kamarainen, A., & Metcalf, S. J. (2014). Extending log-based affect detection to a multi-user virtual environment for science. *Proceedings of the 22nd Conference on User Modelling, Adaptation, and Personalization*, 290–300.

Baker, R. S. J. d., Rodrigo, M. M. T., & Xolocotzin, U. E. (2007). The dynamics of affective transitions in simulation problem-solving environments. *Proceedings of the Second International Conference on Affective Computing and Intelligent Interaction.*

Baker, R., & Siemens, G. (2014). Educational data mining and learning analytics. In Sawyer, K. (Ed.), *Cambridge handbook of the learning sciences* (2nd ed.)(pp. 253–274).

Banawan, M. P., Rodrigo, M. M. T., & Andres, J. M. L. (2015). Investigation of frustration among students using Physics Playground. *Proceedings of the 23rd International Conference for Computers in Education.*

Blikstein, P. (2011). Using learning analytics to assess students' behavior in open-ended programming tasks. In *Proceedings of the 1st International Conference on Learning Analytics and Knowledge* (pp. 110–116). ACM.

Bochner, S., & Hesketh, B. (1994). Power distance, individualism/collectivism, and job-related attitudes in a culturally diverse work group. *Journal of Cross-Cultural Psychology, 25*(2), 233–257.

Bosch, N., D'Mello, S. K., Ocumpaugh, J., Baker, R. S., & Shute, V. (2016). Using video to automatically detect learner affect in computer-enabled classrooms. *ACM Transactions on Interactive Intelligent Systems (TiiS), 6*(2), 17.

Botelho, A. F., Baker, R., Ocumpaugh, J., & Heffernan, N. (2018). Studying affect dynamics and chronometry using sensor-free detectors. *Proceedings of the 11th International Conference on Educational Data Mining*, 157–166.

Carta, J. J., Greenwood, R., Schulte, D., Arreaga-Mayer, C., & Terry, B. (1988). *Code Instructional Structure and Student Academic Response: Mainstream Version (MS-CISSAR).* Kansas City: Juniper Gardens Children's Project, Bureau of Child Research, University of Kansas.

Christ, T. J., Riley-Tillman, T. C., Chafouleas, S., & Jaffery, R. (2011). Direct Behavior Rating: An Evaluation of Alternate Definitions to Assess Classroom Behaviors. *School Psychology Review, 40*(2).

Cohen, J. (1960). A coefficient of agreement for nominal scales. *Educational and Psychological Measurement, 20*(1), 37–46.

Csikszentmihalyi, M. (1990). *Flow: The psychology of optimal performance.*

Daschmann, E. C., Goetz, T., & Stupnisky, R. H. (2011). Testing the predictors of boredom at school: Development and validation of the precursors to boredom scales. *British Journal of Educational Psychology, 81*, 421–440.

Danielson, C. (2011). *Enhancing professional practice: A framework for teaching.* ASCD.

DeFalco, J.A., Rowe, J.P., Paquette, L., Georgoulas-Sherry, V., Brawner, K., Mott, B.W., Baker, R.S., & Lester, J.C. (2018). Detecting and addressing frustration in a serious game for military training. *International Journal of Artificial Intelligence and Education, 28* (2), 152–193.

DiStefano, D. (2018). *How Pre-Service Teachers' Engagement and Affect Informs Instructional Format of an Introductory Methods Course* [Unpublished doctoral dissertation]. Fordham University.

D'Mello, S. K., Lehman, B., & Person, N. (2010). Monitoring affect states during effortful problem solving activities. *International Journal of Artificial Intelligence in Education, 20*(4), 361–389.

D'Mello, S., Dieterle, E., & Duckworth, A. (2017). Advanced, analytic, automated (AAA) measurement of engagement during learning. *Educational Psychologist, 52*(2), 104–123.

D'Mello, S., Picard, R. W., & Graesser, A. (2007). Toward an affect-sensitive AutoTutor. *IEEE Intelligent Systems, 22*(4).

Downer, J. T., Booren, L. M., Lima, O. K., Luckner, A. E., & Pianta, R. C. (2010). The Individualized Classroom Assessment Scoring System (inCLASS): Preliminary reliability and validity of a system for observing preschoolers' competence in classroom interactions. *Early Childhood Research Quarterly, 25*(1), 1–16.

Ekman, P., & Friesen, W. V. (1971). Constants across cultures in the face and emotion. *Journal of Personality and Social Psychology, 17*(2), 124.

Ekman, P., & Friesen, W. V. (1978). *Facial action coding system: Investigator's guide.* Consulting Psychologists Press.

Ekman, P., Friesen, W. V., & Hager, J. C. (Eds.). (2002). *Facial action coding system* (E-book). Salt Lake City, UT: Research Nexus.

Fischer, A. H., & Manstead, A. S. R. (2008). Social functions of emotion. In M. Lewis, J. Haviland-Jones, & L. F. Barrett (Eds.), Handbook of emotions (3rd ed., pp. 456–468). New York: Guilford Press.

Fischer, A. H., Rodriguez Mosquera, P. M., Van Vianen, A. E., & Manstead, A. S. (2004). Gender and culture differences in emotion. *Emotion, 4*(1), 87.

Fredricks, J. A., Blumenfeld, P. C., & Paris, A. H. (2004). School engagement: Potential of the concept, state of the evidence. *Review of Educational Research,74*, 59–109.

Fredricks, J. A., & McColskey, W. (2012). The measurement of student engagement: A comparative analysis of various methods and student self-report instruments. In *Handbook of research on student engagement* (pp. 763–782). Springer.

Furr, R. M., & Funder, D. C. (2007). Behavioral observation. *Handbook of Research Methods in Personality Psychology*, 273–291.

Gadow, K. D., Sprafkin, J., & Nolan, E. E. (1996). *Attention deficit hyperactivity disorder school observation code.*

Gendron, M., Roberson, D., van der Vyver, J. M., & Barrett, L. F. (2014). Perceptions of emotion from facial expressions are not culturally universal: Evidence from a remote culture. *Emotion, 14*(2), 251.

Gobert, J. D., Baker, R. S., & Wixon, M. B. (2015). Operationalizing and detecting disengagement within online science microworlds. *Educational Psychologist, 50*(1), 43–57.

Godwin, K. E., Almeda, M. V., Seltman, H., Kai, S., Skerbetz, M. D., Baker, R. S., & Fisher, A. V. (2016). Off-task behavior in elementary school children. *Learning and Instruction, 44*, 128–143.

Graesser, A. C., McDaniel, B., Chipman, P., Witherspoon, A., D'Mello, S., & Gholson, B. (2006). Detection of emotions during learning with AutoTutor. In *Proceedings of the 28th Annual Meetings of the Cognitive Science Society* (pp. 285–290).

Grawemeyer, B., Mavrikis, M., Holmes, W., Hansen, A., Loibl, K., & Gutiérrez-Santos, S. (2015a). Affect matters: Exploring the impact of feedback during mathematical tasks in an exploratory environment. In *International Conference on Artificial Intelligence in Education*, 595–599. Springer, Cham.

Grawemeyer, B., Mavrikis, M., Holmes, W., Hansen, A., Loibl, K., & Gutiérrez-Santos, S. (2015b). The impact of feedback on students' affective states. In *CEUR Workshop Proceedings* (Vol. 1432). CEUR Workshop Proceedings.

Grawemeyer, B., Mavrikis, M., Holmes, W., & Gutierrez-Santos, S. (2015). Adapting feedback types according to students' affective states. In *International Conference on Artificial Intelligence in Education* (pp. 586–590). Springer, Cham.

Grawemeyer, B., Mavrikis, M., Holmes, W., Gutierrez-Santos, S., Wiedmann, M., & Rummel, N. (2016). Affecting off-task behaviour: How affect-aware feedback can improve student learning. In *Proceedings of the Sixth International Conference on Learning Analytics & Knowledge* (pp. 104–113). ACM.

Grawemeyer, B., Mavrikis, M., Holmes, W., Gutiérrez-Santos, S., Wiedmann, M., & Rummel, N. (2017). Affective learning: Improving engagement and enhancing learning with affect-aware feedback. *User Modeling and User-Adapted Interaction, 27*(1), 119–158.

Grossman, P., Loeb, S., Cohen, J., & Wyckoff, J. (2013). Measure for measure: The relationship between measures of instructional practice in middle school English language arts and teachers' value-added scores. *American Journal of Education, 119*(3), 445–470.

Hamre, B. K., Goffin, S. G., & Kraft-Sayre, M. (2009). *Classroom assessment scoring system implementation guide: Measuring and improving classroom interactions in early classroom settings.*

Harrison, S. E., Riley-Tillman, T. C., & Chafouleas, S. M. (2014). Direct behavior rating: Considerations for rater accuracy. *Canadian Journal of School Psychology, 29*(1), 3–20.

Hill, H. C., Charalambous, C. Y., Blazar, D., McGinn, D., Kraft, M. A., Beisiegel, M., Humez, A., Litke, E., & Lynch, K. (2012). Validating arguments for observational instruments: Attending to multiple sources of variation. *Educational Assessment, 17*(2–3), 88–106.

Hintze, J. M. (2005). Psychometrics of direct observation. *School Psychology Review, 34*(4), 507.

Hofstede, G. (1984). *Culture's consequences: international differences in work-related values* (Vol. 5). Sage.

Hofstede, G. (2003). *Culture's consequences: comparing values, behaviors, institutions and organizations across nations.* Sage publications.

Hofstede, G., & McCrae, R. R. (2004). Personality and culture revisited: Linking traits and dimensions of culture. *Cross-Cultural Research, 38*(1), 52–88.

Hops, H., Davis, B., & Longoria, N. (1995). Methodological issues in direct observation: Illustrations with the living in familial environments (LIFE) coding system. *Journal of Clinical Child Psychology, 24*, 193–203.

Holstein, K., McLaren, B. M., & Aleven, V. (2017). SPACLE: Investigating learning across virtual and physical spaces using spatial replays. In *Proceedings of the Seventh International Learning Analytics & Knowledge Conference* (pp. 358–367). ACM.

Hymavathy, C., Krishnamani, V. R., & Sumathi, C. P. (2014). Analyzing learner engagement to enhance the teaching-learning experience. In *MOOC, Innovation and Technology in Education (MITE), 2014 IEEE International Conference*, 67–70.

Hymavathy, C., Krishnamani, V. R., & Sumathi, C. P. (2015). EDM: Finding answers to reduce dropout rates in schools. *International Journal of Computing Algorithm, 4*(1), 26–29.

Institute for Research on Policy Education and Practice. (2011). *Protocol for language arts teaching observation (PLATO).* http://platorubric.stanford.edu/

Jack, R. E., Garrod, O. G., Yu, H., Caldara, R., & Schyns, P. G. (2012). Facial expressions of emotion are not culturally universal. *Proceedings of the National Academy of Sciences, 109*(19), 7241–7244.

Jiang, Y., Bosch, N., Baker, R. S., Paquette, L., Ocumpaugh, J., Andres, J. M. A. L., . . . & Biswas, G. (2018). Expert feature-engineering vs. deep neural networks: Which is better for sensor-free affect detection? In *International Conference on Artificial Intelligence in Education* (pp. 198–211). Springer, Cham.

Junker, B. W., Weisberg, Y., Matsumura, L. C., Crosson, A., Wolf, M., Levison, A., & Resnick, L. (2005). *Overview of the instructional quality assessment.* Regents of the University of California.

Kai, S., Paquette, L., Baker, R. S., Bosch, N., D'Mello, S., Ocumpaugh, J., Shute, V., & Ventura, M. (2015) A Comparison of video-based and interaction-based affect detectors in Physics Playground. *Proceedings of the 8th International Conference on Educational Data Mining*, 77–84.

Karumbaiah, S., Andres, J. M. A. L., Botelho, A. F., Baker, R. S., Ocumpaugh, J. (2018). The implications of a subtle difference in the calculation of affect dynamics. *Proceedings of the 26th International Conference on Computers in Education*, 29–38.

Karweit, N., & Slavin, R. E. (1982). Time-on-task: Issues of timing, sampling, and definition. *Journal of Educational Psychology, 74*(6), 844.

Kent, R. N., O'Leary, K. D., Diament, C., & Dietz, A. (1974). Expectation biases in observational evaluation of therapeutic change. *Journal of Consulting and Clinical Psychology, 42*(6), 774.

Krumhuber, E. G., Kappas, A., & Manstead, A. S. (2013). Effects of dynamic aspects of facial expressions: A review. *Emotion Review, 5*(1), 41–46.

Lee, S. H., Wehmeyer, M. L., Palmer, S. B., Soukup, J. H., & Little, T. D. (2008). Self-determination and access to the general education curriculum. *The Journal of Special Education, 42*(2), 91–107.

Lewis, T. J., Scott, T. M., Wehby, J. H., & Wills, H. P. (2014). Direct observation of teacher and student behavior in school settings: Trends, issues and future directions. *Behavioral Disorders, 39*(4), 190–200.

Liu, Z., Pataranutaporn, V., Ocumpaugh, J., Baker, R. S. J. d. (2013). Sequences of frustration and confusion, and learning. *Proceedings of the 6th International Conference on Educational Data Mining*, 114–120.

Matsumoto, D. (1991). Cultural influences on facial expressions of emotion. *Southern Journal of Communication, 56*(2), 128–137.

McCall, G. J. (1984). Systematic field observation. *Annual Review of Sociology, 10*(1), 263–282.

McCoy, S., Galletta, D. F., & King, W. R. (2005). Integrating national culture into IS research: The need for current individual level measures. *Communications of the Association for Information Systems, 15*(1), 12.

McCroskey, J. C. (1994). Assessment of affect toward communication and affect toward instruction in communication. In *1994 SCA Summer Conference Proceedings and Prepared Remarks: Assessing College Student Competence in Speech Communication*. Annandale, VA: Speech Communication Association.

Meany-Daboul, M. G., Roscoe, E. M., Bourret, J. C., & Ahearn, W. H. (2007). A comparison of momentary time sampling and partial-interval recording for evaluating functional relations. *Journal of Applied Behavior Analysis, 40*(3), 501–514.

Mesquita, B., & Walker, R. (2003). Cultural differences in emotions: A context for interpreting emotional experiences. *Behaviour Research and Therapy, 41*(7), 777–793.

Miller, W. L., Petsche, K., Baker, R. S., Labrum, M. J., & Wagner, A. Z. (2014). Boredom across activities, and across the year, within reasoning mind. In *Workshop on Data Mining for Educational Assessment and Feedback (ASSESS 2014).*

Mulqueeny, K., Kostyuk, V., Baker, R.S., & Ocumpaugh, J. (2015) Incorporating effective e-learning principles to improve student engagement in middle-school mathematics. *International Journal of STEM Education, 2*(15).

Nelson, N. L., & Russell, J. A. (2013). Universality revisited. *Emotion Review, 5*(1), 8–15.

Nock, M. K., & Kurtz, S. M. (2005). Direct behavioral observation in school settings: Bringing science to practice. *Cognitive and Behavioral Practice, 12*(3), 359–370.

Ocumpaugh, J., Andres, J. M. L., Baker, R., DeFalco, J., Paquette, L., Rowe, J., Mott, B., Lester, J., Georgoulas, V., Brawner, K., Sottilare, R. (2017). Affect dynamics in military trainees. *Proceedings of the 18th International Conference on Artificial Intelligence in Education*, 238–249.

Ocumpaugh, J., Baker, R. S. J. d., & Rodrigo, M. M. T. (2012). *Baker-Rodrigo Observation Method Protocol (BROMP) 1.0. Training manual version 1.0* [Technical report]. New York: EdLab. Manila, Philippines: Ateneo Laboratory for the Learning Sciences.

Ocumpaugh, J., Baker, R. S., & Rodrigo, M. M. T. (2015). *Baker Rodrigo Ocumpaugh Monitoring Protocol (BROMP) 2.0 technical and training manual.* New York and Manila, Philippines: Teachers College, Columbia University and Ateneo Laboratory for the Learning Sciences.

Okur, E., Aslan, S., Alyuz, N., Esme, A. A., & Baker, R. S. (2018). Role of socio-cultural differences in labeling students' affective states. *Proceedings of the 19th International Conference on Artificial Intelligence in Education*, 367–380.

Ornstein, A. C. (1990). A look at teacher effectiveness research—theory and practice. *NASSP Bulletin, 74*(528), 78–88.

Ortony, A., Clore, G. L., & Collins, A. (1990). *The Cognitive Structure of Emotions.* Cambridge University Press.

Ostrov, J. M., & Hart, E. (2014). Observational methods. *The Oxford handbook of quantitative methods in psychology: Foundations, 1*, 286.

Paquette, L., Ocumpaugh, J., & Baker, R. S. (2015). Simulating multi-subject momentary time sampling. In *EDM* (pp. 586–587).

PACT Consortium. (2012). *PACT (Performance Assessment for California Teachers).* http://www.pacttpa.org/_main/hub.php?pageName=Home

Palaoag, T. D., Rodrigo, M. M. T., Andres, J. M. L., Andres, J. M. A. L., & Beck, J. E. (2016). Wheel-spinning in a game-based learning environment for physics. In *International Conference on Intelligent Tutoring Systems* (pp. 234–239). Springer, Cham.

Pardos, Z. A., Baker, R. S., San Pedro, M. O. C. Z., Gowda, S. M., & Gowda, S. M. (2014). Affective states and state tests: Investigating how affect and engagement during the school year predict end of year learning outcomes. *Journal of Learning Analytics, 1*(1), 107–128

Patikorn, T., Heffernan, N. T., & Baker, R. S. (2018). ASSISTments longitudinal data mining competition 2017: A preface. *Proceedings of the Workshop on Scientific Findings from the ASSISTments Longitudinal Data Competition, International Conference on Educational Data Mining.*

Pekrun, R., Goetz, T., Daniels, L., Stupnisky, R. H., & Perry, R. (2010). Boredom in achievement settings: Exploring control–value antecedents and performance outcomes of a neglected emotion. *Journal of Educational Psychology, 102*, 531–549.

Pianta, R. C., La Paro, K. M., & Hamre, B. K. (2008). *Classroom assessment scoring system: Manual K–3.* Paul H Brookes Publishing.

Piburn, M., & Sawada, D. (2000). *Reformed teaching observation protocol (RTOP) reference manual* (Technical report).

Planalp, S. (1998). Communicating emotion in everyday life: Cues, channels, and processes. *Handbook of communication and emotion: Research, theory, applications, and contexts* (pp. 29–48).

Porter, R. E., & Samovar, L. A. (1996). Cultural influences on emotional expression: Implications for intercultural communication. In *Handbook of communication and emotion* (pp. 451–472).

Reschly, A. L., & Christenson, S. L. (2012). Jingle, jangle, and conceptual haziness: Evolution and future directions of the engagement construct. In *Handbook of research on student engagement* (pp. 3–19). Boston, MA: Springer.

Reyes, L., & Fennema, E. (1981). *Classroom processes observer manual.*

Reynolds, C., & Kamphaus, R. (2004). *Behavior assessment system for children, (BASC-2) handout.* AGS Publishing, 4201, 55014-1796.

Richards, L. C., Heathfield, L. T., & Jenson, W. R. (2010). A classwide peer-modeling intervention package to increase on-task behavior. *Psychology in the Schools, 47*(6), 551–566.

Riley-Tillman, T. C., Kalberer, S. M., & Chafouleas, S. M. (2005). Selecting the right tool for the job: A review of behavior monitoring tools used to assess student response to intervention. *The California School Psychologist, 10*(1), 81–91.

Rodrigo, M. M. T., & Baker, R. S. J. d. (2009). Coarse-grained detection of student frustration in an introductory programming course. *Proceedings of ICER 2009: the International Computing Education Workshop.*

Rodrigo, M. M. T., & Baker, R. S. J. d. (2011). Comparing learners' affect while using an intelligent tutor and an educational game. *Research and Practice in Technology Enhanced Learning, 6* (1), 43–66.

Rodrigo, M. M. T., Baker, R. S., Agapito, J., Nabos, J., Repalam, M. C., Reyes, S. S., & San Pedro, M. O. C. (2012). The effects of an interactive software agent on student affective dynamics while using; an intelligent tutoring system. *IEEE Transactions on Affective Computing, 3*(2), 224–236.

Rodrigo, M. M. T., Baker, R. S. J. d., & Rossi, L. (2013) Student off-task behavior in computer-based learning in the Philippines: Comparison to prior research in the USA. *Teachers College Record, 115*(10), 1–27.

San Pedro, M. O. Z., Baker, R. S. J. d., Bowers, A. J., & Heffernan, N. T. (2013). Predicting college enrollment from student interaction with an intelligent tutoring system in middle school. *Proceedings of the 6th International Conference on Educational Data Mining*, 177–184.

San Pedro, M. O. C. Z., Baker, R. S. d., & Rodrigo, M. M. T. (2011). Detecting carelessness through contextual estimation of slip probabilities among students using an intelligent tutor for mathematics. In *International Conference on Artificial Intelligence in Education* (pp. 304–311). Berlin, Heidelberg: Springer.

San Pedro, M. O. Z., Baker, R. S. J. d., & Rodrigo, M. M. T. (2014). Carelessness and affect in an intelligent tutoring system for mathematics. *International Journal of Artificial Intelligence in Education, 24*, 189–210.

Sayette, M. A., Cohn, J. F., Wertz, J. M., Perrott, M. A., & Parrott, D. J. (2001). A psychometric evaluation of the facial action coding system for assessing spontaneous expression. *Journal of Nonverbal Behavior, 25*(3), 167–185.

Sawada, D., Piburn, M. D., Judson, E., Turley, J., Falconer, K., Benford, R., & Bloom, I. (2002).Measuring reform practices in science and mathematics classrooms: The reformed teaching observation protocol. *School Science and Mathematics, 102*(6), 245–253.

Schutz, P., & Pekrun, R. (Eds.) (2007). *Emotion in education.* New York: Academic Press.

Shapiro, E. S., & Heick, P. (2004). School psychologist assessment practices in the evaluation of students referred for social/behavioral/emotional problems. *Psychology in the Schools, 41*, 551–561.

Skinner, C. H., Rhymer, K. N., & McDaniel, E. C. (2000). Naturalistic direct observation in educational settings. In E. S. Shapiro & T. R. Kratochwill (Eds.), Conducting school-based assessments of child and adolescent behavior (pp. 21–54). New York: Guilford Press.

Soukup, J. H., Wehmeyer, M. L., Bashinski, S. M., & Bovaird, J. A. (2007). Classroom variables and access to the general curriculum for students with disabilities. *Exceptional Children, 74*(1), 101–120.

Smith, M. K., Jones, F. H., Gilbert, S. L., & Wieman, C. E. (2013). The classroom observation protocol for undergraduate STEM (COPUS): A new instrument to characterize university STEM classroom practices. *CBE-Life Sciences Education, 12*(4), 618–627.

Stanley, S. O., & Greenwood, C. R. (1981). *CISSAR: Code for instructional structure and student academic response: Observer's manual.* Kansas City, University of Kansas, Bureau of Child Research, Juniper Gardens Children's Project.

Tabanao, E., & Rodrigo, M. M. (2016). A comparison of the experience of confusion among Filipino and American learners while using an educational game for physics. *Proceedings of the 24th International Conference on Computers in Education*. India: Asia-Pacific Society for Computers in Education.

Tsai, J. L., & Levenson, R. W. (1997). Cultural influences on emotional responding: Chinese American and European American dating couples during interpersonal conflict. *Journal of Cross-Cultural Psychology, 28*(5), 600–625.

Volpe, R. J., DiPerna, J. C., Hintze, J. M., & Shapiro, E. S. (2005). Observing students in classroom settings: A review of seven coding schemes. *School Psychology Review, 34*(4), 454.

Volpe, R. J., & McConaughy, S. H. (2005). Systematic direct observational assessment of student behavior: Its use and interpretation in multiple settings: An introduction to the miniseries. *School Psychology Review, 34*(4), 451.

Walker, H. M., & Severson, H. H. (1990). *Systematic Screening for Behavior Disorders: Users guide and administration manual*. Longmont, CO: Sopris West.

Walkington, C., & Marder, M. (2013). Classroom observation and value added models give complementary information about quality of mathematics teaching. *Designing teacher evaluation systems: New guidance from the measures of effective teaching project*, 234–277. San Francisco: Josey Bass.

Waxman, H. C., & Padron, Y. N. (1994). Alternative models for evaluating technology-enriched professional development schools. In *Society for Information Technology & Teacher Education International Conference* (pp. 199–202). Association for the Advancement of Computing in Education (AACE).

Waxman, H. C., & Padron, Y. N. (2004). The uses of the Classroom Observation Schedule to improve classroom instruction. *Observational research in US classrooms: New approaches for understanding cultural and linguistic diversity*, 72–96.

Wessel, D. (2015) The potential of computer-assisted direct observation apps. *International Journal of Interactive Mobile Technologies, 9*(1), 31.

Wigfield, A., & Cambria, J. (2010). Students' achievement values, goal orientations, and interest: Definitions, development, and relations to achievement outcomes. *Developmental Review, 30*, 1–35.

Wilson, M. S., & Reschly, D. J. (1996). Assessment in school psychology training and practice. *School Psychology Review, 25*, 9–23.

Wragg, T. (2002). *An introduction to classroom observation*. Routledge.

ABOUT THE AUTHORS

Ryan Baker is associate professor at the University of Pennsylvania and director of the Penn Center for Learning Analytics. Baker has developed models that can automatically detect student engagement in over a dozen online learning environments, and he co-led the development of the BROMP field observation protocol. He was the founding president of the International Educational Data Mining Society and currently is editor of the journal *Computer-Based Learning in Context* and codirector of the MOOC Replication Framework (MORF).

Jaclyn Ocumpaugh is the associate director of the Penn Center for Learning Analytics at the University of Pennsylvania, where her work centers on affective learning processes, often in STEM. Prior to her work in learning analytics, Ocumpaugh earned degrees in linguistics. She is currently collaborating on several projects in the learning sciences that make broader use of this early training.

Juliana Ma. Alexandra L. Andres earned her BA in psychology at the Ateneo de Manila University in 2017. She worked as a research assistant in the Ateneo Laboratory for the Learning Sciences. She began working as a research assistant in the Penn Center for Learning Analytics and earned her MSEd from the University of Pennsylvania. She is currently pursuing her EdD at the University of Pennsylvania.

CHAPTER 6

Science of Learning and Learning Engineering: Advancing the Relationship Between Learning Sciences and Teaching Practice

Melina R. Uncapher
Neuroscape Center, Department of Neurology, University of California, San Francisco; and Institute for Applied Neuroscience

Britte Haugan Cheng
Menlo Education Research

ABSTRACT

A growing movement of researchers, educators, and policy makers are recognizing that education may be our most important applied science, and that insights from the science of learning can inform decision making in education policy and practice. However, scientific disciplines that make an impact in the world do so not primarily through their scientists, but rather through their associated engineers, whose role is to translate scientific findings and engineer solutions to real-world problems (while also advancing scientific discovery). This chapter will introduce a recent initiative that aims to launch the engineering analog to learning sciences: the discipline of *learning engineering*. This discipline aims to create bidirectional, generative dialogue between researchers and educators to leverage: (1) *principles* of the science of learning, (2) *processes* of human-centered design (i.e., engineering), and (3) *platforms* of technology and social infrastructures, to co-create solutions to persistent challenges in education, whether the challenges are problems of practice, problems of research, or problems of scale. In the process, learning engineering has the potential to reshape educational practice and policy, learning sciences, and technology and program development, and thus, may fundamentally transform our understanding of how people learn and our understanding of how best to support teaching and learning across the variety of contexts that is our education system.

There is an emerging movement across the globe to integrate the multidisciplinary research base on the science of how people learn, in service of translating these research insights into effective teaching and learning practices. These efforts are beginning to bring together research findings from educational psychology, cognitive science, neuroscience, social science, affective science, developmental science, diversity science, the science of the individual, and more. However, efforts to unidirectionally translate research findings *to* educational practice will likely have limited utility and sustainability if they do not close the feedback loop and bring the wisdom of educators into research practices. In this chapter, we discuss promising science of learning efforts around the globe, raise concerns around the extant waterfall models translating research to practice, and propose a novel model that not only allows the science of learning to inform prototypes that can be tested, evaluated, and iterated in local contexts for unique populations across diverse settings, but also affords equal voice to educators who provide the wisdom of practice and the knowledge of local context to impact implementation. This new model of *learning engineering* relies on a new process of *inclusive R&D* to provide a means by which we may deliver on the promise of the emergent field of the science of learning.

A GLOBAL CHALLENGE

Scientific inquiry into how people learn has a long and rich tradition, ostensibly beginning in the late 1800s with Ebbinghaus (1885/1964) and Fechner (1860/1966). Herr Ebbinghaus famously developed methods to objectively study learning and memory in order to prove wrong his philosopher contemporaries who argued that an experimental science of higher mental processes such as learning and memory was impossible. In doing so, he established foundational methods and principles that launched the experimental investigation of learning, which has since branched into the cognitive, social, affective, neurobiological, educational, and developmental sciences, and more. Despite this proliferation of the sciences of learning, the scientific insights about how people learn have largely remained siloed in the halls of academia, separate from the practitioners who would benefit from—and indeed significantly contribute to—an evidence-based or evidence-informed understanding of how students learn. Practitioners can contribute to the science of learning by (a) identifying problems of practice that are most challenging, and (b) providing needed understandings about how innovations may need to be designed, evaluated, and iterated in response to their context (i.e., principles and practices of local implementation).

This persistent chasm between learning sciences research and education practice is likely a root cause that hinders efforts to improve the quality of teaching and learning around the world. Indeed, there is increasing attention not just in the United States but around the globe on how education leaders make decisions about which programs, curricula, and technologies to bring into their districts and schools. While there has certainly been more attention paid in the United States to using student data to inform school practice since the No Child Left Behind act of 2001, student data may not be the primary driver of decision making in schools. Moreover, for leadership to propose strategic initiatives to address any trends revealed by student data, means of evaluating initiatives or educational research itself are needed. Honig and Coburn's 2008 literature review points to the social, organizational, and political complexities of school and district efforts to search for, identify, and access research evidence, as well as to the local knowledge required to interpret and align evidence with ongoing challenges, reform efforts, and existing conditions. Given these complexities and frequent lack of capacity within schools or districts to conduct the required processes to sufficiently vet a program, curriculum, or tool, huge amounts of financial, time, and people resources may be poured into programs, curricula, and tools that are not based on the science of learning and may have no evidence of effectiveness. In many cases, they may be doing more harm than good by siphoning precious fiscal and personnel resources from programs that do show effectiveness.

Both policy making (which exerts forms of systemic pressure for evidence-based decision making that may not recognize local knowledge) and educational research (which produces a significant body of information that must be interpreted to be useful) are implicated in this enduring challenge. As we will argue, in order to best support practitioners in their endeavors, a realignment of policy making, practitioner, and research communities toward impact on everyday teaching and learning in situ is required, including the explicit goal of aggregation and dissemination of evidence generated by practitioners themselves.

A GLOBAL SOLUTION?

There is a growing movement of researchers (Bruer, 1997; Fishman, Penuel, Allen, Cheng, & Sabelli, 2013; Uncapher, 2016; Stafford Brizard,

Cantor, & Rose, 2017), practitioners and policy makers (The Council of Chief State School Officers (CCSSO), 2017), developers (Bevan, Ryoo, Vanderwerff, Petrich, & Wilkinson, 2018), and funders (e.g., US Department of Education, National Science Foundation, William T. Grant Foundation, etc.) that are advocating for a revolution in education similar to that which occurred in medicine two centuries ago, when medical practitioners partnered with researchers who studied the human body. Very rapidly after forming this research-practice partnership in medicine, the efficacy of medical practice improved dramatically. The prevalence of using, for instance, leeches and burr-holes to the skull to treat all manner of ills shifted in favor of more evidence-based and evidence-informed practices, such as applying germ theory to improve medical protocols: prescribing penicillin and sterile surgical procedures dramatically improved medical outcomes in a very short period of time.

So the pressing question is: *What are the leeches and what are the penicillins in modern education?* The science of learning and its various contributing disciplines (cognitive science, social science, neuroscience, developmental science, etc.) have been revealing clues to answer this question. Among the "leeches," the concept of *learning styles*—that students learn best in their preferred modality of auditory, visual, or kinesthetic presentation—is consistently documented as the most frequent misconception about how students learn (e.g., Dekker, Lee, Howard-Jones, & Jolles, 2012; Howard-Jones, 2014). Other highly believed misconceptions include ideas about left brain/right brain learners, coordinated exercises to increase left and right brain integration, and that dyslexia results only from students perceiving letter reversals. The science of learning tells us that these are our modern-day leech concepts: widely believed but without empirical basis for practice. So what are the "penicillin" concepts that have strong evidence of effectiveness but may not be widely practiced yet?

We advocate that education should be considered an applied science, much like medicine. And indeed there have been explicit calls to action for many decades to bridge science of learning research and education practice, with an influential treatise by John Bruer in 1997 (Bruer, 1997) and the creation of the field of Mind, Brain, and Education. Recent educational research reveals that what works is a matter of for whom and under what conditions (Means & Penuel, 2005). Research and development in education, then, should reflect the complexities of educational systems and implement iterative cycles of innovation that respect, aggregate, and leverage knowledge about the interactions between variables and characteristics of contexts (e.g., student population characteristics) and design of innovations.

From an iterative design and development perspective (see Figure 6.1), foundational principles of how people learn could (and we argue, should) be incorporated as part of product or tool development, which itself is conducted according to best practices. Products or tools are designed to support pedagogical approaches of teachers. In the use of products or tools, instructional activities reflect each of these design antecedents, an instantiation of learning principles, translated through the filters of design and teaching practices. In day-to-day practice, multiple innovations are often employed, requiring practitioners to coordinate sets of approaches. Finally, the context of use (classroom, school, or district) is itself a system of affordances and constraints that must be considered by designers and coordinated by teachers and students (Jacobson & Wilensky, 2006; Lemke & Sabelli, 2008).

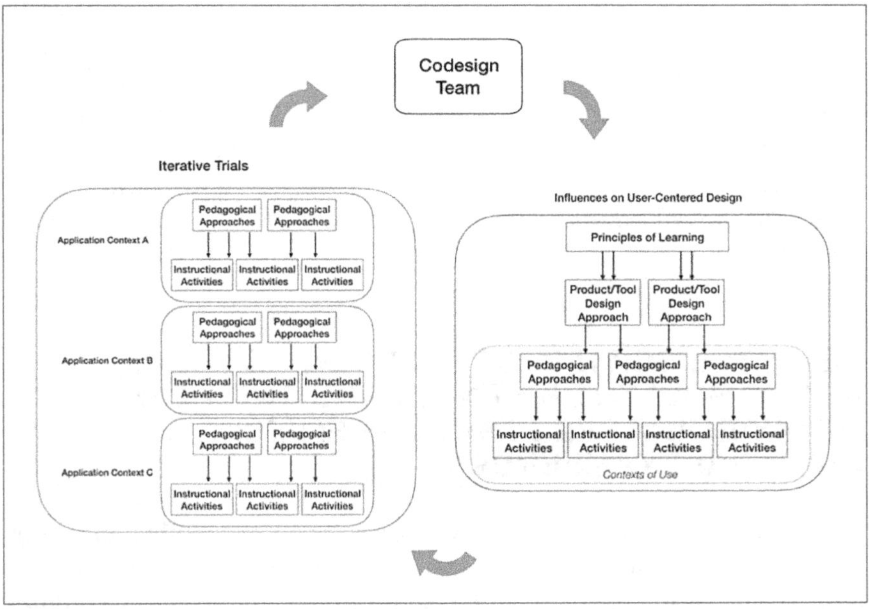

FIGURE 6.1 An iterative codesign and development process of educational products and/or tools includes a team composed of all stakeholders of the design (e.g., researchers, designers, teachers, students, school and district leadership, parents, etc.). User-centered design reflects principles of learning, state-of-the-art design principles appropriate for the innovation being developed (e.g., universal design for learning; Rose & Meyer, 2002), and alignment to anticipated contexts of use including the pedagogical approaches and specific instructional activities, as well as the educational systems in which the activities will take place.

The penicillin concepts are, then, innovations that have been designed to accommodate, or indeed leverage, variation in contexts of use (i.e., educational systems) such that principles from learning sciences operate to support effective teaching and learning across contexts; in particular, instances where a range of stakeholders are involved in the design process to anticipate variation of contexts of use and impacts of that variation (Blumenfeld, Fishman, Krajcik, Marx, & Soloway, 2000; Roschelle & Penuel, 2006). Educational leech concepts, by contrast, are innovations that have not been designed to accommodate a variety of implementation contexts as a core principle. In fact, it has been argued that the multitude of innovations that have been shown to be effective in initial trials but have not been successful when studied at scale have failed in large part due to the absence of such a design-based approach (Fishman et al., 2013).

To best study and understand the impacts of contextual variables on innovation designs, researchers and developers have begun working in networked communities, along with practitioners, with the aim of collectively developing, implementing, and analyzing solutions to best anticipate and interpret interactions with specific context characteristics in an agile, reciprocal process. Later, we offer a view of this type of coordinated, iterative work and discuss its potential to address long-standing educational challenges.

WHAT THE SCIENCE OF LEARNING REVEALS ABOUT HOW THE BRAIN LEARNS AND HOW IT MAY GUIDE THE DESIGN OF EFFECTIVE LEARNING EXPERIENCES

Increasing interactions across the various sciences of learning and development have revealed some fascinating—and actionable—principles of how people learn. For instance, the fields of social, affective, and cultural neuroscience show us clearly that *context matters*, in that the context in which a student learns can have as much influence on the developing brain as does biological maturation (e.g., Choudhury & Slaby, 2016). However, despite the infinite variability that learning contexts impart, cognitive neuroscience also reveals that learners have more in common than the contexts that individuate us: The neural mechanisms of how our distinct experiences are transformed into long-lasting learning are actually the same across individuals. In other words, *while every brain processes a unique set of experiences (generated from distinct life experiences, mindsets, and personal histories), the way those experiences are transformed into long-lasting learning is remarkably consistent across human brains.* Here we provide an overview of the neurobiological consistencies across learning, and what these consistencies tell us about how to effectively design learning environments and learning experiences for all learners, while respecting how individual and contextual differences influence the learning process.

There are many ways and levels that the brain learns about the world it lives within (for a popular taxonomy of learning and memory, see Squire, 2004). For instance, there are networks in the brain that allow us to learn procedures such as how to ride a bicycle (termed *procedural, nondeclarative learning*), and these are partially separable from the brain networks that allow us to learn facts over time such as where bicycles were invented (*semantic, declarative* learning), and still yet are the brain networks that allow us to learn and remember individual events such as where we traveled on our last bicycle ride (*episodic, declarative* learning). When we discuss learning, particularly in K–16 education, we typically mean various combinations of all three types of learning. Ideally, these types of learning are coordinated within instructional activities according to pedagogical principles. Learning can thus be considered the individual and cumulative experiences that transform the brain in such a way that the learner can access the right information at the right time in service of her educational goals, and in a measurable way. Our current understanding of how these learning and memory systems work and interact is summarized below (for more detail, see, e.g., Addis, Barense, & Duarte, 2015; National Academies of Sciences, EngineeringMedicine, 2018; Rugg, Johnson, & Uncapher, 2015).

Three major stages of learning and memory can be conceptualized as (1) *encoding*: when a learning experience is first recorded into memory, (2) *storage*: when this learning is stored or consolidated into long-term memory, and (3) *retrieval*: when this learning is retrieved from long-term memory (Figure 6.2). There are different levels of description of these stages (from what happens at the cellular level of neurons to how the different neural systems interact), but here we focus on the neurocognitive aspects of learning and memory that may be relevant for educators and learners to know in order to design effective learning experiences and assessments of learning progress.

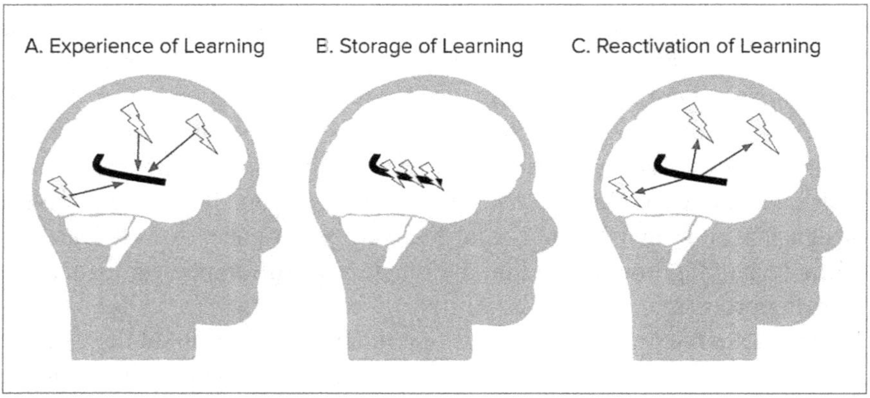

FIGURE 6.2 The three stages of learning in the brain include the neural activity that occurs when (A) the event is first experienced and that activity is recorded by the hippocampus and surrounding medial temporal lobe (MTL), (B) the event is being solidified and stored in long-term memory by consolidation processes in the hippocampus and throughout the brain, and (C) the event is reinstantiated from long-term memory (remembered), triggering a reactivation of the original pattern of activity that initially allowed the learner to experience the event.

Stage 1: Encoding

When we experience an event or encounter new information, the various aspects of the experience—what we see, hear, smell, feel, think, and so forth—are processed by their respective brain networks (visual, auditory, olfactory, affective, semantic networks, etc.). This distributed, yet coordinated symphony of brain activity is what allows us to experience our world in its rich multidimensionality. And while we are busy experiencing our world via the activity of our brain, this symphony of activity is simultaneously being recorded into memory by intricate neural structures called the hippocampus and the cortex that surrounds the hippocampus in the medial temporal lobes (MTL; one in each brain hemisphere). The hippocampus and MTL thus continually log a neural record of our lived experiences throughout the day, in real time (at millisecond-level speeds) (see Figure 6.2A). We call this first stage of learning *encoding*, as in the event is *encoded into memory*. This means that every awake human is learning something during every second of every day, and what is being encoded into memory is what is being experienced (i.e., what the learner is thinking, feeling, sensing, attending to, etc.). Thus, while the *content of what is learned* is highly variable and entirely dependent on the lived experience and personal history of the learner, the way in which that lived experience is encoded into memory is highly conserved (similar) across learners.

This idea can provide the beginnings of resolution to the cognitive dissonance that can arise when educators are taught practices to teach all students, and yet with experience and careful observation of how students learn, they come to the inevitable conclusion that there are individual differences in how students learn. An understanding of the first stage of learning can begin to parse this apparent tension: We can understand where individual differences arise (in the experiences being encoded), and also understand that the way each experience is encoded into memory is the same across students. We next dive deeper into how the brain encodes our experiences in order to highlight some specific principles that can be used to guide practice.

Cognitive science and cognitive neuroscience have been revealing many consistent principles that can lead to deeper, longer-lasting learning. In general, the stronger the neural signal that the hippocampus and MTL receive during learning, the more durable and sustainable the learning. Factors that can enhance the neural signals that the hippocampus and MTL receive during learning include paying selective attention to the information to be learned, reducing external and internal distractions, deep processing of the information to be learned (e.g., by making meaning or relevance), making meaningful connections between the information to be learned and existing ideas or frameworks (schemas), and incorporating social, affective (emotional) and motivational aspects into the learning process. Again, each of these principles is likely to strengthen learning regardless of what is being learned and across contexts. Thus they can be seen as a few of the guiding principles by which to design education innovations for all students that still respect the local contextual and individual differences in experience of our learners.

Stage 2: Storage

Once an experience is encoded by the hippocampus and MTL, cascades of processes are initiated to store that experience into long-term memory. These storage processes are referred to as *consolidation* mechanisms and function as a way for our brain to determine which of our millions of daily episodes are worthy of storing for later use (Figure 6.2B). An everyday analogy for this consolidation process can be the process of placing liquid gelatin (such as Jell-O) inside a refrigerator to initiate a transformation of the liquid gelatin into a more solid state. In the brain, there are many cellular- and systems-level neural mechanisms that serve to solidify the labile learnings of each day, but one of the most important (and actionable) is the process of sleep. Recent advancements in sleep neuroscience have revealed that sleep—specifically, rapid eye movement (REM) sleep—functions as a way for the brain to *replay* the important or salient experiences of each day, thereby initiating memory consolidation processes for those replayed experiences. The process of replaying experiences during REM sleep strengthens the long-term storage of those learnings. In practice, this suggests (with decades of corroborating cognitive scientific evidence) that putting REM sleep cycles in between learning and retrieval can lead to deeper learning and more successful retrieval (i.e., performance on tests).

Developmental neuroscience has also revealed that our circadian rhythms (sleep/wake cycles) shift during the transition to and through adolescence (for review, see Kelley, Evans, & Kelley, 2018). The onset of puberty initiates later sleep and wake times, and yet our middle and high school start times do not yet account for this significant biological transition. This can lead to temporal misalignment between our students' daily readiness to learn and our expectations of their readiness to learn. Such misalignment may be behind the consistent findings that health, mental health, and academic performance of middle and high school students are impacted when schools start earlier than 8:30 a.m. (Kelley et al., 2018). Thus, many groups including the Centers for Disease Control, the American Medical Association, and American Academy of Pediatrics are calling for strong consideration of later school start times for our middle and high schools (Adolescent Sleep Working Group, Committee on Adolescence, and Council on School Health, 2014).

Another important factor that serves to consolidate learning is *time*. The transformation of learning into long-term memories takes time, because the formation of these durable memories requires a series of physical processes to occur: to strengthen the neural pathways of the learned information into a long-term memory, specific cellular mechanisms need to be activated, which in turn activate the production of proteins that strengthen the connections made between the different components of the memory stored throughout the brain. This process gives us a neurobiological understanding of one of the oldest learning science principles, *spaced practice* (also known as *distributed practice*): how the same amount of learning or studying, when spaced out over time, can result in much stronger learning (for review and practical considerations, see Cepeda et al., 2009).

Stage 3: Retrieval

After an experience has been encoded into memory by the hippocampus and MTL, and solidified into long-term memory by consolidation processes, the learned experience then needs to be reinstated in order to be useful at a later, appropriate time. Reinstatement happens when a retrieval cue (e.g., "Where did I park my bicycle this morning?" or, "How did I solve this equation yesterday?") triggers the hippocampal representation of the initial learned experience, which then reactivates the initial pattern of activity stored in the different parts of the brain that first processed the learned experience (Figure 6.2C). This reactivated pattern of activity allows us to reexperience the learned event in the form of a memory.

There are many factors that influence our ability to reactivate the right learning at the right time, but perhaps the most relevant factor for K–16 education is that *retrieving learning from long-term memory is one of the most powerful methods to strengthen learning.* Every time we retrieve learned information from long-term memory, the retrieval process physically changes the nature of the memory itself, which has a dual impact: it both strengthens the memory and makes the memory easier to retrieve again later. These are the neurobiological bases for another powerful learning science principle, *retrieval practice* (also known as *the testing effect*), which is that trying to remember something from long-term memory can strengthen the learning more effectively than further studying of the information (e.g., Agarwal, Bain, & Chamberlain, 2012). Importantly, even if students remember incorrectly or unsuccessfully, they can still secure a *retrieval benefit* as long as they receive corrective feedback (Kornell, Hays, & Bjork, 2009). The role of feedback is well documented in a multitude of classroom studies conducted over decades (Bransford, Brown, & Cocking, 2000; Hattie, 2008).

There is much more that is known about the various types of learning. Here, we focus mainly on how students learn information that can be explicitly discussed later, or *episodic declarative* learning. A fuller treatment of other types of relevant learning such as semantic declarative and procedural nondeclarative can be found (for example, in Renoult, Davidson, Palombo, Moscovitch, & Levine, 2012; and in Gupta & Cohen, 2002, respectively) and a deep review of the many other influences on learning can be found (in National Academies of Sciences, Engineering-Medicine, 2018).

That said, this three-stage model of how the brain learns about much of the world—encoding, storage, retrieval—can provide an initial framework that students, educators, designers, and policy makers can use as a scientifically informed starting point to design effective learning experiences and assessments of learning. Importantly, this framework may prove helpful in understanding and addressing the tension between how to teach many students while respecting the variability of context and lived history of each learner. Specifically, while the experiences that each brain has will be wildly variable across individuals, all neurotypical brains encode, consolidate, and retrieve the same way. With this foundational basis of how people learn, we next turn to global efforts that aim to bring these sciences of learning to bear on educational practices and policies.

GLOBAL SCIENCE OF LEARNING NETWORK EFFORTS: BRINGING TOGETHER SCIENCE, RESEARCH, AND DEVELOPMENT

Recognizing the need for networks of stakeholders to coordinate their work to bring "penicillin concepts" to everyday use, including principles about the learning brain, there are many emerging efforts around the world to bring researchers and practitioners into mutual conversation and learning. In Australia, systemic research-practice translation efforts are led by the Science of Learning Research Centre; in Brazil, by the Brazilian Network of Science for Education; in Hong Kong, by the University of Hong Kong. In the United States, we have several parallel and complementary efforts, foundationally influenced by the National Science Foundation's Science of Learning program, which resulted in six centers and over a dozen collaborative networks. These programs laid the foundations for more recent efforts, including learning engineering initiatives. These initiatives include the first author's EdHub initiative bridging researchers at Stanford, UC Berkeley, and UC San Francisco with Bay Area practitioners (Uncapher, 2016), Harvard's higher education learning engineering initiative (Dede, Richards, & Saxberg, 2019; Dede, 2019), the Institute of Electrical and Electronics Engineers (IEEE) Industry Consortium on Learning Engineering (https://standards.ieee.org/industry-connections/industry-consortium-learning-engineering.html), a Science of Learning and Development (SoLD) initiative (Cantor, Osher, Berg, Steyer, & Rose, 2018; Uncapher, 2018), and an Adolescent Science Translation Project (ASTP; http://dahl-lab.berkeley.edu/research). For more, see the "What Is Learning Engineering?" section below.

In some—but not all—of these global efforts, a primary output of the effort has been to foster partnerships among *researchers* across diverse disciplines. While these *research-research* partnerships support the aggregation of knowledge among researchers, effective translational efforts will require *research-practice* partnerships (RPPs; Coburn, Penuel & Geil, 2013) to integrate the science of learning into effective teaching and learning practices. We define RPPs as long-term, mutually beneficial collaborations that promote the production and use of rigorous research to help solve problems of practice. In an RPP structure, knowledge is shared across research and practitioner communities to ensure the success of an intervention, be it a new tool or practice, for use within an educational system. The increasing prevalence of RPPs is a significant step; programs that will likely make a significant and scalable impact begin with the recognition of the unique lens and skill sets that practitioners bring to the study of learning, to transform a predominantly unidirectional conversation (from research to practice) into a bidirectional one. This recognition informs our understanding of how promising principles from the science of learning may be applied within ecologically valid learning contexts, but can also help us design more authentic methods to assess and intervene within real-world learning environments.

Despite these advances, we argue that many RPPs do not yet go far enough, as they primarily focus on fostering the transfer of research into practice, relying on practitioners to help identify important problems of practice and to bring knowledge of local context to support implementation. We argue that real progress will be made when researchers and practitioners engage in true bi-directional dialog to up-level both disciplines. Among those RPPs that do engage in codevelopment of innovations, the majority do so with the goal of implementing within a specific context; thus leaving implicit the principles of implementation that are so desperately needed across the field—knowledge about how to develop for success across *multiple, dynamic contexts.*

Linked RPPs

In a few cases, RPPs have been organized to support learning about development and implementation across multiple contexts (i.e., *linked RPPs*). This linked RPP model is a more robust model that goes beyond the study of the translation of principles of how people (and brains) learn to the transformation of the research, development, and implementation (practice) endeavors (Carlile, 2004).

Examples of US organizations fostering linked RPPs are Digital Promise's Education Innovation Clusters, The Carnegie Foundation for the

Advancement of Teaching, American Institutes for Research, Rice University's National Network of Education Research-Practice Partnerships (NNERPP), as well as funding agencies such as the National Science Foundation (e.g., Math Science Partnership (MSP) Network), US Department of Education (Regional Educational Labs; Proger, Bhatt, Cirks, & Gurke, 2017) and William T. Grant Foundation. The Carnegie Foundation for the Advancement of Teaching, for example, developed a practice of *improvement science* among its Networked Improvement Communities (NICs), a term introduced in 1992 by Douglas Engelbart, an engineer who saw the promise of using collective action to improve the functioning of systems (Engelbart, 1992). Carnegie's NICs employ plan-do-study-act cycles in which participants (representing a range of system stakeholders) engineer a solution to a problem of practice, employ shorter implementation and evaluation processes than would typically be used, and then, if the solution is demonstrated to be effective, spread that solution throughout the network. The Foundation sees this process as one of *continuous improvement*, drawing heavily from health and organizational sciences in an education-focused approach its researchers refer to as improvement science.

Remaining Challenges to Linked RPPs

The most important lesson to learn from even these exemplary efforts and any others undertaking similar work is how, when, and why knowledge about specific solutions, and their implementation across contexts, is aggregated, disseminated, and taken up by education leaders who need this information to make decisions about how to best support their teachers and students. Carnegie's work focused on educational challenges that were identified a priori (e.g., remedial college mathematics). The Foundation sought and used grant funding to support work within the NICs and to spread innovation throughout its members. Statway, a product emerging from the Foundation's NIC work, with demonstrated evidence of impact at scale (Huang & Yamada, 2017), could thus be considered, in a manner of speaking, a penicillin of remedial math. Dissemination beyond the NICs is still a challenge, however. The Carnegie Foundation holds an annual summit of its NIC members, where a number of nonmembers are invited to participate. In the case of federally funded networks like RELs or MSPs, typical dissemination mechanisms are expected to do this work.

A second challenge to linked RPPs is the need for a more systematic effort to integrate *developers* of programs, curricula, and technologies to ensure that, as key stakeholders in educational innovation, they are also working reciprocally with researchers and practitioners to prototype, implement, evaluate, and iterate on programs and tools in authentic educational settings. *Learning engineering* aims to provide a multidisciplinary solution to address these challenges.

FROM LEARNING SCIENCES TO LEARNING ENGINEERING

The term *learning engineering* was first introduced 50 years ago by Nobel laureate Herb Simon in his presidential address at the President's Institute held at Princeton in 1966 (Simon, 1967) as a way to describe methods by which to move higher education institutions from the "contemporary amateurism of the college to the professional design of learning environments and learning experiences," but—ironically—the concept is only recently moving from concept to application. There are several recent conceptualizations of the term (Hess & Saxberg, 2014; Uncapher, 2018; Dede et al., 2019), each bringing varied perspectives. In the following sections, we discuss our perspective on what learning engineering can be and do, and what are possible next high-impact steps for this emerging field.

What Is Learning Engineering?

Learning engineering is a way to allow researchers, practitioners, and developers of educational curricula, tools, and programs to solve problems of practice using evidence-based strategies from learning science, problem-solving processes of user-centered design (from engineering), and platforms of social and technological infrastructures to design and continuously improve educational environments and experiences to produce optimal learning outcomes.

What learning engineering is *not*: it is not a prescriptive set of input-to-output solutions or a one-size-fits-all set of practices that will ensure every student can learn anything. Rather, learning engineering is a way to describe the sets of activities (many of which are already in existence) that allow us to be generative in creating prototypes to address local problems of practice in education based on the science of learning and the art of teaching. It requires us to move from a linear transfer model (translating research to practice), into a multidirectional model where researchers, practitioners, developers of educational curricula, programs, and tools (and policy makers and funders, where appropriate) work together in a user-centered design process (the core of engineering) to transform the collective practice. In this way, we may develop knowledge in a new shared, theoretical space (Carlile, 2004). This user-centered design process allows for more rapid, virtuous cycles of continuous improvement for education innovations, but also allows the participants to learn from each other (e.g., design-based implementation research; Fishman et al., 2013). For example, **researchers** working with educators to understand the various contexts, affordances, and constraints of teaching and learning in authentic educational settings may refine their research questions, methods, and interpretations. Likewise, **educators** working with learning scientists may gain a deeper understanding of why certain teaching practices are effective and why others are not. **Developers** of curricula, programs, and tools may gain deeper insights into the contexts of use of their products, and how to design for *variability of implementation* rather than fidelity of implementation. Learning about key variations of implementation is made possible with the appropriate social and technical infrastructure of a networked (or linked RPP) community, where coordinated study of use across contexts can be undertaken. Thus, the key components and activities for a learning engineering effort are:

1. ***Scientific principles*** *that come out of empirical investigations of how people learn.* These principles will come from cognitive science, neuroscience, social and affective science, diversity science, developmental science, educational psychology, the science of the individual, and more.

2. ***User-centered design processes*** *that enable scientific principles to help solve real-world problems.* These processes involve mapping the local context (e.g., the school, classroom, teachers, students), co-creating prototypes of potential solutions, evaluating which components of the prototype work for whom, when, where, and in what dosage, and rapid-cycle iterating the prototype to produce measurable improvement on outcome measures. See Figure 6.1 for an example.

3. ***Social and technological infrastructures*** *to support implementation and learning across many contexts of use.* These infrastructures support the multiple stakeholder groups in coming together to map the problems to be solved together, the potential solution space, the resources available and needed in each context to implement, evaluate, and iterate potential solutions, and methods to share learnings across multiple implementation contexts.

There is increasing interest and movement toward building learning engineering as a novel field, with new organizations supporting much of the work described above. For example, MIT's Open Education Policy Initiative (OEPI) has called for investment in the profession of learning engineering (Willcox et al., 2016), Boston College's Lynch School of Education has introduced a new master's program in learning engineering (bc.edu/learningengineering), Design Tech High School in the San Francisco Bay Area offers a learning engineering summer institute for teachers (co-created from the first author's learning engineering bootcamp in collaboration with TNTP; Digital Promise, 2017), Northwestern University's Digital Learning program has introduced a learning engineering program (https://digitallearning.northwestern.edu/article/2017/10/24/meet-northwestern's-learning-engineers), the Institute of Electrical and Electronics Engineers (IEEE) has introduced a new industrywide consortium on learning engineering specifically intended to define the new profession of learning engineering and support working learning engineers (https://standards.ieee.org/industry-connections/industry-consortium-learning-engineering.html), and Harvard's Graduate School of Education and Division of Continuing Education have compiled extensive perspectives on how to deploy learning engineering for improving educational outcomes in online learning in higher education (Dede et al., 2019; Dede, 2019).

What Does a Learning Engineer Do?

Innovations in education that contribute improved and scalable educational outcomes may require a new role: engineers who are skilled in understanding both the problems of practice and the insights of research and practice, and can apply scientific principles to planning, prototyping, deploying, and iterating sustainable solutions to practical real-world problems. Such learning engineers will come into the profession from many entry points: in-service educators who aim to generate scientifically informed practices in the design of learning experiences will likely enter through courses offered by colleges of education or in professional development programs (e.g., through some of the emerging programs outlined in the previous section), preservice educators may be trained in learning engineering as a part of their teacher training, researchers may be educated as they interact with educators when designing and implementing in-school research studies (though they will be well served by formal training in learning engineering in authentic educational environments), and developers of educational curricula, programs, and tools may be educated by interactions with researchers and developers when designing around the context of use (although again, they may be well-served by formal training in learning engineering).

Regardless of how the learning engineer enters the profession, the primary activities of learning engineers will be to leverage promising principles from the science of learning, together with design processes from engineering, and the platforms of technology (where appropriate) and social infrastructures to co-create and test rapid-cycle, iterative solutions to persistent challenges in education practice and learning science research. By this definition, learning engineering can be thought of as serving a *boundary agent* function (Beauchamp & Beauchamp, 2013), which moves the field away from a one-sided, linear transfer of research into practice and toward a more bidirectional, action-research based conversation between researchers and practitioners (and where appropriate, developers and policy makers).

In this way, learning engineers will be able to advance the field to move away from disconnected cycles of research and development toward integrated R&D rapid-cycle iterations (Figure 6.3). One advantage of bringing researchers, practitioners, and developers together into co-creative R&D cycles is that it will dramatically reduce the amount of time it takes to prototype, evaluate, and improve evidence-based practices. For example, even the best current translation cycles can take 6 to 15 years for the scientific insights to be researched (2 to 5 years at best), then to be developed into curricula, tools, and programs (2 to 5 years at best), and then to be sustainably implemented in practice for improved educational outcomes (2 to 5 years at best). Again, this current model of linearly translating research to practice—handing off research insights to developers to create programs that practitioners then have to figure out how to implement in their local contexts—suffers from both time lags as well as communication challenges associated with the handoffs across researchers, developers, and practitioners. Thus, learning engineering aims to move from this linear translation model to a transformation model that collapses the separate cycles of research, development, and implementation into a continuous, virtuous cycle of improvement (Figure 6.3, right). This promises to reduce the amount of time it currently takes to prototype evidence-based practices: at the most optimistic, from 6 to 15 years, by which time we've already lost an entire generation of children through the K–12 cycle (Figure 6.3, left)—to the learning engineering cycle of 2 to 5 years (Figure 6.3, right). From a neurodevelopmental perspective, there are more opportunities to influence learning with more cycles of improvement (Figure 6.3, bottom).

FIGURE 6.3 A model for how the best of the current linear transfer model (left) may be transformed into a more bi- or tri-directional model where researchers, developers, and practitioners co-create education innovations in much more rapid cycles of continuous improvement (right). This provides the benefit of enabling more opportunities to influence learning from a neurodevelopmental perspective (bottom); in other words, the longer cycles of improvement in the extant model allow an entire generation to progress through the K–12 cycle before research insights are implemented in practice, whereas the learning engineering model of inclusive R&D allows for many more cycles of evidence-based improvement.

Not only does this learning engineering model promise to reduce the time it takes to translate research insights to practical application of those insights, but it also promises to improve the quality of implementation of those practices. Bringing together researchers, practitioners, and developers into co-creative activities enables each stakeholder group to learn from each other across boundaries and over time. This multi-directional learning will certainly improve the questions, methods, and outcomes for each stakeholder group, with the optimal goal of improving educational outcomes across the many varied contexts of teaching and learning.

Other important elements of the learning engineering approach are (1) the interdisciplinary nature of the sciences of learning (and development), (2) that learning is the shared interaction between (and thus the shared responsibility of) the learner, the educator, and the context, and (3) perhaps most importantly, that the science of the individual is critical for any efforts to scale science of learning to education practices, and to accurately study how people learn across contexts.

This latter concept of the science of the individual is emerging as a critical lens by which to understand and measure how people learn. According to contemporary leaders in the emerging field, "The science of individuality . . . starts with the premises that individuals vary in how they learn, behave, and develop; that these processes vary according to context; and that there are patterns within that variability" (Rose & Meyer, 2002). A primary challenge of studying and educating the individual has been how to create a methodological approach that could crack one of the biggest challenges in education: how to create effective educational experiences at scale. To scale any educational intervention, one needs to consider and design around the many varied contexts (personal, classroom, school, district, etc.) that comprise the lived experience of each child. The "analyze then aggregate" approach of Rose and Meyer (2002) first identifies individual differences in learning—as well as how those differences vary according to where, when, and with whom learning is occurring—and then uses those individual differences as a foundation by which to model more generalizable principles that can be applied at scale. By recognizing the factors that contribute to individual differences in learning, and describing methods by which to understand and accommodate those individual differences, leaders in the science of the individual are paving a way forward for how to truly bring the science of learning to scale in the form of learning engineering.

What Are the Next Steps for the Field?

How do we build on existing infrastructure, and what new infrastructure is needed? While learning engineering can take place in a variety of contexts employing an array of partnership models, the networked RPP model is ideal given the need to better understand variety in contexts of use of education innovations. Thus, structures to create and support linked RPPs are critical resources in education. Federal grants to create linked RPPs from scratch have been offered, but given the expense, have been few in number. The National Science Foundation (NSF), for example, funds organizations to create hubs among their grantees for just this reason, and these hubs have been successful in creating community among grantees, though the evidence of their ability to support aggregation of theory, findings, and practical application is nascent. A "hub" organization, like NSF's Center for Innovative Research in Cyberlearning (https://circlcenter.org/), might be a potential mechanism for creating the kind of linked RPP network that could be a good host for learning engineering endeavors if the hub focused on creating needed infrastructure among RPPs, including research methods and guidelines, capacity and frameworks to evaluate and share research findings, high-quality preparation and training programs for learning engineers, and coordination with leadership and policy dimensions (and stakeholders) of learning engineering.

First and foremost, a set of *vetted methodologies or guidelines to conduct learning engineering* (embedded within RPPs) will need to be developed to ensure that efficient and responsible R&D is taking place (e.g., design-based implementation research, DBIR; Fishman et al., 2013). These methods might include a form of preregistration of designs and studies to better share theory and results among learning engineering projects and their stakeholders, but also to ensure that efforts do not overlap in concerning ways (e.g., too many initiatives in any one setting that could overburden practitioners or students, initiatives that might create conflicting practices or pressures, etc.). These efforts should consider that any form of preregistration needs to be carefully structured to avoid any implicit preference toward any methods or designs created by the process or forms of documentation (i.e., qualitative or mixed-methods studies should be as valued—amenable to documentation in any preregistration system—as quantitative studies). Among these methods, linked working groups will need to promote a common language to describe the components of application contexts that interact with designs of products or tools, such that a growing body of knowledge about implementation variation can be shared and used to develop future designs. In conjunction with methods, understandings of the obligations of this form of research and development—the principles and ethics that guide the work in order to be responsive to the needs and roles of all stakeholders—must be developed and form the foundation of the field. These guidelines will need to be articulated in partnership by stakeholders and will need to be continuously examined as learning engineering studies take on new challenges and functions in educational systems.

Second, *structures for evaluating and sharing results of studies* within and beyond the home network will be critical to the impact of learning engineering on the broader field. Review criteria will need to be developed, linked to vetted methodologies mentioned above, and will need to solicit cadres of knowledgeable reviewers. As we envision these studies to unfold over shorter timelines than typical research studies, dissemination vehicles must reflect agile research and development cycles and clearly delineate the maturity (or prior research findings) of a particular design, so that findings can be responsibly interpreted by all stakeholders.

Third, as with any emerging field, high-quality training and preparation of learning engineers will be critical. We envision learning engineering as a professional education endeavor, and thus a shared understanding among training programs about how best to prepare learning engineers in the field would accelerate the development of this field. Existing programs mentioned above are well positioned to co-develop training approaches and programs of content, including science of learning, human-centered design, implementation science theory and methods, and educational systems theory, practices, and policy.

Finally, perhaps the most needed change to infrastructure of current educational research and development is a framing of the need for, guidelines of conduct, and potential use of the kind of research and development we are calling for: learning engineering. Indeed, framings that speak to the various stakeholders of education research and development would need to be developed and socialized such that learning engineering's role, methods (including its iterative, agile nature), and its possible outcomes (including failure) are understood and valued. Policy makers, school leadership, teachers, students, and parents, as well as researchers and developers, will all need to be part of discussions that set the stage for each of these consumers of learning engineering, such that they continue to call for and participate in learning engineering projects.

Among these reframings, of critical importance will be the increased recognition of the value of this growing body of evidence of how products and tools are best implemented in various teaching and learning contexts. While education leadership may already use local evidence in their decision making (Honig & Coburn, 2008), accountability policies and frameworks continue to prioritize large-scale evaluation studies that are designed to control for variation of context through large samples rather than examine variation to identify how best to support teaching and learning. Local knowledge and evidence is, for the most part, not considered rigorous, and its use is not recognized. As coordinated learning engineering studies compile evidence of what works for whom under which conditions, the consistency of effectiveness of a particular design and its associated practices can be established to speak to audiences seeking evidence at scale. We have argued that generation of large-scale evidence in this manner is a more efficient process than typical research and development, one that will generate many insights about implementation and about the study contexts themselves that can more immediately serve stakeholders. Partnerships conducting learning engineering research will need to expand their work to include supporting school and district (and possibly regional or state) leaders to develop strategies to integrate learning engineering studies into their workflows and accountability structures.

Pathways to establishing this infrastructure will take time to identify and forge, as many of our current academic and R&D institutions and processes are built around linear transfer models. However, as we have argued, movement toward RPPs, RPP networks, and learning engineering have already begun. This chapter points to the need to coordinate these approaches to bring the best of the sciences of learning and the best of teaching and learning together in a transformational approach to improving education.

REFERENCES

Addis, D. R., Barense, M., & Duarte, A. (Eds.). (2015). *The Wiley handbook on the cognitive neuroscience of memory.* Chichester, UK: John Wiley & Sons. http://doi.org/10.1002/9781118332634

Adolescent Sleep Working Group, Committee on Adolescence, and Council on School Health. (2014). School start times for adolescents. *Pediatrics, 134*(3), 642–649. http://doi.org/10.1542/peds.2014-1697

Agarwal, P. K., Bain, P. M., & Chamberlain, R. W. (2012). The value of applied research: Retrieval practice improves classroom learning and recommendations from a teacher, a principal, and a scientist. *Educational Psychology Review, 24*(3), 437–448. http://doi.org/10.1007/s10648-012-9210-2

Beauchamp, C., & Beauchamp, M. H. (2013). Boundary as bridge: An analysis of the educational neuroscience literature from a boundary perspective. *Educational Psychology Review, 25*(1), 47–67. http://doi.org/10.1007/s10648-012-9207-x

Bevan, B., Ryoo, J. J., Vanderwerff, A., Petrich, M., & Wilkinson, K. (2018). Making deeper learners: A tinkering learning dimensions framework. *Connected Science Learning, 17.* Retrieved from: http://csl.nsta.org/2018/07/making-deeper-learners/

Blumenfeld, P., Fishman, B. J., Krajcik, J., Marx, R. W., & Soloway, E. (2000). Creating usable innovations in systemic reform: Scaling up technology-embedded project-based science in urban schools. *Educational Psychologist, 35* (3), 149–164.

Bransford, J. D., Brown, A. L., & Cocking, R. R. (Eds.). (2000). *How people learn: Brain, mind, experience, and school.* Washington, DC: National Academy Press.

Bruer, J. T. (1997). Education and the brain: A bridge too far. *Educational Researcher, 26*(8), 4–16. http://doi.org/10.3102/0013189X026008004

Cantor, P., Osher, D., Berg, J., Steyer, L., & Rose, T. (2018). Malleability, plasticity, and individuality: How children learn and develop in context. *Applied Developmental Science, 1*(4), 1–31. http://doi.org/10.1080/10888691.2017.1398649

Carlile, P. (2004, September–October). Transferring, translating, and transforming: An integrative framework for managing knowledge across boundaries. *Organization Science, 15*(5), 555–568.

Cepeda, N. J., Coburn, N., Rohrer, D., Wixted, J. T., Mozer, M. C., & Pashler, H. (2009). Optimizing distributed practice. *Experimental Psychology, 56*(4), 236–246. http://doi.org/10.1027/1618-3169.56.4.236

Choudhury, S., & Slaby, J. (Eds.) (2016). *Critical neuroscience.* Oxford, UK: John Wiley & Sons. http://doi.org/10.1002/9781444343359

Coburn, C. E., Penuel, W. R., & Geil, K. E. (2013). *Research-practice partnerships: A strategy for leveraging research for educational improvement in school districts.* New York, NY: William T. Grant Foundation.

The Council of Chief State School Officers (CCSSO). (2017). Advancing school improvement in SEAs through research practice partnerships. Retrieved from https://www.ccsso.org/sites/default/files/2017-10/AdvancingSchoolImprovementSEAsThroughResearchPracticePartnerships.pdf

Dede, C., Richards, J., & Saxberg, B. (Eds.). (2019). *Education at scale: Engineering online teaching and learning.* New York: Routledge.

Dede, C. (2019). Improving efficiency and effectiveness through learning engineering. In C. Dede, J. Richards, & B. Saxberg (Eds.). (2019). *Education at scale: Engineering online teaching and learning* (pp. 1–14). New York: Routledge.

Dekker, S., Lee, N. C., Howard-Jones, P., & Jolles, J. (2012). Neuromyths in education: Prevalence and predictors of misconceptions among teachers. http://doi.org/10.3389/fpsyg.2012.00429/abstract

Digital Promise. (2017). Learning by design: How Design Tech High School uses research. *White Paper for Research at Work*, 1–8.

Ebbinghaus, H. (1964). *Memory: A contribution to experimental psychology.* New York: Dover. (Originally published, 1885.)

Engelbart, D. C. (1992, August). Toward high-performance organizations: A strategic role for groupware. In *Proceedings of the GroupWare, 92*, 3–5.

Fechner, G. T. (1860/1966). In H. E. Adler (Transl.), *Elements of psychophysics.* New York: Holt, Rinehart, and Winston. (Original work published 1860). [*Elemente der psychophysik.* 1860. Leipzig: Breitkopf und Hertel.]

Fishman, B. J., Penuel, W. R., Allen, A.-R., Cheng, B. H., & Sabelli, N. (2013). Design-based implementation research: An emerging model for transforming the relationship of research and practice. In B. J. Fishman, W. R. Penuel, A.-R. Allen, & B. H. Cheng (Eds.), *Design-based implementation research: Theories, methods, and exemplars.* National Society for the Study of Education Yearbook. New York, NY: Teachers College Record.

Gogtay, N., Giedd, J. N., Lusk, L., Hayashi, K. M., Greenstein, D., & Vaituzis, A. C., et al. (2004). Dynamic mapping of human cortical development during childhood through early adulthood. *Proceedings of the National Academy of Sciences, 101*(21), 8174–8179. http://doi.org/10.1073/pnas.0402680101

Gupta, P., & Cohen, N. J. (2002). Theoretical and computational analysis of skill learning, repetition priming, and procedural memory. *Psychological Review, 109*(2), 401–448. http://doi.org/10.1037//0033-295X.109.2.401

Hattie, J. (2008). *Visible learning: A synthesis of over 800 meta-analyses relating to achievement.* New York: Routledge.
Hess, F. M. A., & Saxberg, B. A. (2014). *Breakthrough leadership in the digital age : using learning science to reboot schooling.* Thousand Oaks, CA: Corwin.
Honig, M. I., & Coburn, C. (2008). Evidence-based decision making in school district central offices: Toward a policy and research agenda. *Educational Policy, 22*(4), 578–608.
Howard-Jones, P. A. (2014). Neuroscience and education: myths and messages. *Nature Reviews Neuroscience, 15*, 817. http://doi.org/10.1038/nrn3817
Huang, M., & Yamada, H. (2017). *Maintaining success rates: Does Statway sustain its impact as it scales to new classroom and institutions.* Carnegie Math Pathways Technical Report. Stanford, CA: Carnegie Foundation for the Advancement of Teaching. Retrieved from: https://www.carnegiefoundation.org/wp-content/uploads/2017/02/Carnegie_Pathways_MSR_Mar2017.pdf
Jacobson, M., & Wilensky, U. (2006). Complex systems in education: Scientific and educational importance and implications for the learning sciences. *The Journal of the Learning Sciences, 15*(1), 11–34.
Kelley, P., Evans, M. D. R., & Kelley, J. (2018). Making memories: Why time matters. *Frontiers in Human Neuroscience, 12*, 400. doi:10.3389/fnhum.2018.00400
Kornell, N., Hays, M. J., & Bjork, R. A. (2009). Unsuccessful retrieval attempts enhance subsequent learning. *Journal of Experimental Psychology-Learning Memory and Cognition, 35*(4), 989–998. http://doi.org/10.1037/a0015729
Lemke, J., & Sabelli, N. (2008). Complex systems and educational change: Towards a new research agenda. *Educational Philosophy and Theory, 40*(1), 118–129.
Means, B., & Penuel, W. R. (2005). Research to support scaling up technology-based innovations. In C. Dede, J. Honan, & L. Peters (Eds.), *Scaling up success: Lessons from technology-based educational improvement,* pp. 176–197. New York: Jossey-Bass.
National Academies of Sciences, Engineering, Medicine. (2018). *How people learn II: learners, contexts, and cultures.* Washington, DC: National Academies Press. http://doi.org/10.17226/24783
Proger, A. R., Bhatt, M. P., Cirks, V., & Gurke, D. (2017). *Establishing and sustaining networked improvement communities: Lessons from Michigan and Minnesota* (REL 2017–264). Washington, DC: U.S. Department of Education, Institute of Education Sciences, National Center for Education Evaluation and Regional Assistance, Regional Educational Laboratory Midwest. Retrieved from http://ies.ed.gov/ncee/edlabs
Renoult, L., Davidson, P. S. R., Palombo, D. J., Moscovitch, M., & Levine, B. (2012). Personal semantics: At the crossroads of semantic and episodic memory. *Trends in Cognitive Sciences, 16*(11), 550–558. http://doi.org/10.1016/j.tics.2012.09.003
Roschelle, J., & Penuel, W. (2006). Co-design of innovations with teachers: Definition and dynamics. *Proceedings of the 7th International Conference on Learning Sciences* (p. 606–612), June 27–July 1, 2006, Bloomington, Indiana.
Rose, D. H., & Meyer, A. (2002). *Teaching every student in the digital age: Universal design for learning.* Alexandria, VA: ASCD.
Rugg, M. D., Johnson, J. D., & Uncapher, M. R. (2015). Encoding and retrieval in episodic memory. *The Wiley handbook on the cognitive neuroscience of memory* (Vol. 36, pp. 84–107). Chichester, UK: Wiley-Blackwell. http://doi.org/10.1002/9781118332634.ch5
Simon, H. A. (1967). The job of a college president. *Educational Record, 48*, 68–78.
Squire, L. R. (2004). Memory systems of the brain: A brief history and current perspective. *Neurobiology of Learning and Memory, 82*(3), 171–177. http://doi.org/10.1016/j.nlm.2004.06.005

Stafford Brizard, K. B., Cantor, P., & Rose, L. T. (2017). Building the bridge between science and practice: essential characteristics of a translational framework. *Mind, Brain, and Education, 11*(4), 155–165. http://doi.org/10.1111/mbe.12153

Uncapher, M. R. (2016). *Bridging research and practice: Closing the loop with learning engineering.* White House Symposium on the Future of Education R&D and Digital Learning, 30–32.

Uncapher, M. R. (2018). From the science of learning (and development) to learning engineering. *Applied Developmental Science, 48*, 1–4. http://doi.org/10.1080/10888691.2017.1421437

Willcox, K., Sarma, S., & Lippel, P. (2016) *Online Education: A Catalyst for Higher Education Reforms.* Final report of the MIT Online Education Policy Initiative.

ABOUT THE AUTHORS

Melina Uncapher, PhD, is an assistant professor in the Department of Neurology at UC San Francisco, director of the Education Division for UCSF's Neuroscape Center, and is leading a national initiative to bring inclusive R&D to the field of education, funded by the Bill and Melinda Gates Foundation and the Chan Zuckerberg Initiative. She also holds an affiliation with Stanford's Psychology Department and is a MacArthur Scholar. She has studied the brain mechanisms of how students learn for 20 years.

Britte Haugan Cheng, PhD, is principal and founder at Menlo Education Research. She holds a PhD in cognition and development from the University of California Berkeley and has been leading research in the learning sciences for over 15 years.

CHAPTER 7

The Learning Sciences and Education Schools

Susan H. Fuhrman
President Emerita, Teachers College, Columbia University

ABSTRACT

Growth in the reach, sophistication, and number of fields devoted to the study of learning has implications for all educational endeavors, and especially for education schools. Education schools prepare future educators; increasingly learning to teach involves learning about learning and how to support it. Integrating new findings from fields such as anthropology, human development, sociology, and cultural psychology about the cultural nature of learning and discoveries about brain processes from fields such as neuroscience, machine learning, artificial intelligence, computer-based learning, and data analytics are critical to assure that future teachers are well equipped to boost learning. Incorporating these fields suggests that research conducted in education schools will expand in disciplinary reach. Schools should promote interdisciplinary work. Applying that work in real educational settings, another consistent aspect of education school missions, will mean more support for schools in using technology effectively and, in turn, more data to help school personnel assess learning and make adjustments to better support it.

Over the past 30 to 40 years, studies of how people learn and the conditions that best promote learning have expanded in number, size, and scope. According to the National Academies of Science (2018), "the past several decades have seen an explosion of research that has substantially expanded understanding of brain processes and what they mean for individual learning, schooling, and policy" (p. ix). This explosion has implications for all educational sectors and institutions. The entire PreK–adult learning enterprise is focused on enhancing knowledge, skills, and understanding among individuals and the citizenry at large. When it comes to universities, specifically, the growth in the number, force, and interaction of disciplines devoted to learning is evident in all corners of the research enterprise. A large number of researchers studying learning are in engineering schools—working on machine learning and artificial intelligence (AI), natural language processing, and robotics. Another large group are housed in medical schools and related bioscience departments, studying how the brain works, how the body can learn to adjust to lost limbs and other trauma, and how devices can assist the body, learning its operations and providing feedback to generate improvement. Still others are business schools, studying, for example, how consumers or investors learn information that affects their behavior.

All this activity may obscure the part of the university that is most affected by the growth in learning sciences: education schools or departments. This chapter focuses on the implications of the growth in the learning sciences for education schools for (1) the preparation of future educators, (2) the research enterprise at education schools, and (3) the approaches to school improvement that education schools study and then work with schools to implement.

To state the obvious, education schools are all about learning. Of course, education schools include many allied disciplines, like the economics or politics of education, but the very mission of education schools—improving education (through educator preparation, research, and service, as most education school missions state) implies a focus on how to teach to enhance learning and on understanding learning, in the lab and the field.

PREPARING EDUCATORS

Historically, those learning to teach have been schooled in what the field has known about learning. Mostly through courses on education psychology and developmental psychology, but also in courses on curriculum development, instructional methods, and assessment, education school faculty have built their programs of study on accumulated knowledge about learning. Theories of learning developed by icons of psychology such as Piaget, Dewey, Bloom, Bruner, and Vygotsky have influenced how prospective teachers (and their teachers) organize material, design learning activities, and assess student learning for most of the last century.

In the 1980s, researchers in fields such as cognitive psychology, developmental psychology, social psychology, and neurosciences began to interact with new pioneering studies in computer science, machine learning, AI, robotics, and data analytics to broaden the research and the potential for understanding how people learn (Fischer, Hmelo-Silver, Goldman, & Reimann, 2018). At the same time, there has been and continues to be significant growth in research focusing on the social context of learning. According to the National Academy of Sciences (2018), research derived from "fields such as anthropology, cultural psychology, cognitive science and neuropsychology is a recognition of the cultural nature of learning and development for all learners throughout life" (p. 136). Now, all those fields are contributing to the "learning sciences" and exponentially increasing the knowledge we have about the learning process and potential approaches to enhancing learning.

Research Influencing Educator Preparation

With this expanded view, it's fair to say that only a portion of the insights the learning sciences are contributing today are affecting the instruction educators in preparation receive. For example, understandings of how context shapes learning, including student cultures and classroom diversity, have led to new attention to pedagogies that build on student assets and speak to their life experiences. Culturally relevant pedagogy, a concept dating back at least to the 1990s (Ladson-Billings, 1994) is recently emerging as a central aspect of courses about teaching various disciplines or working with students at various stages of development.

The research drawn from computer-based learning studies and related disciplines is a bit slower in exerting an influence. For example, teachers learning how to organize material for students are likely to be guided by hierarchies, taxonomies, or theories of cognitive load that were in use 20 years ago and for years before that. They are much less likely to venture into subject-specific learning progressions, for example, which are currently being explored through software that permits analysts to identify cognitive maps or paths through material to achieve better understanding.

Therefore, courses in math or science education may not draw on the latest hypotheses about organizing material and learning activities (Corcoran, Mosher, & Rogat, 2009; Daro, Mosher, & Corcoran, 2011). So, the first implication of the learning sciences for education schools is the necessity of better integrating them into teacher and administrator preparation.

Before suggesting specific implications of the learning sciences for teaching teachers and principals, it's important to inquire about the gap between what we are learning from new and evolving fields and what's currently incorporated in teacher education. In part the gap is simply a function of time. There is always a lag between research and practice, a time during which research gets translated for a generalist rather than specialist audience and gets disseminated into textbooks and other outlets aimed at users. In part, the disjuncture is disciplinary; education schools have historically been dominated by psychologists, and many have yet to incorporate analytics, neuroscience, and machine learning as fields of study. In part, the issue speaks to different philosophical orientations.

Many who teach teachers, often former K–12 teachers themselves, value research that speaks to their own experiences. They are strongly influenced by the cognitive and developmental and social learning fields of the late 60s, 70s, and early 80s when they went to education school. They see teachers as active learners themselves who know best about their own particular students, reflective practitioners who are much more likely to rely on their own insights to, for example, group students at similar levels for learning, than on software-driven feedback that suggests placement choices.

The learning sciences emerging from newer fields, such as artificial intelligence, are much less well known by teacher educators. The newer, typically *big data* driven studies, might appear to some as a return to the behavioral era where the emphasis was on categorization and differentiation, not on appreciating varied individual student strengths and how they relate to the context of learning. They may lump new fields with positivism, relying on data-derived findings despite possible biases in the design and conduct of the research, some of which might be implicit and not acknowledged, even by the researchers conducting the work.

The challenge for the future is to enhance the influence of newer research so teachers of tomorrow know the most recent findings about learning and are exposed to this growing interdisciplinary field. In addition to continuing critical research from cognitive and developmental psychology, the contributions of newer research on cultural context and culturally responsive pedagogies and the explosion of knowledge coming from computer-based learning fields must be incorporated into teacher preparation.

What The Learning Sciences Say About Learning and Teaching

The National Academies of Sciences' new volume, *How People Learn II*, stresses the integration of psychological research, neuroscience, sociocultural research, and insights from newer computer science fields. The Academies highlight five conclusions of learning research for learning in school (2018, p. 160–161):

1. Effective educators must understand the interaction among what learners bring with them—prior knowledge, experience, motivations, interests, cognitive skills, language skills—their own prior experience and cultural influences; and the cultural, social, cognitive, and emotional characteristics of the learning environment.

2. Self-activated or self-directed learning is critically important, with guidance from teachers in setting appropriate goals, designing appropriate challenges, and giving targeted feedback.

3. Curricula and instructional activities should support learners in connecting what they do in and outside of school and through learning approaches leveraged for each learner.

4. Provide purposeful teaching of the language and practices particular to disciplines.

5. Use well-designed assessments to diagnose current student learning and direct a path to advancing to desired levels.

Linda Darling-Hammond similarly draws from various disciplines to identify what the learning sciences suggest for classroom instruction. In a talk to education school deans, convened in March 2018 by the Carnegie Corporation, she listed the key findings that should guide educators: "Conversation and experiences create neural pathways; learning is social; emotion and learning are linked; authentic tasks motivate effort; feedback shapes learning; and language generates thinking (as well as representing it)."

Integrating Current Learning Sciences Research into Educator Preparation

How do we promote the integration of newer research and its implications for pedagogy into educator preparation?

First, we probably need to rethink the profession of "teacher educator." Most now in this role received doctorates in specific disciplines, such as art education or math education (Goodwin, Smith, Souto-Manning, Cheruvu, Tan, Reed, & Taveras, 2014). They did not study how to teach adults, how to supervise practice, how to link practical experiences of their students with college coursework, and many other elements that fall under their charge. At Teachers College, we started a multicourse series on teaching teachers that we hope will influence this field over time. Learning science research should be included as part of the special curriculum for teacher educators, so they can then include it in the curriculum for their own students. Importantly, we must go beyond exposing them to new findings and focus on working with them to identify and develop tools applying the knowledge.

Second and related, we must create more structure around the content of teacher education, across and within disciplines. Teacher education varies significantly across education schools, just as college and university curricula in general vary. The traditions of autonomy and faculty governance in higher education promote professorial control over what and how various subjects are taught. One can find course titles (e.g., American History) that are almost universal, but that doesn't guarantee identical syllabi. The precise content is very much a function of the particular professor and department. In teacher education, courses in classroom management, for example, can differ in assigned readings, the order of subtopics, the amount of practice and rehearsal included in the class meetings, and so on. A number of leading researchers in teacher education are trying to create more consensus about what prospective teachers should learn, specifying "core" or "high leverage" practices that all teachers should know and be able to do and all teacher candidates should learn. These scholars also disseminate effective approaches to teaching these central practices (Grossman, 2018; Loewenberg Ball & Forzani, 2009). The practices they specify, such as assessing student thinking and prior understandings, are grounded in the learning sciences. The movement toward core practices can, therefore, boost the influence of the learning sciences.

Third, we need to address another historic pattern in teacher education, where we rely on the (typically) one psychology course and an education psychology textbook to cover much of the psychologically derived knowledge about learning and development. Therefore, the pedagogical, instructional, or classroom management implications of what we know about learning or child development has often been isolated, rather than integrated throughout courses on teaching math, leading discussions in social studies, and the like. If we can move to greater integration of the newer research emanating from learning sciences, we will find better application of findings throughout teacher education.

Fourth, a segregation of materials reflects the teaching arrangements for teacher education. Typically, this is a separate faculty, in a separate department from the psychologists, neuroscientists, and (now) machine learning scholars who are joining education school faculties. It's difficult to promote interdisciplinary cooperation in any field as people need to learn how to understand new methodologies and approaches to have informed discussions. But arguably, the segregation between teacher education faculties (whose research typically focuses on classroom studies to illuminate learning) and faculties directly involved in studying learning through other approaches is particularly troubling as it is the next generation of teachers who can best use emerging findings to improve education in the next generation of students. And to compound the challenge to integration, teacher education faculty are often not granted the same stature and respect as other education school faculty despite their centrality. Many scholars have argued that this disjuncture reflects gender discrimination, as teacher education and teaching are mostly female fields, more so than other disciplines in education schools such as economics or instructional technology (Cochran-Smith & Zeichner, 2009).

Such scholars point to the lack of status of the teaching field in general and highlight its reflection among university faculty. Also, teacher education is a deeply clinical field; faculty are called on to supervise their students' practice as a key aspect of their instruction. This makes teacher educators very different from psychologists, economists, sociologists, and other education school scholars who may also spend some of their time in the field, but for research, not for supervision, and who are expected to provide cutting-edge findings, not to focus on applying findings in practice. The divide is similar to the medical school differentiation between "regular," tenured faculty (many working mostly in the laboratory) and clinical nontenured faculty (who do research, but very applied, practice-oriented work). Some very distinguished education schools use clinical faculty for teacher education because tenure-track faculty are expected to produce research at a pace and of a quality that may not be compatible with significant time supervising students in the field.

The intersection of status issues and the applied nature of much research conducted by teacher educators has led to a vicious cycle in which teacher education research as a field has received significantly less funding than other education research fields and therefore cannot be equal in scope and scale. In turn, the lack of scale, the frequent reliance on very-low-cost individual classroom case studies, and the consequent limits on generalizability interact with a paucity of data about different teacher education programs and their effects to lead to the labeling of teacher education research as less rigorous than other fields (Cochran-Smith & Zeichner, 2009).

It is clear that if newer knowledge derived from a wide array of disciplines is to affect teacher education, scholars from various fields must interact with respect and generosity. To promote that exchange and openness, it's imperative that education school faculties diversify and then engage in interdisciplinary research.

Before moving to the topic of education school research and learning sciences, I want to share an example of an effort to integrate new knowledge about learning into teacher education. Dr. Herbert Ginsburg, a distinguished developmental psychologist, recently retired from the faculty of Teachers College, Columbia University. Building on his research on intellectual development, mathematics education, and testing and assessment, he pioneered a course on early mathematics teaching (including using cognitive interviews to assess student understanding and teaching concepts through gaming) for Teachers College preservice teachers. It's unusual for a psychologist to teach a course in how to teach a specific discipline, focusing on how students learn math rather than exclusively on how to teach math. It suggests an approach to integration that should be emulated.

RESEARCH IN EDUCATION SCHOOLS

In order to enhance learning science research and improve the likelihood of impact, most education schools will need to expand the disciplines they encompass and encourage faculties within existing disciplines to broaden their horizons. They may need to add, for example, new faculty in neuroscience and education, learning analytics, or data science. Existing faculty in some fields, for example, instructional technology and cognitive psychology, will find useful data coming from new sources—large databases derived from software use across millions of students.

Most critically, as we have seen, learning science is an interdisciplinary field. Psychologists should pair with data scientists and neuroscientists to get deeper insights into learning; learning specialists need to partner with sociologists and anthropologists who study the social context of learning. Some joint work will occur naturally, but there is an important role for incentives at the university or school level. Many colleges run competitive grants for researchers to get started on new projects, perhaps when a gift makes new research possible. Leadership can tweak existing competitions to award additional credit to proposals that draw investigators across disciplines and start new competitions in the learning sciences that require collaborative work. Colleges can also sponsor centers and institutes that bring scholars together across fields to focus on the learning sciences. Similarly, departments and programs can be constructed to promote integration of related fields. Northwestern's School of Education and Social Policy has a Learning Sciences department that includes cognitive psychologists, computer scientists, developmental psychologists, and scholars of education policy, multilingualism, cultural context, technology design, and learning in specific disciplines.

Finally, leadership can interest donors in gifts that promote interdisciplinary work. As donors learn about the implications of a much greater understanding of learning, their excitement can be harnessed into supporting research with great potential impact. Leaders must work with them to help them understand the essentially interdisciplinary nature of work with significant promise, and the need for incentives to encourage scholars used to working in their own fields to form new collaborations. Even when government competitions or foundation grants are designed for cross-field collaborations, scholars with little background in such work might still need internal incentives to cooperate on a joint proposal.

The specialization of faculty that makes interdisciplinary work challenging is a symptom of a long-standing trend in higher education. Because academia puts a premium on new, unique, cutting-edge research, to encourage scholars to forge their own individual paths in advancing knowledge, all the incentives are in favor of greater specialization, the search for subareas that no one else has explored. There are few rewards for synthesis or replication, two essential aspects of "good science" in any commonsense understanding.

The pattern starts with doctoral-level research, where dissertations are supposed to show unique individual promise for the future scholar, and continues through hiring, tenure, and promotion. Candidates are cited for their distinctive contributions and less favored if their work builds too much on or reflects others. In this manner, much research becomes increasingly arcane as its narrow focus leaves it less relevant. The pattern is reinforced by peer-reviewed journals, which themselves become increasingly specialized and their audiences narrowed. As for collaborative work, even within a narrow subspecialization, reviewers and university committees find multiple authorship of articles and books a challenge in assessing individual candidates. There is always much discussion in such committees over whether other coauthors are students being mentored by the candidate rather than established scholars who might be carrying much of the load. It matters if the candidate is "first author" (or "last" in a laboratory the candidate supervises), rather than a name in the middle of a string of collaborators.

The structure the academy has developed around specialization is especially problematic for interdisciplinary work. Such research is hard for specialized journals and reviewers to assess and may therefore result in fewer peer-reviewed articles, in turn jeopardizing the hiring, tenure, and promotion of scholars who work across disciplines. Tenure and promotion review committees intent on determining a candidate's individual merit might find collaborative, interdisciplinary work particularly challenging to evaluate. Those committees themselves may not be broad enough to understand work that extends beyond existing specializations.

If the learning sciences are to be promoted, the few interdisciplinary journals and associations that exist must be supported. The necessity of incentives to encourage scholars to engage in such work is obvious. And, as what we know about learning depends on drawing together what is learned in many fields as well as designing research deliberately involving a cross-disciplinary team, we must rethink the place of synthesis in our valuation of research contributions. Synthesis is essential to bringing research to lay audiences; users must understand the weight of the evidence. What does accumulated knowledge tell us? As new studies emerge, how do the new findings fit in with, or possibly contradict, previous understandings? How much weight does one give the new finding when compared to prior relevant studies? What are the implications of the body of current research for practice?

IMPLICATIONS FOR WORK WITH SCHOOLS

Education schools stress contact with the field and an obligation to use knowledge to improve education, from early childhood to opportunities for adults. Mission statements use phrases such as "in partnership with schools and communities," "working with a wide range of local settings," and "commitment to service" to indicate that these schools see themselves as contributing not only well-prepared professionals, but also knowledge that will be of use to educators already in practice and to policy makers who design and support the education system.

Clearly, some of what is being learned about learning can (and does) make its way into the field directly, through professional development opportunities, many of which are conducted by education school faculty; through comentoring of student teachers by university and school faculty; and through publications that bring research to wider audiences. Work on culturally relevant pedagogy is, for example, featured in many in-service activities and user-friendly books. An example of this is Souto-Manning and Martell's (2016) book *Reading, Writing, and Talk: Inclusive Teaching Strategies for Diverse Learners, K–2*.

In addition to preparing professionals, education school researchers influence practice by focusing on the implications of their own work for learning settings throughout the system. Some researchers who consider their work (e.g., on memory or executive function or motivation) fairly basic, providing the underpinnings for future more applied work, are uncomfortable with specifying implications. But many learning scientists choose to join education school faculties because they want to influence practice; they could lodge themselves in an arts and sciences psychology department but have chosen an education school specifically to be close to and immersed in the field. Their knowledge of the field puts them in a good position to tease out suggestions for both future research and practice, even from more basic work.

Educational Technology: Use and Research

A good example of translation and work with practitioners concerns education technology. Many learning platforms—tutoring systems, games, simulations—are developed by computer scientists on the faculty or staff of engineering schools. These tools may not draw sufficiently on what is known about how students learn, for example, how they learn better if text and pictures are closely associated or how they may be distracted by certain sidebar activities. Computer scientists working in instructional technology, however, will know these things. It is they who are best suited both to design new technologies (perhaps in collaboration with engineering school machine learning faculty) and to advise schools on how best to use technology to enhance learning.

We know from summaries of many studies that technologies should be closely aligned to particular instructional goals, with some tools best suited to provide opportunities for practice and repetition and others better for active learning or engaging students in collaborative activities. We know that these aligned tools must be integrated with other instructional approaches, including teacher- and student-led activities; that educators must learn how best to chose and integrate various tools; and that implementation must be carefully planned (National Academies of Science, 2018, Chapter 8). Education school faculty can help schools design and implement technology use with these optimal conditions (and they can prepare preservice teachers with this emerging knowledge). They also serve the field by evaluating products that emerge from the private sector and determining their effectiveness.

According to the National Academies (2018), technology use decisions by instructors and institutions should be based on evidence of positive impact, in situations that are similar (to the deciding school or teacher) with respect to learning goals, learner characteristics, the environments for learning, the social and cultural context, and the levels of support for students and teachers in using the technology (p.196). Clearly, providing the evidence suggested by this recommendation is an important task for education school researchers, or for teams of those people and other specialists in technology. Only those with a firm grounding in education will understand both the particular technology's promise for learning and the features of the environment and context that are relevant to the technology's success.

Data About Student Performance

Another implication of the growth of the learning sciences for the field centers on the corresponding growth of data about student performance. Instructional technologies are developing rapidly, derived from growth in learning science fields such as machine learning, artificial intelligence, and natural language processing. Of course, their use also reflects the expansion of broadband and the development of school user friendly hardware. Many new technologies provide real-time evidence of student learning, giving feedback to teachers and students of their mastery of material, achievement of competencies, and satisfaction of learning objectives. New technologies can probe deeper into student understanding than was possible previously; for example, educators now have much more access to data about student thinking processes since new tools give students an opportunity to show all their work as well as the answer. Data derived from these software tools can be critically important to teachers in deciding the next instructional steps, in assigning students to appropriate groupings or methodologies, and in determining the success of their own instructional strategies.

These data, and other evidence derived from more formalized digital assessments, perhaps given periodically and covering multiple lessons and competencies, are new to a system that historically relied on paper products and expensive one-shot standardized tests for judging student learning. The abundance of data presents decisions for the instructor about which is more important or valid, reliable, and easy to use.

New data about performance also creates much more evidence of student learning potentially available to and shareable with higher authorities who can alter resources to help teachers and schools succeed. But the data could also be used to hold schools responsible for learning. In the language of educators, these new data could be used for accountability purposes.

However, we have learned in the last two decades that "too much accountability" can be harmful. When schools are judged on what can be tested, the curriculum is invariably narrowed. During the era of No Child Left Behind (2001–2009), single tests in mathematics and in reading were the basis for state judgment of whether a school was succeeding or not, and, if not, whether it required additional remedies, like mandating schools to hire supplemental services or giving students the option of choosing another school, or, eventually, closure. During the following years of the Obama administration, states were given incentives to use those single student achievement tests for teacher evaluation as well. Therefore, schools and teachers focused as much attention as possible on the particular knowledge and skills that were tested. Student placement in grades came to be largely dependent on these tests in many districts. Nontested subjects, such as elementary school social studies or science, were squeezed to the side, given less and less instructional time (Jennings & Rentner, 2006). Further, because standardized tests typically took a shallow view of proficiency defined in terms of the skills needed to succeed on relatively short and, too often, quite artificial test items (i.e., with little direct connection to real-world contexts; Bennett & Gitomer, 2009, p.3), many argued that these tests were dumbing down the curriculum. It became a major challenge to aim high while testing low.

A critical lesson from this period is that whatever can be easily measured gets the most attention. Once tests that enabled comparisons across schools and districts became available, the scores were an easily accessible, understandable, and concrete indicator, regardless of the quality of the assessment itself. Further we learned that if stakes or consequences are attached to a measure, those measured often employ strategies to raise scores that do not actually promote learning. The measure becomes perverted. For example, in addition to focusing narrowly on tested items rather than teaching the whole curriculum, in those years some educators literally cheated by altering scores (Strauss, 2015).

The presence of new achievement data that could be used by schools, districts, and states to make evaluative judgments could mean higher-level accountability almost all the time. Every test can be consequential; comparisons will be made even when premature and inappropriate. This is a worry with new, mostly software-based assessments that are given regularly. Even daily reports from tutoring platforms, games, simulations, and so on that should provide diagnostic information that will help teachers make adjustments (like increased focus on some areas or changing a strategy and approach) might be tempting to higher-level authorities. For example, many schools now use computer-based formative tests throughout the year, ostensibly to suggest instructional improvements likely to lead to greater performance in the long run. In some schools, teachers say that these formative assessments are used by school authorities to assess teacher progress and to intervene if judged necessary, treating the assessments as mini summative assessments. Knowing this, teachers might make short-term changes in their activities intended to raise formative scores rather than use the scores as information that can improve student learning over the long term. This unintended use of formative assessments can pervert the measure, making it less accurate for diagnostic or predictive purposes (Shepard, 2005).

The upside is that the availability of new data about learning might alleviate the reliance on narrow measures. Now all the student work (in class and at home), always so critical to teacher grades, can be much more easily judged and aggregated through e-portfolios. Now, all the data provided by software can alleviate the situation of reliance on narrow tests. In fact, a number of states are examining the idea of periodic computer-based assessments that can be combined into an aggregate score for units, semesters, or years of school (e.g., Louisiana Department of Education, 2018). These assessments would be relatively unobtrusive and curriculum embedded, so the danger of narrowing the curriculum is considerably less as compared to a one-shot test.

CONCLUSION

Growth of the learning sciences shows us that as a society there is much more to know about learning. New findings are continually emerging. Enabled by new technologies, we will understand more about thinking processes, the cognitive maps learners create within domains (e.g., Koedinger, D'Mello, McLaughlin, Pardos, & Rose, 2015), and how to motivate and continue to engage students (e.g., Baker, D'Mello, Rodrigo, & Graesser, 2010), for example. The final implication for the field, and for education schools, is to treat much of what we think we know and emerging new findings more as hypotheses than as confirmed knowledge. Old assumptions will be challenged by new insights, areas we never truly understood will become clear, and entirely new domains will develop. New approaches (such as ordering content by learning progressions) should be seen through an experimental lens, and opportunities to validate them should be designed. Education school and preK–20 educators should work together to study and confirm, to set up contrasts we can learn from, and to spread knowledge of effective approaches. Many scholars have encouraged educators to take an inquiry or research stance toward their own practice, using the knowledge gained to improve their approaches (e.g., Lytle & Cochran Smith, 1992). Expanding the data and analytic reports available to school-based educators should enhance their effectiveness as researchers.

The learning sciences have many implications for teacher education, for education school research, and for partnerships with the field. The ability of the field to apply and benefit from new findings and new learning technologies will depend on collaborations with education schools, and the latter's relevance will depend on their openness to new knowledge and disciplines. If this has always been the case, the explosion in the learning sciences makes it an imperative.

REFERENCES

Baker, R. S., D'Mello, S. K., Rodrigo, M. M. T., & Graesser, A. C. (2010). Better to be frustrated than bored: The incidence, persistence, and impact of learners' cognitive–affective states during interactions with three different computer-based learning environments. *International Journal of Human-Computer Studies*, 68(4), 223–241.

Bennett, R. E., & Gitomer, D. H. (2009). Transforming K–12 assessment: Integrating accountability testing, formative assessment and professional support. In *Educational assessment in the 21st century* (pp. 43–61). Dordrecht: Springer.

Corcoran, T., Mosher, F., & Rogat, A. (2009). Learning progressions in science: An evidence-based approach to reform. CPRE Research Report #RR-63. Philadelphia: Consortium for Policy Research in Education. doi:10.12698/cpre.2009.rr63

Cochran-Smith, M., & Zeichner, K. M. (Eds.). (2009). *Studying teacher education: The report of the AERA panel on research and teacher education.* Routledge.

Daro, P., Mosher, F., & Corcoran, T. (2011). *Learning trajectories in mathematics: A foundation for standards, curriculum, assessment, and instruction.* CPRE Research Report #RR-68. Philadelphia: Consortium for Policy Research in Education.

Fischer, F., Hmelo-Silver, C. E., Goldman, S. R., & Reimann, P. (Eds.). (2018). *International handbook of the learning sciences.* Routledge.

Goodwin, A. L., Smith, L., Souto-Manning, M., Cheruvu, R., Tan, M. Y., Reed, R., & Taveras, L. (2014). What should teacher educators know and be able to do? Perspectives from practicing teacher educators. *Journal of Teacher Education, 65*(4), 284–302.

Grossman, P. (2018). *Teaching core practices in teacher education.* Cambridge, MA: Harvard Education Press.

Jennings, J., & Rentner, D. S. (2006). Ten big effects of the No Child Left Behind Act on public schools. *Phi Delta Kappan, 88*(2), 110–113.

Koedinger, K. R., D'Mello, S., McLaughlin, E. A., Pardos, Z. A., & Rose, C. P. (2015). Data mining and education. *Wiley Interdisciplinary Reviews: Cognitive Science, 6*(4), 333–353.

Ladson-Billings, G. (1994). *The dreamkeepers: Successful teachers of African American children.* San Francisco: Jossey-Bass.

Loewenberg Ball, D., & Forzani, F. M. (2009). The work of teaching and the challenge for teacher education. *Journal of Teacher Education, 60*(5), 497–511.

Louisiana Department of Education (2018, July 27). *Louisiana ESSA innovative assessment pilot first to receive federal approval.* Retrieved from https://www.louisianabelieves.com/newsroom/news-releases/2018/07/27/louisiana-essa-innovative-assessment-pilot-first-to-receive-federal-approval

Lytle, S., & Cochran-Smith, M. (1992). Teacher research as a way of knowing. *Harvard Educational Review, 62*(4), 447–475.

National Academies of Sciences, Engineering, and Medicine. (2018). *How people learn II: Learners, contexts, and cultures.* National Academies Press.

Shepard, L. A. (2005, October). Formative assessment: Caveat emptor. In *ETS Invitational Conference The Future of Assessment: Shaping Teaching and Learning, New York.*

Souto-Manning, M., & Martell, J. (2016). *Reading, writing, and talk: Inclusive teaching strategies for diverse learners, K–2.* Teachers College Press.

Strauss, V. (2015). How and why convicted Atlanta teachers cheated on standardized tests. Retrieved from https://www.washingtonpost.com/news/answer-sheet/wp/2015/04/01/how-and-why-convicted-atlanta-teachers-cheated-on-standardized-tests/?

ABOUT THE AUTHOR

Susan Fuhrman is president emerita of Teachers College, Columbia University, a founding director of the Consortium for Policy Research in Education (CPRE), and past-president of the National Academy of Education. Previously, she was dean of the University of Pennsylvania's Graduate School of Education, where she was also the school's George and Diane Weiss Professor of Education.

PART III

From Theory and Research to Educational Practice

CHAPTER 8

Advancing the State of Online Learning: Stay Integrated, Stay Accessible, Stay Curious

Korinn S. Ostrow and Neil T. Heffernan
Worcester Polytechnic Institute

ABSTRACT
Learning environments are constantly evolving; where once students relied on textbooks, paper, and pencil, they now complete the majority of their assignments online (Lu, 2008). Demand for the integration of computer-based systems into existing instructional practices and curricula has led recent usage of online tools and content to spike (Pawlowski & Bick, 2012). However, prominent gaps in our collective understanding of how to best develop, evaluate, and disseminate educational technologies pose significant risks for consumers. These environments are only as good as the quality, quantity, and accessibility of their content.

ASSISTments is an online learning platform designed to provide students with immediate feedback and teachers with robust assessments. A free public service of Worcester Polytechnic Institute supported through more than $25 million in public and private funding, ASSISTments is primarily used for middle and secondary mathematics, supporting the delivery, collection, and grading of classwork and homework. Keeping abreast of recent advances in the learning sciences, ASSISTments has improved educational outcomes by focusing on three ideologies: staying integrated, staying accessible, and staying curious. This chapter explores how the ASSISTments team has worked to apply each of these ideologies, the lessons learned in the process, and why others in the learning sciences should do the same.

THE MODERN CLASSROOM: *TURN ON* THE TECH, *TUNE IN* TO EFFICACY

Learning environments are constantly evolving; where once students relied on textbooks, paper, and pencil, they now complete the majority of their assignments online (Lu, 2008). Demand for the integration of computer-based systems into existing instructional practices and curricula has caused usage of online tools and content to spike in recent years (Pawlowski & Bick, 2012). In the United States, more schools than ever before have the infrastructure and capacity necessary to use tech-based learning tools; the *New York Times* reported that schools across the country had purchased 8 million Chromebooks during the 2017 academic year (Singer, 2017). Students are also far more likely than ever before to use the Internet for academic pursuits. A recent study by the nonprofit broadband advocacy group EducationSuperHighway revealed that more than 44 million students learn in classrooms with high-speed Internet connections, compared to 4 million just 5 years ago (Herold, 2018). With connected hardware in place, software options can grow abundant and even overwhelming. Companies like LearnPlatform are gaining traction as they seek to help teachers and administrators navigate a sea of more than 5,000 educational technology products now available for classroom instruction. The modernization of the American classroom is upon us.

However, prominent gaps in our collective understanding of how to best develop, evaluate, and disseminate educational technologies pose significant risks for consumers. A seemingly endless list of learning management systems, online tutoring platforms, and other learning applications are marketed to school administrators, teachers, and parents, touting abilities to enhance scholastic achievement and advance students' performance by entire grade levels within particular domains. As it stands, these systems are developed independently, with little—if any—communication of effective practices. As such, the field suffers from a lack of emphasis on universal measures of productive outcomes. In addition, robust evaluation of educational technologies has generally been limited to tools that serve higher education (VanLehn, 2006). This leaves administrators, teachers, and parents responsible for "grading" K–12 products by establishing closed communities to track and discuss "best practices" without applying rigorous scientific methods. How can consumers make informed decisions about a learning tool without validated and unbiased proof of the system's efficacy? What is it that makes one tutoring system or learning application outperform another? Should school districts place greater value on benchmarked achievement outcomes, increases in engagement and motivation, easily attainable parent interaction, or the underlying costs of delivering educational technologies to their students?

Commercialized educational technologies are also quick to claim progress in actualizing "personalized" learning, despite the deficit of *scientific evidence* that pertains to personalization. Developers may publish conference proceedings or produce white papers on the results of an efficacy trial or independent research project, but most fail to publish null results (aka the "file drawer problem" that contributes to why most research findings are false; Ioannidis, 2005) that would put a damper on the commercial success of their product. Plus, internal studies often fail to meet standards for rigor set forth by government-funded policy leaders like the What Works Clearinghouse (Institute of Education Sciences, 2003; What Works Clearinghouse, 2008). Although these standards were created to drive policy, if used more broadly, they could serve as powerful resources to help administrators, teachers, and parents make educated decisions about the application of technology in the classroom. The learning sciences community essentially needs the equivalent of the Food and Drug Administration—not to strictly regulate educational technology, but to oversee its efficacy in a manner that promotes a universal language for systemic change through an understanding of effective measures and principles.

Requiring that educational technologists communicate universal definitions of student success (learning, affect, engagement, etc.) would offer consumers a more concise way to measure and compare the efficacy of these systems. However, to seek even greater gains, learning scientists should rethink how technology is applied in the classroom. Technology has historically been used to replace outdated methods rather than to innovate new classroom practices (Bush & Mott, 2009). As such, the efficacy of educational technologies has often been compared to expert human tutors or traditional homework practices (Anderson, Corbett, Koedinger, & Pelletier, 1995; Kulik & Kulik, 1991; Mendicino, Razzaq, & Heffernan, 2009; Oxman & Wong, 2014; Shute, 1993; VanLehn, 2006; Woolf, 2009). Designers of these tools develop content and interventions to chase the ever-evasive 2 sigma problem cited by Bloom (1984) as the pinnacle of expert human tutoring. However, these technologies offer new insights into how students learn that could not be measured by human tutors or through paper and pencil approaches. Broadening our views of the capabilities of educational technologies will help advance the state of online learning by translating findings into significant implications for educational policy.

The treasure trove of student data collected by educational technologies could be leveraged to improve student learning and achieve *evidence-based* personalization. Beyond natural data collection, linking rigorously designed hypothesis tests to these environments would further benefit users (teachers and students), stakeholders in the learning process (administrators and parents), and educational researchers. The quality of research in the field would flourish, and platforms would grow from iterative improvements to their design and content. Commercialized products maintain their footing by embracing AB testing and other forms of market research that help stakeholders accumulate, assess, and retain users through minimally invasive changes to the user experience (Kohavi, Longbotham, Sommerfield, & Henne, 2009). However, most educational technologies were not designed to leverage these approaches to explore how different learning strategies affect different students.

Vast potential for this type of work is expanding in parallel with the growing popularity of learning applications and online learning platforms. The ASSISTments team envisions a future in which universal standards allow for the comparative evaluation of educational technologies and establish a safer marketplace for administrators, teachers, and parents, while driving personalization through evidence-based interventions. Best practices could be identified within platforms and outcomes could be compared across platforms, with successful, platform-specific interventions replicated and assessed for generalizability to other educational technologies. To create the kind of systemic change necessary to achieve this vision, educational technologies and the classrooms they serve need to evolve together and embrace open science. The rest of this chapter discusses the ASSISTments team's efforts to model the future of online learning.

ASSISTMENTS: A RESEARCH-DRIVEN ONLINE LEARNING ENVIRONMENT

ASSISTments is an online learning platform that supports the delivery, collection, and grading of classwork and homework. ASSISTments is a free public service of Worcester Polytechnic Institute, developed through more than $25 million from the IES, the NSF, the US Department of Education, and various private foundations. This funding has supported 16 years of codevelopment with teachers and researchers, resulting in an evidence-based teacher-paced learning resource and a shared scientific instrument that can be used to conduct randomized controlled experiments at multiple granularities to determine what works in online education (Ostrow, Heffernan, & Williams, 2017). Funding has also allowed the platform to remain free to teachers and students, increasing its practical relevance and ease of adoption. As such, ASSISTments has routinely doubled its user base each year since its inception in 2003. During the 2017–2018 academic year, ASSISTments was used by more than 1,300 teachers and more than 50,000 students from more than 400 schools in 38 US states and six foreign countries. Students solved nearly 9 million problems from more than 150,000 assignments. A recent review on the efficacy of educational technologies by MIT's Poverty Action Lab concluded that ASSISTments was one of the most promising educational interventions currently available in the United States (Escueta, Quan, Nickow, & Oreopoulos, 2017) based on the results of a recent efficacy trial (Roschelle, Feng, Murphy, & Mason, 2016) conducted by independent research firm SRI International.

Although ASSISTments began as a tool for middle school mathematics, it has grown to include a wide variety of K–12, advanced placement, and college-level content. Use of ASSISTments has been shown to reliably improve students' mathematics learning in comparison to traditional paper and pencil approaches (Kelly, Heffernan, & Heffernan et al., 2013; Koedinger, McLaughlin, & Heffernan, 2010; Mendicino, Razzaq, & Heffernan, 2009; Singh et al., 2011; Soffer et al., 2014). Growing repositories of science content are being built to support physics, chemistry, and electronics teaching and learning, and recent expansions to the platform are even allowing ASSISTments to be leveraged in English and history classrooms. For instance, DocAssist, a Google Drive plug-in that integrates with ASSISTments, allows teachers to define a writing rubric within a Google Doc that adds accountability to the revision process by requiring students to address comments and feedback while the system tracks their revisions. By responding to the needs of teachers, ASSISTments retains flexibility that other educational technologies tend to lack.

ASSISTments provides students with immediate feedback and supplemental tutoring while providing teachers with robust student- and class-level reports. Immediate feedback is most commonly presented as *correctness feedback*, or notification of whether an answer was right or wrong. Students may also receive supplemental tutoring including hint messages (a series of progressively detailed clues to the problem's solution), scaffolding problems (smaller questions meant to break the problem down into steps), worked examples (examples showing how to solve a similar problem), or mistake messages (hint-like messages tailored to specific common wrong answers). Teachers can also assign content with feedback turned off, transforming ASSISTments into an assessment tool for exit tickets, quizzes, tests, and proficiency benchmarks. Student-level reports then provide teachers with an in-depth analysis of students' performance on their classwork, homework, and assessments, highlighting their accuracy, feedback usage, and completion time. Class-level reports help teachers pinpoint shared areas of struggle by flagging common wrong answers (errors that were made by at least 10% of students in the class) and can be anonymized to facilitate guided homework reviews or class discussions.

ASSISTments also keeps the teacher in charge of curriculum decisions and assignment protocol. Content libraries are available for more than 20 of the top seventh-grade mathematics textbooks in the United States, supplementing book content with correctness feedback without infringing on copyright by requiring that students use their textbooks to access the problems. Equivalent libraries are now being built to support some of the most popular open educational resources (OERs). Teachers can also write their own problems and feedback with ease, or can take advantage of a repository of more than 300 mastery-based "Skill Builders" (tailored by the ASSISTments team to the Common Core State Standards for Mathematics; NGACBP & CCSSO, 2010). Teachers can assign prebuilt problem sets directly from these libraries or can combine and/or alter copies of prebuilt problems to create unique problem sets. Because ASSISTments was also designed to support randomized controlled experimentation (Heffernan & Heffernan, 2014), researchers also use these content libraries, modifying problems or feedback to examine best practices in online learning.

ASSISTments also features support for spaced practice and computer-adaptive skill testing. The *Automatic Reassessment and Relearning System* (ARRS) measures students' retention days to weeks after their completion of mastery-based learning assignments (Skill Builders) and delivers remediation assignments as necessary (Xiong & Beck, 2014). ARRS has been proven effective in significantly enhancing longitudinal skill retention (Soffer et al., 2014; Wang & Heffernan, 2014). *PLACEments*, a computer-adaptive prerequisite skill training system, allows teachers to create and assign assessments that pinpoint gaps in students' prior knowledge to guide relearning and strengthen understanding of skill relationships (Adjei & Heffernan, 2015; Whorton, 2013). These features and others have been developed to align with a strong, research-based foundation. The ASSISTments team credits the enduring success of the platform to the six theory-based rationales highlighted in Table 8.1. Ongoing research is being conducted to prove these rationales as the mechanisms underlying the efficacy of the platform and its interventions.

TABLE 8.1 Likely Mechanisms Driving the Efficacy of ASSISTments

- **Immediate Feedback**
  Studies have found meaningful learning gains for students that are exposed to different types of computer-driven feedback (e.g., Jaehnig & Miller, 2007; McDaniel, Wildman, & Anderson, 2012; Shute, 2008; Thomas, Alexander, Jackson, & Abrami, 2013). In their meta-analysis of 22 studies, Azevedo and Bernard (1995) found that immediate feedback provided the greatest instructional advantage compared to other interventions. Findings suggested that students benefitted from both the confirmation of correct answers and the knowledge of where they erred. Studies have isolated similar effects within the context of ASSISTments (Kelly, Heffernan, Heffernan et al., 2013; Mendicino, Razzaq, & Heffernan, 2009).

- **Mastery Learning**
  In mastery learning, students must meet a predefined threshold of proficiency in a skill or learning objective before advancing to a subsequent skill or objective. Mastery learning programs have been shown to lead to higher student achievement compared to more traditional forms of skill training (Anderson, 2000; Koedinger & Aleven, 2007). A positive-effect size was reported in favor of mastery learning in a meta-analysis of 103 studies (Kulik, Kulik, & Bangert-Drowns, 1990). ASSISTments Skill Builders offer students a mastery learning environment for fluency practice.

- **Spaced Practice**
  Studies have repeatedly shown the benefits of spaced practice (Cepeda et al., 2009; Dunlosky, Rawson, Marsh, Nathan, & Willingham, 2013) and have recommended attending to the spacing of practice over time (Pashler et al., 2007). Rohrer (2009) also noted that spaced practice is underutilized in mathematics instruction. Studies have isolated similar effects in the context of ASSISTments (Ostrow, Heffernan, Heffernan, & Peterson, 2015; Soffer et al., 2014; Wang & Heffernan, 2014). The Automatic Reassessment and Relearning System supports spaced practice and remediation in ASSISTments (Xiong & Beck, 2014).

- **Cognitive Diagnostic Assessment (CDA)**
  Leighton and Gierl (2007) define CDAs as measures of students' specific knowledge structures and processing skills that highlight cognitive strengths and weaknesses. When teachers can diagnose the mistakes made by their students, both can take concrete actions in response. Further, awareness of common wrong answers can help students cognitively and motivationally (Azevedo & Bernard, 1995). Pellegrino, Chudowsky, and Glaser (2001) recommended integrating best practices from the realms of cognitive psychology and psychometrics into CDA.

- **Homework**
  In their 2006 meta-analysis, Cooper, Robinson, & Patall argued that homework was generally effective, particularly in mathematics and particularly at the secondary level. Steenbergen-Hu & Cooper (2013) suggested that the majority of K–12 classroom applications of intelligent tutoring systems were ineffective and actually worsened achievement gaps. However, they noted that use of these systems for *homework* could lead to growth (Steenbergen-Hu & Cooper, 2013). It has also been shown that online homework increases students' motivation to complete assignments (Hunter, 2015). Studies have isolated similar effects within the context of ASSISTments (Kelly, Heffernan, Heffernan et al., 2013).

(Continued)

TABLE 8.1 Likely Mechanisms Driving the Efficacy of ASSISTments, *continued*

• **Formative Assessment** The practice of formative assessment requires that teachers measure students' performance in actionable ways. Subsequent instruction can then be tailored to students' performance. Many studies have documented moderate effect sizes for formative assessment (Black & Wiliam, 2007; Brookhart, 2007; Guskey, 2007; Hattie, 2009; Heritage & Popham, 2013; Kingston & Nash, 2011; Shavelson, 2008; Speece, Molloy, & Case, 2003; Thum, Tarasawa, Hegedus, Yun, & Bowe, 2015). Paschal, Weinstein, & Walberg (2003) showed that homework could serve as formative assessment if students received the appropriate feedback.

Keeping abreast of recent advances in the learning sciences, the ASSISTments team also feel that the platform has improved educational outcomes by focusing on three ideologies: staying integrated, staying accessible, and staying curious. The following sections discuss how the team has worked to apply each of these ideologies, lessons learned in the process, and why others in the field should do the same.

STAY INTEGRATED: TEACHER PACING, OPEN EDUCATIONAL RESOURCES, AND LMS INTEGRATION

One-to-one programs are gaining popularity across the country, linking students with technology and tearing down the digital divide, an issue commonly interpreted as a lack of *access* to hardware and online infrastructure in impoverished and disadvantaged communities. However, an exhaustive review by the MIT Poverty Action Lab of randomized controlled trials assessing the effects of access to technology revealed that *access alone* was not associated with greater student learning (Escueta et al., 2017). If access alone is not effective, it is necessary to begin asking about *what* is being accessed—the learning programs that are taking over our classrooms. Studies have shown that many of these programs fail to effectively improve student learning (Campuzano, Dynarski, Agodini, & Rall, 2009), and that some even exacerbate achievement gaps (Steenbergen-Hu & Cooper, 2013). Researchers believe that these effects stem from the fact that these technologies are commonly used to *replace* instruction during class time (Steenbergen-Hu & Cooper, 2013). It is common practice in one-to-one environments for departments to replace existing textbooks with self-paced learning activities. When students demonstrate mastery in a unit, they are advanced to the next unit, out of sync with their classmates.

Self-pacing is most effective for strong students with strong "prior knowledge, self-regulation skills, learning motivation, and experience with computers" (Steenbergen-Hu & Cooper, 2013). Underperforming students struggle to keep up in self-paced environments and can fall behind even more than in a structured class environment. Despite this, student pacing is currently hailed as the basis for "personalized" instruction. The disconnect created by this type of "personalization" also hampers the pivotal role that teachers play in students' academic achievement (RAND Education, 2012). Researchers have found that the quality of student-teacher interaction informs classroom organization and instructional support, two variables that correlate with numerous measures of students' cognitive, emotional, and social engagement (Hughes, Cavell, & Willson, 2001; Rimm-Kaufman, Baroody, Larsen, Curby, & Abry, 2015). When online learning systems "personalize" instruction by relying on student pacing, the teacher functions more as a one-on-one tutor and the class structure changes almost entirely.

Despite these issues, *teacher-paced* educational technologies, rather than students' self-paced systems, are uncommon. Teacher pacing allows the teacher to remain in control of the class topic, with content assigned to students at the teacher's discretion. Teacher pacing offers a more powerful way to incorporate computers into the classroom by retaining class structure and organization.

ASSISTments is valuable because of its teacher-paced initiatives. Rather than developing a new curriculum, ASSISTments flexibly supports teachers' existing initiatives by working with their curricula and textbooks. ASSISTments allows teachers to enhance any classwork or homework assignment with immediate feedback and detailed performance reports, providing flexible support for greater ease of use. Exit tickets, tests, quizzes, and other assessments can also be administered using ASSISTments (with or without feedback), allowing teachers to access robust reports of student performance to strengthen subsequent lesson preparation. The vignette in Figure 8.1 explores how Ms. Kelly, a seventh-grade math teacher, uses ASSISTments to assign a homework assignment and prepare for subsequent class review. She uses an Item Report to spot shared misconceptions among her students that she might have otherwise overlooked. Where once the types of conclusions she draws from the Item Report would have been difficult if not impossible to summarize in time for her subsequent class review, ASSISTments grades student content and highlights common issues, saving Ms. Kelly time and effort while allowing her to better serve her students.

The problems in Ms. Kelly's vignette were adapted from open educational resources (OERs). Support for OERs is a relatively new feature of ASSISTments that allows further flexibility in supporting existing classroom initiatives. Educause, a nonprofit membership organization that supports the use of OERs for higher education, explains the practice of OERs as "ubiquitous access to high-quality, effective learning materials that can be easily tailored and freely adapted, revised, expanded, translated, and shared with educators and learners around the world" (Green, Illowsky, Wiley, Ernst, & Young, 2018). OERs abide by the five R's to help provide accessible and effective learning opportunities to all students: materials can be retained, reused, revised, remixed, and redistributed (Green et al., 2018). At the middle school level, OERs typically take the form of digitized textbooks and curricula that are released under an intellectual property or Creative Commons license that allows the materials to remain free and flexible.

MS. KELLY'S HOMEWORK ASSIGNMENT

On Monday, Ms. Kelly assigned two problems for homework using ASSISTments. The next morning, she prepared for class by assessing the assignment's Item Report (shown on the next page). The Item Report highlights class- and student-level performance to help guide Ms. Kelly's homework review and subsequent instruction. The excerpt from the Item Report shows the answers of eight students in Ms. Kelly's class.

Problem #1 was a straightforward systems of equations exercise. However, the problem was challenging for Ms. Kelly's students; only 27% answered the problem accurately, and 66% of students who got it wrong responded with an answer of "0." Responses led her to believe that students arrived at this common wrong answer by overlooking the sign change when subtracting a negative: $9 - 9 = 0$ rather than $9 - (-9) = 18$.

Problem #2 was broken into five parts requiring students to calculate the cost for two ski trip charters based on 72 skiers attending, write equations to express both rates, and justify their choice of the least expensive charter in an open response problem. The Item Report shows that some students (Gangi, Courtney, and Carl) had trouble with all five parts, while others (Lalit and Linda) had misconceptions on #2a before self-correcting. Skimming responses to #2e, Ms. Kelly notices that the students who struggled, and even some who came up with the correct responses (like Wei and Wakeeta), thought that Mountain Charter would *always* be the better option for the local ski club's travel needs, failing to understand how transportation rates were influenced by the number of skiers attending.

Ms. Kelly decides to begin with these two misconceptions in her homework review to guide subsequent instruction.

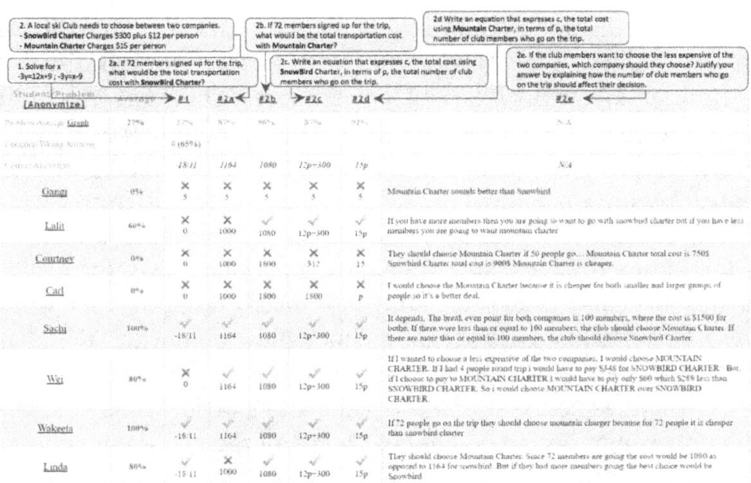

FIGURE 8.1 A vignette describing how ASSISTments can be used to supplement preexisting classroom initiatives.

The nation's embrace of OERs is relatively recent, with the Hewlett Foundation establishing its Open Educational Resources Initiative in 2002, citing educational materials from the 1990s as failing to promote enhanced learning or incorporate the latest technological and pedagogical advances (Atkins, Brown, & Hammond, 2007). The goal of this initiative was "to use information technology to help equalize the distribution of high-quality knowledge and educational opportunities for individuals, faculty, and institutions within the United States and throughout the world" (Atkins, Brown, & Hammond, 2007). According to a review of their progress (Atkins, Brown, & Hammond, 2007), the foundation invested $68 million in OERs between 2002 and 2007. Nearly two decades later, teachers remain focused on the quality and accessibility of OERs today. Educause's 2018 "Key Issues in Teaching & Learning," a survey of more than 900 members in the teaching and learning community, revealed that open education was the 10th most popular issue, with accessibility and universal design of educational technologies rated 2nd, and the evaluation of tech-based instructional innovations ranking 9th (Educause, 2018). Integrating educational technologies and OERs will help assure that all learners have access to free and effective learning materials.

OER curricula for middle school mathematics are gaining traction across the country (Tepe & Mooney, 2018) as teachers and districts turn away from costly textbooks and powerhouse publishers. According to *EdWeek*, EngageNY is the fastest growing curriculum in the United States (Heitin, 2016), with a recent study by RAND revealing that more than half of the teachers in the United States have used materials from EngageNY (Kaufman et al., 2017). In addition, EngageNY is acclaimed for its alignment to Common Core State Standards, making it easy for teachers to make the switch (EdReports, 2018). As such, building on OERs like EngageNY can allow educational technologies to consider the changing market for how learning is happening, as well as the resources and organizational structures necessary for the wider adoption and implementation of learning principles and interventions. Many of the classrooms that access EngageNY content are also using ASSISTments as instructional support to provide formative assessment opportunities, technology integration, and problem-solving interactions. By supporting OERs, ASSISTments synergistically enhances EngageNY content with its trademark capacities for feedback and reporting, making both the curriculum and the learning platform even more useful to teachers as they digitize their classrooms.

ASSISTments also integrates with learning management systems (LMSs; e.g., Canvas or Moodle) to promote ease of use. The most popular LMS integration at the middle school level is the platform's accessibility via Google Classroom. Google Classroom is a free service of Google that can be accessed with a Google account. Many districts that purchase Chromebooks also leverage the Google suite (including Gmail, Google Drive, and Google Classroom). The ASSISTments team harnessed Google's APIs to develop an application that would allow teachers and students to use Google Classroom to access ASSISTments content effortlessly by using their Google accounts rather than requiring separate log-in information for ASSISTments. Teachers can assign content to students' "Streams" and decide which assignments to port back to their "Gradebook." A wide and continuously growing range of ASSISTments content is available through Google Classroom, including Common Core aligned fluency practice (Skill Builders), content for AP statistics, chemistry, and physics, and EngageNY content for Grades 3–12. Educational technologies are only as good as the quality, quantity, and accessibility of their content, and ASSISTments has found success by addressing each of these issues through flexible classroom integration.

STAY ACCESSIBLE: FREE SERVICE COMBATS THE DIGITAL DIVIDE AND ACHIEVEMENT GAPS

Although accessibility is still considered a critical issue in educational policy reform, research has yet to support the idea that hardware *alone* can eliminate the achievement gap (Escueta et al., 2017). Consider the one-to-one initiative in the state of Maine. The program has provided all seventh- and eighth-grade students with laptops since 2002. Despite this access, the Nation's Report Card by the National Assessment of Educational Progress (www.nationsreportcard.gov/) shows that math scores across the state have remained largely unaffected and achievement gaps in mathematics have actually grown. Since 2000, Maine's average eighth-grade math scores have improved by only three points, compared to the national gain of seven points on average. For students on Free or Reduced Lunch Plans (FRLP)—an indicator of lower socioeconomic standing and the status of 44.7% of Maine students in 2015—math performance actually *fell* by one point while similar students across the nation exhibited a 13-point gain on average. These students have lost considerable traction in comparison to their FRLP noneligible peers who gained nine points over the same period. Thus, a 16-point difference between FRLP eligible and noneligible students in 2000 became a 25-point difference by 2017. In this example, closing the digital divide by targeting access alone is *not* creating equity in mathematics education.

Beyond accessibility, factors like device compatibility and a lack of Internet access can also be limiting for students using educational technologies. ASSISTments has found success by tackling these issues directly. The platform can be accessed from a variety of devices including computers, tablets, and cell phones, is supported on all popular browsers, and has its own iOS and Android applications. When integrated with Google Classroom or other LMSs, ASSISTments retains the compatibility of its host. Internet access is not a limiting factor for the use of ASSISTments either. Students can download their assignments at school and work offline at home, helping to make the system practical regardless of potential discrepancies in accessibility brought about by a students' socioeconomic status.

Devices used to support student-paced learning environments that cut the teacher out of the picture tend to exacerbate achievement gaps, stalling performance in underprivileged and underperforming students (Steenbergen-Hu & Cooper, 2013). Once accessible, educational technologies should instead support the role of the teacher in working with students of all performance levels in a unified class setting. Technology should amplify, rather than minimize, the impact of the teacher and her classroom organization and structure. Essentially, the goal should not be to provide *students* with a learning environment, but to provide *teachers* with the technologies necessary to more effectively monitor, communicate with, and motivate their students. In this sense, accessibility and integration go hand in hand when establishing ease of use—by using a flexible approach that integrates with existing classroom initiatives and curriculum, ASSISTments has been able to move beyond *literal* accessibility into *practical* accessibility.

As such, a critical aspect of *practical* accessibility is the cost of supporting online learning. Whereas many educational technologies—often those marketed as curriculum replacement strategies—charge districts for use of their systems, ASSISTments is completely free. Since its inception, ASSISTments has been maintained as a free public service of Worcester Polytechnic Institute through more than $25 million in grant funding from public and private institutions. Early funding helped establish a baseline of the platform's efficacy, develop its flexible infrastructure, create a strong repository of content, and grow and maintain a reliable user population. After more than a decade of growth, the pursuit of larger grant lines, including funding for the IES efficacy trial summarized in Table 8.2, has helped maintain the platform's commitment to remain free.

The ASSISTments efficacy trial, conducted by SRI International, concluded that among a vast sample of seventh-grade students in Maine, those randomly assigned to use ASSISTments for classwork and homework scored 70% higher on a standardized assessment than otherwise expected ($p < .008$). In addition, use of the system closed achievement gaps; students scoring below the median on their sixth-grade state math test exhibited more than a full grade level of growth from use of ASSISTments (Roschelle et al., 2016). This finding is unique among the majority of K–12 online learning systems in mathematics (Steenbergen-Hu & Cooper, 2013). A potential mechanism for observed gains? Teachers using ASSISTments reliably changed their approaches to homework review. They spent the same amount of time reviewing homework as teachers in the control condition (on average), but their reviews focused on a smaller number of more difficult problems, tailored to students' specific misconceptions (Roschelle et al., 2016). These results were thought to have practical importance because use of ASSISTments aligned to existing school policies and practices (Fairman, Porter, & Fisher, 2015) utilized a free, easily accessible resource, and had a meaningful impact on student achievement. As such, SRI concluded that ASSISTments offered an easy-to-implement intervention that nearly doubled student learning and helped to close achievement gaps (Roschelle et al., 2016).

TABLE 8.2 Sample, Design, Measures, Fidelity and Attrition, Analysis, and Results of the ASSISTments Efficacy Trial (Roschelle et al., 2016)

- **Sample**
  - Schools: 46
    - Normally distributed by school size and prior mathematics achievement
  - Teachers: 87 (seventh grade)
  - Students: 2,867 (seventh grade)
- **Design**
  - Clustered, school-level random assignment
  - Schools assigned to condition for 2 years
  - Treatment
    - Year 1—Teachers received PD and practiced using ASSISTments
    - Year 2—Teachers used ASSISTments with the student-level study population
  - Control
    - Years 1 and 2—Teachers delivered homework using traditional methods
- **Measures**
  - TerraNova Common Core Mathematics Assessment
    - Standardized, end-of-year outcome
    - No effort made to align ASSISTments content to test content
  - Supplemental measures
    - Interviews with teachers and school principals
    - Teacher observations, surveys, and logs
    - System data from ASSISTments
- **Fidelity and Attrition**
  - Substantial use of ASSISTments during the school year
    - 14 hours (on average)
    - 967 problems
  - Attrition rates were low
    - School-level attrition rate of 6.5% (3.8% differential)
    - Student-level attrition rate of 10.1% (5.7% differential)
- **Analysis**
  - 3-Level Hierarchical Linear Model
  - Covariates:
    - Standardized sixth-grade assessment scores
    - Free and Reduced Lunch Status
    - Individualized Education Plan Status

(Continued)

TABLE 8.2 Sample, Design, Measures, Fidelity and Attrition, Analysis, and Results of the ASSISTments Efficacy Trial (Roschelle et al., 2016), *continued*

- **Results**
  - Convergent evidence of reliable effects on teaching practices
    - Treatment teachers focused their homework reviews
      - Targeted on fewer, more difficult problems
      - Targeted on common wrong answers and misconceptions
  - Significantly different mean scores on TerraNova ($p < .01$, $g = .18$)
    - Expected yearly gain of 11 points (on average)
    - Treatment associated with +8.84 points gained, nearly one full grade-level equivalent
  - Effect more prominent for students with sixth-grade math scores below the median
    - Underperforming students experienced significantly greater gains ($p < .05$, $g = .28$)
    - More than one full grade-level equivalent

In response to the effects observed in the efficacy trial, ASSISTments recently received nearly $7 million in funding from the IES to replicate this work (R305A170137) and to conduct a follow-up effectiveness trial (R305A170243). These next steps will test whether the platform is a reliably effective learning tool at scale and whether observed effects will generalize to student populations across the United States. Pursuing funding of this magnitude has allowed ASSISTments to remain free for teachers and students as the platform has gained momentum, allowing the ASSISTments team to continue fighting for equity in education.

STAYING CURIOUS: HOW ASSISTMENTS HAS HARNESSED RIGOROUS RESEARCH

Traditional approaches to educational research have lost their footing in today's fast-paced, tech-driven landscape. Despite increases in the demand for rigorously controlled experimentation (US Department of Education, 2010; Pashler et al., 2007), researchers often stray from conducting this type of work due to its high costs, perceptions of its intrusion into "normal instructional practice," its potentially critical stakes with regard to fidelity of implementation, and difficulty achieving reliable and replicable results (National Research Council, 2002). Further, researchers may find it difficult to integrate their traditional, rigorous methods with the growing prevalence of educational technologies.

Educational technologies have the potential to play a key role in allowing educational researchers to conduct randomized controlled trials more efficiently in modern learning environments. However, developers of these resources fail to realize how supporting a collaborative research environment could inform best practices within their platform while broadly influencing the field. Similarly, funders fail to realize that research-infused platforms have the potential to drastically reduce costs, promote the development and application of universal measures, and strengthen capacity for replication, all while influencing practice and policy.

Take, for instance, the simplified "pipeline" structure for scientific investigation upheld by the Institute of Education Sciences, summarized in Table 8.3 on the next page (IES & NSF, 2013). Within this structure, many small grants are allotted for Exploratory Research projects meant to contribute to fundamental knowledge on educational outcomes by testing, developing, and refining theory and methodologies or by examining relationships among important constructs in education to form a basis for future interventions (IES & NSF, 2013). Development and Innovation grants then support larger projects that draw on existing evidence to develop and pilot interventions to achieve a specific goal (IES & NSF, 2013). The most sought-after IES funding tracks include their Efficacy and Replication or Effectiveness and Scale-up Grants, which contribute to evidence of the impact of fully developed interventions tested through rigorous designs, with clear outcome measures and powerful statistical analyses (IES & NSF, 2013). Efficacy trials that test interventions under "ideal" circumstances cost the IES upwards of $3 million each, while Effectiveness Trials meant to assess interventions in more "typical" circumstances are valued upwards of $4 million each. Despite their high price tags, it is rare for these projects to result in significant implications for practice and policy. Educational technologies could be used to alleviate some of this monetary burden, but first they must be accepted as tools for scientific inquiry..

While other learning technologies have the potential to provide many of the same classroom benefits as ASSISTments, none are comparable in terms of allowing educational researchers to design and implement content-based experimentation with ease. Research within ASSISTments began to flourish in 2014, through the development of the ASSISTments Testbed, shared research infrastructure that brought researchers together with students and teachers to study effective learning interventions while iteratively improving ASSISTments' content and user experience. Developed under an SI2 grant from the NSF (1440753), the ASSISTments Testbed allowed researchers from around the world to examine basic learning interventions by embedding randomized controlled experiments

TABLE 8.3 IES Research Goals, Grant Durations, and Distributions, Compared to the Projected Support of a Single Educational Technology Platform Used for Research

IES RESEARCH GOAL	GRANT DURATION (YEARS)	GRANT SIZE	TOTAL AWARDS (LIFETIME)	IES YEARLY CAPACITY	ED TECH YEARLY CAPACITY
Exploration	2–4	$600K–1.4M	196	15.9	25–50+
Development and Innovation	4	$1.4M	344	20.5	10–20+
Efficacy and Replication	3–5	$700K—3.3M	318	22.5	10+
Effectiveness/ Scale-Up	5	$4M	17	0.9	5+
Measurement	4	$1.4M	108	7.9	25–50+

within students' classwork and homework assignments. The Testbed gave researchers unprecedented access to learning content that could be experimentally manipulated (within the boundaries of normal instructional practice) and randomly assigned to students. The process of study creation was relatively simple and did not require skill in computer programming, nor did it necessarily require research-specific skills; teachers could (and did) use the Testbed to conduct simple studies in their classrooms.

The Testbed brought together student-level randomization of content and feedback with detailed log files of student- and class-level features to help researchers tease apart treatment effects and understand the context within which interventions worked. Through the Assessment of Learning Infrastructure (ALI), the reporting tool associated with the ASSISTments Testbed, researchers could access automated reports that provided basic analyses and preprocessed CSV files featuring the raw data logged by ASSISTments as students worked through the experiment-embedded assignment (Ostrow et al., 2016). ALI offered data at four granularities to suit different research needs: action-level, problem-level, student-level, and student-problem-level data. These data sets could also be combined with ALI's covariate file that provided anonymized student-, class-, and school-level data linked to participating students' prior performance within ASSISTments (i.e., prior to their random assignment into the study).

The ASSISTments Testbed hosted more than 150 randomized controlled experiments that sought to understand the effects of cognitive, metacognitive, and socioemotional interventions embedded in content, feedback, games, activities, and surveys. Exemplary work has included studies examining whether feedback medium (text vs. video) influences student learning (Ostrow & Heffernan, 2014), the influences of desirable difficulties and interleaved rather than blocked content (Ostrow et al., 2015), and the motivational effects of Dweckian mindset videos (Kelly, Heffernan, D'Mello, Namias, & Strain, 2013). In addition to the Testbed's broad impact for researchers, the ASSISTments team's subsequent capacity to analyze multiple studies simultaneously has opened new doors for the data mining community, inspiring researchers to model treatment effects in new ways. Working with statisticians from the University of Texas–Austin, Harvard, and the University of Michigan, the team is combining deep learning techniques that model student data with statistical methods to predict homework completion in order to more accurately estimate treatment effects in randomized controlled experiments. When applied to data from a set of 22 experiments running in the ASSISTments Testbed, standard errors were reduced by at least 40% across eight experiments (Sales, Botelho, Patikorn, & Heffernan, 2018). Essentially, this translates to the use of cutting-edge techniques to develop methodological improvements in measuring the effectiveness of learning interventions, extending the potential for evidence-based personalized learning.

SI2 funding set the groundwork for a more recent NSF DIBBs project (1724889) that is scaling the ASSISTments Testbed's research capacity to support researchers across disciplines through automated supports for study creation, implementation, data reporting, and analysis, thereby increasing the efficiency, reliability, and cost effectiveness of investigations. Specifically, recent work is automating the process of study creation and data analysis through the development of the *Template Tool*, infrastructure that supports the capacities of the ASSISTments Testbed and that will help address research implementation issues. From experience helping researchers implement their experimental designs within the Testbed, the team discovered that most research questions brought to the platform could be assessed using a set of design patterns or templates. Therefore, the Template Tool was developed to help researchers access and populate experimental design templates, making the study creation process user-friendly. The team is now working to merge the Template Tool with ALI to provide more robust automated analyses that will supplement the infrastructure's preprocessed data files. Continued funding from the NSF has allowed the Testbed's research capacity to grow, supporting researchers across disciplines in conducting randomized controlled experiments. Some of the first projects from researchers without association to WPI are beginning to reach publication (Fyfe, 2016; Clinton, Walkington, &

Sparks, 2019), proving the platform's value as a shared research instrument and suggesting the need for our continued efforts in its development and growth.

In its current form, the ASSISTments Testbed is decentralized, with researchers leveraging ASSISTments while juggling interactions with various resources offered by Google that support the platform's capacities for data reporting and analytics. In addition, researchers commonly request information about content availability and usage prior to developing their studies—information that is currently only accessible by programmers on the ASSISTments team, but that could be made readily available through centralized queries and visualizations. As such, the ASSISTments research environment must continue to evolve.

The future of research within ASSISTments will include a more sophisticated, *centralized* research instrument capable of offering myriad features and functions that extend beyond those currently available in the ASSISTments Testbed. The team's vision for the future includes rebranding the ASSISTments Testbed into E-TRIALS, an *EdTech Research Infrastructure to Advance Learning Science*. E-TRIALS will serve as a natural extension of prior work with the ASSISTments Testbed, effectively streamlining the process of online educational research by establishing a centralized research interface with more robust capacities to better serve our research community. E-TRIALS will improve the accuracy and reliability of the data collection practices currently utilized by the Testbed, while simultaneously expanding the tool's breadth of application and emphasizing a sense of user-friendliness that is currently missing from the platform's research protocol.

While it is true that not *all* educational research is suited for online learning environments, educational technologies offer an opportunity to reduce strain on funding agencies and help accelerate the scientific process by offering authentic environments for randomized controlled experimentation. After transforming ASSISTments into a shared research infrastructure, the team believes that other educational technologies have an untapped potential to support collaborative research at scale. By applying randomized controlled experimentation to these environments, researchers can learn "what works, for whom, and when," thereby improving educational technologies for teachers and students (Ostrow, Heffernan, & Williams, 2017). The field is at a critical turning point for funders and developers of educational technologies to effect change. Shared research instruments like E-TRIALS could serve as a critical first step in a larger evolution of thought and practice for the learning sciences.

A CALL FOR THE LEARNING SCIENCES: TARGET EFFECTIVE LEARNING BY STAYING INTEGRATED, STAYING ACCESSIBLE, AND STAYING CURIOUS

Keeping abreast of recent advances in the learning sciences, ASSISTments has improved educational outcomes by harnessing three ideologies: staying integrated, staying accessible, and staying curious. In terms of integration, ASSISTments flexibly supports teachers' existing classroom initiatives. The teacher-paced platform adds immediate feedback and robust reports to homework, classwork, and assessments and offers support for more than 20 of the nation's leading middle school mathematics textbooks as well as full OER curricula (e.g., EngageNY). Materials can be accessed directly from ASSISTments or through other popular LMSs like Google Classroom and Canvas. In terms of accessibility, ASSISTments is maintained as a free public service of Worcester Polytechnic Institute, in part through more than $25 million in funding from various public and private sources. The platform is available on a wide variety of devices, and students can download materials and work offline, making the system practical for the everyday learner. Remaining free to teachers and students has helped ASSISTments address achievement gaps and fight for equity in education. ASSISTments also operates at the forefront of educational research, with the ASSISTments Testbed challenging the standards of funding, practice, and policy in educational research by leveraging the platform as a shared scientific instrument. The future of this shared research environment, E-TRIALs, will aim to challenge conventions and revitalize how the field approaches research in modern classrooms.

As learning environments continue to digitize and educational technologies flourish, it will grow critical for researchers and developers in the learning sciences to reassess the goals of these platforms. Educational technologies should not be thought of as tools to replace traditional classroom practices, but should instead be leveraged in flexible ways that harness the best of both the classroom and the technology. Educational technologies are also only as good as the quality, quantity, and accessibility of their content. To target these issues, developers must remain cognizant of how their platforms integrate with existing content, curricula, and practices, while striving to break down barriers in access and understanding that keep students from equitable achievement. The future of educational research, and therefore implications for both policy and practice, will likely also be heavily engrained in technology. Understanding the potential value of these platforms as shared scientific instruments will be critical if they are to effectively take up this charge.

Designing educational technologies with the goals of staying integrated, accessible, and curious will require a revolution in thought regarding the way these systems serve classrooms. In theory, upholding these three ideologies has the potential to influence research and policy in ways that would impact all students, teachers, and administrators of tomorrow. As a learning scientist, the fate of modern education rests in your hands. May you make it your motto to stay integrated, accessible, and curious forever more.

REFERENCES

Adjei, S. A., & Heffernan, N. T. (2015). Improving learning maps using an adaptive testing system: PLACEments. *Proceedings of the 17th International Conference on Artificial Intelligence in Education, 9112*, 517–520.

Anderson, J. R. (2000). *Learning and memory: An integrated approach.* New York: John Wiley and Sons, Inc.

Anderson, J. R., Corbett, A. T., Koedinger, K. R., & Pelletier, R. (1995). Cognitive tutor: Lessons learned. *The Journal of the Learning Sciences, 4*(2), 167–207.

Atkins, D. E., Brown, J. S., & Hammond, A. L. (2007). *A review of the Open Educational Resources (OER) movement: Achievements, challenges, and new opportunities.* Report to the William and Flora Hewlett Foundation.

Azevedo, R., & Bernard, R. M. (1995). A meta-analysis of the effects of feedback in computer-based instruction. *Journal of Educational Computing Research, 13*(2), 111–127.

Black, P., & Wiliam, D. (2007). A theoretical foundation for formative assessment. In J. H. McMillan (Ed.), *Formative classroom assessment: Theory into practice.* New York: Teachers College Press.

Bloom, B. S. (1984). The 2 Sigma problem: The search for methods of group instruction as effective as one-to-one tutoring. *Educational Researcher, 13*(6), 4–16.

Brookhart, S. (2007). Expanding views about formative classroom assessment: A review of the literature. In J. H. McMillan (Ed.), *Formative classroom assessment: Theory into practice* (pp. 43–62). New York: Teachers College Press.

Bush, M. D., & Mott, J. D. (2009). The transformation of learning with technology: Learner-centricity, content and tool malleability, and network effects. *Educational Technology, 49*(2), 3–20.

Campuzano, L., Dynarski, M., Agodini, R., & Rall, K. (2009). Effectiveness of reading and mathematics software products: Findings from two student cohorts—executive summary (NCEE 2009-4042). Washington, DC: National Center for Education Evaluation and Regional Assistance, Institute of Education Sciences, U.S. Department of Education.

Cepeda, N. J., Coburn, N., Rohrer, D., Wixted, J. T., Mozer, M. C., & Pashler, H. (2009). Optimizing distributed practice: Theoretical analysis and practical implications. *Experimental Psychology, 56*(4), 236–246.

Clinton, V., Walkington, C., & Sparks, A. (2019). The effect of modifying the language of mathematics story problems on problem-solving measures. Presented at *The 2019 Annual Meeting of the American Educational Research Association*, Toronto, Canada.

Cooper, H., Robinson, J. C., & Patall, E. A. (2006). Does homework improve academic achievement? A synthesis of research, 1987–2003. *Review of Educational Research, 76*(1), 1–62.

Dunlosky, J., Rawson, K., Marsh, E., Nathan, M., & Willingham, D. (2013). Improving students' learning with effective learning techniques: Promising directions from cognitive and educational psychology. *Psychological Science in the Public Interest, 14*(1), 4–58.

EdReports. (2018). Math reports: Compare K–8 math materials. Reports Center. Retrieved from https://www.edreports.org/math/reports/compare-k8.html

Educause. (2018). Key issues in teaching & learning. *Educause Learning Initiative.* Retrieved from https://www.educause.edu/eli/initiatives/key-issues-in-teaching-and-learning

Escueta, M., Quan, V., Nickow, A. J., & Oreopoulos, P. (2017, August). Education technology: An evidence-based review. NBER Working Paper No. 23744. JEL No. I20, I29, J24.

Fairman, J., Porter, M., & Fisher, S. (2015). Principals discuss early implementation of the ASSISTments online homework tutor for mathematics: ASSISTments Efficacy Study Report 2. Menlo Park, CA: SRI.

Fyfe, E. (2016). Providing feedback on computer-based algebra homework in middle-school classrooms. *Computers in Human Behavior, 63*, 568–574.

Green, C., Illowsky, B., Wiley, D., Ernst, D., & Young, L. (2018). 7 things you should know about open education: Content. *Educause Learning Initiative.* Retrieved from: https://library.educause.edu/~/media/files/library/2018/6/eli7157.pdf

Guskey, T. R. (2007). Formative classroom assessment and Benjamin S. Bloom: Theory, research, and practice. In J. H. McMillan (Ed.), *Formative classroom assessment: Theory into practice* (pp. 63–78). New York: Teachers College Press.

Hattie, J. (2009). *Visible thinking: A synthesis of over 800 meta-analyses relating to achievement.* New York: Routledge.

Heffernan, N., & Heffernan, C. (2014). The ASSISTments ecosystem: Building a platform that brings scientists and teachers together for minimally invasive research on human learning and teaching. *International Journal of Artificial Intelligence in Education, 24*(4), 470–497.

Heitin, L. (2016). Creators of EngageNY start new archive of free Common-Core materials. *Education Week.* Retrieved from http://www.edweek.org/ew/articles/2016/05/18/creators-of-engageny-start-new-archive-of.html.

Heritage, M., & Popham, W. J. (2013). *Formative assessment in practice: A process of inquiry and action.* Cambridge, MA: Harvard Education Press.

Herold, B. (2018). Schools see "incredible progress" on Internet Connectivity, report says. *Education Week.* Retrieved from https://www.edweek.org/ew/section/multimedia/schools-see-incredible-progress-on-internet-connectivity.html

Hughes, J. N., Cavell, T. A., & Willson, V. (2001). Further support for the developmental significance of the quality of the teacher–student relationship. *Journal of School Psychology, 39*(4), 289–301.

Hunter, S. (2015). Does online homework increase motivation to complete homework? [Unpublished thesis]. United States Military Academy, West Point.

IES & NSF. (2013). Common guidelines for education research and development: A report from the Institute of Education Sciences, U.S. Department of Education, and the National Science Foundation.

Institute of Education Sciences. (2003). Identifying and implementing educational practices supported by rigorous evidence: A user friendly guide. Washington, DC: U.S. Department of Education.

Ioannidis, J. P. A. (2005). Why most published research findings are false. *PLoS Med, 2*(8), e124.

Jaehnig, W., & Miller, M. (2007). Feedback types in programmed instruction: A systematic review. *The Psychological Record, 57*, 219–232.

Kaufman, J. H., Davis, J. S., Wang, E. L., Thompson, L. E., Pane, J. D., Pfommer, K., & Harris, M. (2017). *Use of open educational resources in an era of common standards: A case study on the use of EngageNY.* Santa Monica, CA: RAND Corporation.

Kelly, K., Heffernan, N., D'Mello, S., Namias, J., & Strain, A. (2013). Adding teacher-created motivational video to an ITS. *Proceedings of the Twenty-Sixth International Florida Artificial Intelligence Research Society Conference*, 503–508.

Kelly, K., Heffernan, N., Heffernan, C., Goldman, S., Pellegrino, J., & Soffer Goldstein, D. (2013). Estimating the effect of web-based homework. In H.C. Lane, K. Yacef, J. Mostow, & P. Pavlik (Eds.), *Artificial intelligence in education.* Lecture Notes in Computer Science, 7926.

Kingston, N., & Nash, B. (2011). How many formative assessment angels can dance on the head of a meta-analytic pin: .2. *Educational Measurement: Issues and Practice, 31*(4), 18–19.

Koedinger, K., & Aleven, V. (2007). Exploring the assistance dilemma in experiments with Cognitive Tutors. *Educational Psychology Review, 19*(3), 239–264.

Koedinger, K., McLaughlin, E., & Heffernan, N. (2010). A quasi-experimental evaluation of an on-line formative assessment and tutoring system. *Journal of Educational Computing Research, 43*(4), 489–510.

Kohavi, R., Longbotham, R., Sommerfield, D., & Henne, R. M. (2009). Controlled experiments on the web: Survey and practical guide. *Data Mining and Knowledge Discovery, 18*(1), 140–181.

Kulik, C., & Kulik, J. (1991). Effectiveness of computer-based instruction: An updated analysis. *Computers in Human Behavior, 7*, 75–91.

Kulik, C., Kulik, J., & Bangert-Drowns, R. (1990). Effectiveness of mastery learning programs: A meta-analysis. *Review of Educational Research, 60*(2), 265–306.

Leighton, J. P., & Gierl, M. J. (2007). Why cognitive diagnostic assessment? In J. P. Leighton & M. J. Gierl (Eds.), *Cognitive assessment for education: Theory and applications* (pp. 3–18). New York: Cambridge University Press.

Lu, J. (2008). Effects of traditional and digital media on student learning in space design. *The Scholarship of Teaching and Learning at EMU, 2*(5), 75–90.

McDaniel, M. A., Wildman, K. M., & Anderson, J. L. (2012). Using quizzes to enhance summative-assessment performance in a web-based class: An experimental study. *Journal of Applied Research in Memory and Cognition, 1*(1), 18–26.

Mendicino, M., Razzaq, L., & Heffernan, N. T. (2009). A comparison of traditional homework to computer supported homework. *Journal of Research on Technology in Education, 41*(3), 331–358.

National Governors Association Center for Best Practices (NGACBP) & Council of Chief State School Officers (CCSSO). (2010). Common Core State Standards. Washington, DC: Authors.

National Research Council. (2002). *Scientific research in education.* Washington, DC: The National Academies Press.

Ostrow, K. S., & Heffernan, N. T. (2014). Testing the multimedia principle in the real world: A comparison of video vs. text feedback in authentic middle school math assignments. In Stamper, Pardos, Mavrikis, & McLaren (Eds.), *Proceedings of the 7th International Conference on Educational Data Mining*, (pp. 296–299).

Ostrow, K., Heffernan, N., Heffernan, C., & Peterson, Z. (2015). Blocking vs. interleaving: examining single-session effects within middle school math homework. In Conati, Heffernan, Mitrovic, & Verdejo (Eds.), *Proceedings of the 17th International Conference on Artificial Intelligence in Education*, (pp. 388–347).

Ostrow, K. S., Heffernan, N. T., & Williams, J. J. (2017). Tomorrow's edtech today: Establishing a learning platform as a collaborative research tool for sound science. *Teachers College Record, 119*(3), 1–36.

Ostrow, K., Selent, D., Wang, Y., Van Inwegen, E., Heffernan, N., & Williams, J. J. (2016). Assessment of Learning Infrastructure (ALI): The theory, practice, and scalability of automated assessment. *Proceedings of the 6th International Conference on Learning Analytics and Knowledge*, 279–288.

Oxman, S., & Wong, W. (2014). White paper: Adaptive learning systems. DV X Innovations, DeVry Education Group, and Integrated Education Solutions.

Paschal, R., Weinstein, T., & Walberg, H. (2003). The effects of homework on learning; a quantitative synthesis. *Journal of Educational Research, 78*(2), 97–104.

Pashler, H., Bain, P., Bottge, B., Graesser, A., Koedinger, K., McDaniel, M., & Metcalfe, J. (2007). *Organizing instruction and study to improve student learning* (NCER 2007–2004). Washington, DC: National Center for Education Research, Institute of Education Sciences, U.S. Department of Education.

Pawlowski, J. M., & Bick, M. (2012). Open educational resources. *Business and Information Systems Engineering, 4*(4), 209–212.

Pellegrino, J. W., Chudowsky, N., & Glaser, R. (2001). *Knowing what students know: The science and design of educational assessment.* Washington, DC: National Academy Press.

RAND Education. (2012). *Teachers matter: Understanding teachers' impact on student achievement.* Santa Monica, CA.

Rimm-Kaufman, S. E., Baroody, A., Larsen, R., Curby, T. W., & Abry, T. (2015). To what extent do teacher-student interaction quality and student gender contribute to fifth graders' engagement in mathematics learning? *Journal of Educational Psychology, 107*(1), 170–185.

Rohrer, D. (2009). The effects of spacing and mixing practice problems. *Journal for Research in Mathematics Education, 40*(1), 4–17.

Roschelle, J., Feng, M., Murphy, R. F., & Mason, C. A. (2016). Online mathematics homework increases student achievement. *AERA Open, 2*(4), 1–12.

Sales, A., Botelho, A. F., Patikorn, T., & Heffernan, N. T. (2018). Using big data to sharpen design-based inference in A/B tests. *Proceedings of the Eleventh International Conference on Educational Data Mining*, 479–485.

Shavelson, R. J. (2008). Guest editor's introduction. *Applied Measurement in Education, 21*(4), 293–294.

Shute, V. J. (1993). A macroadaptive approach to tutoring. *Journal of Artificial Intelligence in Education, 4*(1), 61–93.

Shute, V. (2008). Focus on formative feedback. *Review of Educational Research, 78*(1), 153–189.

Singer, N. (2017, May 13). How Google took over the classroom. *The New York Times.* Retrieved from: https://www.nytimes.com/2017/05/13/technology/google-education-chromebooks-schools.html

Singh, R., Saleem, M., Pradhan, P., Heffernan, C., Heffernan, N., Razzaq, L., Dailey, M., O'Connor, C., & Mulchay, C. (2011). Feedback during web-based homework: The role of hints. In Biswas, Bull, Kay, & Mitrovic (Eds.), *Proceedings of the 15th International Conference on Artificial Intelligence in Education*, 6738: 328–336.

Soffer, D., Das, V., Pellegrino, G., Goldman, S., Heffernan, N., Heffernan, C., & Dietz, K. (2014). Improving long-term retention of mathematical knowledge through automatic reassessment and relearning. *American Educational Research Association.* Division C—Learning and Instruction / Section 1c: Mathematics.

Speece, D. L., Molloy, D. E., & Case, L. P. (2003). Responsiveness to general education instruction as the first gate to learning disabilities identification. *Learning Disabilities: Research & Practice, 18*(3), 147–156.

Steenbergen-Hu, S., & Cooper, H. (2013). A meta-analysis of the effectiveness of intelligent tutoring systems on K–12 students' mathematical learning. *Journal of Educational Psychology, 105*(4), 970–987.

Tepe, L., & Mooney, T. (2018). Navigating the new curriculum landscape: How states are using and sharing open educational resources. Council of Chief State Officers.

Thomas, T., Alexander, K., Jackson, R., & Abrami, P. (2013). The differential effects of interactive versus didactic pedagogy using computer-assisted instruction. *Journal of Educational Computing Research, 49,* 403–436.

Thum, Y. M., Tarasawa, B., Hegedus, A., Yun, X., & Bowe, B. (2015). Keeping learning on track: A case-study of formative assessment practice and its impact on learning in Meridian School District. Research Report. Portland, OR: Northwest Evaluation Association.

US Department of Education. (2010). Transforming American education: Learning powered by technology, the national educational technology plan. Washington, DC: Office of Educational Technology.

VanLehn, K. (2006). The behavior of tutoring systems. *International Journal of Artificial Intelligence and Education, 16*, 227–265.

Wang, Y., & Heffernan, N. (2014). The effect of automatic reassessment and relearning on assessing student long-term knowledge in mathematics. In Trausan-Matu, Boyer, Crosby, & Panourgia (Eds.), *Proceedings of the 12th International Conference on Intelligent Tutoring Systems*, 8474, (pp. 490–495).

What Works Clearinghouse. (2008). What Works Clearinghouse procedures and standards handbook (Version 2.0). Washington, DC: Institute of Education Sciences, US Department of Education.

Whorton, S. (2013). Can a computer adaptive assessment system determine, better than traditional methods, whether students know mathematics skills? (Master's thesis, Computer Science Department, Worcester Polytechnic Institute). Retrieved from http://www.wpi.edu/Pubs/ETD/Available/etd-041913-095912/

Woolf, B. P. (2009). *Building intelligent interactive tutors.* Burlington, MA: Morgan Kaufman.

Xiong, X., & Beck, J. E. (2014). A study of exploring different schedules of spacing and retrieval interval on mathematics skills in ITS environment. In Trausan-Matu, Boyer, Crosby, & Panourgia (Eds.), *Proceedings of the 12th International Conferences on Intelligent Tutoring Systems*, 8474, (pp. 504–509).

ABOUT THE AUTHORS

Korinn S. Ostrow, PhD, is a research scientist at Worcester Polytechnic Institute. She recently completed her dissertation on the potential of leveraging technology to conduct educational research at scale. Her work also focuses on the causal mechanisms underlying students' learning, retention, motivation, and engagement in educational technologies.

Neil T. Heffernan, PhD, is a professor of computer science and the director of the Learning Sciences and Technologies Program at Worcester Polytechnic Institute, and the creator of ASSISTments. He has extensive experience in machine learning, intelligent tutoring systems, artificial intelligence, cognitive science, and mathematical cognition.

ACKNOWLEDGMENTS

The authors of this work have been supported by the following grants and funding partners: the National Science Foundation (1316736, 1252297, 1109483, 1031398, 0742503, 1440753, 1535428, 0742503, 0231773, 0448319, 1724889, 1636782, and 1822830), the Institute of Education Sciences (R305A180401, R305A120125, R305C100024, R305K03140, R305A07440, R305A170137, R305A170243), the Graduate Assistance in Areas of National Need program (P200A120238 & P200A150306), the Office of Naval Research (STEM Grand Challenges, N00014-13-C-0127, N00014-18-1-2768), the Spencer Foundation, and the Bill and Melinda Gates Foundation. The views presented in this work are those of the authors and are not necessarily endorsed by these funders.

CHAPTER 9

Designing Immersive Authentic Simulations That Enhance Motivation and Learning: EcoLearn

Chris Dede, Tina Grotzer, Amy Kamarainen, and Shari Metcalf
Harvard Graduate School of Education

ABSTRACT

Over the past decade, our team has completed and studied three curricula: EcoMUVE (a middle school curriculum based on two immersive virtual ecosystems), EcoMOBILE (a curriculum that blends EcoMUVE with experiences in real ecosystems infused with digital resources), and EcoXPT (an extension of EcoMUVE that includes experiment-based inquiry authentic to ecosystem science). This chapter describes affordances of immersive media (multi-user virtual environments, augmented realities) for motivation and learning and how the design of these three curricula draws on theoretical and conceptual principles from the learning sciences.

EcoLearn (http://ecolearn.gse.harvard.edu) is a design-based research group at the Harvard Graduate School of Education that explores the use of advanced immersive technologies to support learning about the process of scientific inquiry and the complex causal dynamics of ecosystems. Thus far, we have developed three completed curricula: EcoMUVE (a middle school curriculum based on two immersive virtual ecosystems), Eco-MOBILE (a curriculum that blends EcoMUVE with experiences in real ecosystems infused with digital resources), and EcoXPT (an extension of EcoMUVE that includes experiment-based inquiry authentic to ecosystem science). Not discussed in this chapter is our ongoing development of Eco-MOD, a third-grade curriculum that pairs computational modeling with an immersive virtual ecosystem.

THEORETICAL AND CONCEPTUAL BASES OF THE ECOLEARN CURRICULA

This section describes principles from the learning sciences that have guided our EcoLearn development. Curricula designed to teach advanced knowledge and skills are often based on "guided social constructivist" theories of learning (Palincsar, 1998), in which students strive to master authentic tasks in realistic situations. Meaning is constructed by each person, so students add skills and understandings based on what they already know and can do, which is shaped by their developmental level, their prior experiences, and their sociocultural background and context. Teachers act as coaches and mentors to foster learning by providing rich, loosely structured experiences and guidance that encourage meaning-making. This type of learning is usually social; students build their knowledge and skills based on group experiences and collaborative interactions.

Immersive media have affordances that enable guided social constructivism even in barren settings like classrooms. Psychological immersion is the mental state of being completely absorbed or engaged with something. For example, a well-designed game in a multi-user virtual environment (MUVE) draws viewers into the world portrayed on the screen, and they feel caught up in that virtual environment. Each participant can influence what happens in the digital world and can interact with others who are virtually present; the use of narrative and symbolism creates credible, engaging situations (Dawley & Dede, 2013). Head-mounted displays can add sensory immersion to induce virtual presence (place illusion), the feeling that you are at a location in the virtual world (Slater, 2009).

Immersion aids motivation and learning in some ways, but used indiscriminately it can undercut understanding. For example, in mastering complex knowledge and sophisticated skills, students learn well in a cycle in which first they prepare for an experience that involves doing something they want to master, then they attempt that performance, then they observe the results of that attempt, and finally they assess what went well, what did not, why, and what they need to learn in order to execute a more successful repetition of the cycle (Kolb, 1984). Immersion is helpful in the acting and observing parts of the cycle, but unless used carefully it can interfere with the planning and reflecting parts of the cycle, which require metacognition that the sensory immediacy of the virtual environment can overwhelm. This—and numerous other factors—makes effective instructional design for immersive learning complicated.

Psychological immersion in completely virtual settings or in mixed reality (partially digital) contexts enables situated learning. Mastering knowledge and skills takes place in the same or a similar context to the target context to which it will later be applied, and the setting itself tacitly helps to develop skills through experience and modeling. For example, in a medical internship, both the contextual supports and the team activities in a hospital surgical operating room promote situated understanding.

Situated learning requires authentic settings, activities, and assessments linked to guidance that involves coaching, modeling, mentoring, and "legitimate peripheral participation" (Wenger, 1998). As an example of legitimate peripheral participation, graduate students work within the laboratories of expert researchers, who model the practice of scholarship. Novice students interact in research with colleagues who understand the sophisticated processes of scholarship to varying degrees. While in these settings of authentic practice, students gradually move from novice researchers to more advanced roles, developing skills and evolving expectations for their performance.

Related to situated learning is embodied cognition, an instructional strategy positing that retrieving a concept from memory and reasoning about it is enhanced by creating a mental, perceptual, and psychomotor simulation of it (Barsalou, 2008). For example, research shows that second-grade students who acted out stories about farms using toy farmers, workers, animals, and objects increased their understanding and memory of the narrative. Steps involving grounded cognition as a strategy for learning include having an embodied experience (which could be created by immersive interfaces), learning to imagine that embodied experience as a mental perceptual simulation, and imagining that experience when learning from symbolic materials, thus bridging from the concrete to the abstract.

Potentially quite powerful, situated learning is seldom used in formal instruction because creating tacit, relatively unstructured learning in complex real-world settings is difficult. However, MUVE, augmented reality (AR), and mixed reality (MR) experiences can draw on the power of situated learning by creating immersive, authentic experiences with problems, roles, and settings similar to or embedded in the real world (Dede, Jacobson, & Richards, 2017). In particular, these immersive interfaces provide the capability to create communities in which participants can gain knowledge and skills through interacting with other participants who have varied levels of skills, enabling legitimate peripheral participation driven by social and collaborative interactions.

Situated learning is important in part because of the crucial issue of transfer. Transfer is the application of knowledge learned in one situation to another situation, demonstrated if instruction on a learning task leads to improved performance on a transfer task, typically a skilled performance in a real-world setting. For example, statistical reasoning learned in a classroom can potentially aid with purchasing insurance or interpreting weather forecasts. A major criticism of instruction today is the low rate of transfer generated by conventional instruction. Even students who excel in school or training settings often are unable to apply what they have learned to similar real-world contexts. Situated learning addresses this challenge by making the setting in which learning takes place similar to the real-world context for performance in work or personal life. Learning in well-designed digital contexts can lead to replication in the real world of behaviors successful in simulated environments (Fraser et al., 2012; Grotzer, Metcalf, Tutwiler, Kamarainen, Thompson, & Dede, 2017; Harrington, 2011; Mayer, Dale, Fraccastoro, & Moss, 2011; Norman, Dore, & Grierson, 2012).

Moreover, the evolution of an individual's or group's identity is an important type of learning for which simulated experiences situated in immersive interfaces are well suited (Gee, 2003; Turkle, 1997). Reflecting on and refining an individual identity is often a significant issue for students of all ages, and learning to evolve group and organizational identity is a crucial skill in enabling innovation and in adapting to shifting contexts. Identity "play" through trying on various representations of the self and the group in virtual environments provides a means for different sides of a person or team to find common ground and the opportunity for synthesis and evolution (Laurel, 1993; Murray, 1998).

Immersion is important in this process of identity exploration because virtual identity is unfettered by physical attributes such as gender, race, and disabilities (Slater, 2009). A related attribute that makes immersive learning different, and potentially more powerful than real-world learning, is the ability to create interactions and activities in mediated experience that are not possible in the real world. These include, for example, teleporting within a virtual environment, enabling a distant person to see a real-time image of your local environment, or interacting with a (simulated) chemical spill in a busy public setting.

In our EcoLearn design-based research, we draw on these and other principles from the learning sciences, as illustrated by the three curricula described next.

ECOMUVE

The EcoMUVE middle grades curriculum focuses on the potential of immersive authentic simulations for teaching ecosystems science concepts, scientific inquiry (collaborative and individual), and complex causality (Metcalf, Kamarainen, Tutwiler, Grotzer, & Dede, 2011; Grotzer, Kamarainen, Tutwiler, Metcalf, & Dede, 2013; Metcalf et al., 2018). The curriculum has two MUVE-based modules, which center on pond and forest virtual ecosystems. Each module consists of ten 45-minute lessons and represents an ecological scenario involving complex causality. The curriculum is inquiry-based; students investigate research questions by exploring the virtual ecosystem and collecting data from a variety of sources over time, assuming roles as ecosystems scientists.

Overall, EcoMUVE enables internship-like experiences in immersive simulated ecosystems that support authentic scientific practices, including collaborative inquiry, with the teacher and peers providing mentoring on performance. The description below focuses on the EcoMUVE Pond curricular module; the Forest module is similar in its curricular approach.

The Learning Objectives of EcoMUVE Pond

EcoMUVE Pond represents a pond and its surroundings, including a nearby golf course and housing development. Students visit the pond over a number of virtual days, using their avatars to explore, see realistic organisms in their natural habitats, chat with other members of their research team, and collect water, weather, and population data. This avatar-based immersion can occur from either a first-person or third-person perspective.

During a virtual summer, changes occur within the pond. These changes are subtle but detectable both visually and through measurements of water quality variables. Eventually, an easily discernable "event" occurs—the larger fish in the pond die overnight. Known as a fish kill, it may be viewed as part of a larger process in play or as an event that grabs one's attention and requires explanation.

In most problem-based scenarios, students are given the problem to solve. However, in EcoMUVE they need to discern it. This design feature was included to help students learn the importance of focusing on processes and change over time. As students time-travel over 6 virtual weeks, they may notice the subtle visual changes as the water clarity shifts and fish swim closer to the surface. Eventually the fish kill captures students' attention.

EcoMUVE Pond simulates an extreme eutrophication scenario in which the proximal cause of the fish kill is low dissolved oxygen concentrations in the pond during a particularly warm and windless night, but the ultimate cause is the process of eutrophication driven by excessive fertilizer runoff followed by algae growth and decomposition. As they examine the virtual world, students learn about processes that lead to an increase (e.g., photosynthesis and mixing) or decrease (respiration, in particular bacterial respiration, and warming temperatures) in dissolved oxygen concentrations in a pond. To fully understand the fish kill, students must also recognize distant drivers of change, like fertilizer that was applied in the watershed and washed into the pond during a recent rainstorm.

The following affordances for recognizing change over time and process-oriented versus event-based causality are built into EcoMUVE. A time-traveling calendar tool allows students to go back and forth in time to see the subtle changes that they may have missed. They may talk to residents or collect data and clues. Data they've collected is stored in a table so that they can analyze temporal trends using a built-in graphing function. They can use digital tools (an Atom Tracker and a Food Web) that support understanding the flows of matter and of energy through the ecosystem.

The curriculum supports students' learning about typical ranges for water quality measurements and helps students see how ecological processes and interactions result in variation in the measurements over time. Students conclude the unit by constructing concept maps, which represent their understanding of the ecosystem components related to the fish kill, and are asked to support the relationships they've identified with evidence they've collected.

Immersive Features of the MUVE-Based Pond Curriculum

Moving through the Pond virtual environment offers an opportunity to realize its features (Figure 9.1). Avatars can walk uphill to the housing development and down along a drainage ditch where water is flowing into the pond; this provides a way to reinforce students' perceptions of the topography, which is very important in understanding the dynamics of a watershed.

FIGURE 9.1 Students can collect water, weather, and population data, as well as chat with members of their research team.

Virtual agents (for instance, a park ranger, a local dog walker, and a landscaper) offer pieces of information. Physical artifacts, such as a bag of fertilizer, also provide valuable data. Linked visual representations reinforce abstract concepts (Kamarainen, Metcalf, Grotzer, & Dede, 2015);

students can measure pond turbidity and link the measurements to their experiences by seeing how murky the water looks on different days). Using a "submarine" tool, they can also shrink to microscope size to see organisms within the pond that are invisible at normal scale (Figure 9.2). The submarine tool is implemented so that students can travel directly up and down in the pond and zoom to observe organisms at various levels of magnification.

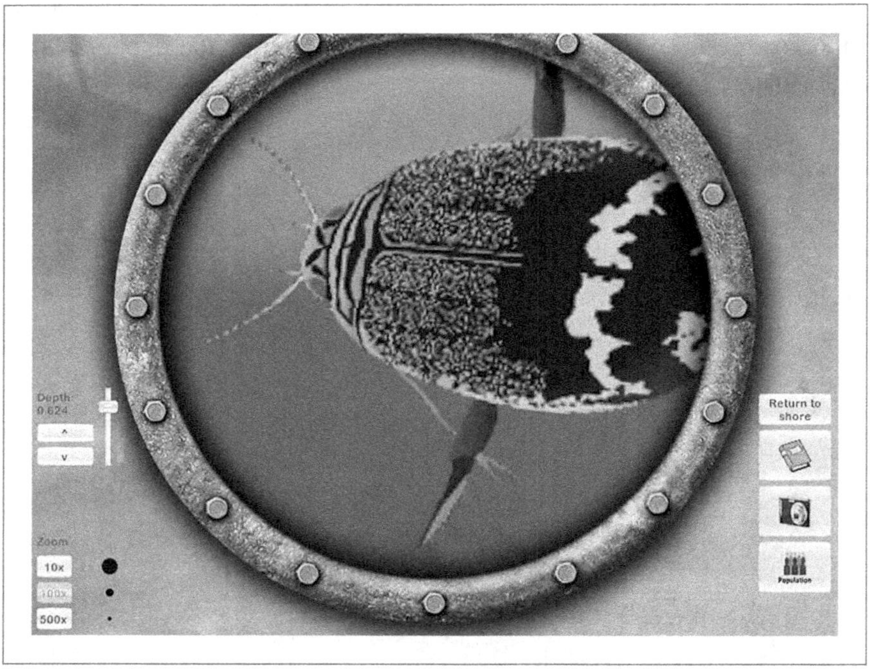

FIGURE 9.2 The submarine tool allows students to see and identify microscopic organisms.

Students measure environmental variables to collaboratively complete a Data Table that numerically reveals changes over time; they can then display longitudinal graphs showing correlations among the data they have collected (Figure 9.3).

Based on entries in the Field Guide from organisms they have found, students can also construct a Food Web to show the flow of energy through the ecosystem. In addition, they can view an Atom Tracker feature to show the flow of matter over time (Figure 9.4). Both of these dynamics, not apparent through sensory information, are important in understanding the

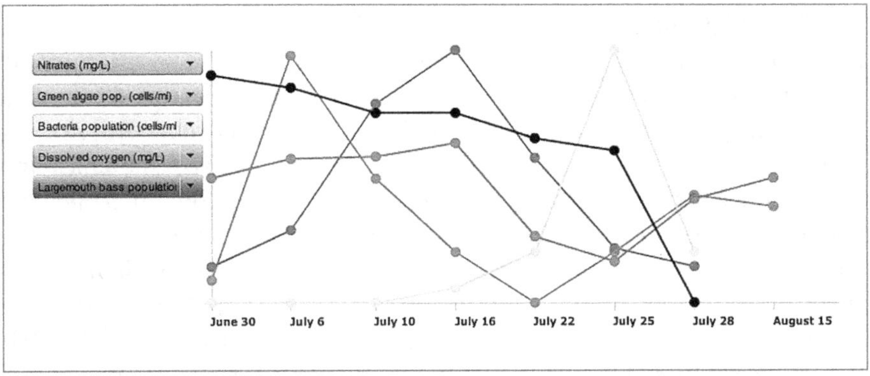

FIGURE 9.3 Graphs display correlations in how variables change over time.

causality of ecosystems. Students can use six interactive learning quests, implemented outside the virtual world, to learn more about content related to pond dynamics (Chlorophyll α, Turbidity, pH, Nitrates and Phosphates, Dissolved Oxygen, and Bacteria).

FIGURE 9.4 An oxygen molecule describes a stage of its journey through the ecosystem.

The Pond curriculum uses a "jigsaw" pedagogy; students work in teams of four and are given complementary roles (naturalist, microscopic specialist, water chemist, private investigator). Each student performs data collection specific to his or her role in the virtual pond ecosystem, sharing these data with teammates within the immersive interface via tables and graphs. Each team works collaboratively to analyze the combined data and understand the ecosystem relationships. The curriculum culminates in each team creating an evidence-based concept map representing their understanding of the causal relationships in the ecosystem and presenting it to the class (Figure 9.5). A video showing the "look and feel" of EcoMUVE is available at http://ecolearn.gse.harvard.edu/ecoMUVE/video.php.

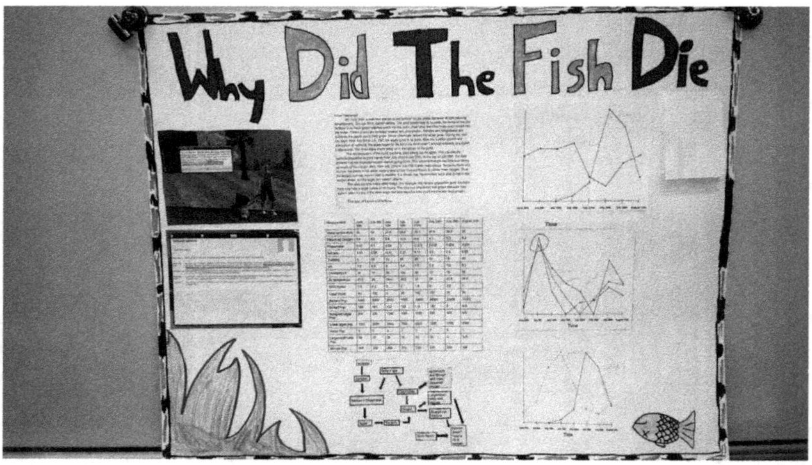

FIGURE 9.5 Team's explanation including data and concept map.

When students have collected all of the data, they will start to notice patterns in the graphs of the data over time. Students may notice changes in phosphates, nitrates, chlorophyll α, oxygen, turbidity, weather variables, and population sizes. These changes are related to one another, and many of these changes give hints about what caused the fish to die.

In order to put the pieces of the puzzle together, students are asked to examine what variables have changed over time. In efforts to explain why these changes are happening in the pond, the students will draw on observations and information they have gathered elsewhere in the environment. The EcoMUVE environment provides an open forum in which students can use scientific inquiry to pursue their own path of discovery. Below we provide a few potential paths by which students could uncover important parts of the fish kill story.

As the students visit the pond on different days, most notice dramatic changes in the color of the pond. By talking to one of the people in the world, the students find out that the pond is not usually so green. Students may wonder what is causing the pond to be so green. By using the water measurement tools and the submarine, students will learn the connection between the green color and the tiny floating plants (algae) in the pond. They realize that the pond is so green because the algae population has increased.

Using the data tools, students may also notice that the level of the phosphates changed quite a bit over time. As students try to understand why the phosphate concentration changes over time, they may notice that the fertilizer that is being used in the watershed contains phosphate. During their first visit, they see the landscaper preparing to apply a fresh load of fertilizer to the lawns near the pond. Students who visit the pond on July 6th will notice that there is plenty of rain falling near the pond.

Reading the information on the fertilizer bag, and gathering information from the Atom Tracker tool, students will learn that phosphates that have not been used by plants can be washed off of the ground when it rains. The Atom Tracker tool will also help students recognize the critical role that phosphate plays in supporting the growth of plant populations. Thus, students will discover that phosphates likely had something to do with why the algae population increased.

Using the population tool, or observing organisms in the submarine, students may notice a dramatic change in the number of bacteria that are in the pond. The bacteria population increases manyfold just days before the dead fish are found. Because many students recognize that bacteria can cause diseases, some students may think that the bacteria caused the fish kill. When students use the Field Guide to learn more about bacteria, they will find out that many bacteria that live in ponds are decomposers. Students may begin to think of the increase in bacteria as an effect rather than a cause. Students will learn more about the role of bacteria through the Atom Tracker and Field Guide and find out that bacteria thrive on dead plants and animals. Students will also discover that bacteria use a lot of oxygen during the process of decomposition. With this new information, the decline in oxygen on July 25 begins to make sense.

Students may also notice that not all the fish died between July 25 and July 28. On July 28, students can still find fathead minnows in the pond. If students use the Field Guide to learn more about fathead minnows, the students will find that these fish happen to be tolerant of high temperatures, high turbidity, and low oxygen concentrations. This may give students a clue about the variables that might have caused the other fish to die. The change in dissolved oxygen that immediately precedes the fish kill may be a strong connection that draws the students' attention. Further, the Atom Tracker tool will give the students clues about the importance of dissolved oxygen for fish health.

Thus, in keeping with authentic science, there are multiple pathways that students may take as they discover components that contribute to the fish kill. Rich hints and clues are provided through each of the tools and nonplayer character interactions built into the MUVE.

The final part of the EcoMUVE involves students in generating multiple possible explanations and working as a group to decide which hypothesis best explains the fish kill. The process of exploring multiple explanations challenges students to support their ideas with evidence; the teacher provides guidance as needed to accomplish this. The group discussion will also help students construct an understanding of the pond ecosystem that incorporates the complex causal relationships highlighted above. Each group must then present their best, most-detailed explanation, along with supporting evidence, to the rest of the class.

Overall, the curriculum offers complementary opportunities for observational fieldwork. A teachers' guide is available for helping students learn via the EcoMUVE curriculum, including an overview of the ecosystems content, causal understanding goals, pedagogical methods, technical information, and a detailed day-by-day lesson plan (Metcalf, Kamarainen, Tutwiler, Grotzer, & Dede, 2013).

Our research measures include students' motivation to do science and feelings of self-efficacy about their abilities as scientists, students' understanding of ecosystems science content and practices, students' abilities to perform individual and collaborative scientific inquiry, and students' understanding of complex causality (Metcalf et al., 2014; Chen, Metcalf, & Tutwiler, 2014; Chen, Tutwiler, Metcalf, Kamarainen, Grotzer, & Dede, 2016; Grotzer et al., 2013; Kamarainen et al., 2015; Metcalf, Kamarainen, Torres, Grotzer & Dede, 2018). We also have studied teachers' perceptions of the practicality and effectiveness of the EcoMUVE curriculum (Metcalf et al., 2016). We have found significant gains in all the factors listed above (Metcalf, Kamarainen, Torres, Grotzer, & Dede, 2018). (For reasons of space, the detailed results of the numerous studies we have conducted on EcoMUVE are referenced in our citations rather than summarized here.)

ECOXPT

EcoMUVE is a first-generation ecosystems science curriculum that focuses on the observational methods of ecosystems science. We later designed and developed EcoXPT as a second-generation, more complex curriculum that builds on EcoMUVE but adds new components to the digital ecosystem and includes six types of experimental and investigative tools authentic to ecosystems science, enabling students to reason about causes (Dede, Grotzer, Kamarainen, & Metcalf, 2017). In addition to the environmental features in EcoMUVE Pond, a farm, a second pond, a second housing development, and a stream have been added. While immersed in the virtual world, students can assess the slope of the land, thereby gaining a tacit understanding of landscape topography and the boundaries between watersheds. They can further explore the influence of slope on the transport of materials through the ecosystem by using a "tracer tool" to track where water, and the fertilizer it carries, flows on a rainy day. Water flows in a variety of directions, and determining this becomes important in understanding the causes of the fish kill. Students collect environmental and population data over time and conduct a variety of experiments in the virtual ecosystem. Teams of students construct hypotheses, supporting their arguments with data and experimental results.

Reasoning in purely observational environments, like EcoMUVE Pond, tends to be inferential, based on visual information, measurements, and correlations observed over time. In EcoXPT, we are studying whether the ability to conduct experiments in order to test various causal hypotheses about variables and relationships will support students in evidence-based reasoning. Further, by situating the simulated experimental tools within the context of the virtual ecosystem, we are studying whether students can adopt more sophisticated approaches to investigation that mirror the thinking moves that ecosystem scientists use when investigating environmental problems. We hypothesize that EcoXPT will give students opportunities to extend their observational learning by applying their experimental findings to building hypotheses about the ecosystem scenario.

EcoXPT invites students into immersive experimentation with multidimensional experiences situated in an unfolding eutrophication scenario in which students learn new information through their observations over space and time, from virtual characters in the world, and from gathering information in the field guide and other sources. As with EcoMUVE, multiple varied forms of representation convey perceptual and graphical data, but EcoXPT also makes experimental data available to the students, allowing them to intervene and manipulate certain variables, enabling them to systematically investigate relationships between variables. The use and interpretation of varied forms of representation is further supported by two more new features in EcoXPT, a digital notebook and a concept mapping tool, which help students integrate various forms of evidence into their scientific arguments. EcoXPT illustrates the capacity of immersive simulations to enable extended, multidimensional, authentic experiences based on principles from the learning sciences. Videos showing the "look and feel" of EcoXPT are available at https://ecolearn.gse.harvard.edu/ecoXPT/video.php.

EcoXPT Enables Students to Use the Tools and the Inquiry Practices of Ecosystem Scientists

The learning sciences emphasize helping students to understand that science is not just a body of facts to be memorized, but also a set of practices used collaboratively to expand on what is known about the natural world. EcoXPT supports this integration of knowledge and practice by promoting engagement in use of scientific tools, while aiding reflection on the value of using those tools in conjunction with larger investigative strategies in order to develop and support an evidence-based argument.

EcoXPT tools that illustrate situated experimentation include:

- ***Tolerance Tanks***. Students adjust the levels of an environmental factor, such as fertilizer, in three tanks containing different species of fish (e.g., minnow, bluegill), to determine the level (if any) at which each type of fish is affected by that factor (Figure 9.6).

- ***Tracers.*** Chemical markers show the movement of matter in the environment. Adding tracers to bags of fertilizer lets students test how the spatial layout and topography affect fertilizer runoff when it rains.

- ***Comparison Tanks.*** Students configure one to three tanks with experimental factors and collect measurements—e.g., discovering that a tank with algae has a higher dissolved oxygen level than one without algae.

- ***Weather Simulator.*** This enables students to model the effect of various environmental factors (e.g., wind, temperature) on the level of dissolved oxygen in water (Figure 9.7).

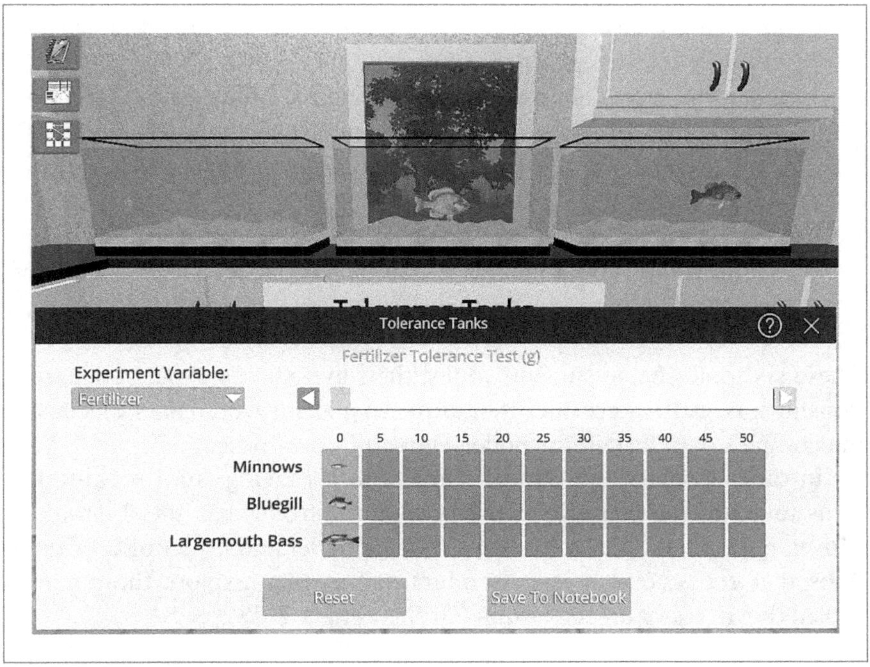

FIGURE 9.6 Tolerance Tank tool

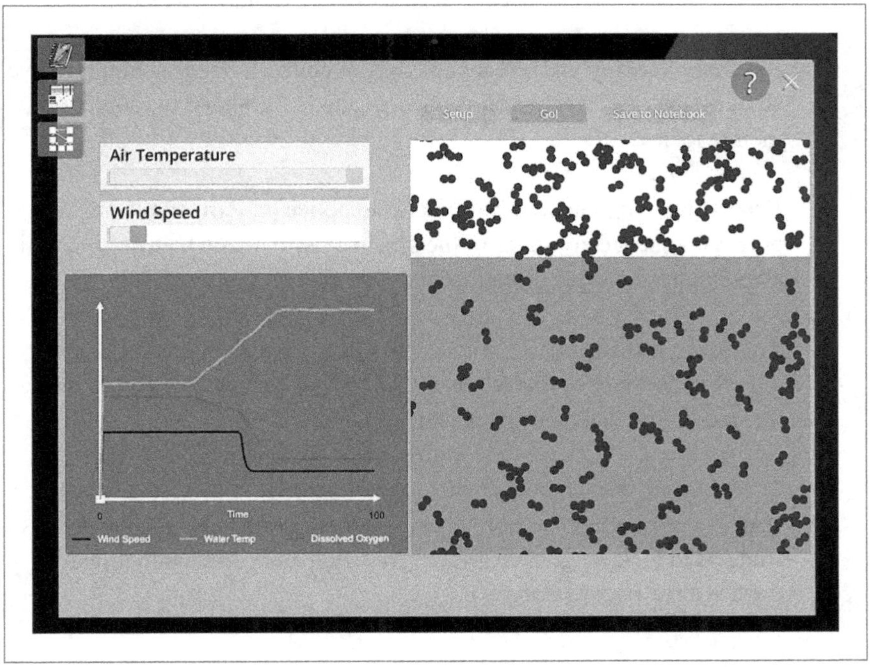

FIGURE 9.7 Weather Simulator

- ***Mesocosms*** are containers in an outside location that provide a smaller environment that is similar to the pond. This enables the investigator to assess the impact of variables of interest (e.g., addition of fertilizer) in addition to environmental factors (e.g., sunlight, weather) in ways that more closely mirror the pond than small, indoor tolerance and comparison tanks can.

- ***Sensor Buoy***. A buoy immersed in the pond provides a steady stream of data about water quality over time.

These six tools enable students to test their hypotheses about simple relationships as well as conduct multidimensional measurements that reveal the complex causality in the pond's dynamics over time.

In order to learn the thinking inherent in moving from seeking patterns to analyzing causality, the curriculum introduces a set of Thinking Moves posters and videos to help students understand the kinds of questions that ecosystems scientists might ask as they explore the potential causal dynamics of an ecosystem (Grotzer et al., 2017):

- ***Deep Seeing*** encourages students to consider the natural history of the ecosystem and to engage in careful observation of what is there. It asks them to look while being careful to set their assumptions aside.

- ***Evidence Seeking*** encourages students to collect evidence from multiple sources, to seek corroborating evidence, and to evaluate the sources of their evidence.

- ***Pattern Seeking*** encourages students to notice patterns in the ongoing processes and steady states of the system and to notice how certain variables change together or not.

- ***Analyzing Causality*** asks students to use experimental evidence and intervention to try to impact change in the patterns in an effort to discern the underlying mechanisms at work.

- ***Constructing Explanations*** encourages students to develop the best "story" or explanation that they can from the available evidence. It asks students to look for gaps in their explanation and to assess their explanations against rival explanations.

Early Research Results on Effectiveness

Studies of a full version of EcoXPT in terms of its usability and effectiveness in classroom settings are now being conducted. Below are summarized findings from pilot studies on earlier, partial versions of the curriculum. In 2016, a pilot study of EcoXPT was conducted with four teachers who taught a total of 14 classes of seventh-grade students (N = 280) using an early version of the 2.5 week curriculum (Metcalf, Kamarainen, Grotzer, & Dede, 2016; Thompson, Kamarainen, Tutwiler, Metcalf, Grotzer, & Dede, 2016). Data collected included a pre-post content survey measuring content knowledge in ecosystems science, consistent with the US Next Generation Science Standards (National Research Council, 2013) for this grade level, as well as the students' final presentations, which included concept maps hypothesizing causal relationships. The pre-post content survey (Thompson et al., 2016) found statistically significant gains ($t_{188} = 9.5045$, $p < 0.001$) in ecosystem science content knowledge. This provides evidence that the learning sciences precepts used were successful in enhancing students' knowledge of ecosystems science concepts, as well as their understanding of complex causality.

Quotes from student presentations demonstrate ways in which students drew conclusions from their experiments:

- "An experiment we did in the mesocosms showed that the bacteria ate the dead matter which is the dead plants. Bacteria is able to do respiration so the bacteria uses the dissolved oxygen. So the bacteria use all of the limited dissolved oxygen, so both the bacteria and the fish die."

- "We used tracers to trace the fertilizer, the fertilizer ran off of the ground and into the pond. When the fertilizer got to the pond it caused the algae to grow, because the algae are plants."

Digital concept maps representing teams' hypotheses illustrate sophisticated learning about the ecosystem relationships and evidence-based reasoning about causal mechanisms. This type of evidence-based reasoning indicates the success of design strategies based on the learning sciences in achieving strong student outcomes (Metcalf, Reilly, Kamarainen, King, Grotzer, & Dede, 2018). Process data from longitudinal log files as the digital concept maps are constructed helps us analyze students' stages of understanding.

Two studies using mixed-methods analyses (including log file data, video, and think-aloud interviews) about students' use of and strategies toward experimentation using a set of virtual experimental fish tanks revealed diverse strategies for experimentation (Thompson et al., 2016) and found that students used more expert strategies for experimentation over time (Metcalf, Kamarainen, Grotzer, & Dede, 2016). These cases provided a rich basis for developing supports for effective design of virtual experiments that support development of both conceptual knowledge related to important ecosystem relationships, as well as support for more effective and appropriate strategies for experimentation (Grotzer et al., 2017). These findings indicate the value of designing learning sciences principles into EcoXPT.

ECOMOBILE

The EcoMOBILE project explored the unique affordances of AR, as well as the capabilities of data collection probeware, to support setting-enhanced learning in environmental science education (Kamarainen et al., 2013). The EcoMOBILE curriculum is a blend of the EcoMUVE learning experiences with field-based activities. The ability to understand ecosystems is enriched by experiences in real environments, and combining the MUVE with real-world experiences offers powerful opportunities for situated application of classroom knowledge, thus opening the door to transfer (Grotzer et al., 2014).

The focus of the Ecosystems Mobile Outdoor Blended Immersive Learning Environment (EcoMOBILE) project was to design and study a set of learning experiences in which students use mobile broadband devices (smartphones, tablets) to access virtual information and simulated experiences while outside, immersed in real, local ecosystems. EcoMOBILE developed outdoor AR experiences in which information, simulations, and videos were superimposed on through-the-camera-lens views of natural phenomena.

In EcoMOBILE activities, the technology components have included an AR experience running on wireless-enabled mobile devices, along with either water measurement test kits or environmental probes. The AR experiences can be accessed from mobile devices (smartphones or tablets) with wireless connectivity and GPS capabilities. Location-based triggers are placed on a map of the physical setting, and these hotspots become accessible to students at the real location in the field (Figure 9.8). At a location-based trigger, students can experience AR visualizations overlaid on the real environment, as well as interactive media including text, images, audio, video, 3-D models, and multiple-choice or open-ended questions (Kamarainen, Metcalf, Grotzer, Brimhall, & Dede, 2016). Students also used probeware to collect real-world data, just as ecosystem scientists would (Figure 9.9, see next page). A video showing the "look and feel" of EcoMOBILE is available at http://ecolearn.gse.harvard.edu/ecoMOBILE/video.php.

FIGURE 9.8 A green location-based trigger showing the direction and distance to the next location.

EcoMOBILE explored the utility of AR and mobile technologies to support the following themes related to the learning sciences:

- Offering situated support for student engagement in authentic ecosystem science inquiry and investigation
- Symbolic representations of data and scientific phenomena that help students "see the unseen" and connect multiple representations to make sense of phenomena across scales and context

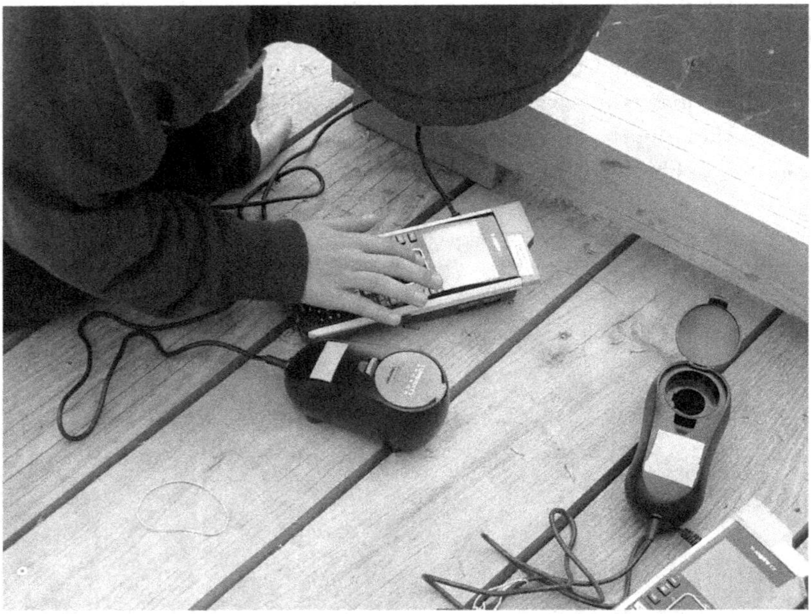

FIGURE 9.9 Collecting water quality data on turbidity using digital probes.

- Scaffolded reflection and targeted prompting to promote the transfer of thinking moves and habits of mind from the classroom context to the real world

While inquiry-based activities and the freedom they grant are valuable, it is easy for students to get lost or confused without some amount of guidance during the process. The step-by-step procedures many learners are used to following in "cookbook" laboratory activities are too restrictive, but simply being left unguided at a pond for an hour would not result in optimal learning for students. Providing the right amount of scaffolding for each learner is difficult in a classroom, and it is much more challenging in a field trip with learners spread out and investigating different phenomena or questions. EcoMOBILE provides sufficient structure to stay on-task and focused but not too much that would stifle creativity and inquisitiveness. Hints and definitions of terms are only a few clicks away at any point in the activity, and points of reflection and synthesis are provided for students to think about their investigation and what they've uncovered thus far.

Using EcoMOBILE, we aimed to help students to see an ecosystem "through the eyes of an ecologist." Ecologists bring to bear sophisticated background knowledge and powerful thinking moves when they observe or study natural systems (Eberbach & Crowley, 2008; Kamarainen & Grotzer, 2019). These perspectives can help scientists identify patterns, notice the unusual, foreground relevant information, and put their observations in the context of the cycles and seasons that are typical of a place. Students who have completed EcoMUVE or EcoXPT get an introduction to these powerful perspectives, and EcoMOBILE provides a situated experience in which students can apply their knowledge to the real world.

Augmented reality has been shown to support student engagement in scientific practices, like inquiry (Dunleavy, Dede, & Mitchell, 2009; Kamarainen et al. 2013; Klopfer & Squire, 2008), and also supports the logistics involved in delivering outdoor learning experiences (Dunleavy et al., 2009; Kamarainen et al., 2013). Having learning take place in real world settings can lead to more positive attitudes about nature and a more direct connection to students' local environment, but it can also result in distraction, a lack of focus, and an overwhelming amount of information to process.

Augmented reality can support learning through revealing hidden or invisible aspects of a system and linking multiple representations or visualizations of a phenomenon across scales. Dunleavy and Dede (2014) refer to using AR to "see the unseen" as a general principle for designing impactful AR for learning. Prior research shows that helping students to notice and reflect upon processes that are responsible for patterns and change in natural systems can support students in shifting from static or event-based notions of causality toward process-based explanations (Grotzer et al. 2013; Lindgren & Moshell, 2011). Location-based AR can prompt students to observe an object, pattern, or phenomenon that they might not otherwise notice—for example, a nesting cavity created by a woodpecker, or a pile of scat left behind by a deer. Eberbach and Crowley (2008) describe that scientific observation is more challenging than generally appreciated and requires coordination of disciplinary knowledge, the scientific practice of observation, and the application of one's attention. Novices often don't know what to look for, so they may quickly give up or overlook interesting aspects of the world around them. AR can be used to alert students to an opportunity to observe something meaningful that connects with ideas they've been learning about in class; and tips, reminders, and reflective prompts embedded in the experience can encourage students to adopt practices of observation that mirror those used by experts (Dunleavy & Dede, 2014; Klopfer & Squire, 2008; Grotzer et al., 2015).

AR can also be used to overlay or link multiple representations of a system or phenomenon (Zimmerman & Land, 2014; Kamarainen et al., 2016). Many ecological changes are driven by organisms or processes that are too small to see, while emergent patterns or outcomes may be best visualized from a whole system perspective. Prior research shows that when making sense of scientific visualizations, students benefit from viewing multiple forms of representation (Wu & Shah, 2004; Ainsworth, 1999), engaging in metacognition and reflection related to the visualizations (Wu & Shah, 2004; Chang, Quintana, & Krajcik, 2009), and making links among representations (Wu & Shah, 2004). Augmented reality can support this by juxtaposing multiple representations or overlaying them with a physical pattern or phenomenon, which allows the user to easily connect and compare the representations without having to hold one in mind while accessing a second (Radu, 2014; Tang, Owen, Biocca, & Mou, 2003; Pathomaree & Charoenseang, 2005).

AR visualizations can be used to communicate changes over time by embedding views or narratives that describe the history of a place (Zimmerman & Land, 2014; Grotzer et al., 2014), or by pointing to evidence of change over time that may be present within the landscape. Using AR to provide visitors with time lapse, before-and-after, or "what if it were winter" views of a place that they may only visit once can provide a powerful shift in perspective.

By introducing and overlaying virtual information on top of these real-world settings, we can direct student attention to specific features that may not even be visible with the naked eye or may occur over long periods of time. Instead of adding a source of distraction (as many teachers fear when using technology with their students), the mobile device ends up focusing students' attention, increasing their engagement, and guiding their inquiry. Far from being detrimental, the addition of technology to the field trip helps maximize learning gains in a set amount of time with minimal distraction from the cognitive load of having too much to see or observe. The EcoMOBILE activity allows students and teachers to reap the benefits of real-world, situated learning while minimizing the potential downsides. By supporting authentic engagement in ecosystem science practices as well as carrying forward symbolic representations of scientific phenomenon, the EcoMOBILE activities are carefully designed to support transfer of classroom ideas into the broader world. Our work has shown that it is critical to consider the type of cueing and prompts that are integrated into the AR experience to support students in making connections across contexts (Grotzer et al., 2014; Kamarainen et al., 2018).

We designed EcoMOBILE activities to maintain some symbolic and conceptual congruence between the tools available in the virtual and real worlds during inquiry. These tools were designed to help students consider and apply practices and habits of mind they were exposed to in the classroom. For example, the virtual water measurement tools students are exposed to in EcoMUVE include dissolved oxygen, temperature, turbidity, pH, and phosphate and nitrate probes. While on an EcoMOBILE field trip, students use handheld probes to measure dissolved oxygen, temperature, and turbidity. Meanwhile, the Atom Tracker tool in EcoMUVE allows students to track carbon, oxygen, and phosphorus atoms through the virtual world, while the EcoMOBILE Atom Tracker module allows students to track virtual atoms through the real world. Finally, EcoMOBILE explored the use of Virtual Binoculars and a Time Transporter tool to help students reason through causal complexity by encouraging them to think about distant as well as local causes, and to think about changes over long periods of time (Grotzer et al., 2014).

Overview of EcoMOBILE Modules

A set of three-to-five-day curricular units, coupled with teacher professional development, were created to understand the strengths and limits of AR, as well as to develop effective instructional design strategies for this type of learning. For each EcoMOBILE unit, students' outcomes in motivation and learning were studied. The goal was to enhance the educational achievements of students and teachers while adding to the knowledge of designers, researchers, and practitioners about effective practices in motivation, instruction, and learning.

Most of the EcoMOBILE experiences were designed to complement the EcoMUVE curriculum discussed earlier. Learning in EcoMUVE includes a supported introduction to ecosystem science inquiry within immersive simulated ecosystems designed to help students learn the systems dynamics and causal complexity inherent in ecosystems processes. In conjunction with EcoMUVE, the EcoMOBILE curricula allow students to synthesize and share information that they collect in the field; to visit geo-referenced locations to access important ecosystems information; and to engage with simulations that illustrate aspects of causal complexity. As discussed by Grotzer and colleagues (2014), a study contrasting two science classes of fifth and sixth graders (n = 38) found that the class that used EcoMUVE and then EcoMOBILE transferred their learning to the real world, but both classes made substantial gains in their use of EcoMOBILE at the pond.

Collectively, the EcoMOBILE activities offer new visions for learning. They offer ways of supporting student inquiry as students grapple with real-world data and the messiness of their inherent complexity and variability. Our findings indicate that augmented realities such as EcoMOBILE enhance learning in the real world by offering prompts, multiple representations, scaffolding graphics, and other guidance that collectively give students a deep understanding of the ecosystems dynamics. By aiding understanding of the real world through using digital devices, our research places learning in authentic contexts, so students no longer need to learn to apply concepts to settings outside the classroom on their own. Our research shows that augmenting reality, placing learning in authentic contexts, and offering scaffolds as students are learning all have a significant positive impact on their educational outcomes, including their motivation in STEM (science, technology, engineering, and mathematics).

Providing extended, mentored real-world activities outside classrooms is difficult, particularly for younger students. AR and mobile, just-in-time scaffolding, such as that provided by EcoMOBILE, offer opportunities for students to access expert knowledge and habits of mind in relevant disciplines. This offers many more students the chance to develop knowledge, skills, and motivation for a STEM career.

Organisms and Food Webs Module

In the Organisms and Food Webs module, students embark on a series of quests at a local ecosystem to discover the relationships between types of organisms (producers, consumers, and decomposers), as well as the relationship between these organisms and their habitats and other abiotic factors. QR codes are placed in the environment to act as a trigger for the mobile devices.

The Organisms and Food Webs module provides situated support for authentic inquiry in that students engage in observation of the real world and are prompted to record observations in order to make claims about relationships among components of the ecosystem. Also, the activities support transfer between the classroom and real world, as students find real examples of producers, consumers, and decomposers, and upon returning to the classroom, integrate these into a canonical representation of a food web that represents the feeding relationships in their neighborhood ecosystem that mirrors the visual format common in middle school curricula.

Atom Tracker Module

The Atom Tracker EcoMOBILE module invites students to follow a carbon atom or an oxygen molecule through the real environment. It also includes exploring the movement of water through the water cycle with the AR app directing students to examine specific objects (the water in a pond, or the bark of a tree), observe ecosystem processes (like transpiration, photosynthesis, and respiration), providing explanations for what they see, prompting reflection on how different facets of the ecosystem relate to each other, and allowing students to document what they observe via pictures, audio, video, and text.

The Atom Tracker module focuses on supporting students in "seeing the unseen" through multiple representations of atoms and their cycles at various scales. Students physically move around the environment tracing the pathways of oxygen and carbon. Embodying the movement of molecules gives students a more dynamic perception of material cycling (Lindgren & Moshell, 2011; Rogers & Price, 2008). Atom Tracker aims to give a tacit sense that atoms and molecules, though not directly visible, are all around us. Students are prompted to look for and notice features of the environment (e.g., look for duckweed) that connect directly with the movement of their virtual atom. A QR code attached to the trunk of a tree activates an animation of photosynthesis, represented by molecules of carbon dioxide and water rearranging to form glucose and oxygen within a chloroplast (Kamarainen et al., 2016). Through layering of multiple representations—images and animations with real objects (water, trees, duckweed)—students can situate and visualize otherwise hidden processes like transpiration, photosynthesis, and respiration.

Water Quality Measurement Module

The Water Quality Measurement module invites students to collect real-world data from a pond or ponds and to observe the variation in those data. It encourages them to compare this to the "standardized" data in the EcoMUVE pond. Students look for factors that might influence their findings. Depending upon the locale, they might also compare multiple real-world ponds and consider the factors leading to variation between those ponds. This involves collecting water quality data, similar to those that students can collect in EcoMUVE, using wireless probes and sensors or water quality test kits.

Students engage in authentic approaches to scientific practice, as the experience guides students to use environmental probes to collect and make sense of their own data. These data are then displayed in a visual representation that allows the aggregation and sharing of data from multiple people, times, and locations. In our case, we used physical visual poster-based displays available in the environment. Such activities can be leveraged to support students in analyzing highly variable data and applying appropriate statistical techniques to make sense of the spatial and temporal patterns in these data.

Watershed Tour Module

The Take a Tour module helps students reflect on watersheds, the pathways water may flow in through an ecosystem, and how flowing through certain pathways may affect the quality of that water. An experience that starts out as a "Watershed Tour" led by Ranger Susan soon turns into a mystery in which the students are prompted to assist in the investigation. Students investigate the pathways for movement of water in their school's ecosystem, collect evidence of where and how water travels through that ecosystem, and build an argument about what contaminants the water might collect. The experience concludes by asking students to use information on water quality indicators and the evidence they collected on the field trip to determine what path the water followed.

The water cycle plays out in dynamic ways on real landscapes and leads to both visible and hidden aspects that are revealed and investigated during the Watershed Tour. Water pools in depressions where it can evaporate or sink into the groundwater, or during heavy rains it may rush through a stream or run off of a road carrying sediment and pollutants as it goes. Students examine the landscape for visual evidence of where water flows, documenting the slope, as well as the presence of land where water can soak into the groundwater versus surfaces that are paved and therefore over which water would run off. Finding a storm water drain leads students to view visual representations of the hidden, engineered infrastructure beneath the ground that carries water to the nearest stream. Thus, students apply the abstract ideas about the water cycle, about the shape of a landscape, evaporation, infiltration, and rainfall to the real and situated context of their backyards.

Knowing Black's Nook Module

While the other EcoMOBILE activities can be played in any ecosystem with the appropriate physical and ecological features, Knowing Black's

Nook is situated specifically at the Black's Nook pond in Cambridge, Massachusetts. Students use "thinking tools" to think about environmental cause and effect from different perspectives. "Virtual Binoculars" help students think about how distant causes (e.g., things happening in other parts of the watershed) might affect the water quality in the place they are standing. Also, a "Time Machine" helps students think about what the field trip location was like in the past and how that history might carry forward to affect what we see today.

The special virtual tools featured in Knowing Black's Nook are extensions of important causal reasoning habits of mind that students are implicitly introduced to during the EcoMUVE curriculum. Thus, Knowing Black's Nook provides an opportunity for students to explicitly apply these ecological perspectives to an ecosystem in order to better understand how things that happened far away and long ago affect it. As discussed by Grotzer and colleagues (2014), a study contrasting two science classes of fifth and sixth graders ($n = 38$) found that the class that used EcoMUVE and then EcoMOBILE transferred their learning to the real world but both classes made substantial gains in their use of EcoMOBILE at the pond. (For reasons of space, the detailed results of the numerous studies we have conducted on EcoMOBILE are referenced in our citations rather than summarized here.)

CONCLUSION

All three of the EcoLearn curricula are based on principles from the learning sciences. These include:

- Guided social constructivist theories of learning involving collaborative development of shared meaning.
- Immersive simulations involving embodied cognition and based on narratives about authentic real-world challenges, enabling identity exploration.
- Situated learning with coaching, modeling, mentoring and legitimate peripheral participation.
- Inquiry and thinking moves based on cycles of plan/attempt/observe/reflect and on evidence-based explanation.
- Scaffolding for transfer of learning.

Using modern immersive media, we have demonstrated that curricular models based on these learning sciences principles are effective for student motivation and learning. Teachers report our curricula are practical, affordable, and desirable in their classroom settings.

As described in the US National Research Council report *Education for Life and Work in the 21st Century* (National Research Council, 2012), cognitive, intrapersonal, and interpersonal dimensions of knowledge and skills are best developed in tandem. Table 9.1 categorizes a broad range of knowledge and skills vital in the 21st century according to these dimensions (Dede, 2014). In contrast to industrial-era schooling with its emphasis on multiple-choice and short-answer testing, mastery for a global, knowledge-based, innovation-centered economy requires the ability to apply knowledge and skills in real-world contexts—for which all three dimensions are important—demonstrating proficiency via effective, authentic performances. Our EcoLearn curricula serve as demonstrations of concept, showing that by applying principles from the learning sciences this type of instruction can be achieved at scale in typical classroom settings.

TABLE 9.1 Dimensions of Knowledge and Skills

COGNITIVE OUTCOMES	INTRAPERSONAL OUTCOMES	INTERPERSONAL OUTCOMES
Cognitive processes and strategies	Intellectual openness	Teamwork and collaboration
Knowledge	Work ethic and conscientiousness	Leadership
Creativity	Positive core self-evaluation	Communication
Critical thinking	Metacognition	Responsibility
Information literacy	Flexibility	Conflict resolution
Reasoning	Initiative	
Innovation	Appreciation of diversity	

REFERENCES

Ainsworth, S. (1999). The functions of multiple representations. *Computers & Education, 33*(2–3), 131–152.

Barsalou, L. W. (2008). Grounded cognition. *Annual Review of Psychology, 59*, 617–645.

Chang, H.-Y., Quintana, C., & Krajcik, J. S. (2009). The impact of designing and evaluating molecular animations on how well middle school students understand the particulate nature of matter. *Science Education*. doi:10.1002/sce.20352

Chen, J. A., Metcalf, S. J., & Tutwiler, M. S. (2014). Motivation and beliefs about the nature of scientific knowledge within an immersive virtual ecosystems environment. *Contemporary Educational Psychology, 39*(2), 112–123.

Chen, J. A., Tutwiler, M. S., Metcalf, S. J., Kamarainen, A., Grotzer, T., & Dede, C. (2016). A multi-user virtual environment to support students' self-efficacy and interest in science: A latent growth model analysis. *Learning and Instruction, 41*, 11–22.

Dawley, L., & Dede, C. (2013). Situated learning in virtual worlds and immersive simulations. In J. M. Spector, M. D. Merrill, J. Elen, & M. J. Bishop (Eds.), *Handbook of research for educational communications and technology* (4th ed., pp. 723–734). New York: Springer.

Dede, C. (2014). *The role of digital technologies in deeper learning.* New York, NY: Jobs for the Future. http://www.jff.org/publications/role-digital-technologies-deeper-learning

Dede, C., Grotzer, T., Kamarainen, A., & Metcalf, S. (2017). EcoXPT: Designing for deeper learning through experimentation in an immersive virtual ecosystem. *Educational Technology & Society, 20*(4), 166–178.

Dede, C., Jacobson, J., & Richards, J. (2017). Introduction: Virtual, augmented, and mixed realities in education. In D. Liu, C. Dede, R. Huang, & J. Richards, (Eds.). *Virtual reality, augmented reality, and mixed reality in education* (pp. 1–18). Hong Kong: Springer.

Dunleavy, M., Dede, C., & Mitchell, R. (2009). Affordances and Limitations of Immersive Participatory Augmented Reality Simulations for Teaching and Learning. *Journal of Science Education and Technology* 18, 1 (February), 7–22.

Dunleavy, M., & Dede, C. (2014). Augmented reality teaching and learning. In J. M. Spector, M. D. Merrill, J. Elen, & M. J. Bishop (Eds.), *The handbook of research on educational communications and technology* (4th ed.) (pp. 735–745). New York: Springer.

Eberbach, C., & Crowley, K. (2009). From everyday to scientific observation: How children learn to observe the biologist's world. *Review of Educational Research, 79*(1), 39–68.

Fraser, K., Ma, I., Teteris, E., Baxter, H., Wright, B., & McLaughlin, K. (2012). Emotion, cognitive load and learning outcomes during simulation training. *Medical Education, 46*(11), 1055–1062.

Gee, J. P. (2003). *What video games have to teach us about learning and literacy.* New York: Palgrave Macmillan.

Grotzer, T. A., Kamarainen, A., Tutwiler, M. S., Metcalf, S., & Dede, C. (2013). Learning to reason about ecosystems dynamics over time: The challenges of an event-based causal focus. *BioScience, 63*(4), 288–296.

Grotzer, T. A., Metcalf, S. J., Tutwiler, M. S., Kamarainen, A. M., Thompson, M., & Dede, C. (2017, April). *Teaching the systems aspects of epistemologically authentic experimentation in ecosystems through immersive virtual worlds.* San Antonio, TX: National Association for Research in Science Teaching (NARST).

Grotzer, T. A., Powell, M., Kamarainen, A. K., Courter, C., Tutwiler, M. S., Metcalf, S., & Dede, C. (2014). Turning transfer inside out: The affordances of virtual worlds and mobile devices in real world contexts for teaching about causality across time and distance in ecosystems. *Technology, Knowledge, and Learning, 19*(3). doi:10.1007/s10758-014-9241-5

Harrington, M. C. R. (2011). Empirical evidence of priming, transfer, reinforcement, and learning in the real and virtual trillium trails. *Learning Technologies, IEEE Transactions on Issue, 4*(2), 175–186.

Kamarainen, A. M., & Grotzer, T. A. (2019, July). Constructing causal understanding in complex systems: Epistemic strategies used by ecosystem scientists. BioScience, *69*(7), 533–543. https://doi.org/10.1093/biosci/biz053

Kamarainen, A., Metcalf, S., Grotzer, T. A., Brimhall, C., & Dede, C. (2016). Atom tracker: Designing a mobile augmented reality experience. *International Journal of Designs for Learning, 7*(2), 111–130.

Kamarainen, A. M., Metcalf, S., Grotzer, T., Browne, A., Mazzuca, D., Tutwiler, M. S., & Dede, C. (2013). EcoMOBILE: Integrating augmented reality and probeware with environmental education field trips. *Computers & Education, 68*, 545–556. https://doi.org/10.1016/j.compedu.2013.02.018.

Kamarainen, A., Metcalf, S., Grotzer, T., & Dede, C. J. (2015). Exploring ecosystems from the inside: How immersion in a multi-user virtual environment supports epistemologically grounded practices in ecosystem science instruction. *Journal of Science Education and Technology, 24*(2), 148–167.

Kamarainen, A. M., Thompson, M. M., Metcalf, S. J., Grotzer, T. A., Tutwiler, M. S., & Dede, C. (2018, June). Prompting connections between content and context: blending immersive virtual environments and augmented reality for environmental science learning. In D. Beck, C. Allison, L. Morgado, J. Pirker, F. Khosmood, J. Richter, & C. Gütl (Eds.), *Immersive Learning Research Network: Fourth International Conference, iLRN 2018, Missoula, Montana, June 24–29, 2018. Proceedings* (Vol. 840) (pp. 36–54). Springer.

Klopfer, E., & Squire, K. (2008). Environmental detectives: The development of an augmented reality platform for environmental simulations. *Educational Technology Research and Development, 56*(2), 203–228.

Kolb, D. A. (1984). *Experiential learning: Experience as the source of learning and development* (Vol. 1). Englewood Cliffs, NJ: Prentice-Hall.

Laurel, B. (1993). *Computers as theatre.* New York: Addison-Wesley.

Lindgren, R., & Moshell, J. M. (2011, June). Supporting children's learning with body-based metaphors in a mixed reality environment. In *Proceedings of the 10th International Conference on Interaction Design and Children* (pp. 177–180). ACM.

Mayer, B. W., Dale, K. M., Fraccastoro, K. A., & Moss, G. (2011). Improving transfer of learning: Relationship to methods of using business simulation. *Simulation & Gaming, 42*(1), 64–84.

Metcalf, S. J., Chen, J. A., Kamarainen, A. M., Frumin, K. M., Vickrey, T. L., Grotzer, T. A., & Dede, C. J. (2014). Shifts in student motivation during usage of a multi-user virtual environment for ecosystem science. *International Journal of Virtual and Personal Learning Environments, 5*(4), 1–15.

Metcalf, S. J., Kamarainen, A. M., Cooke, C. B., Turkay, S., Grotzer, T., & Dede, C. (2016). Teacher perceptions of the practicality and effectiveness of immersive ecological simulations. In K. Terry & A. Cheney (Eds.), *Utilizing virtual and personal learning environments for optimal learning* (pp. 22–45). Hershey, PA: Information Science Reference. doi:10.4018/978-1-4666-8847-6.ch002

Metcalf, S. J., Kamarainen, A. M., Grotzer, T. A., & Dede, C. J. (2016). Changes in student experimentation strategies within an inquiry-based immersive virtual environment. Paper presented at American Educational Research Association (AERA) San Antonio, TX, April–May 2016.

Metcalf, S. J., Kamarainen, A., Tutwiler M. S., Grotzer, T. A., & Dede, C. J. (2011). Ecosystem science learning via multi-user virtual environments. *International Journal of Gaming and Computer-Mediated Simulations, 3*(1), 86–90.

Metcalf, S. J., Kamarainen, A., Tutwiler, M. S., Grotzer, T. A., & Dede, C. J. (2013). Teacher perceptions of the practicality and effectiveness of immersive ecological simulations as classroom curricula. *International Journal of Virtual and Personal Learning Environments, 4*(3), 66–77.

Metcalf, S. J., Reilly, J. M., Kamarainen, A. M., King, J., Grotzer, T. A., & Dede, C. (2018, October). Supports for deeper learning of inquiry-based ecosystem science in virtual environments: Comparing virtual and physical concept mapping. *Computers in Human Behavior, 87,* 459–469.

Metcalf, S. J., & Tinker, R. F. (2004). Probeware and handhelds in elementary and middle school science. *Journal of Science Education and Technology, 13*(1), 43–49.

Metcalf, S., Kamarainen, A., Torres, E., Grotzer, T., & Dede, C. (2018). EcoMUVE: A case study on the affordances of MUVEs in ecosystems science education. In J. Qian (Ed.), *Integrating multi-user virtual environments in modern classrooms* (pp. 1–25). New York: IGI Global.

Murray, J. H. (1998). *Hamlet on the holodeck: The future of narrative in cyberspace.* Cambridge, MA: MIT Press.

National Research Council. (2012). *Education for life and work: Developing transferable knowledge and skills in the 21st century.* Washington, DC: The National Academies Press. http://www.nap.edu/catalog.php?record_id=13398

National Research Council. (2013). *Next Generation Science Standards: For States, by States.* Washington, DC: The National Academies Press. https://doi.org/10.17226/18290

Norman, G., Dore, K., & Grierson, L. (2012). The minimal relationship between simulation fidelity and transfer of learning. *Medical Education, 46*(7), 636–647.

Palincsar, A. S. (1998). Social constructivist perspectives on teaching and learning. *Annual Review of Psychology, 49*(1), 345–375.

Pathomaree, N., & Charoenseang, S. (2005). Augmented reality for skill transfer in assembly task. *IEEE International Workshop on Robot and Human Interactive Communication*, 500–504.

Radu, I. (2014). Augmented reality in education: A meta-review and cross-media analysis. *Personal and Ubiquitous Computing, 18*(6), 1533–1543.

Rogers, Y., & Price, S. (2008). The role of mobile devices in facilitating collaborative inquiry in situ. *Research and Practice in Technology Enhanced Learning, 3*(3), 209.

Slater, M. (2009). Place illusion and plausibility can lead to realistic behaviour in immersive virtual environments. *Philosophical Transactions of the Royal Society of London, 364*, 3549–3557.

Tang, A., Owen, C., Biocca, F., & Mou, W. (2003). Comparative effectiveness of augmented reality in object assembly. In *Proceedings of the Conference on Human Factors in Computing Systems—CHI '03* (p. 73).

Thompson, M., Kamarainen, A., Tutwiler, M. S., Metcalf, S., Grotzer, T., & Dede, C., (2016). *Examining middle school students' pathways through experimentation via a virtual simulation.* Paper presented at NARST, Baltimore, MD, April 2016.

Turkle, S. (1997). *Life on the screen: Identity in the age of the Internet.* New York: Simon and Schuster.

Wenger, E. (1998). *Communities of practice: Learning, meaning, and identity.* Cambridge, England: Cambridge University Press.

Wu, H. K., & Shah, P. (2004). Exploring visuospatial thinking in chemistry learning. *Science Education, 88*(3), 465–492. doi:10.1002/sce.10126

Zimmerman, H. T., & Land, S. M. (2014). Facilitating place-based learning in outdoor informal environments with mobile computers. *TechTrends, 58*(1), 77–83.

ABOUT THE AUTHORS

Chris Dede is the Timothy E. Wirth Professor in Learning Technologies at Harvard University. His fields of scholarship include emerging technologies, policy, and leadership. He is a fellow of the American Educational Research Association and has served as a visiting expert at the National Science Foundation Directorate of Education and Human Resources.

Tina Grotzer is a member of the Faculty of Education at Harvard University and a senior researcher at Project Zero where she directs the Cognition in a Complex World Lab. Her research focuses on complex causal reasoning interacts and on developing supports for learning causal complexity and understanding of science.

Amy Kamarainen is a senior research manager at the Harvard Graduate School of Education where she manages research related to both the EcoMOBILE and EcoXPT projects. She is an ecosystem scientist who holds a BS in zoology from Michigan State University and a PhD from the University of Wisconsin–Madison.

Shari Metcalf is a senior researcher at the Harvard Graduate School of Education and project director for EcoLearn. Her research centers on the design and evaluation of computer–based tools for science education using scaffolded, immersive environments in which students engage in authentic learning activities.

ACKNOWLEDGMENTS

EcoMUVE was supported by the Institute of Education Sciences, US Department of Education, grant R305A080514 to Chris Dede and Tina Grotzer, and the National Science Foundation, grant REC-0845632 to Tina Grotzer. EcoMOBILE was supported by the Qualcomm, Inc. Wireless Reach initiative, National Science Foundation grant DRL-1118530 to Chris Dede and Tina Grotzer, and Texas Instruments. EcoXPT was supported by the National Science Foundation Grant No. 1416781 to Tina Grotzer and Chris Dede. All opinions, findings, conclusions, or recommendations expressed here are those of the authors and do not necessarily reflect the views of the funders.

CHAPTER 10

MIT BLOSSOMS—High School OER STEM Lessons Leading to Deep Learning, for Students *and* Teachers

Richard C. Larson and M. Elizabeth Murray
Massachusetts Institute of Technology

ABSTRACT

The MIT BLOSSOMS program has created over 200 interactive video lessons for high school STEM teachers, for use in their classes. The technology is video, downloadable from the web, simple and sustainable in developing as well as developed countries. A BLOSSOMS lesson is shown on a screen in front of the class and moves in short 2-to-4-minute segments, each challenging the students to a STEM problem they have not seen before. After each segment, the video is turned off, and the in-class teacher guides the class through a phenomenon-motivated, inquiry-based, active learning exercise. The students experience a "Teaching Duet," with teaching done both by the BLOSSOMS video teacher and their regular teacher. To solve the challenges, students need to figure out how to apply concepts from their traditional lecture courses.

We describe the evidence-based reasons for the design of BLOSSOMS, including the full involvement of in-class teachers. We discuss the motivation and history of BLOSSOMS, as well as education "systems" issues that often inhibit educational initiatives. We conclude with two new BLOSSOMS initiatives: (1) BLOSSOMS lessons as the trigger for Project-Based Learning (PBL), as a means to challenge students even more deeply as they act and think like scientists and engineers, in addressing multifaceted complex real problems; and (2) BLOSSOMS-motivated blended Teacher Professional Learning (TPL) workshops. The efforts—PBL and TPL—are meant to help address two needed changes in our US education system: (1) adding student portfolios to high school records, the portfolios serving as new assessment vehicles for college admission and/or job application; and (2) developing new, creative ways of doing teacher "Professional Development," focused on nonlecture pedagogy that supports active, inquiry-based learning.

LEARNING IS SO MUCH MORE THAN FORMULAS, MORE THAN MEMORIZATION

An investment in knowledge pays the best interest.

—Benjamin Franklin

A Radio Land Trip

Let's start in Lake Wobegon, that fictional town in Minnesota made popular on *Prairie Home Companion*, Garrison Keillor's former national radio show (Minnesota Public Radio, 2018). At the close of each show, Keillor said, "And that's all from Lake Wobegon, where all the women are strong, all the men are good looking and *all the children are above average*." (Keillor, 2000; emphasis added). Let's ask a middle school math class: "Is it possible or impossible for all the students of Lake Wobegon to be above average?" Imagine an active classroom, where the teacher becomes mentor and coach, not lecturer. First, Mike puts on the blackboard the mathematical definition of average, a sum of *N* numbers divided *N*. There is active discussion. Virtually everyone is saying, "No, it's impossible." "But how do we demonstrate that?" Then Susan exclaims: "I've got an idea. Let's seven of us stand in front of the blackboard and arrange ourselves in a line from shortest to tallest. We find the average and we demonstrate that it's impossible! We can't all be taller than average!" The class cheers as they do the exercise and successfully show the result (Figure 10.1).

FIGURE 10.1 Blackboard demonstration that not all students can be above average height.

We thank the image copyright holder, LearnZillion, for giving permission to utilize this figure. Retrieved from https://learnzillion.com/resources/287740/

But then the teacher breaks into the class: "News flash from the *Lake Wobegon Chronicle*: Every member of the senior class of Lake Wobegon High School has graduated and each has been accepted into an Ivy League university!" She asks, "Now, is it possible for all the (senior class) students of Lake Wobegon to be above average?" At first the class seems stumped. Then Nancy says, "Wait, very few Minnesotans get into Ivy League universities! I'll bet that all the graduating seniors from Lake Wobegon are above average for Minnesota." And Carl chips in, "Right, and above average for the United States!" The class cheers again, and then the students reflect on what they have learned.

This Lake Wobegon challenge is the opening segment of an interactive video lesson of our MIT BLOSSOMS program where BLOSSOMS stands for Blended Learning Open Source Science Or Math Studies. The lesson is, *Averages, Still Flawed* (Livengood & Jordan, 2014).

A "plug-and-chug" approach to computing averages would not have led to such an active class. The concept of average goes beyond the algebraic formula. A major mind shift: *"The answer" is not "the answer" but rather "the process" is the answer.* It's the process of investigation and creative critical thinking that we want to get across to students. Math is not simply how to give input data (e.g., student heights) to a computational algorithm and then churn out a numerical result. But, unfortunately, many students experience it that way.*

Relevance of STEM to Students' Lives

Research has shown that many secondary school students drop out of STEM learning due to their feeling that STEM (science, technology, engineering, and mathematics) is boring, difficult, and/or not relevant to their lives (Pinxten, De Laet, Soom, & Langie, 2015). Some say it bluntly: "Mathematics is perceived as a tricky, tedious, and boring subject by almost everybody from the beginning of their school life" (Bishara, 2016).

In BLOSSOMS lessons, we try to include examples that teenagers can relate to: "On average, do your friends on Facebook have more friends than you do?" Jeffrey exclaims, "Wow, that's a weird question! How to

* Research has shown that on any given day typically 70% of students in a class have not done the assigned reading. In STEM classes with "plug-and-chug" type homework, students often go to the end-of-chapter assigned problems first, then page back through the unread chapter to find the paragraph or two that explains the mechanical steps for solving that problem. Needless to say, this behavior does not lead to deep conceptual learning. But it may be encouraged in courses that teach to the test, where test problems are of the plug-and-chug variety. See "How Do You Get Your Students to Do the Assigned Reading?" (Hall, 2016).

approach it?" Perhaps the in-class teacher suggests dividing students into small teams and creating "friendship networks" within each team. The networks would have to reflect the randomness of actual friendship networks. We can't all be friends with everyone else—too boring! The students develop a way to do this. They draw a picture of their groups' friendship network. Then they have to decide exactly what the term *on average* means in this instance. To their surprise, they will discover that each and every group-created friendship network has this property! OK, experimental verification, but how do we prove it mathematically? That's the main question, and the process of teacher-mentored discovery takes the students though a bit of graph theory and into senior level mathematics. For details, see, *The Friendship Paradox: Why We Can't All Be Popular* (LaCurts & Ousterhout, 2018).

Math Was Created to Solve Real Problems!

Unfortunately, mathematicians write most math textbooks! Most love the intellectual beauty and rigor of math, but care little for applications, perhaps not even knowing many applications. Therein we see a mismatch with the needs of typical high school students. It's safe to speculate that the most probable number of future mathematicians in any given high school math class is zero! Yes, there will be a few future mathematicians over a large collection of math classes, but the vast majority of students in any given class will only need to use math intelligently and creatively once they graduate from formal education.

To help motivate students, why not, whenever possible, introduce a new STEM concept or method via an application? Describe the real problem first, without any math or science, and let the STEM thinking follow naturally. Education scholars call this, "phenomenon-based learning" or "phenomenon-motivated learning" (AmplifyScience, 2018). The history of mathematics demonstrates that almost all math discoveries were phenomenon-motivated. The same is true in physics and engineering, and often in chemistry and biology.

Consider the famous Pythagorean theorem, "The sum of the squares of the legs (the two shorter sides) of a right triangle is equal to the square of the hypotenuse (the longest side)." Students may ask, "But why do we care? And when did anyone care?" Here the teacher could describe in a motivational way that past societies found the need to create right triangles. Over 4,000 years ago, the Babylonians, Indians, and Chinese already knew that a right triangle could be created with the sides of 3, 4, and 5 units, and that the sum of the squares of the two shorter sides equaled the square of the longer side (Barron et al., 1998; Moyer, n.d.; Symeonidis & Schwarz, 2016): $3^2 + 4^2 = 9 + 16 = 25 = 5^2$. "3-4-5" is now called a Pythagorean triplet. Using small knots, by partitioning a string or rope into 12 equal-length pieces and then laying it into a triangle so that one side contains three equal-length segments, the second side four and the last side five segments, they could easily construct a right angle ("Pythagorean Theorem–Egyptian Pyramids," n.d.; Gardner, 2009). The Chinese used this approach in land surveying and astronomy. The Egyptians used this to assure that the slopes of their pyramids were correct and—as surveyors—to reestablish property rights along the Nile River after annual floods (Gonczy, 2003; Martzoff, 1996).

Historians report that Pythagoras visited Egypt, saw these applications of the rope partitioning, and then generalized the 3-4-5 result to an arbitrary right triangle (Haupt, 2013; "Pythagorean Theorem–Egyptian Pyramids," n.d.) hence the name, Pythagorean theorem.

For more, see the BLOSSOMS lesson *The Pythagorean Theorem: Geometry's Most Elegant Theorem* (Haupt, 2013). Following the students' mastery of the Pythagorean theorem, the teacher may challenge them with related BLOSSOMS lessons, such as *How Tall Is That?* (Liang, 2015), or *The Parallax Activity: Measuring the Distance to Nearby Stars?* (Black, 2012), or *Pythagoras and the Juice Seller* (Marmash, 2010). Each of these problems can be solved with the Pythagorean theorem, but the students must discover that, and then identify the right triangle and move forward to a solution.

As students learn more mathematics, they may first be exposed to the types of agriculture and trade problems that gave rise to the Chinese inventing systems of linear equations (Budd & Sangwin, 2004a). Or, they may see that designing grazing fields for livestock prompted ancient civilizations to invent the quadratic equation (Budd & Sangwin 2004b). Or, in thinking of the mathematics of insurance, gambling, population growth, jury sizing, and more, students should consider this respected quote: "The driving force behind the development of probability theory and statistics was pressure from society to obtain solutions to important problems of practical use" (Hald, 2004). Phenomena have driven mathematics.

City Streets

Now let's go back to the 1700s, to visit another BLOSSOMS lesson, *Taking Walks, Delivering Mail: An Introduction to Graph Theory*, as presented by Karima Nigmatulina (Nigmatulina, 2009):

(Let's) take ourselves back to the 1700s, to the city of Königsberg, . . . a wealthy trading city in Prussia. . . . You can see (in Figure 10.2) a map of the city of Königsberg from that time. Königsberg was divided into four parts by a river called Pregel. The top part of the city was called Alstadt. The middle island part of the city was called Kneiphof. The lower part of the city was called Vorstadt, and the right middle part of the city was called Lomse. These four city parts were connected by seven bridges, and these bridges are shown . . . on the diagram (in Figure 10.3). So here is what the city of Königsberg looked like in the 1700s.

The citizens of the city really enjoyed their city and they would walk around the city a lot. They created a game for themselves. The game was: Could they start in one part of the city, walk around in such a way that they crossed all the bridges exactly once—not more, not less—and come back to that original spot where they started? . . . This is the problem that we're going to start with today. Do you think that such a route exists? Can we start in one point of the city, walk around, cross all the bridges exactly once and come back to that original starting point? Take some time with your teacher. See if you can come up with such a route and please let me know if you think that you can, or if you think that you can't. Tell me in five minutes. See you soon.

The video fades to black and the in-class teacher, who is serving in a "teaching duet" role with Karima, now guides and mentors the class in active, inquiry-based learning. Because the teacher studied Karima's teacher's guide before the class, she decides to divide the class into four competing teams, each representing one of the four parts of Königsberg. The teacher gives each team copies of downloaded maps (Figures 10.2 and 10.3). Then the teacher runs a contest: The team that finds such a path first wins a prize! The winning team's prize is a dinner at a fancy restaurant, paid for by the teacher!

Now the students are truly committed and *engaged*! They are working on graph theory's famous *Seven Bridges of Königsberg Problem*, introduced in 1736 by Leonhard Euler (Alexanderson, 2006), inventor of graph theory. In this very accessible lesson, our BLOSSOMS in-class students will soon discover the basics, including a graph depiction of the problem as shown in Figure 10.4. To their chagrin, they will eventually become convinced that there is no feasible solution to the problem. They will conclude that for there to be a solution, each of the four sections of Königsberg must have an exit bridge to accompany each entrance bridge. This means that the number of bridges touching each section of the city must be an

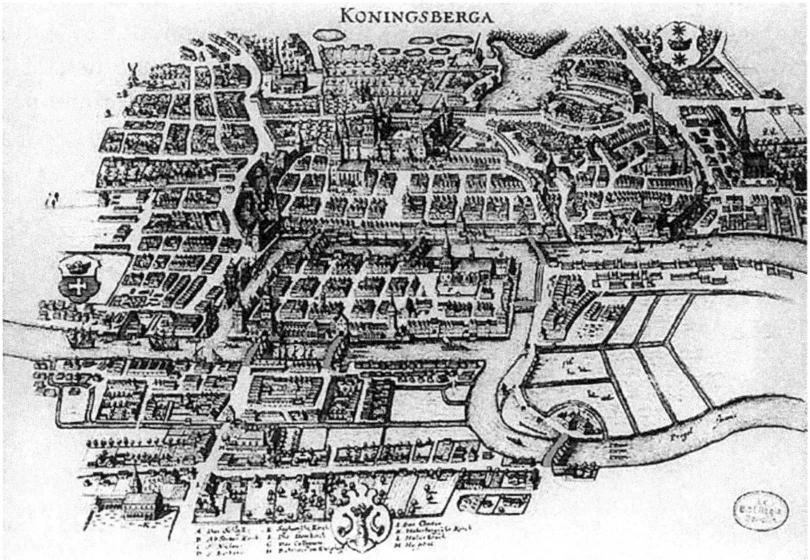

FIGURE 10.2 Historical map of Königsberg

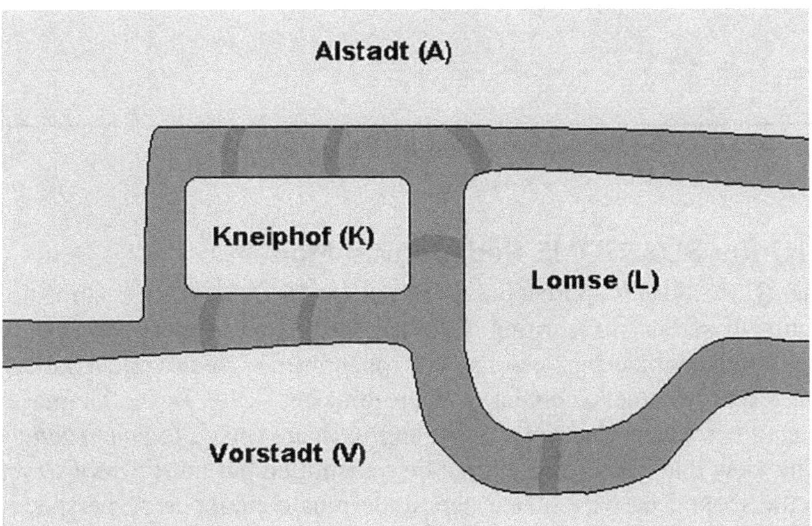

FIGURE 10.3 Another depiction of Königsberg

even number. Königsberg did not have this property! No student team will go off to a free dinner! But the students will now be committed to learning more about graph theory and its applications. In the second half of this lesson, they will eagerly learn how graph theory is used to route postal workers.

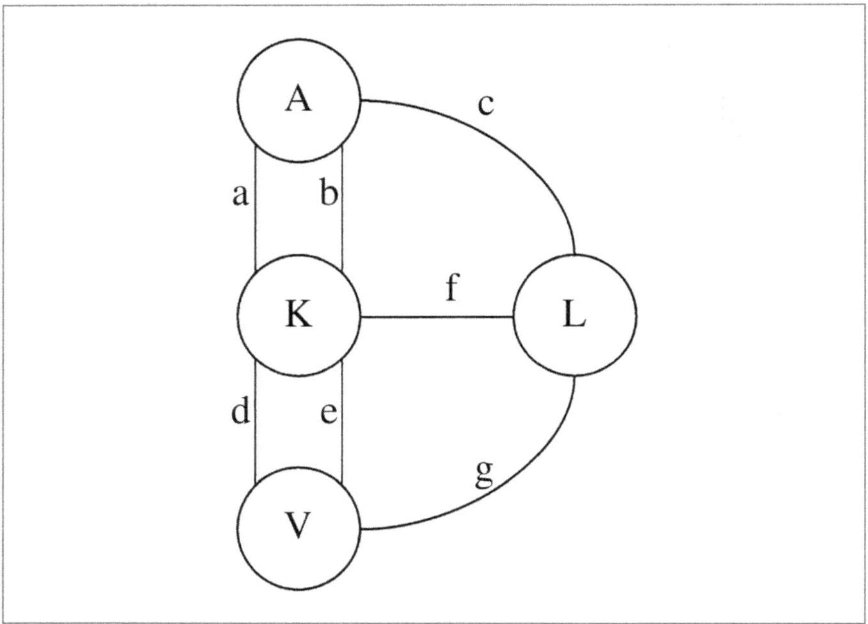

FIGURE 10.4 Graph depiction of Königsberg

Why the BLOSSOMS Pedagogical Model

The BLOSSOMS approach has been designed to engage students in inquiry-based active learning (Colburn, 2000) and to motivate math, science, and engineering lessons with phenomena—real-world challenges that require the development of deep thinking skills. In the language of education science, the roots of this approach are linked to *constructivism*, "The view that knowledge cannot be transmitted but must be *constructed* by the mental activity of learners underpins contemporary perspectives on science education" (Driver, Asojo, Leach, Mortimer, & Scott, 1994). Education researchers, using evidence-based approaches, have found that *collaborative, phenomenon-motivated, inquiry-based active learning*, the pedagogy of BLOSSOMS, usually yields successful classroom implementation of the constructivist philosophy (Michael, 2006). For instance, in one famous study involving 2,084 control students (traditional lectures) and 4,458 experimental students (active learning), the active learning students in follow-on tests outperformed the traditional students by two standard deviations (Hake, 1998)!

This is not to argue for the elimination of textbooks and/or lectures. Students must obtain foundational knowledge in mathematics and science, and often the most efficient way to instill that information is via lectures and textbooks. But deep learning, building on fundamentals, is fostered with the constructivist approach.

MIT BLOSSOMS, THE ORIGINS

Teaching is the profession on which all other professions depend.

—Linda Darling-Hammond

October 19, 2004: Northwest China, Ningxia Hui Autonomous Region, Yuanzhou District. The two authors are visiting a middle school in one of the poorest regions in China.* Before entering the school we saw a satellite dish near the entranceway. We were told that this was used to download, from a fixed-position satellite, educational lectures by excellent teachers, usually from Shanghai and Beijing. Each school we visited had a satellite dish.

In the classroom, the teacher was showing a downloaded video of a biology lecture. Suddenly, the teacher stopped the video and for the next several minutes engaged the class in the science they just saw. The students were active, enthusiastic, and vocal. Then the teacher returned to the video lecture, only to stop it again several minutes later to interact once more with the class. The entire biology class period worked this way—video snippets of a lecture interspersed with active class discussions. The students remained alert, attentive, and engaged throughout.

* This section and the next are adapted from the paper "STEM Education: Inferring Promising Systems Changes from Experiences with MIT BLOSSOMS," Richard C. Larson and M. Elizabeth Murray, *Systems Research and Behavioral Science*, published in Wiley Online Library. doi:10.1002/sres.2411. 2016. In the trip to China in 2004, Professor KANG Feiyu and his colleagues at the School of Continuing Education of Tsinghua University hosted us. They generously set up for us a sequence of visits to distance learning centers and technology-equipped primary and secondary schools.

Standing in the back of this classroom, we had a sudden thought, an "aha moment": *Might it be possible to create video lessons that are predesigned to be interrupted?* That is, could we move away from long video lectures randomly stopped by the in-class teacher and toward an integrated lesson providing video content interspersed with recommended teacher-facilitated classroom activities for students? And so was born an idea that 3 years later emerged as the MIT BLOSSOMS Project.

MIT BLOSSOMS—The First 10 Years

MIT BLOSSOMS began in 2008 and by 2019 had developed an online repository of over 200 freely available lessons in mathematics, biology, chemistry, physics, and engineering, created by volunteers from more than 10 countries, with quality assured by MIT staff.

The BLOSSOMS program has a somewhat different interpretation of "blended learning." Most often this term represents a classroom having a regular teacher, with students having direct access to online computers. Some of the learning is directly from the teacher, as usual, and the rest of it is via the student using her computer (Clayton Christensen Institute, n.d.). With BLOSSOMS, the "blend" is the BLOSSOMS video-recorded teacher plus the live in-class teacher, performing in a "teaching duet." The primary role of the Internet is to serve as an efficient BLOSSOMS lesson delivery mechanism for the teacher. The classroom need not have Internet connection, as the teacher can download the video from any Internet-connected facility.

A BLOSSOMS video lesson is shown on a screen in front of the class and moves in short 2-to-4-minute spurts, each segment challenging the students to some STEM problem they have not seen before. After each segment, the video is turned off, and the in-class teacher carefully guides the class through an inquiry-based active learning exercise. Most lessons are phenomenon-motivated, so the students need to figure out what concepts learned from their traditional lectures may be relevant to solving the challenges. Our intent is not to replace lectures, but to supplement them with BLOSSOMS active learning classes, especially at the start and/or ends of multiclass "content blocks." In our view, an ideal STEM class utilizing BLOSSOMS would experience a BLOSSOMS lesson two or three times per month.

MIT BLOSSOMS was initially designed as a program to work with educators in developing countries. Via video, we sought above all to introduce STEM teachers in those countries to a new way of teaching—moving away from a scripted lecture format with its emphasis on memorization for tests toward a more active, student-centered approach that encourages deep learning. BLOSSOMS other major goals are:

1. To have students begin to act, think, and do as scientists, mathematicians, and engineers
2. To teach students the skills and mindset required for critical and creative thinking and problem solving
3. To demonstrate the relevance of STEM in students' daily lives
4. To make STEM subjects fun
5. To develop within the students an awareness and appreciation for diverse cultures

In historical order, these are our 10 partner countries: the United States, Jordan, Pakistan, Saudi Arabia, Lebanon, Brazil, Malaysia, China, Japan, and Mexico. Since an important goal of BLOSSOMS is to encourage universities to reach out in assisting local high schools, we first develop a relationship with one or more universities in a partnering country. This is only logical, since the "outputs" from high schools represent the "inputs" to universities. Well-prepared high school graduates become superb university freshmen. We also like to have relationships established with ministries of education and/or a large local company. The probability of implementation success is increased with multiple in-country supporting stakeholders.

In 2010, recognizing that teachers across the United States were also in need of this kind of resource, we began to interact with US schools at the same level as out-of-country schools. We have worked with teachers in many states, including Massachusetts, Rhode Island, Florida, Utah, and Washington, DC.

Since teacher training is essential to deliver BLOSSOMS lessons, MIT BLOSSOMS staff members have provided face-to-face training to over 2,000 high school teachers in seven countries.

Quality Assurance

Quality control of BLOSSOMS lessons is highest priority. Our BLOSSOMS teachers are usually unpaid volunteers—professors, high school teachers, students of all ages, and practicing professionals. They may be located near us in Cambridge, Massachusetts, or anywhere; one is literally on the other side of the world in Singapore. Over the first two years of BLOSSOMS, we developed and continue to use a six-step design and production process (Larson & Murray, 2016). The six steps are (1) concept of the lesson; (2) lesson architecture; (3) pseudo-script; (4) storyboard (videographer-created); (5) videotaping the lesson; (6) background information including a teacher's guide. Anyone creating a BLOSSOMS lesson needs our permission to move from one step to the next. This often requires two or three iterations at each stage. We have found that the six-step production control process yields excellent quality of the final learning product—a new BLOSSOMS lesson.

Education Systems

Teachers everywhere appear to face the same challenges and constraints in practicing their profession. The majority of schools today—even those well equipped with new technologies—use pedagogies and classroom management techniques that haven't changed much since our great-grandparents were in school! The industrial model of "product creation" (i.e., producing educated young people) is similar to that of a Henry Ford mass production plant circa 1915. It appears that a majority of schools worldwide face similar barriers in equipping their young people with the knowledge and skills vital for a changing world. These are "systems" barriers, established over decades, and they will require some time to change.

By getting into the live classroom with a novel pedagogical model, requiring a new set of skills for the teacher and encouraging full engagement of the students, BLOSSOMS attempts to make several systems changes at once in the secondary school educational system. Our international partners (Malik, 2016a; Malik, 2016b; Abdullah & Shukor, 2016) and we have had both successes and failures, with some outcomes in between. From these experiences, many still active and ongoing, in this chapter we attempt to extrapolate to the next higher level—making several broader systemic recommendations to improve secondary school STEM education. The discussion leads to two major new BLOSSOMS initiatives: moving to project-based learning (PBL) and to teacher professional learning (TPL), each with a BLOSSOMS orientation.

Experience to Date: OER and Teacher's Choice for Using BLOSSOMS

Being freely available, BLOSSOMS lessons are downloaded, viewed, and used in classrooms worldwide. In addition to implementation activities of official MIT BLOSSOMS partners, reports of use are via e-mails, YouTube messages, ShareMyLesson.com, and entries on social media. For example, the comment "Thanks for the video Emma!! I really like the visual examples. I will apply someday with my students!" was posted on YouTube for *An Introduction to the Physics of Sailing* (Ferris, 2017), and "This video is awesome. Huge respect!" was posted for *The Physics of Pool* (Formaggio & Machuca, 2011). We have multiple distribution channels, including YouTube and MIT as well as ShareMyLesson.com. Some individual lessons have been viewed and/or downloaded over 50,000 times just via YouTube. But the choice to use BLOSSOMS in the classroom, or to study a lesson and then present it oneself, continues to be an individual teacher's choice.

In our own extensive work in classrooms, we usually receive enthusiastic responses from teachers and students. For example, in response to the BLOSSOMS lesson *The Broken Stick Experiment: Triangles, Random Numbers and Probability* (Larson, 2008) that was delivered to a mathematics class at the Arlington High School, Arlington, Massachusetts, the in-class teacher reported, "I found the video to be extremely effective in engaging the students in my class. . . . With lessons like this one, many concepts are incorporated into one cohesive problem and because of the teacher and the video's clarity and strong teaching method, we had no need for textbooks or outside resources." The students from the class were also supportive and enthusiastic. For instance, a student named Alex remarked, "The project we did on Tuesday was interesting and engaging. As we worked with our group mates, we were working together to solve a complex problem. It was helpful to refer back to the video and see whether we were right on our discovery. If we were wrong or headed in the right direction, the video clearly explained the problem in a slow and steady pace. . . . I appreciate MIT for presenting us this video that allowed us to engage in the problem solving and learn how to break down a difficult problem into clear stages."

One might reasonably ask, "Why has there not yet been a formal assessment or evaluation of BLOSSOMS, with a statistically significant sample size?" Good question! The answer is multifaceted. First, BLOSSOMS remains a bottom-up rather than top-down implementation endeavor. To our knowledge, no one school has adopted BLOSSOMS in a schoolwide initiative. For this reason, until now it has been difficult to achieve a credible evaluation. However, with our new Teacher Professional Learning initiative discussed below, we are planning to conduct such a formal assessment. Once we implement that TPL workshop series with a large number of teachers in several states, we will be able to evaluate one major goal of BLOSSOMS—to train and encourage STEM teachers to move away from a traditional lecture format toward adoption in their own teaching of an active, inquiry-based pedagogy that leads to deeper learning. A second reason there has been no formal assessment is tied to the fact that the ultimate benefit to students of BLOSSOMS-type active learning lessons may not be visible for some time, as the students' problem-solving methods evolve and as their general interest in STEM subjects grows. No instant assessment is possible, since large time constants are involved. Because of this and other related concerns, we feel the best way to assess student impact of a given BLOSSOMS video lesson in the short term is to follow it up with a small-group project-based learning lesson, as will be discussed later.

TODAY'S EDUCATION SYSTEMS, OPERATING UNDER NEWTON'S LAWS

Nothing happens until something moves.

—Albert Einstein

The Physics of Nearly Everything

For any BLOSSOMS teachers who want to introduce Newton's laws of motion to their class, many different phenomena can be understood by students reasoning like Newton. In our portfolio of BLOSSOMS lessons, we have *The Physics of*. . .

Pool: https://blossoms.mit.edu/videos/lessons/physics_pool

Donkey Carts: https://bit.ly/2MSeHTf

Boomerangs: https://blossoms.mit.edu/videos/lessons/physics_boomerangs

Sailing: https://bit.ly/2MnR7Rd

Soap Bubbles: https://bit.ly/2nHGkDq

Racing Cars: https://blossoms.mit.edu/videos/lessons/physics_racing_cars

Kite Flying: https://bit.ly/2vGpfOD

Footballs: https://bit.ly/2nG3LwN

Consider donkey carts from Lahore, Pakistan. The road traffic in Lahore includes donkey carts, each with one donkey, one driver, two wheels, one axle, a flat wooden platform for cargo, and no brakes! How does it function? With no brakes, Newton says, "An object in motion tends to stay in motion." That is a challenge for the driver, who must stop at intersections and otherwise navigate dense traffic. Newton also tells us, "An object at rest tends to stay at rest." Another challenge for the driver—to motivate the donkey to start moving! And if the driver does not know about *center of mass*, a pivot point concept derived from Newton's laws, too much weight may be placed behind the axle and the poor donkey may find his front legs dangling in the air (Figure 10.5)! Yes, this happens in practice, and its inclusion in the lesson brings some fun to the students studying physics. It's also an opportunity for students worldwide to experience some of the rich way of life of Pakistan—learning physics and getting to know and appreciate a distant country's culture.

FIGURE 10.5. In Pakistan, driver not knowing about center of mass. (Qayyum, 2015)

The Physics of Education

Newton's laws can also be applied, perhaps metaphorically, to institutions (Conte, 2017). Reviewing Newton's laws of motion:

1. An object in motion tends to stay in motion, and an object at rest tends to stay at rest.
2. $\mathbf{F} = m\mathbf{a}$, where $\mathbf{F}$ is the force on an object, m is its mass, and $\mathbf{a}$ is its acceleration.
3. For every action, there is an equal and opposite reaction.

The education delivery establishment in most countries, over decades, has accumulated huge mass. Numerous stakeholders have developed vested interests in maintaining the status quo. These stakeholders include teachers' unions; teachers' colleges; for-profit companies; local, regional, and federal governments; the "testing establishment," and so on. A few countries such as Finland are counterexamples (Martin, 2018). The accreted mass develops in part because it is much easier to add things to the system than to subtract them.

The huge system mass gives it immense inertia, and Newton's laws suggest that any significant movement from status quo would require substantial force. *An object at rest tends to stay at rest.* And combating substantial change, *For every action, there is an equal and opposite reaction.* But what is at risk here? It is the very future of our young people, meaning the future of our country, of every country. From working with educators with BLOSSOMS in various countries, we believe that substantial change is required, and huge force must be applied to the educational establishment in order to provide improved education to our young people. Is there any better investment in our collective and individual future than in education? Together, we can move mountains; Newton tells us so!

The system has many parts, interconnected in complex ways. Where to start? How do we get significant movement? From our BLOSSOMS work, we identify two system components of prime importance: (1) standardized multiple-choice tests; and (2) STEM teachers—their recruitment, training, and work conditions. If these two subjects can be addressed in a substantial way, changing significantly for the better, we believe that we will see consequential positive movement.

"The Standardized Test—Not a Magic Bullet!"

In speaking with high school STEM teachers, we are convinced that the current "magic bullet" trend to evaluate students based on a single number, a score from a standardized multiple-choice test, is a huge mistake. Many researchers and practitioners agree (Archbald & Newman, 1988). For instance, consider this representative teacher's statement about state exams: "state tests have resulted in a narrowing of the taught curriculum; a prevalence of drill-and-fill instructional practices; a proliferation of ineffectual benchmark assessment systems that significantly reduce instructional time; and an incessant mimicking of multiple-choice item format on classroom assessments" (Ferlazzo, 2018).

How many of us in careers feel that we could accurately be evaluated by a single number? Not many, I presume. How should we evaluate you and your career accomplishments? Our answer (and yours, too, we guess): *a representative portfolio of your accomplishments.* In talking with adult audiences about education, we often ask this question: "In high school you undoubtedly took many STEM classes and did well, most likely A's and B's. If I were to select now a STEM test that you took in high school, do you think you could pass it today? Raise your hands if you think you could." Rarely do we see a raised hand. And yet, the folks in the audience view themselves as educated accomplished adults. How can this be if they would *fail the STEM tests* they aced in high school? We say it's because education is not about memorizing facts but rather becoming knowledgeable about framing and formulating creative approaches to new problems. It's all about the systematic process of attacking problems, not the regurgitation of memorized content.

Even current honor students have short testing memories. Researchers report (Heath & Heath, 2018; Dintersmith & Wagner, 2015) that students at an elite private high school in New Jersey averaged B+ on a test in June, but when they retook it in September, the average plummeted to F. Test knowledge is not permanent knowledge. Perhaps Einstein had true insight: "Education is what remains after one has forgotten what one has learned in school."

If portfolio assessment is good for us adults, why is it not good for our children? Is it simply that the cost would be too high? That getting a computer-scanned number on a test taken by many thousands is much less expensive for the "system" to process? Whatever cost savings can be gained here will be swamped by the negative unintended consequences of applying the magic bullet approach.

Teachers have come up to one of us (Larson) saying things like this: "Dick, we would love to bring compelling STEM lessons like BLOSSOMS into our classrooms to develop critical and creative thinking skills, lessons not in textbooks and not on the mandated test-focused curriculum, but we can't. I fear that at the next PTA meeting, a parent might come up to me and threaten a lawsuit because I spent a class session on a mind-expanding STEM lesson, not focusing on the next standardized test, and as a result 'Little Johnnie' might score 2 points lower on the SAT test." The focus has been on the test, a focus that is all-encompassing, as many teachers work only on test preparation for days or even weeks before the students take it. How is that for developing critical and creative thinking skills, the type required of STEM professionals?

Tests can foster cheating. When a single number evaluates a human, there is great temptation to cheat. Some students cheat. Some teachers cheat. We have all read the news stories, from urban school districts where some teachers erase and correct wrong answers, to tony suburbs, where a test-savvy imposter will take an SAT test for someone for the price of $2,500. In 2019 there was the infamous "Operation Varsity Blues," including not only fraudulent SAT scores but also massive bribery, detailed in the largest-ever FBI investigation of college application cheating (Medina, Benner, & Taylor, 2019). Magic bullet solutions almost always lead to cheating, because there is so much at stake and it is so easy to cheat.

Donald Campbell in 1979 proposed an axiom now known as *Campbell's law*:

> The more any quantitative social indicator is used for social decision-making, the more subject it will be to corruption pressures and the more apt it will be to distort and corrupt the social processes it is intended to monitor. . . . When test scores become the goal of the teaching process, they both lose their value as indicators of educational status and distort the educational process in undesirable ways. (Campbell, 1979)

Portfolios are currently used to evaluate some students. At MIT, the Department of Architecture requires each student to develop a portfolio of works. The content of the portfolio is used to evaluate each architecture student. In K–12 settings, it is not unusual to evaluate with portfolios a student's abilities in art, music, and other "creative" endeavors. But why not math and science, both very creative?

Portfolios demonstrate diversity. A single-number assessment scheme ignores diversity in students' interests, capabilities, and accomplishments.

Which "B student" is better: a straight B student or a student with 50% C's and 50% A's? If the A's of the second student were related to the student's passion, interests, and accomplishments in biology, then a portfolio showing his biology skills and research would demonstrate that (Geweertz, 2018). We should celebrate a student's targeted excellence. Portfolios celebrate diversity of interests, talents, and accomplishments. The single-number scheme is a *flaw of averaging*, ignoring diversity in abilities within each student. In terms of underrepresented groups, the demonstration of diverse interests would allow a supportive teacher to note relative strengths and interests in a student and encourage that student to go far. As one example, California's High Tech High celebrates diversity and encourages students to pursue their passions, emphasizing development of student portfolios created via project-based learning (High Tech High, n.d.).

We are not suggesting discarding standardized tests altogether. They are needed to ascertain that certain fundamental knowledge has been mastered. But we are saying, *Let's give student portfolios a significant fraction of weight when evaluating students, their academic knowledge, achievements, and potential.* Our favorite weights: 50–50.

We need to encourage our young people to explore the wonder of math and science, to ask questions that relate to their everyday lives. Students should be able to *frame*, *formulate*, and attempt to *solve* math and science problems that are awakened in them as a result of something they have seen, experienced, or dreamed about. The student then adds her proposed solution to her *portfolio of accomplishments*, and later submits that portfolio to her college of choice, along with her SAT, ACT, and AP scores!

There is positive momentum. As one example, we cite Mastery Transcript Consortium (MTC) (n.d.) that is working with more than 200 schools to redesign student transcripts to "reflect the unique skills, strengths, and interests of each learner." While the final design for the new transcripts has not been decided at the time of this writing, there is the hope that they will in some way facilitate student portfolios (Avallone, 2018).

STEM Teachers

There are no more important components of the education system than human teachers. Not computers, not games, not AI, not smartphones, not robot teachers. We can all remember that one special teacher who motivated us in a given direction and changed our lives irrevocably for the better. We can hope that each school-age child today will experience an equivalently transformative teacher during his or her K–12 days.

Students need excellent STEM teaching now more than ever: "In the next decade, almost all of the 30 fastest-growing occupations will require intermediate or advanced knowledge of science, technology, engineering, and/or mathematics" (Moritz & Weiss, 2018). Successful life fulfillment of our future graduates depends on superlative STEM education. But the current situation with US STEM teachers is troubling.

First, there is the severe shortfall in numbers of STEM teachers (EnCorps, 2018):

- 25% of students attend schools that do not offer calculus
- 15% of students attend schools that do not offer physics
- 15% of students attend schools that do not offer advanced mathematics
- 10% of students attend schools that do not offer chemistry

Worse, economically disadvantaged school districts are often "STEM deserts," having far greater than average shortages of STEM teachers.* The State of Rhode Island provides a glimpse of on-the-ground reality:

> East Providence High School hasn't had a physics teacher in 2½ years. The district has had to offer the course online.
>
> Supt. Kathryn Crowley said it's so hard for her district to find qualified high school math and science teachers that she "poaches" them from other districts, a practice that other school leaders privately acknowledge.
>
> High school math and science teachers, especially those in chemistry and physics, are in such demand that they get multiple job offers, and they can ask for top salaries. "The labor market for math and science teachers is as brutal as it's ever been," said Jeremy Chiappetta, executive director of Blackstone Valley Prep, . . . "People are basically hopping around. You make an offer. They accept. A week later they say, 'I'm not going to take this offer.' " (Borg, 2018)

We have read similar reports from other states.

* "A quarter of high schools with the highest percentage of African American and Latino students don't offer Algebra II—a prerequisite for many higher-level STEM courses—and a third of these schools do not offer chemistry. Given the existence of these STEM deserts, it's no surprise that people of color are significantly underrepresented in the growing STEM workforce" (Moritz & Weiss, 2018).

Second, even with the shortfalls and high demand for STEM teachers, there is the insufficient training of many current STEM teachers. With the education system moving from teaching facts to be memorized toward active deep learning, the content knowledge and pedagogical expertise required of STEM teachers has never been greater. But unfortunately, only a minority of STEM teachers studied a STEM field as first major in college. As a result, many science, math, and engineering teachers are not certified to teach the subjects they teach. Here are the data for high school students taught by teachers with no major and no certification in their subject area in year 2000: math—31%, biology—45%, chemistry—61%, physics—66%, and earth and planetary science—79% (EnCorps STEM Teachers Program, 2018; see also Hill & Gruber, 2011). Limitations of teacher content knowledge have often forestalled use of BLOSSOMS lessons in classrooms, as giving an active learning BLOSSOMS class requires deep content and pedagogical knowledge.

Third, poor work conditions for STEM teachers give rise to many early career abandonments. We have met scores of great secondary school STEM teachers. But many of them are frustrated with "the system" and its bureaucratic constraints—limited flexibility in the classroom; large class sizes; ever-changing flavors of desirable content and pedagogy leading to constant retooling; low pay compared to the private sector; low respect (in contrast to other countries such as Finland and Japan); lack of a compelling career path; assignment to problem schools for which they have no training; and so on. These are the conditions that lead to high teacher turnover (Darling-Hammond, Sutcher, & Carver-Thomas, 2016).*

As a consequence of the problems above, content and pedagogical knowledge of many current STEM teachers is shallow, not deep. This limits the type of teaching they feel comfortable with to scripted lectures with little student engagement (University of Vermont, 2018). Such one-way content delivery is not good for students who need to develop critical thinking skills. Let's recall Socrates' (n.d.) saying: "Education is the kindling of a flame, not the filling of a vessel."

Recently, 47% of students report being disengaged at school (Tucker, 2016). Yet *student engagement* is vital to learning: It's "the degree of attention, curiosity, interest, optimism, and passion that students show

* "The concept of 'student engagement' is predicated on the belief that learning improves when students are inquisitive, interested, or inspired, and that learning tends to suffer when students are bored, dispassionate, disaffected, or otherwise 'disengaged.' *Stronger student engagement* or *improved student engagement* are common instructional objectives expressed by educators" (EnCorps 2018; its source: teach.com; see also Hill & Gruber, 2011).

when they are learning or being taught, which extends to the level of motivation they have to learn and progress in their education" ("Student engagement," n.d.).

Many US public school teachers belong to teachers' unions, the two largest being the NEA (National Education Association, http://www.nea.org) and AFT (American Federation of Teachers, https://www.aft.org). Contrary to some popular perceptions, these unions strive to help teachers to teach in many ways, including sharing lessons and best practices, operating social professional networks to discuss and compare teaching experiences, and more. Since the BLOSSOMS program produces—free of charge—STEM lessons for use *by the teacher* in the classroom in front of the regular students, both the NEA and AFT support BLOSSOMS and feature BLOSSOMS on their websites. The AFT operates ShareMyLesson.com https://sharemylesson.com), where BLOSSOMS lessons are offered. This AFT website is an example of "lesson-study-created" shared lessons (Hird, Larson, Okubo, & Uchino, 2014). BLOSSOMS staff members have given invited BLOSSOMS STEM webinars on ShareMyLesson.com (Larson, 2018). Thousands of STEM teachers have benefited from the programs of ShareMyLesson.com and from the professional networking operated by the NEA. Some positive system forces are moving in the right direction!

But more change is needed. Policywise, we have both near-term and long-term problems. Near term, we must find better ways to retain current STEM teachers and to improve their STEM teaching. Longer term, we need to change certain aspects of the current system that so many STEM teachers and would-be STEM teachers find unattractive. We must free up the bureaucratic nature of the system, increase pay, offer compelling career paths, and—by raising the professional status of teachers—increase their standing and respect in the eyes of the general public.

Regarding the near-term problem, the great majority of teachers we have met want to improve themselves, in content knowledge, in pedagogy, in engaging the students, in handling difficult situations, in sharing lesson plans, and more. But during the school year, time is precious and there is little time for effective teacher professional development (PD). And what PD is offered is often thought of, by teachers, as an expensive waste of time—not effective. In this chapter we suggest how BLOSSOMS can help create compelling workshops aimed at Teacher Professional Learning (TPL) (see the section with this heading), a proposed new form of PD aimed at training teachers in the active, inquiry-oriented learning pedagogy espoused by BLOSSOMS. This is especially important with the current introduction of Next Generation Science Standards (NGSS; http://www.nextgenscience.org).

Newton's laws contain optimism: "An object in motion tends to stay in motion." Getting key components of the education system moving in a good direction creates positive momentum that can then lead to additional constructive change.

PROJECT-BASED LEARNING

You've got to be very careful if you don't know where you are going, because you might not get there.

—Yogi Berra, Hall of Fame catcher for the New York Yankees (Scott, 2015)

The Motivation

We have argued for several interrelated changes in typical high school STEM teaching, learning, and student assessment:

1. In the "system," have assessments of student academic achievement and potential rely less on standardized tests and more on a student's portfolio of accomplishments.

2. Encourage active, inquiry-based learning, where students are motivated to act and think as scientists, engineers, and mathematicians.

3. Introduce new topics and problems as phenomenon-based, where the need is to solve a real-world problem, and the science, math, and/or engineering is derived from that need.

4. Provide opportunities for students to "go deep" in aspects of STEM, both individually and in small teams, the end result being student-created reports, artifacts, and presentations.

Project-based learning (PBL) is a type of extended learning undertaking, usually carried out in small student teams, that responds to (2), (3), and (4) above, the end result—when successful—providing rich portfolio additions to assist in (1) above. PBL means many things to many people. Usually there is a phenomenon or set of phenomena that students are to study collaboratively, both inside and outside of the classroom. The teacher's statement of the problem is usually more expansive, lacking sharp boundaries, than a typical homework or in-class lecture problem. There are no right or wrong answers. Rather there is a process of student research and discovery, applying new configurations of fundamental knowledge learned in class to frame, formulate, and develop insights for the stated problem, hopefully leading to recommended ameliorative action on the problem. The duration of a PBL assignment can be as short as a day to as long as a full academic year.

Why BLOSSOMS and PBL?

While there is substantial agreement on the positive student learning aspects of PBL, there are problems implementing PBL in practice. Its use is far less than one might like. The major problem appears to be lack of appropriate teacher training on how to define a project for PBL and—critically—how to implement PBL, especially how to navigate the various issues that are bound to arise during the multiweek period of student PBL work (Glenn, 2016). One illustrative issue is the need to monitor student teams to assure that each team member does his or her fair share of work. Another is that students often become frustrated working on a problem that has no right or wrong answers.

Some existing BLOSSOMS lessons can be used as the jumping-off point for a multiweek PBL exercise. The BLOSSOMS lesson introduces the STEM content and problem to a class and—via interactive, inquiry-based learning—starts the students thinking critically about issues raised in the lesson. This gets the teacher "off the hook" in terms of needing to "seed the problem," that is, to provide STEM content and define the problem. Teachers also need easy-to-understand, yet comprehensive "scaffolding" resources to help them navigate the next few weeks of the student PBL activities, so that they feel confident guiding the students and advising them through both exciting and difficult stretches. This is our newest BLOSSOMS initiative.

In a recent paper, we discuss the need for a rubric for the teacher to frame the overall approach to the PBL (Cammarata & Larson, 2018):

> A rubric should be created before the project starts and provide clear criteria that define the extent to which a team meets expectations in terms of learning, cooperation, collaboration, presentation, content completeness, language, visual appeal, and marketing. . . . A rubric should be relatively specific to the BLOSSOMS session at hand. (pp. 18, 19)

The following section gives an example of a project-based learning exercise.

The Tragedy of the Commons

Imagine that the Boston Commons opens for cow grazing in the year 1640. Citizens of Boston are now allowed to graze their cows on the Commons. There is no charge for this privilege. First one, then two, and eventually say 20 citizens each bring one cow to graze on the Commons. All is fine, as the cows remain healthy, giving plenty of milk, and the grass on the Commons remains strong. Then Citizen 1 thinks to himself, *Well, all 20 cows are fine, I think I'll bring a second cow to the Commons.* He does this, and the others soon follow, leading to 40 cows on the Commons. All is still fine. But eventually this pattern repeats several times, and we soon find 100 cows grazing on the Commons. The cows eat the grass faster than it can replenish, and none of the cows get enough to eat. The milk production of each cow is now down significantly, and eventually the system crashes, leading to no cows and a now-barren Commons. This is the Tragedy of the Commons, as explained from the point of view of early Bostonians.

This story is a metaphor for the overuse and abuse of freely available public resources, not just grasslands. Most of us have heard of this problem in some form. Professor Garrett Hardin introduced it, first at a meeting in 1968 (Hardin, 2005) and later in the magazine *Science* (Hardin, 1968).

Seeing the applicability of this metaphor in virtually all parts of the globe, in 2013 the BLOSSOMS team created a BLOSSOMS lesson, *Tragedy of the Commons* (Horn & Peña-Alcaraz, 2013). The production took place on the grounds of the Eastleigh Dairy Farm in Framingham, Massachusetts (https://eastleighfarm.wixsite.com/eastleighfarm), filmed among about 200 cooperating cows! We quote from the BLOSSOMS website:

> In this lesson, students . . . will become comfortable with the concept of problems of shared resources—and will learn to recognize, and seek out, examples all around them. . . . Students will work with their groups to discuss the logic behind the tragedy of the commons, to consider some options for preventing this tragedy and to examine examples of problems of shared resources that are relevant to them. They will also come up with (mathematical) functions that fit behavior described in the video, and be asked to think about the behavior of functions provided in the video and accompanying materials.

To motivate and facilitate mathematical thinking, the lesson includes an animated simulation using mathematical models depicting the eventual depletion of resources (*Tragedy of the Commons*, 2013).

Following the logic of *Tragedy of the Commons*, depletion of freely available shared resources occurs virtually everywhere on Earth. The lesson offers the opportunity for students to apply it in a multiweek PBL exercise, focused on a local problem of overuse of shared resources. Their final reports and presentations can involve invited decision makers from local governments and industries. Parents also should be invited! Numerous projects are possible, including:

- Air pollution
- Water pollution
- Overfishing
- Overallocation of water entitlements
- Chemical and nutrient pollution
- Traffic congestion

Information related to other BLOSSOMS PBL packages is located on the MIT BLOSSOMS website (https://blossoms.mit.edu).

A final element of the BLOSSOMS PBL lesson packages will enable teachers and students around the world to share their PBL research, findings, and final products with students in other countries—students working from the same BLOSSOMS kickoff video lesson. As an international education initiative, Global Learning is a high priority for BLOSSOMS.

BLOSSOMS PBL projects, if done with care, dedication, and imagination—mentored by well-prepared and confident teachers—should yield strong additions to students' portfolios of accomplishments.

TEACHER PROFESSIONAL LEARNING (TPL)

Teaching is a learning experience.

—Numerous teachers

Teachers as Students

Suppose we have 25 students sitting in a classroom. They are all high school physical science *teachers*. At the head of the class is an exemplary BLOSSOMS physics teacher who is about to show a physics experiment via video. But first he describes the experiment and asks the students to guess what will happen and to explain their reasoning using Newton's laws of motion. Here is the described experiment:

> *There are two identical 2-kg weights hanging by equivalent equal-length threads from a horizontal secure steel beam above. Below each hanging weight is another identical thread, with nothing tied to it. (See Figure 10.6 on the next page.) Now the in-class teacher is about to pull at the bottom of the lower thread of the left half of the setup, the pulling being done very slowly but continuously increasing in force magnitude. Eventually one of the threads breaks. Then, on the right half of the setup he pulls the lower thread as quickly as he can, with great force. One of the threads breaks.*
>
> ***Question to the class:*** *If I were to conduct this experiment in front of you, pulling each of the two threads as described, which of the four thread segments breaks in each case, and why?*

One can imagine that there is a lively discussion, as each student records a guess before the experiment is carried out. The students in this teacher class are learning just as they want their own students to learn—as in a few days or weeks these "students" will again become teachers and offer the identical BLOSSOMS lesson to their own physics students.

Getting with the Program

Our new TPL program, *Teacher as Learner: A Blended Model of Professional Learning for STEM Teachers*, focuses on high school science teachers charged with teaching in the style of Next Generation Science Standards (NGSS; https://www.nextgenscience.org). NGSS is new and potentially transformational. The three dimensions of NGSS are "Core

FIGURE 10.6 Hanging by a thread: The experimental setup—2 identical weights, 4 identical strings

Source: Lenox, 2018

Ideas, Crosscutting Concepts, and Science and Engineering Practices," all predicated on phenomenon-motivated learning (Next Generation Science, n.d.). Teaching in an NGSS classroom requires teachers to study intently the conceptual structure of NGSS, especially the incorporation of cross-cutting concepts and the associated supportive active learning pedagogy. This is a difficult mountain to climb for most teachers. However, we have found that these same teachers agree that the NGSS teaching framework will greatly improve K–12 science education—teaching their students to think and act like scientists and to move beyond "chug-and-plug," "drill-and-kill" exercises to deep subject knowledge. Responding to what we see as a lack of available training resources around NGSS for these teachers, MIT BLOSSOMS has worked to design a blended Teacher Professional Learning (TPL) package that is at once highly accessible (online) and widely scalable. Our project involves the creation of new BLOSSOMS lessons, each aligned with NGSS phenomenon-driven, three-dimensional learning and designed specifically for the purpose of scalable TPL.

The new TPL lessons represent the four NGSS disciplinary domains: life sciences, engineering, earth and space science, and physical sciences. In these lessons, the video breaks are used to engage *teachers* who are in the TPL program. These students, returned as NGSS-trained science teachers, will use the same BLOSSOMS lessons in their own classrooms. Currently most NGSS training is labor intensive, face-to-face, and non-scalable with only a limited number of expert NGSS trainers.

As of this writing, we are beginning to build from the new BLOSSOMS video lessons toward a scalable blended TPL system to educate secondary school science teachers to become skilled practitioners of NGSS. We are leveraging the successful MIT BLOSSOMS "teaching duet" instructional approach to create this new blended model for TPL *that can be used by school districts or small professional development learning groups anywhere*. The new model will provide TPL that engages teachers by immersing them in professional learning that is NGSS-mandated three-dimensional.

The Online, Downloadable "Package"

Each of the new BLOSSOMS lessons serves as the anchor for an online, downloadable "TPL package" for that specific domain. Along with this anchor BLOSSOMS lesson, each domain online TPL package includes:

1. An edited video of that lesson being taught by a master teacher in a live classroom to real high school students

2. Video clips of follow-on conversations with the master teacher who taught the lesson

3. Video clips of conversations with students who experienced this master teacher's live class

In addition to the video content, there are accompanying informative textual materials.

The Blended Professional Learning Cycle

While any teacher can download the TPL package and learn from it, we prefer its first use be in a one- or two-day TPL workshop. Experienced NGSS facilitators would integrate the BLOSSOMS TPL packages into comprehensive TPL workshops offered locally. The "packages" serve as the core of four different workshops, training teachers in each of the four NGSS disciplinary domains. This blended professional learning model begins with teachers experiencing the NGSS-style (three-dimensional) BLOSSOMS lesson just as their students would. This is followed by an opportunity for teachers to reflect on that experience from their own professional point of view by observing via edited video the same lesson performed by a master teacher with students in an actual classroom.

Some additional features of the TPL workshops include:

1. Participating teachers are required to bring a lesson of their own that they hope to align with the NGSS standards. Time is available for participating teachers to work collaboratively and with the workshop facilitator to improve their lessons, using the EQuIP Rubric for Science (https://bit.ly/2tlr1lr).*

2. The program includes development of a strong online teacher professional community where teachers will feel comfortable sharing and improving their NGSS experiences.

3. After the workshop, the TPL video modules are available online for teachers to use as resource and review tools, as well as in their own classrooms.

4. This style of blended professional learning, facilitated in duet teaching style, is best implemented with follow-up sessions throughout the school year.

5. Teachers are invited to participate in online communities for active collaborative TPL and reflection.

6. Wide use of this blended Teacher Professional Learning model will enable MIT BLOSSOMS to conduct a formal assessment of how successful BLOSSOMS video lessons are in guiding and encouraging

* "The purpose of the rubric and review process is to: (1) review existing lessons and units to determine what revisions are needed; (2) provide constructive criterion-based feedback and suggestions for improvement to developers; (3) identify examples/models for teachers' use within and across states; and (4) to inform the development of new lessons, units, and other instructional materials." ("EQuiP Rubric for Science," n.d.)

teachers to adopt a more active, student-centered, and inquiry-based pedagogy in their own classrooms.

Additional information about the TPL workshops is available on the BLOSSOMS website.

SUMMARY AND CONCLUSIONS

The function of education is to teach one to think intensively and to think critically. Intelligence plus character—that is the goal of true education.

—Martin Luther King Jr.

We have focused on STEM: science, technology, engineering, and mathematics, emphasizing two themes: (1) STEM subject matter must be taught and learned in a new way, one that leverages fundamentals of learning science, and (2) substantial positive impact on student learning requires education systems changes.

Learning Science

Our proposed pedagogical model, brought to reality with MIT BLOSSOMS lessons, entails phenomenon-motivated, active, inquiry-based learning, guided both by the in-class teacher and the video-recorded BLOSSOMS teacher. We have argued that most mathematical and scientific findings were originally motivated by the need to analyze and understand phenomena in the world around us. Students, via discovery, can learn and remember best in such a reality-motivated learning environment. Highly respected in education, schools in Finland utilize phenomenon-based learning and argue strongly for its continued use (Silander, 2015; Northern, 2018). This pedagogical approach also helps ameliorate another problem of current STEM education—early dropouts of students from STEM learning paths, due to their feeling that STEM is boring, hard, and not relevant to their lives. Phenomenon-based learning, appropriately taught, can change all that—truly engaging the students (Huitt, 2011; Volet & Jarvela, 2001). An engaged student is motivated and eager to learn.

Active, inquiry-based learning has been studied and recommended widely. (Kubieck, 2005). Quoting from a widely cited NAS report, "Active learning leads to increases in examination performance that would raise average grades by a half a letter, and . . . failure rates under traditional lecturing increase by 55% over the rates observed under active learning. The analysis supports theory claiming that calls to increase the number of students receiving STEM degrees could be answered, at least in part, by abandoning traditional lecturing in favor of active learning." (Freeman, et. al., 2014). The results are clear and unambiguous, an unusual situation in education research! Finally, we should mention that there is a significant Venn diagram overlap between phenomenon-based learning and active, inquiry-based learning. One can add to the Venn diagram, with even more overlaps, project-based learning (PBL), also highly praised in the learning science literature (Blumenfeld et. al., 1991; Capraro, Capraro, & Morgan, 2013).

Finally, we incorporate dual teaching in the classroom, the "teaching duet" of BLOSSOMS. Why bring an "outsider" into the class? There are at least three reasons. First, teachers spend upwards of 60 hours per week (and often more) just doing what they need to do to "keep their heads above water": prepare for class and teach the required curriculum, grade papers and exams, manage myriad issues that arise, and so forth (Murray, 2013). They do not have time to research and create from scratch a nontextbook deep learning lesson in science or mathematics. Second, research has shown that individual lessons created and heavily vetted by experts, over months, can be superior to those created by single teachers operating in "craft mode." This process of multimonth lesson creation and ultimate sharing is called *Lesson Study*, featured in Japan (Arani, Fukaya, & Lassegard, 2010) as well as the United States (Droese, 2010). BLOSSOMS lessons are Lesson Study lessons (Hird et. al., 2014), their design and creation following a rigorous six-step production process, involving multiple individuals highly qualified in the content and pedagogy, with average time from start to finish being about nine months. Third, BLOSSOMS teachers represent the diversity of teachers throughout the world. They are drawn from many different ethnicities, religions, and cultures. They range in age from 16 to 75. Over 50% are female. Eleven languages are spoken in the BLOSSOMS video repository. The BLOSSOMS video teacher can serve as a role model, hopefully motivating many students—seeing someone who "looks like" and "acts like" them—to attempt to emulate that superlative teacher (Weber, 2011; Shin, Levy, & London, 2016). In a sense, the BLOSSOMS video teacher is a "force multiplier" to the in-class teacher. And the in-class teacher, the most important component in the educational system, is the mentoring guide for students in their active learning and discovery.

Systems Changes

We have argued that, with regard to STEM, the educational systems of the United States and many other countries require substantial change in order to effectively educate the future leaders of the 21st century. With MIT BLOSSOMS being a small program in these huge systems, there is only so much we can contribute. From our 10+ years of in-the-field experiences with BLOSSOMS in multiple countries, we have identified two changes that we believe are critical and mandatory:

1. Reduce the significance of standardized multiple-choice tests as an evaluator of a STEM student's academic abilities, and augment the evaluation with an equally important portfolio of the student's accomplishments.

2. Work to develop improvements in STEM teachers' training, working conditions, salaries, recruitment, and career paths.

With regard to teachers' training, we feel that too many current STEM teachers do not have adequate deep knowledge of the STEM material that they teach, and as a result they feel comfortable only teaching scripted lectures via one-way content delivery. Such lack of deep knowledge prohibits many classes from experiencing active, inquiry-based learning as illustrated by BLOSSOMS lessons.

Our two major new initiatives have been motivated by (1) and (2) above. The first is PBL, Project-Based Learning, using an appropriate BLOSSOMS lesson as the launching event of a multiweek PBL collaborative student team exercise. Comprehensive written and video guidance for the teacher is provided under this new initiative, not only in defining the possible PBL exercises but also in addressing complications that may arise during the weeks of the students' PBL efforts. Students who successfully complete the PBL exercise will experience thinking and learning like a scientist, what it means to "go deep" in a subject, and they will develop important social collaborative skills. The written project plus other student-created artifacts can be added to their portfolio of accomplishments.

The second is TPL, blended Teacher Professional Learning, where new BLOSSOMS lessons in science—using NGSS standards—are used as the anchoring mechanisms for all-day teacher professional learning workshops. The workshop starts with teachers as students, as learners, experiencing the same BLOSSOMS NGSS lesson that they themselves will ultimately teach to their own students. The workshops should demonstrate going deep in a given science phenomenon, using active, inquiry-based learning.

Newton's laws of motion apply to organizations just as they apply to physical objects. We have argued that due to significant system inertia anchored to the status quo, a huge set of forces, all working in one compatible direction, will be required to get "educational establishments" moving in more positive, compelling directions. A program such as BLOSSOMS can only play a limited role, producing a small net force. But we are excited that around the United States and elsewhere, there are myriad other innovative STEM-oriented programs now working in high schools, all adding to the vector force. Each should be considered as a mini experiment from which we can learn. New best practices will be identified, revalidated, fine-tuned, and then brought up to scale. The force is with us!

REFERENCES

Abdullah, Z., & Shukor, N. A. (2016). "Challenges in integrating BLOSSOMS in Malaysia's STEM education system." *Systems research and behavioral science*. Wiley. Published online in Wiley Online Library (wileyonlinelibrary.com). doi:10.1002/sres.2412

Alexanderson, G. L. (2006). Euler and Königberg's bridges: A historical view. *Bulletin of the American Mathematical Society, 43*(4), October 2006, 567–573. Published electronically July 18, 2006. Retrieved from https://bit.ly/2P6csw4

Amplify Science. (2018). What's so phenomenal about phenomena? An introduction to phenomenon-based learning. Lawrence Hall of Science, University of California. Retrieved from https://bit.ly/2KJIxMy

Arani, M. R. S., Fukaya, K., & Lassegard, J. P. (2010). Lesson study as professional culture in Japanese schools: An historical perspective on elementary classroom practices. *Nichibunken Japan Review, 22*, 171–200.

Archbald, D., & Newman, F. (1988). *Beyond standardized testing: Assessing authentic academic achievement in the secondary school*. Reston, VA: National Association of Secondary School Principals.

Avallone, A. (2018, August 27). Competency without compromise: Rethinking the high school transcript. *Education Week*. Retrieved from https://bit.ly/2LDCNzG

Barron, B. J. S., Schwartz, D. L., Vye, N. J., Moore, A., Petrosino, A., Zech, L., & Bransford, J. D. (1998). Doing with understanding: Lessons from research on problem- and project-based learning. *Journal of the Learning Sciences, 7*(3–4), 271–311. https://doi.org/10.1080/10508406.1998.9672056

Bishara, S. (2016). Creativity in unique problem-solving in mathematics and its influence on motivation for learning. Retrieved from https://doi.org/10.1080/2331186X.2016.1202604

Black, D. V. (2012). *The parallax activity: Measuring the distances to nearby stars.* [Video file]. MIT BLOSSOMS. Retrieved from https://blossoms.mit.edu/videos/lessons/parallax_activity_measuring_distances_nearby_stars

Blumenfeld, P. C., Soloway, E., Marx, R. W., Krajcik, J. S., Guzdial, M., & Palincsar, A. (1991). Motivating project-based learning: sustaining the doing, supporting the learning. *Educational Psychologist, 26*(3–4), 369–398. doi:10.1080/00461520.1991.9653139

Borg, L. (2018, August 18). Math, science teachers in short supply in R.I. schools. *Providence Journal.* Retrieved from http://www.providencejournal.com/news/20180818/math-science-teachers-in-short-supply-in-ri-schools

Budd, C., & Sangwin, C. (2004a). 101 Uses of a quadratic equation. *+plus magazine.* Retrieved from http://plus.maths.org/content/os/issue29/features/quadratic/index

Budd, C., & Sangwin, C. (2004b). 101 Uses of a quadratic equation: Part II. *+plus magazine.* Retrieved from http://plus.maths.org/content/101-uses-quadratic-equation-part-ii

Cammarata, L., & Larson, R. C. (2018). Project-based methods for assessment of active learning STEM video lessons. *International Journal on Innovations in Online Education.* Retrieved from http://onlineinnovationsjournal.com/streams/editor-s-choice-articles/17558d930bc39ba2.html

Campbell, D. T. (1979). Assessing the impact of planned social change. *Evaluation and Program Planning, 2*(1), 67–90. doi:10.1016/0149-7189(79)90048-X

Capraro, R. M., Capraro, M. M., & Morgan, J. R. (Eds.). (2013). *STEM project-based learning: an integrated science, technology, engineering, and mathematics (STEM) approach* (2nd ed.). Rotterdam, Boston: Springer Science & Business Media.

Clayton Christensen Institute. (n.d.). Blended learning universe. Retrieved from https://bit.ly/2MYICJt

Colburn, A. (2000, March). An inquiry primer. *Science Scope*, 42–44. Retrieved from http://www.experientiallearning.ucdavis.edu/module2/el2-60-primer.pdf

Conte, S. L. (2017). Newton´s laws applied to organizational change. *How to do business analysis blog.* Retrieved from https://bit.ly/2MG70mh

Darling-Hammond, L. (2018). Teaching is the profession on which all other professions depend. https://ed.stanford.edu/news/teaching-profession-which-all-other-professions-depend-linda-darling-hammond-transforming

Darling-Hammond, L., Sutcher, L., & Carver-Thomas, D. (2016, September 15). A coming crisis in teaching? teacher supply, demand, and shortages in the U.S. *Learning Policy Institute.* Retrieved from https://learningpolicyinstitute.org/product/coming-crisis-teaching

Dintersmith, T., & Wagner, T. (2015). *Most likely to succeed: Preparing our kids for the innovation era.* New York: Simon and Shuster.

Driver, R., Asojo, R., Leach, J., Mortimer, E., & Scott, P. (1994). Constructing scientific knowledge in the classroom. *Educational Researcher, 23*, 5–12.

Droese, S. (2010). *Lesson study in the US: Is it a mechanism for individual and organizational change? A case study of three schools* (Doctoral dissertation). Madison: The University of Wisconsin.

Einstein, A. (n.d.) *Goodreads.* Retrieved from https://www.goodreads.com/quotes/20149-nothing-happens-until-something-moves

Einstein, A. (n.d.). *Brainy Quote.* Retrieved from https://www.brainyquote.com/quotes/albert_einstein_108304

EnCorps STEM Teachers Program. (2018). There is a crisis-level shortage of math and science teachers. https://encorps.org/about/stem-crisis/

Equip rubric for science. (n.d.). Next generation science standards. Retrieved from https://www.nextgenscience.org/resources/equip-rubric-science

Ferlazzo, L. (2018, August 4). Response: Ways to improve state-standardized tests. *Education Week*. Retrieved from https://bit.ly/2webyFY

Ferris, E. (2017). *An introduction to the physics of sailing* [Video file]. MIT BLOSSOMS. Retrieved from https://blossoms.mit.edu/videos/lessons/introduction_physics_sailing

Formaggio, J. A., & Machuca, J. (2011). *The physics of pool* [Video file]. MIT BLOSSOMS. Retrieved from https://blossoms.mit.edu/videos/lessons/physics_pool

Freeman, S., Eddy, S. L., McDonough, M., Smith, M. K., Okoroafor, N., Jordt, H., & Wenderoth, M. P. (2014, June 10). Active learning increases student performance in science, engineering, and mathematics. *PNAS, 111*(23), 8410–8415; published ahead of print May 12, 2014. https://doi.org/10.1073/pnas.1319030111

Gardner, B. (2009). Geometry before Euclid. *Euclid's Elements—A 2,500 Year History*. Retrieved from https://faculty.etsu.edu/gardnerr/Geometry-History/before-euclid.htm

Geweertz, C. (2018, November 12). Importance of SAT, ACT scores dwindling in college admissions. *Education Week*. Retrieved from https://bit.ly/2DDbeqF

Glenn, P. (2016, April 23). Why project-based learning hasn't gone mainstream (and what we can do about it). *EdSurge*. Retrieved from https://bit.ly/1YQ72E9

Gonczy, T. (2003). Ancient Chinese mathematics: right triangles & their applications. Retrieved from https://bit.ly/2MpUOqc

Hake, R. R. (1998). Interactive-engagement versus traditional methods: A six-thousand-student survey of mechanics test data for introductory physics courses. *American Journal of Physics 66*, 64–74.

Hald, A. W. (2004). *A history of probability and statistics and their applications before 1750* (p. 3). Retrieved from https://bit.ly/2yDZ2BN

Hall, Manci. (2016). How do you get your students to do the assigned reading? *The innovative instructor blog*. https://ii.library.jhu.edu/2016/04/01/how-do-you-get-your-students-to-do-the-assigned-reading/

Hardin, G. (1968, December 13). The tragedy of the commons. *Science,162*(3859), 1243–1248. doi:10.1126/science.162.3859.1243

Hardin, G. (2005, March 13). The tragedy of the commons. *The Garrett Hardin Society*. Retrieved from http://www.garretthardinsociety.org/articles/art_tragedy_of_the_commons.html

Hart, R. (2010). *The Chinese roots of linear algebra*. New York: Johns Hopkins University Press.

Haupt, S. (2013). *The Pythagorean theorem: Geometry's most elegant theorem*. MIT BLOSSOMS. Retrieved from https://bit.ly/2OsRZRF

Heath, C., & Heath, D. (2018, January 10). The secret to student engagement. *Education Week*. Retrieved from https://www.edweek.org/ew/articles/2018/01/10/the-secret-to-student-engagement.html

High Tech High. (n.d.). Retrieved from https://www.hightechhigh.org/hth/

Hill, J. G., & Gruber, K. J. (2011). Education and certification qualifications of departmentalized public high school-level teachers of core subjects: Evidence from the 2007–08 schools and staffing survey. U.S. Department of Education, National Center for Education Statistics, Institute of Education Sciences. NCES 2011-317.

Hird, M., Larson, R. C., Okubo, Y., & Uchino, K. (2014). Lesson study and lesson sharing: an appealing marriage. *Creative Education, 5*, 769–779. SciRes. https://file.scirp.org/Html/7-6302167_46993.htm

Horn, A., & Peña-Alcaraz, M. (2013). *Tragedy of the commons* [Video file]. MIT BLOSSOMS. Retrieved from https://blossoms.mit.edu/videos/lessons/tragedy_commons

Huitt, W. (2011). Motivation to learn: An overview. *Educational psychology interactive.* Valdosta, GA: Valdosta State University. Retrieved from http://www.edpsycinteractive.org/topics/motivation/motivate.html

Keillor, G. (2000). *National Geographic: In search of Lake Wobegon.* Retrieved from http://www.garrisonkeillor.com/national-geographic-in-search-of-lake-wobegon/

Kubieck, J. (2005). Inquiry-based learning, the nature of science, and computer technology: New possibilities in science education. *Canadian Journal of Learning and Technology / La Revue canadienne de l'apprentissage et de la technologie, 31*(1), Canadian Network for Innovation in Education. Retrieved from https://www.learntechlib.org/p/42864/.

LaCurts, K., & Ousterhout, A. (2018). *The friendship paradox: Why we can't all be popular* [Video file]. MIT BLOSSOMS math & science video lessons for high school classes. Retrieved from https://blossoms.mit.edu/videos/lessons/friendship_paradox_why_we_can't_all_be_popular

Larson, R. C. (2008). *The broken stick experiment: triangles, random numbers, and probability* [Video file]. MIT BLOSSOMS. Retrieved from https://bit.ly/2Rtfegi

Larson, R. C. (2018). Solving real-world math problems with inquiry-based, collaborative learning. Share my lesson. Retrieved from https://bit.ly/2DhFlzd

Larson, R., & Murray, E. (2016). STEM education: Inferring promising systems changes from experiences with MIT BLOSSOMS. *Systems Research and Behavioral Science, 34*(3). Wiley Online Library. doi:10.1002/sres.2411

Lenox, F. (2018). *Hanging by a thread* [Video file]. MIT BLOSSOMS. Retrieved from https://blossoms.mit.edu/videos/lessons/hanging_thread

Liang, F. (2015). *How tall is that?* [Video file]. MIT BLOSSOMS. Retrieved from https://blossoms.mit.edu/videos/lessons/how_tall

Livengood, D., & Jordan, R. (2014). *Averages: Still flawed* [Video file]. MIT BLOSSOMS math & science video lessons for high school classes. Retrieved from https://blossoms.mit.edu/videos/lessons/averages_still_flawed

Malik, N. A. (2016a). Challenges to high school STEM education in Pakistan. *Systems Research and Behavioral Science, 34*, 307–309. Wiley Online Library (wileyonlinelibrary.com). doi:10.1002/sres.2413

Malik, N. A. (2016b). Naveed A. Malik—LINC 2016 Conference Speaker. Massachusetts Institute of Technology. Retrieved from http://linc2016.mit.edu/program/speakers/naveed-a-malik

Marmash, G. S. A. (2010). *Pythagoras and the juice seller* [Video file]. MIT BLOSSOMS. Retrieved from https://blossoms.mit.edu/videos/lessons/pythagoras_and_juice_seller

Martin, C. (2018, October 1). The U.S. desperately needs to modernize and elevate the teaching profession. Here are some ways to advance the workforce for the next generation. *The 74.* Retrieved from https://bit.ly/2IAnZ4A

Martzoff, J. C. (1996). *A history of Chinese mathematics.* Shanghai, China: Berlin Heidelberg: Springer-Verlag.

Mastery Transcript Consortium. (n.d.). Retrieved from http://mastery.org

Medina, J., Benner, K., & Taylor, K. (2019, March 12). Actresses, business leaders and other wealthy parents charged in U.S. college entry fraud. *New York Times.* Retrieved from https://www.nytimes.com/2019/03/12/us/college-admissions-cheating-scandal.html

Michael, J. (2006). Where's the evidence that active learning works? *Advances in Physiology Education, 30*, 159–167.

Minnesota Public Radio. (2018). A Prairie Home Companion with Garrison Keillor. Retrieved March 7, 2019, from https://www.prairiehome.org/index.html

Moritz, M., & Weiss, E. (2018, April 11). Opinion: The U.S. doesn't have enough STEM teachers to prepare students for our high-tech economy. 4 steps toward addressing that shortage. *The 74 million.* Retrieved from https://bit.ly/2LgtqFX

Moyer, E. (n.d.). Pythagorean knowledge in ancient Babylonia. *Egypt origins*. Retrieved from http://www.egyptorigins.org/babpyth.htm

Murray, C. (2013). How many hours do educators really work? *EdTech Magazine*. Retrieved from https://edtechmagazine.com/k12/article/2013/08/how-many-hours-do-educators-actually-work

Next Generation Science. (n.d.). Three dimensional learning. Retrieved from http://www.nextgenscience.org/three-dimensions

Nigmatulina, K. R. (2009). *Taking Walks, delivering mail: An introduction to graph theory* [Video file]. MIT BLOSSOMS. Retrieved from https://bit.ly/2Bbjg9t

Northern, S. (2018, October 31). Phenomenon-based learning in Finland inspires student inquiry [Blog post]. Retrieved from https://bit.ly/2TuoZzj

Pinxten, M., De Laet, T., Soom, C., & Langie, G. (2015). Fighting increasing drop-out rates in the STEM field. *The European readySTEMgo project*. Retrieved from https://bit.ly/2MZYVpi

Pythagorean Theorem. (n.d.). Retrieved from http://mathematica.ludibunda.ch/pythagoras6.html

Pythagorean Theorem–Egyptian Pyramids. (n.d.). Retrieved from http://pythagoreantheorem-pyramids.tumblr.com

Pythagorean Theorem–Egyptian Pyramids. (n.d.). *BibMe*. Retrieved from http://www.bibme.org/

Qayyum, A. (2015, June 29). 6 hilarious road side activities in Pakistan. *Shugal*. Retrieved from https://www.shughal.com/6-hilarious-road-side-activities-in-pakistan/

Scott, N. (2015, September 23). The 50 greatest Yogi Berra quotes. *USA Today*. Retrieved from https://ftw.usatoday.com/2015/09/the-50-greatest-yogi-berra-quotes

Shin, J., Levy, S., & London, B. (2016, July). Effects of role model exposure on STEM and non-STEM student engagement. *Journal of Applied Social Psychology, 46*(7). doi:10.1111/jasp.12371

Silander, P. (2015). Phenomenon-based learning. Retrieved from http://www.phenomenaleducation.info/phenomenon-based-learning.html

Socrates. (n.d.). *Goodreads*. Retrieved from https://www.goodreads.com/quotes/69267-education-is-the-kindling-of-a-flame-not-the-filling

Stanford Graduate School of Education. (2018, July 21). Retrieved from https://stanford.io/2LmcZrv

Student engagement. (n.d.). In *The glossary of education reform*. Retrieved from https://www.edglossary.org/student-engagement/

Symeonidis, V., & Schwarz, J. F. (2016). A phenomenological perspective on teaching and learning, capturing holistic phenomena. A recent program reform in Finland. *Forum Oświatowe, 28*(2), 31–47.

Tucker, C. (2016, March 2). Letting students lead the learning. Retrieved from https://catlintucker.com/2016/03/students-lead-learning/

Tragedy of the commons [Simulation]. (n.d.). MIT BLOSSOMS. Retrieved from https://blossoms.mit.edu/legacy/tragedy/index.htm

University of Vermont. (2018, July 2). Teachers lacking educational background in science use inquiry-oriented instruction least: Not using the pedagogical approach heralded by the National Research Council could be linked to unfilled STEM jobs. *ScienceDaily*. Retrieved from https://www.sciencedaily.com/releases/2018/07/180702094100.htm

Volet, S., & Jarvela, S. (2001). *Motivation in learning contexts: Theoretical advances and methodological implications*. London: Pergamon/Elsevier.

Weber, K. (2011). Role models and informal STEM-related activities positively impact female interest in stem. *Technology and Engineering Teacher, 71*(3), 18–21.

ABOUT THE AUTHORS

Richard C. Larson, professor at the Massachusetts Institute of Technology, was trained in operations research and systems analysis. He has devoted much of his recent time to STEM education, especially at the high school level. He is a strong advocate for students learning STEM in active learning settings, where they often "discover" key STEM concepts, leading to student engagement, commitment, knowledge retention, and development of critical thinking skills.

Elizabeth Murray started her MIT career as a founding volunteer for MIT LINC—Learning International Networks Consortium—an initiative connecting university educators from developing countries to enrich their knowledge of online distance education. She has been BLOSSOMS project manager since 2008.

ACKNOWLEDGMENTS

As a program that produces freely available open educational resources (OER), BLOSSOMS requires outside funding to do our work. To that end we have received generous funding from a variety of foundations, corporations, individuals and MIT, all cited at the end of each BLOSSOMS video lesson.

For supporting conversations related to this chapter, we thank Peter McLaren, Glenn Strehle, Dan Frey, and all of our BLOSSOMS teachers. The following helped to support the work and ideas reported herein: The Lounsbery Foundation, the Open Education Resources Foundation Inc. of Florida, the MIT Abdul Latif Jameel World Education Lab, NTT Com Asia Ltd., Trumptech (Hong Kong) Ltd., and the Hong Kong Innovation and Technology Fund (ITS/212/16FP) under the HKUST-MIT Research Alliance Consortium. Findings and opinions expressed herein are those of the authors and do not necessarily represent those of the sponsors or of MIT.

CHAPTER 11

The Art of Learning Science at Sesame Workshop

Jennifer A. Kotler, Courtney B. (Wong) Chin, and Rosemarie T. Truglio
Sesame Workshop

ABSTRACT
In this chapter, educational researchers at Sesame Workshop provide insights on preschool children's understanding of educational television through the lens of learning science. The authors describe findings demonstrating *Sesame Street*'s efficacy, the formative research process, and theoretical approaches to helping children comprehend messages from the show. Using examples from their own work with children over the last decade and beyond, they describe guiding principles from learning science that have helped the creators of *Sesame Street* help children learn important cognitive and social skills. Such principles include understanding children's developmental level and background knowledge, tailoring story lines and design features in ways to maximize comprehension and promote motivation and engagement. They describe considerations for nonlinear video as well as for adults who support children's learning. Finally, the authors discuss future directions for learning science.

One of these chapters is not like the others. If you grew up in the late 1960s or early 1970s, the introductory sentence may ring a bell. It is inspired by a popular *Sesame Street* song, "One of These Things Is Not Like the Other," designed to teach sorting and classification skills. This chapter is different from the others in this book, as it focuses on how learning science influences the longest-running preschool educational television program in history. Throughout the chapter we highlight principles and findings from the field of learning science that support children learning from educational video. We share our research findings from *Sesame Street*, which celebrates its 50th anniversary on November 10, 2019, to highlight learning science principles in action.

Sesame Street was conceived by Joan Ganz Cooney in the late 1960s as an educational experiment to use media to teach children school readiness skills. Ms. Cooney noted the incredible allure that popular television advertisements had on children and felt that the same strategies and techniques could be used to prepare children, particularly those who did not have access to high-quality educational support, important skills to help prepare for kindergarten. This idea was sparked around the same time that Head Start became a national program designed to help disadvantaged children become prepared for formal schooling. A grant from the Carnegie Foundation with Lloyd Morrisett as a thought partner, the willingness of PBS to air the show, and a partnership with Jim Henson, a master puppeteer, allowed Joan Ganz Cooney's vision to become a reality (Fisch & Truglio, 2001).

Particularly unique about the program is the collaboration of educators, researchers, and creatives (writers, producers, puppeteers, animators, filmmakers), all of whom play an integral role to produce an engaging and educationally impactful show that meets the needs of young children. This "marriage" between creative, education, and research became firmly embedded as the Sesame Workshop model.

The first two authors of this chapter, Kotler and Shin (née Wong) are researchers. The members of our full-time team of five are responsible for conducting research at various stages of development. We have doctorates and masters degrees and equivalent studies and backgrounds in child development, psychology, education, children's theater, and anthropology. We conduct quantitative and qualitative analyses across a range of methodologies. The third author leads the curriculum and education team. Dr. Truglio holds a PhD in developmental psychology, and her team has backgrounds in education, child development, and psychology at the master's and bachelor's levels. Her team is responsible for developing each season of *Sesame Street* curriculum and working with the production team to guide the writing toward educational outcomes. The production team is the third partner in the marriage, and its members have backgrounds in television production, writing, communication, and other creative fields. They oversee the writers and the development of the scripts.

At the beginning of the 1960s, behaviorism was a popular discipline addressing how children learn that pervaded academic institutions. Cognitive psychology and learning theories started gaining traction as the decade progressed (Goleman, 1987). In conversations with Dr. Lewis Bernstein, who was on the research team early in his career, later the executive producer of *Sesame Street* and then the head of the Education, Research and Outreach group, and Dr. Shalom Fisch, who was vice president of research for over 15 years, there were a variety of learning theories that informed the work. Dr. Bernstein says when he joined the Workshop in 1972, the theoretical underpinning of *Sesame Street* was a "nondogmatic eclecticism," meaning it took the best approaches across theoretical frameworks (Lewis Bernstein, personal communication, January 29, 2019).

The first two years of *Sesame Street* were evaluated for efficacy and impact. The first year evaluation was focused on measurable academic skills (literacy, mathematics, science), as well as cognitive processing skills (logic and reasoning). The second year continued to focus on these skills but expanded the curriculum to include more social and emotional goals. To date, the *Sesame Street* curriculum is revised on an annual basis to ensure that the needs and best practices are integrated into new programming. In both evaluation studies the researchers found that children who watched *Sesame Street* more frequently learned more than nonviewers or less frequent viewers (Ball & Bogatz, 1970; Bogatz & Ball, 1971). Results indicated that *Sesame Street* viewers showed greater gains in areas such as knowledge of the alphabet, numbers, shapes, relational terms, and sorting and classification skills compared to nonviewers. The show reached almost two million homes and continued to grow its audience over those first initial years. Flash forward 50 years, and *Sesame Street* has been present in 150 countries in various iterations including about 35 coproductions.

Numerous research studies of the US-based show since those first initial evaluations in the early 1970s continue to demonstrate *Sesame Street*'s influence in helping children's development. Several independent studies provide evidence of the long-term impact of *Sesame Street* on school readiness, with significant, measurable benefits found after 1, 3, or even 10 years (Fisch, 2000; Fisch & Truglio, 2001; Kotler, Truglio, & Betancourt,

2016). According to one naturalistic longitudinal study, viewing of *Sesame Street* in the preschool years has even been found to be associated with significantly higher grades in English, mathematics, and science in high school (Huston, Anderson, Wright, Linebarger, & Schmitt, 2001). A recent analysis that looked at viewing trends and broadcast availability when *Sesame Street* was first on the air showed that children who had greater access to the show in early childhood did better in school. The impacts were particularly evident for boys, black children, and children living in economically disadvantaged areas, and the benefits remained throughout elementary school (Kearney & Levine, 2015).

While many of the evaluation studies show evidence *that* the program supports positive development and for whom, this chapter intends to go deeper into theoretical and practical applications of *why* the content works and how to improve it. Principles from and research through the lens of learning science has helped the team at Sesame Workshop understand what is working and why. Learning science principles may also help us understand how we may need to modify the content to ensure that we produce the intended positive effects. This chapter will focus on content development and the findings from research with children that help all of us create effective educational content.

FORMATIVE RESEARCH AND POSTPRODUCTION SHOW TESTING METHODS

The collaboration between production, education, and research necessitated that all work together to ensure high-quality content. Sesame Workshop, formerly called The Children's Television Workshop, required that early versions of segments be tested with children to assure that children understood the messages and were engaged by the content before the content was finalized. Formative research played and still plays a strong role in helping us shape what the content becomes. When formative research is not conducted because of time constraints, we often do postproduction episode testing to assess how well we did in conveying the messages and inform future production decisions. Bottom line: As Ms. Cooney says, the children are the real experts, and we must take the time to listen to them.

Formative research is the testing of content while it is being developed. At the individual television episode level, the research team tests early drafts of the content to ensure that the story line is being embraced by the children in the ways that the writers and education team intended and that the content is understood and liked. We sometimes do this by creating a storybook. The design team provides characters and artwork, and the research team creates a storybook based on exact wording in the script. The research team reads the storybook to children, often attempting the character voices, and assesses where children seem particularly engaged or confused. When time and resources allow, we often ask the production team to create a more polished storymatic that allows us to show children a rough draft of the show with moving pictures. The storymatic is rough, the voices might not be those of the actual actors, but the depiction gives children a general sense of what the show will ultimately look like. These early drafts allow the research team to take the content out to children in their schools or in a focus group setting and get an initial sense of what is emerging from the story. The researchers tell the children that the show is not finished yet but that we need them to help us make it as good as it can be.

Our methods vary when working with children. The research team sometimes pretests children individually and sometimes in groups to get a sense of what they might know about a topic beforehand, or sometimes we just show them the draft episode and have them watch it. Most of the time children view the stories in groups of five to eight, although sometimes there are larger or smaller groups depending on the project. After viewing, children are asked questions—many open-ended questions to assess recall, and sometimes we have options to assess recognition. Most children we work with for *Sesame Street* are ages three or four, and we do not expect that all children will want to or be able to speak to us, but the research team gets a sense of what we are hearing and what we are not hearing from the children who feel most comfortable speaking.

When storymatic or storybook creation is too costly or there is not enough time for it, then the research team tests episodes right before they are finalized, or just after they are finalized. Under these circumstances, changes are difficult to make even if some are suggested, but testing these episodes for children's understanding of the story lines helps the creative and content teams prepare for the next season—what worked well and where we need to be better. These tests also help indicate if there needs to be more supporting material around the particular segments to ensure that the intended messages are reinforced more broadly. In a few cases, if an almost finished show tests in a way that is worrisome, that show won't be broadcast or the content will be edited.

The research methods described above sometimes resemble well-controlled quantitative and qualitative research designs and sometimes are more informal conversations. Formative research is usually not designed to be systematic or generalizable for the field at large, but many of our studies are scientifically rigorous and could meet requirements for peer-reviewed journal articles. Most often we do have a protocol of questions that are followed. When percentages are reported, they are based on individual-level coded data. Our group discussions are analyzed with more qualitative approaches.

THEORETICAL ORIENTATION TOWARD LEARNING

Various theoretical approaches have been proposed about how children learn information in the classroom, from engaged others, and from media. Dr. Bernstein described the nondogmatic eclecticism that was present at the Workshop in the early years. This sentiment feels true today as well. Throughout the 50 years of *Sesame Street*'s broadcast, there have been education and research staff coming from a variety of approaches to learning: we have had behaviorist, cognitivist, and constructivist approaches represented in several departments across the history of the organization. Besides theoretical orientation, we have had staff from a variety of disciplines influencing content development including those from child development, various fields within psychology, sociology, anthropology, education, and communications who have brought their wisdom to the various projects Sesame Workshop develops.

Although our curricula may have differed over the years, the importance of understanding child development and applying theory to practice has not. There are some principles, across a variety of disciplines and orientations, that pervade the way we approach content creation and child learning. These principles may have overlapping theoretical underpinnings and can be supported using similar research designs, but they contribute to the lens by which we consider how content is created and evaluated.

One might speculate that having multiple theoretical approaches may be overwhelming and that having a single overriding approach might be valuable. But learning science is multidisciplinary and uses multiple approaches, which is seen as a strength of its discipline—no single theory can best explain learning. Various theoretical approaches allow us to understand learning more deeply and for a broader array of learners. Furthermore, theory guides practice, but it is through research that we are able to test hypotheses and truly see the results of our efforts. Research helps us determine ultimately whether we are going in the right direction.

In the following section we provide some guiding principles about children's development that help the research and education teams at Sesame Workshop understand and think about how children will process new information and how they learn best. Along with guiding principles, we provide examples from our collective knowledge and experiences working with children for the past 10 to 30 years, as well as specific examples from research with children that highlight the various principles in action. These guiding principles and accompanying examples are not an exhaustive list but are meant to be illustrative of the kinds of ways theory informs practice.

Principle 1: Understand the Ages, Stages, and Past Experiences of the Audience

Children make meaning from what they see on television based on their developmental level, as well as their past and current experiences with television and real-world experiences. Drawing from information processing theories, as well as more cognitive developmental schools of thought (such as Piaget), we know that certain topics and portrayals are more readily absorbed and understood than others.

Applying this principle in our research studies, we often look to see whether children understand the main messages of the story line and whether they are able to understand feelings of characters, make connections between events, and have enough background information about the particular topic to respond to the screen and infer information that is not necessarily explicitly demonstrated or discussed. Sometimes we have a sense from the literature that certain portrayals may be very challenging given children's developmental level particularly because children usually attend to one main thing at a time.

Centration and Preoperational Thought

Piaget posited that preschool children are in *preoperational* thought. One particular aspect of this stage of development is *centration*, which is attending to one property of a concept at a time and often ignoring other properties. This often leads to false conclusions. Understanding children's development from a Piagetian perspective helps us understand how children might approach particular content. For example, the team was thinking about creating new segments of *Elmo's World* where children would be asked to play along with Elmo as he played a matching game.

We tested a variety of ways to ask children to match items before any actual content was made. One example we tested was to ask children to match a target "bee" to one of three other bees. No media had been created, so we used some artwork that had been around for other purposes. The target bee had 6 legs, 4 wings, 2 antennae, 1 tail, and a smiley face. One wrong answer bee had 2 legs, 4 wings, 2 antennae, 1 tail, and a smiley face. The other wrong answer bee had 6 legs, no wings, 2 antennae, 1 tail, and a smiley face. The antennae, tail, and smiley face remained constant. The legs and wings changed. If this was difficult for you to keep track of, imagine yourself as a 3-year-old who may not have developed a sense of one-to-one correspondence (the ability to match an item to a number set) and does not have the ability to *subitize* (the ability to assess the number of things at a glance without actually counting). Some children were able to identify the matching bee, but they could not articulate why it was a match. Other children struggled to find the matching bee (Kotler & Wong, 2016). Our advice to the production team was to begin with matching bees that only differed on one dimension such as the number of legs, not on two (legs and wings). We also recommended using simpler designs of bees so children were not distracted by the extraneous features that were not a part of the matching task.

Another example of how the concept of centration could help explain children's understanding of a story is from a street story we tested about a clothing drive (Wong, 2017a). Here the two dimensions that were at play were the concept of fit (I no longer fit into a sweater) and need (I don't have a sweater and need one). In this story, a Muppet named Rudy outgrew his sweater. Even though he loved it, it no longer fit him. The adults around him suggested that he give it to someone else who needs it through a clothing drive. In the rough draft version of the story, Rudy asks different characters if they need a sweater. Each example of his kind gesture showed him attempting to give his sweater to others who were bigger than him and could not fit his sweater. In the original tested version, children reported that the story was about Rudy looking for someone who *fit* his sweater—not specifically for someone who *needed* a sweater—and they did not report much about the clothing drive. The writing team revised the script so that it featured examples of Rudy trying to give away his sweater to those who were similar size or smaller than him but were wearing sweaters, so it would be clear that they could fit the sweater but did not need it. So when Rudy finally found a match, a Muppet who *needed* a sweater and wasn't wearing one, it was clearer to children that this was because she needed a sweater. This was also reinforced by other Muppets at the clothing drive who were giving away clothes to neighbors who needed them. The focus was now more on need than it was on fit. In subsequent research children's responses demonstrated that they now focused more on need than on the fit and their understanding of the central message went up considerably (Wong, 2018).

Scripts and Memory Bias

Just as developmental stages may explain children's responses to the television they view, their own experiences also shape how they interpret characters and story lines. Schema theory, Piagetian principles, and information processing all suggest that children have certain ways in which they process and organize information. Children have certain scripts about sequencing of events, as well as the characteristics that go along with certain known concepts based on what they have seen before even if that means that their interpretation of a new event is hazy.

An example of how children apply their prior experience to a television show in ways that might conflict with their understanding of a new concept was demonstrated well in a *Sesame Street* episode designed to teach children that they do not need any superpowers to be an everyday hero; they can be kind all of the time (Wong, 2016c). The leading character, a human celebrity, comes to *Sesame Street* in a cape and describes himself as the Everyday Hero. The Everyday Hero traverses the neighborhood with his cape demonstrating the kind things he can do for those who encounter him—such as helping with carrying groceries or getting a ball that went into the street. Children watched a storymatic of the episode, and upon the conclusion we asked them to tell us about what happened. The children, who were 3 and 4 years old, focused on the celebrity's superpowers—his cape, his strength, and in one case, gave him "laser eyes" that he did not possess and were nowhere to be seen or heard in the show! While the superpowers of the everyday hero were engaging for the children, the message of being kind in everyday ordinary ways appeared to be buried. This is not surprising given children's prior associations with superheroes. In an effort to engage children with a superhero narrative that we all assumed would be interesting to children, the educational message was lost. To remedy this, the writers rewrote the script making a leading character a "kindness kid"—with no cape or superhero qualities—and in the final episode testing children focused much more on his good deeds of being kind by helping others (Wong, 2017b).

Another example of children using previous knowledge to interpret circumstances in stories is a street story in which Rudy uses Abby's wand

(Abby is a Muppet who is a fairy) to try to cast a healing spell on Grover, who has a cold and cannot stop sneezing (Wong, 2016b). Instead of healing Grover, Rudy (who is a monster and not a fairy) casts a spell that makes Grover's sneezes cause seasons to change! Each time Grover sneezed, a pink frame with yellow and blue stars appeared as a border around the screen, with a "poof" sound effect, as the season changed. The frame and sound effects were designed to signal that magic had occurred. However, many children recalled the frame and sound effects not only as magic, but that a picture was being taken as well. Both of these factors—the magic and the picture, seemed to overshadow the sneeze as the reason for season changing. There was no mention or visual of a camera in the animatic, and the magic wand was not continuously used, yet the idea of picture-taking and successive magic spells likely overshadowed the central idea that Grover's magically influenced sneezing caused the season changes. The research findings suggested that in order to highlight the sneeze as the reason for season changes, having fewer features highlighting the use of magic might help. On the other hand, given that neither magic nor sneezing is a true cause for season changes, and these features were included solely as entertainment to teach more about the seasons, it is not terribly worrisome that magic overshadowed sneezing!

We have seen other examples of children using existing scripts that may explain children's misremembering or misinterpreting of information. For example, in one episode Buzz Aldrin comes to Sesame and talks about his visit to the moon (Kotler, 2005). One child's response to "How come Buzz Aldrin knows so much about the moon?" was "He was the first man to ride the reindeer there." This show testing occurred in the winter around Christmas, so it is possible that the child combined the Santa Claus narrative with the story about Buzz Aldrin! In that same episode, children also seemed unimpressed about the uniqueness of going to the moon. When asked if anyone had gone to the moon, at least one child replied "the cow," likely remembering the nursery rhyme that the cow jumped over the moon.

Emotionally Charged Stories

Not only might children use prior knowledge and schemas inaccurately to apply to new stories, certain scripts may activate certain memories over others. The research team often suggests to writers to include content that is emotionally salient to children. The reason for this is that content that has emotional meaning to children often is associated with more descriptive and accurate memories (Channell & Barth, 2013; Levine & Pizarro, 2004; Canli, Zhao, Brewer, Gabrieli, & Cahill, 2000). There is also a negativity bias in that events that are experienced more negatively are recalled more easily than are ones that are experienced more positively (Kensinger, 2009). Having a sense of the research surrounding the use of emotions to influence memory for a story has been helpful in understanding how children respond to episodes and why emotional story lines are important for impact. The 48th season of *Sesame Street* was focused on cultivating cultural competencies and embracing differences and similarities. For example, the Workshop did an early test of an episode that was designed to teach children that people have all different hair types that can move in different ways, but most importantly to emphasize that not all hair needs to be the same to be beautiful.

In the first tested draft of the story, two friends (an African American female puppet, Gabriela, with tight curly hair, and Prairie Dawn, a Caucasian female puppet with straight blonde hair) make up a dance that is focused on how they can move their hair. But as they choreograph their dance, they quickly realize that Gabriela's hair doesn't flip! At this point in the story, the friends think that they can't dance together until they somehow "fix" Gabriella's hair so it can flip just like Prairie's. Fortunately, Nina, a human female cast member, tells the girls that there's nothing wrong with Gabriella's hair and explains that different hair does different things.

The research group tested this episode with groups of 3- and 4-year-old children, who were mostly black and Hispanic, in a school in New York City. Children were able to pick up on the main character's emotions and the reason for her distress—but they seemed to not be able to recall that in the end she felt better because she realized her hair was great just the way it was and that she can could participate in a dance with the rest of the characters where all of their hair could do different things (Wong, 2016e). Moreover, the language children used to describe the character's hair was troubling. Children described her hair as broken and that it needed fixing, and they repeated that mantra despite the lead researcher attempting to have the children focus on the positive ending. The researcher spent another 10 to 15 minutes telling the children how beautiful each of their hair was. Research on the negativity bias gives context to why children picked up on the negative emotions felt by the character, but the fact that they were not able to remember the rest of the story was worrisome, as certainly the intention was not to leave children with that message.

With the Sesame Workshop Model in action, this information was shared and the script was rewritten. Instead of the focus being on what any one character could or could not do, the episode focused on how each character brought in a unique feature and contributed to the dance to make the dance more inclusive and special (Prairie Dawn flipped her hair, Gabriella wiggled her poofs, Elmo joined and fluffed his fur, Big Bird shook his tail feathers). They acknowledged briefly that their hair did different things and then celebrated the differences. There was no feeling bad about what one's hair couldn't do. When this version was tested in its full episode form, children were better able to tell the researchers the story line accurately and without a focus on any negative characteristics of being different (Wong, 2018). While often an emotional story is important for a hook, too much of a focus on hurt feelings might backfire and instead leave children with an unintended message. We all learned that lesson, and everyone worked together to create a new effective version.

In a similar instance of negativity bias, another script focused on Rudy not wanting to try new foods of different cultural backgrounds and then eventually trying and liking something new at the end (Wong, 2016f). There was a street fair on *Sesame Street* featuring foods from all over the world. Everyone was excited to see and try new foods—except for Rudy. Abby kept trying to get Rudy to try a new food, but he refused. Toward the end, they found saag paneer, which somewhat resembles grilled cheese—a food that Rudy knows and likes. They convince him to try it, he does, and he likes it! Most children, however, focused on Rudy saying no to trying new food at each food booth at the street fair and did not recall him trying any new foods. Research suggested that more emphasis be placed on him trying new foods and liking them.

Principle 2: Tailor Story Line and Design Features to Support Maximum Comprehension

Children learn from contexts that set them up to succeed and provide them with support. Drawing on Vygotskian principles of the zone of proximal development (ZPD), which is the difference between what a learner can do on his or her own and what can be done with the help of a more skilled or knowledgeable peer, and Bruner's work on scaffolding, meaning providing incremental support, it is important that the content provide supportive prompts in the story line and in the design features of the show.

Drawing on cognitive load theory (Sweller, 1988), which describes working memory as being limited in capacity and duration, it is important that as creators of educational media we reduce the "load" on children's processing to make it more likely that they will remember the most critical aspects of a story. In other words, we need to make sure that we are not asking children to process too many things at once and that we are highlighting the important things that the children should focus on. As in the previous examples with the negativity biases, the more we can highlight the positives or what we do want children to focus on, the better chance of overcoming biases or existing scripts that may or may not be accurate for understanding a new story.

Additionally, ensuring that the educational message is central to understanding the plot helps reduce cognitive load. Sometimes the educational messages are buried while an entertaining concept is highlighted. Drawing on the principles of information processing theory, Shalom Fisch has proposed the "capacity model" of television viewing, one that suggests children learn educational messages in television much better when the educational messages are in the plotline (Fisch, 2000). When an educational message is incidental to the main story line, children often miss it because their working memories have to attend to too many things at once.

Production features, the language and syntax of television and video, are a critically important aspect of children's understanding of story lines, conversations, and character portrayals. Often described as formal features, these are the ways that television producers use the camera, light, and sound and other techniques to draw viewers' attention to various aspects of a story or to signal information to the viewer without explanation. Pans, zooms, fades, and crashes all have meaning, and it is incredibly important to know whether children understand their meanings and what those effects do to their understanding of a story. When used effectively, they can draw children's attention to the most important aspects of a story (Huston et al., 1981).

Providing routine, familiarity, repetition, and structure within a show also helps with children's understanding of the content and reduces cognitive load. Segments like letter and number of the day, which are in most episodes, are incredibly popular, and children have learned to sing and dance along. The song and format is exactly the same for each episode. The only thing that changes is the letter or number. *Elmo's World*, which has the same features and segments within the show, was also designed to provide a consistent and familiar format to reduce cognitive load. Within a particular segment, repetition helps children retain critical information, and having characters who are trusted and liked deliver information also helps with learning.

Visual Superiority

One finding that was established early on in the television effects body of work was that for young children, information that is portrayed visually is more likely to be recalled than information that is presented verbally—having both is ideal for maximum input and processing. Information that is presented largely verbally, such as explanations for things that have few corresponding visual cues, will be less likely to be recalled.

One example that supports this contention is children's recall of two different segments of "Cookie Crumby Pictures" (Kotler, 2013). These 5-minute vignettes are parodies of popular family movies whose educational goal is to teach a variety of executive function strategies. In one episode, which is a James Bond 007 parody, Cookie Monster has to remember a pattern in order to open a series of doors to rescue a stolen crown. M (the wise advisor) gives him advice through his wristwatch and reminds him with verbal warnings to remember the strategy (stop and listen to the instructions) before impulsively pressing buttons (which result in chickens falling on his head when the wrong pattern is entered). In a second episode, a parody of *The Karate Kid*, Cookie Monster is asked to follow a particular pattern in order to understand "Biscotti Karate." The strategy that he is taught by the Biscotti Master is "Eyes watch, ears listen, voice quiet, body calm," and we see Cookie Monster and the Biscotti Master use nonverbal gestures to provide visual reinforcement for each component of the strategy. When we tested these episodes with children, while both tested pretty well for recall of the strategy, the one on the Biscotti Kid tested even better in understanding the overall transferable strategy. The children who watched the James Bond segment were more likely to recall the buttons used to open the doors but not the fact that Cookie Monster needed to listen, whereas the children who watched the Biscotti Kid vignette could not recall Biscotti Karate but could recall the strategy for paying attention. While there may be a variety of reasons why children recalled the strategy better in the Biscotti Kid version, we attribute much of this to what was most visually salient in the episode. The information about the strategy in the James Bond vignette came mostly from M, who was a small figure within a watch, and her advice was mostly verbal, whereas the Biscotti Kid vignette had advice from a co-located character, the Biscotti Master, who demonstrated the strategy visually and had Cookie Monster model the strategy.

Another example of the importance of visual emphasis is an episode about the Yip Yips' visit to *Sesame Street* (Wong, 2016g). The Yip Yips are aliens who marvel at all things that humans take for granted. In this episode, their job was to come to *Sesame Street* to learn about people and find out what was the same about all of them. They discovered four points of difference: people's size, skin color, physical ability (i.e., fully able vs. using a wheelchair), and language. The Yip Yips were sad because they could not seem to find what was the same about all people—only what was different. Elmo realized a Yip was sad and declared that that's what's the same about *everyone*—Earth people, monsters, and Martians all have feelings. Characters then sang a song about everyone having feelings, with little visual support to illustrate this message. What children recalled from this episode was that aliens were looking for people, and people have different sizes and skin colors—which were the two most strongly visually represented differences. Given that feelings are internal states, these are likely more difficult to model. However, increasing focus on the visual aspects of feelings such as facial expressions helped improve comprehension.

Principle 3: Ensure That Content Is Engaging and Motivating

Children learn more when they are motivated, cognitively engaged, and actively processing the information in front of them than if they do not connect with the content. Children cannot learn if they do not watch; therefore, we need to make the content as engaging as possible. Constructivists suggest that children make meaning of all learning material. In order to ensure that the content is meaningful, we need to provide content that is salient and participatory (children are focused intently on the screen and talk to the screen or follow instructional prompts such as "dance along with me." When children are invited in to join in the fun by a beloved character, we often see them respond.

The game moments in *Elmo's World* are an example of this engagement. Elmo's tablet fills the screen, and we can see Elmo's hand moving as he plays a game on the tablet and asks the children for help. He asks them to help him complete a simple task or set of tasks, with all of the information they need visible on-screen. After he asks each question, children's voices encourage him or give him suggestions about what to do next. The research team frequently sees children drop toys they are playing with and look up at the screen once they hear children's voices responding. They too join in and point at correct answer options, get up and touch the screen to "select" the correct answer, or shout helpful answers to Elmo.

Humor also plays an important role in children's continued engagement with the content. There are a variety of things children find funny. One of the segments of *Sesame Street* that gets consistent laughs is Mr. Noodle (an adult live character in *Elmo's World*), who is a mime who often gets things very wrong. Voice-overs of children and Elmo ask Mr. Noodle to do a variety of tasks like put on a shoe or use a jump rope, and he usually does something initially ridiculous with an earnest attempt. Eventually, with the help of Elmo and the children, he gets it right and he is very proud. Mr. Noodle demonstrates a variety of things that are funny to children. He uses exaggerations and clownish humor, he uses known objects the wrong way, he violates expectations (what adult doesn't know that you can't put a shoe on your arm!), and he earnestly seems to have no idea that he's making a mistake, making the children feel expert at something an adult is not.

Humor to Enhance or Detract from Learning

Humor is one of the hallmarks of *Sesame Street*. But humor must be used with caution given what we know about cognitive load and children's ability to focus on only one dimension of a problem at a time. The way humor is used varies, and we find from testing that certain aspects of humor help children understand the message and certain aspects of humor may interfere with children's comprehension of the intended message. What preschool children find humorous is usually based on some sort of incongruity—something out of place, something highly exaggerated, something unexpected for the setting (Lyon, 2006). According to instructional humor processing theory (Wanzer, Frymier, & Irvin, 2010), which is integrated from several learning theories, in order for students to learn from humor, they need to perceive and then resolve the incongruity in a humorous instructional message. If students do not resolve the incongruity, they may experience confusion instead of humor (Banas, Dunbar, Rodriguez, & Liu, 2011)

In the aforementioned episode about Buzz Aldrin, the main thesis of the story is that Cookie Monster wants to go to the moon because he thinks it's a giant cookie—it looks like a giant cookie, so he thinks it must be one. Cookie Monster spends a large portion of the episode trying to figure out a way to eat that giant cookie. Then Buzz Aldrin comes to *Sesame Street* and explains that the moon is made of rocks, and is not a cookie. Before showing children the episode, the research team asked them what they thought the moon was made of. Most did not know. One or two said rocks. No child said cookies. Upon watching the episode, it was clear that some of the children seemed to get the humor right away, laughing that Cookie Monster thought the moon was a cookie. Even if they had little understanding about what the moon was made of, they had a sense that it was not a giant cookie. At posttest, about 30% of the children were able to articulate that the moon is made of rocks. But about 15% of the children said the moon is made of cookies (Kotler, 2005). The researchers did not record whether children spoke such answers with a smile or laugh to indicate that they were laughing with us, but the sense we got when chatting with the children was that some of them were indeed confused about the actual composition of the moon. In this case, children had little prior knowledge of what the moon is made of, and the humor may have detracted from children learning the actual message, either because it gave them the wrong information or because it was just much more salient as part of the episode.

We have considered this and other examples of silly or ridiculous humor to cautiously review early drafts of scripts that may similarly center on a concept that is silly and possibly challenging to understand. Recall the episode about Rudy trying new foods. In the initial draft of the story, the focus was on Oksana, Oscar the Grouch's niece, coming to *Sesame Street* and not wanting to try new yummy foods (Wong, 2016d). Who would not want to try new yummy foods? As a relative of Oscar the Grouch who loves yucky things, it would make sense to us adults that his niece would also only like yucky and not yummy foods. However, the goal of the episode was to encourage children to try new, different foods that they had never tried before. With a focus on a repetition of Oksana not wanting to try yummy foods and only liking grouchy foods, theory would suggest that children would focus only on that silliness and miss the only somewhat related intended message about trying *new* foods, not just trying new *yummy* foods. In response, the writers changed the script to feature Rudy (who plays it seriously and is not a trash-loving character) not wanting to try new foods, removing the possibly detracting silly yucky/grouchy versus yummy humor.

Another study we conducted that makes the point about the role of humor as an enhancer or distractor was designed to understand children's comprehension of Global Grover 2.0 segments (Kotler, 2010). These segments are designed to teach children about different science, technology, engineering, and math (STEM) concepts with Super Grover as the hero who experiments in a very clumsy way in order to highlight an actual concept.

One vignette was designed to teach children how to use a ramp to get down from a high place when one cannot use the stairs. In this episode a cow can't get down from a higher place because the only way down is stairs and cows cannot physically walk down stairs. The second showed how a pole can be used as a lever to help a chicken get over a high wall. The last vignette we tested showed how to balance a boat that has an elephant at one end and a small sheep at the other end. The solution, after many failed attempts, is to bring more sheep aboard and finally get the boat balanced.

Before viewing, children were pretested on the different concepts and asked what tools and techniques they would use to solve the problems posed above. Children then watched the three vignettes. After each vignette children were interviewed about the concepts contained within that vignette and posttested on the vignette-specific problem. The order in which children were shown the vignettes was counterbalanced. The results of the study showed that for the ramp and lever episodes, children were more likely to identify a picture of a ramp and a lever and what they are used for after seeing the vignette than before. However, this was not the case for identifying that something is balanced. Children were asked to choose from four pictures of something that is balanced. Their multiple-choice answers did not increase significantly from pretest to posttest. They were also asked to identify how they know if something is balanced, and their ability to articulate this difference did not change from pretest to posttest either. This could be because that the concept of something being balanced is more complicated than being able to identify something that can be used as a ramp or a lever. But other answers lie in how the children explained the story back to us.

In the ramp and the lever episodes, the humor came from discovering how they were used. In the ramp vignette, a cow cannot walk downstairs, but when a big piece of wood falls from where the cow is, onto Grover who is at the bottom of the stairs, it creates a ramp, allowing the cow to walk down to the bottom, while Grover gets squashed under it. Children get to see a ramp being created and laugh as it is being created. In the pole as lever, as Grover learns to use the pole, we see him getting flung around, and then the chicken is able to fling herself across the wall, showing children that the pole can be used in this way to scale over a large object. By contrast, the vignette about balance showed a perfectly balanced boat with many sheep on one side and an elephant on another. However, the animals then realized that they couldn't get the boat to actually move, so in order to get it moving, the elephant adjusts himself to paddle and, in doing so, flings all of the sheep (including Grover, now dressed as a sheep) into the water. Because the part where the animals ultimately were balanced was not funny but the falling off of the boat was, it is possible that children's attention was not directed toward the balancing part of the lesson. Indeed, when we asked children what happened in the story, over 25% of the children said they all fell in the water (which was just in the very end of the story and only lasted a few seconds).

Another example where humor was used well to further the story and enhance learning is a Street story called "Rocking Rollie" (Wong, 2016a). In this story, two Muppet characters, Zoe and Rosita, are tasked with babysitting a baby seal named Rollie. Baby Rollie would cry unless he was constantly rocked in his cradle, which meant Zoe and Rosita needed to continuously rock him. Their arms became tired from rocking, but when they stopped, baby Rollie would start crying. The exaggerated attempts by Zoe and Rosita to continuously rock the cradle demonstrated the problem very well, and children both laughed at and deeply understood the dilemma they were in. What saved the day was a pulley system that allowed the characters to rock the cradle with less effort. Researchers found that children provided a very rich account of the story, even more so than other stories they had tested. The silliness of exaggerated motions and loud crying coupled with a solution that made the characters' troubles go away was an effective use of humor to drive the story line and engage the children.

BEYOND LINEAR VIDEO, BEYOND PRESCHOOLERS

While Sesame Workshop is known best for its television shows and linear video content for young children, the organization does a lot more. Our web- and app-based content as well as our print materials and educator and caregiver training resources are also used around the globe. Learning science informs how those assets are developed and used as well. While many of the principles mentioned in this chapter apply to children understanding portrayals in media, we have also had to expand our knowledge about how to work with adult learners and users. While our preschool audience is in Piagetian stages of preoperational thought, their parents and caregivers are in the formal operational stage.

Our work with educators and parents has encouraged us to investigate other learning strategies for adults that do not focus necessarily on comprehension and understanding but rather on interest and use. Given that adults have much more choice about what content they use, motivational and behavioral strategies are particularly important. The content can be well received and understood, but getting educators or parents through an intervention requires an understanding of how to get adults to use an intervention. The Fogg behavior model (Fogg, 2009) suggests that three components influence the degree to which a new behavior is adopted or an old one is modified. The three factors are motivation, ability, and a trigger. Motivation has three levels—physical, emotional, and social—and focuses on the drive that a person has to take on the behavior change. Ability means whether it is simple for a person to engage in a particular behavior at a certain point in time; it is not an assessment of someone's overall skills or abilities. Finally, the trigger is some sort of prompt or call to action that assists the learner to act on the behavior.

One of the ways the Workshop applied principles of this model (even before we knew its specifics) with adult behavior is a mobile phone study that encouraged 80 parents to increase literacy conversations with their children in a fun engaging manner (Horowitz et al., 2006.) Parents were given a video-capable phone and committed to doing three or four literacy activities with their children per week over an 8-week period. Parents received a text message four times a week. The text message contained an audio message delivered by Maria, a human character from *Sesame Street*, asking the adults to do a simple activity with their child like look around the living room and find all of the things that start with *C*, like the *couch*, the *chair*, the *carpet*. Then the adult was asked to hand the phone to the child, who received an audio message from a character as well as a video about the letter that the child would be asked to find with the parent. There were also three letters or postcards sent to parents to remind them to participate throughout the project.

We can see from the design of this intervention that there was initial motivation on the part of the parents to do an activity with their child—they signed up to participate and agreed to the activities. The activities themselves were simple and used everyday moments to support parent-child interaction. The triggers—in the form of a text, a friendly message from a celebrity, and an activity from a delightful Muppet character, along with letters and postcards, helped remind parents to do the activities and prompted action.

Analysis of the usage data suggested that use was highest right after the text messages were received and then declined steadily afterward but that in general compliance with the intervention (or at least viewing the text message and listening to the audio and video) was higher than expected.

Parents said that they increased their discussion of letters and words as a function of the study and that their children's letter recognition and letter sound knowledge had increased as a function of participating (Horowitz et al., 2006; Druin, 2009). This type of research design, using mobile technology to reach parents, has gained traction in more recent years, with a larger-scale study showing that when parents received texts that suggested literacy activities with their children, their children's literacy scores on standardized measures increased (York, Loeb, & Doss, 2018).

Another example of the application of the Fogg behavior model is engagement with a Sesame Workshop initiative called *Sesame Street In Communities* (SSIC), which offers resources, training, and strategies to parents and educators with a comprehensive website (www.sesamestreetincommunities.org) and organization support. Early formative research in three communities suggested that parents, educators, and community leaders saw the need for content particularly about how to cope with trauma and difficult life events (Phoenix Marketing International, 2016). Participants in the research study hoped to fill that need. They looked at early drafts of the materials and felt that the content was in the right direction. Once the content was developed, local organizations were trained on how to use the SSIC resources and we conducted additional research to assess how providers were using the materials. In our conversations with providers, it was clear that the content still resonated very well and that when they used the content it was effective, but they often did not remember to use the content, and it did not fit into their existing daily routines or practices in a systematic way. These issues point to a motivation, ability, and trigger limitation of our original implementation plans, which provided a lot of choice for the organizations and participants rather than imposing a set structure. We did not provide extra motivational incentives or reminders.

After receiving feedback that the organizations and providers were not using the content as frequently and consistently as we had hoped, the team decided to provide more motivational supports and triggers to remind use. First, we now have more plans in place to get organizations on board with stronger commitment devices to encourage use. Second, we are increasing the communication opportunities across participants so that they have a social environment in which to discuss and trade experiences. Third, finding ways to systematize the experience and reward completion such that participants complete a course and receive continuing education credits and/or a certificate of completion will likely increase adherence and use of the materials. Fourth, we are creating more check-ins, reminders, and refresher courses to help support providers and organizations to ensure that they use the materials in ways that most effectively support the families and communities that they serve.

CONCLUSION AND LOOKING FORWARD

Throughout its 50-year history, *Sesame Street*, both the show and its accompanying digital educational content, has addressed all aspects of children's development to help them grow "Smarter, Stronger, and Kinder" to be successful in school and in life. Staying current on theories of and trends in education, child development, and social policy is essential for us in understanding how and where our content can be most useful.

Learning science has contributed to the way *Sesame Street* is created, but this contribution is bidirectional. Our methods and our results have also contributed to the field of learning science. First, Sesame Workshop pioneered the collaboration of researchers, writers, and creatives working together to produce quality educational television. The formative research process that Sesame Workshop developed helped spawn a larger industrywide practice. Many other production companies have adopted and adapted the model of collaboration and of research that began with Sesame Workshop. Many of the other strong educational media properties that have helped children learn a variety of skills applied the formative research model to help ensure their content is strong. Second, much of the research that exists on the positive effects of educational television comes from empirical studies of *Sesame Street*, the domestic show and many of its international coproductions, conducted by academics and scholars around the world. It is highly unlikely that any academic or popular press article would discuss the positive benefits of educational television without mentioning the vast amount of research conducted on *Sesame Street*. This body of research has supported practitioners and creators who want to use their content for good. Third, the research on positive effects of *Sesame Street* has been used to promote policies that support educational television programming (Children's Television Act of 1990), public funding for such programming (PBS, CPB), and research funding for understanding the role of media in children's lives (CAMRA Act). The success of *Sesame Street* is promising for the learning science community as it highlights how content that is both educational and entertaining can be successful for decades but also demonstrates how the results of its effectiveness can be used to inform policy and garner further support for similar initiatives.

While many of the commonly used theories in media research and the ones we discussed here provide an understanding of broad categories of learners (preschool children, parents, educators), many of these theories do not guide us in creating for individual differences particularly in linear video. When making content that is intended to appeal to a large variety of learners, it is important that we understand what is appealing and engaging for the masses, but we must also spend more time looking at the variation across individuals to assess how different content resonates with different learners.

In his book *The End of Average*, Dr. Todd Rose (2016), a researcher at Harvard, argues that the concept of "average" is inherently flawed and that we need to find alternative ways to measure success that work for individuals. The more those who work in service of positive development for all children can find ways to tailor content to maximize learning and assessment for a variety of learners, the more we will deliver on our educational missions. Learning scientists are tackling this very issue, and we expect to see a lot more about individualization and personalized learning from this academic community in the upcoming decades.

As various theories and methodology have advanced our understanding of children and how they learn, the researchers and educators at Sesame Workshop will continue to assess the science, as well as listen to the children, to ensure that the content is as strong and meaningful as it can be. In order to most effectively serve learners' needs, it is critical that we assess new ways of capturing learning, iterate on our content, and ensure that we create content that resonates with and includes all children. We will continue to work with the *Sesame Street* writing and creative teams who, year after year, conceive and write story lines, portrayals, and characters that delight audiences and teach important life skills.

As a formal discipline, learning science is relatively young, but its multidisciplinary approach to design and education will become increasingly important as new technologies emerge that may promise greater results in less time. Truly understanding how to reach a variety of learners, at a variety of developmental stages and cultural experiences, requires the contribution of scientists with a variety of perspectives and expertise. We look forward to being part of this community as it grows and look forward to contributing our knowledge of children's learning through educational media as well as learning and applying best practices from other scholars.

REFERENCES

Ball, S., & Bogatz, G. A. (1970). *The first year of* Sesame Street*: An evaluation*. Princeton, NJ: Educational Testing Service.

Banas, J. A., Dunbar, N., Rodriguez, D., & Liu, S. (2011). A review of humor in education settings: Four decades of research. *Communication Education, 60*(1), 115–144.

Bogatz, G. A., & Ball, S. (1971). *The second year of* Sesame Street*: An evaluation*. Princeton, NJ: Educational Testing Service.

Canli, T., Zhao, Z., Brewer, J., Gabrieli, J., & Cahill, L. (2000). Event-related activation in the human amygdala associates with later memory for individual emotional response. *Journal of Neuroscience, 2000*(20), RC99.

Channell, M. M., & Barth, J. M. (2013). Individual differences in preschoolers' emotion content memory: The role of emotion knowledge. *Journal of Experimental Child Psychology, 115*, 552–561. doi:10.1016/j.jecp.2013.01.012

Druin, A. (2009). *Mobile technology for children: Designing for interaction and learning*. Burlington: Morgan Kaufmann.

Fisch, S. M. (2000). A capacity model of children's comprehension of educational content on television. *Media Psychology*, 2(1), 63–91.

Fisch, S. M., & Truglio, R. T. (2001). Why children learn from *Sesame Street*. In S.M. Fisch & R. T. Truglio (Eds.), *"G" is for growing: Thirty years of research on children and* Sesame Street (pp. 233–244). Mahwah, NJ: Lawrence Erlbaum Associates.

Fogg, B. J. (2009). A behavior model for persuasive design. *Persuasive'09*, April 26–29, Claremont, California.

Goleman, D. (1987, August 25). Embattled giant of psychology speaks his mind. *New York Times*. https://www.nytimes.com/1987/08/25/science/embattled-giant-of-psychology-speaks-his-mind.html

Horowitz, J. E., et al. (2006). *Evaluation of the PBS ready to learn cell phone study: Learning letters with Elmo*. Los Alamitos, CA: WestEd.

Huston, A. C., Anderson, D. R., Wright, J. C., Linebarger, D. L., & Schmitt, K. L. (2001). *Sesame Street* viewers as adolescents: The recontact study. In S. M. Fisch & R. T. Truglio (Eds.), *"G" is for .growing: Thirty years of research on children and* Sesame Street (pp. 131–144). Mahwah, NJ: Lawrence Erlbaum Associates.

Huston, A. C., Wright, J. C., Wartella, E., Rice, M. L., Watkins, B. A, Campbell, T., & Potts, R. (1981). Communicating more than content: Formal features of children's television programs. *Journal of Communication, 31*(3), 32–48.

Kearney, M. S, & Levine, P. B. (2015). Early childhood education by MOOC: Lessons from *Sesame Street*. NBER Working Paper No. 21229, JEL No. I24, J24.

Kensinger, E. A. (2009). Remembering the details: Effects of emotion. *Emotion Review, 1*(2), 99–113.Kotler, J. A. (2005, March). *Season 36 testing research findings* [Unpublished internal document]. Sesame Workshop.

Kotler, J. A. (2010, November). *Research on Super Grover 2.0: Ramp, lever & balance*. Unpublished internal document]. Sesame Workshop.

Kotler, J. A. (2013, May 14). *Cookie Monster format testing* [Unpublished internal document]. Sesame Workshop.

Kotler, J. A, Truglio, R. T., & Betancourt, J. (2016). R is for responsive: How *Sesame Street* meets the changing needs of children in the United States. In Cole, C., & Lee, J. (Eds.), *The Sesame effect: The global impact of the longest street in the world* (pp. 72–91). New York: Routledge.

Kotler, J. A., & Wong, C. B. (2016, July 18). *Elmo's world games paper testing: Final report* [Unpublished internal document]. Sesame Workshop.

Levine, L., & Pizarro, D. (2004). Emotion and memory research: A grumpy overview. *Social Cognition, 22*, 530–554.
Lyon, C. (2006). Humour and the young child. *Televizion*, 4–9.
Phoenix Marketing International. (2016, February 29). Sesame Street *in communities target end users evaluate the website and supplemental content: A Final report of qualitative research findings* [Unpublished internal document].
Rose, T. (2016). *The end of average: How we succeed in a world that values sameness.* San Francisco, CA: HarperOne.
Sweller, J. (1988). Cognitive load during problem solving: Effects on learning. *Cognitive Science, 12*(2), 257–285.
Wanzer, M. B., Frymier, A. B., & Irwin, J. (2010). An explanation of the relationship between instructor humor and student learning: Instructional humor processing theory. *Communication Education, 59*(1), 1–18.
Warren, R. (2003). Parental mediation of preschool children's television viewing. *Journal of Broadcasting & Electronic Media, 47*(3).
Wong, C. B. (2016a, February 25). *Script testing top lines: Rocking Rollie & ready for today* [Unpublished internal document]. Sesame Workshop.
Wong, C. B. (2016b, March 3). *Script testing top lines: The four sneezons* [Unpublished internal document]. Sesame Workshop.
Wong, C. B. (2016c, April 11). *Script testing top lines: Everyday heroes* [Unpublished internal document]. Sesame Workshop.
Wong, C. B. (2016d, September 1). *4807 Street food first draft—notes* [Unpublished internal document]. Sesame Workshop.
Wong, C. B. (2016e, October 13). *Hair training & Rapunzel gets a haircut Storymatic research report* [Unpublished internal document]. Sesame Workshop.
Wong, C. B. (2016f, November 4). *Street food & sneaky shoes Storymatic research report* [Unpublished internal document]. Sesame Workshop.
Wong, C. B. (2016g, December 2). *Martian mission Storymatic research report* [Unpublished internal document]. Sesame Workshop.
Wong, C. B. (2017a, February 6). *Clothing drive Storymatic research report* [Unpublished internal document]. Sesame Workshop.
Wong, C. B. (2017b, March 15). *Season 47 January/February show test* [Unpublished internal document]. Sesame Workshop.
Wong, C. B. (2018, April 30). Sesame Street *season 48 full episode testing report* [Unpublished internal document]. Sesame Workshop.
York, B.. Loeb, S.. & Doss, C. (2018). One step at a time: The effects of an early literacy text messaging program for parents of preschoolers. *Journal of Human Resources, 53*(4).

ABOUT THE AUTHORS

Jennifer A. Kotler is the vice president of content research and evaluation at Sesame Workshop. Dr. Kotler leads a team that conducts research and evaluation projects across the globe to support Sesame Workshop in achieving its goal of helping children become smarter, stronger, and kinder.

Courtney Wong Chin is the director of content research and evaluation at Sesame Workshop where she is responsible for assessing the educational content of Sesame Workshop projects across multiple media platforms (e.g., television, web, apps, print).

Rosemarie T. Truglio is the senior vice president of curriculum and content at Sesame Workshop. Dr. Truglio is responsible for the development of the interdisciplinary curriculum on which Sesame Street is based and oversees content development across platforms.

CHAPTER 12

How to Increase Learning While Not Decreasing the Fun in Educational Games

Valerie Shute, Fengfeng Ke, Russell Almond, Seyedahmad Rahimi, Ginny Smith, and Xi Lu
Florida State University

ABSTRACT
In this chapter we discuss a next-generation learning game—*Physics Playground*—that successfully blurs the distinction between assessment and learning to promote STEM competency development. We are using evidence-centered design to integrate game-based learning, problem-based learning, personalized learning, and learning by design, linking the activities to both informal and formal physics knowledge. Our focus in this chapter is on the design of various in-game learning supports that offer just-in-time explanations when students succeed and encouragement and instructional scaffolding when they struggle. Our current learning supports include worked examples, physics animations, constructed definitions, short videos, and relevant formulas. This chapter informs researchers in computer and learning sciences on the design and development of effective in-game learning supports and the methodology of data mining that can potentially drive a dynamic delivery of learning supports. Moreover, this chapter will inform science educators in developing effective education programs for youth.

Fun from games arises out of mastery. It arises out of comprehension. It is the act of solving puzzles that makes games fun. In other words, with games, learning is the drug.

—Raph Koster

The big problem that we are tackling with the research discussed in this chapter is that the United States has been a global leader in STEM-related areas, but this top-tier position is currently threatened by a decreasing number of US students choosing to pursue expertise in STEM fields and an inadequate supply of teachers skilled in those subjects (US Department of Education [USDOE], 2015). According to the President's Council of Advisors on Science and Technology (2012), economic projections indicate the need for about 1 million more STEM professionals than we will actually produce over the next decade. Unfortunately, the math and science data of our students suggest we are not on track to reach our projected needs. The United States now lags behind other nations in STEM education at the elementary and secondary levels (Hanushek, Peterson, & Woessman, 2012; Programme for International Student Assessment [PISA], 2012; Trends in International Mathematics and Science Study [TIMSS], 2011).

To keep the United States competitive in the global economy, we need to increase the number and diversity of students entering into STEM areas. Our work, described in this chapter, focuses on achieving two goals that could have the largest impact on meeting this challenge. The first goal is to get more children excited about and interested in science—specifically physics. Recognizing that interest alone is not enough, our second goal is to identify ways to facilitate and deepen science-related learning in immersive and meaningful learning environments. Well-designed digital games represent a promising vehicle for meeting both goals: capturing children's interest in STEM fields like physics and supporting active, contextualized learning.

REVIEW OF RELEVANT LITERATURE

Digital Games in Education

Besides being a popular activity across all gender, ethnic, and socioeconomic lines, playing digital games has been shown to be positively related to various competencies, attributes, and outcomes such as visual-spatial abilities and attention (e.g., Green & Bavelier, 2007, 2012; Shute, Ventura,

& Ke, 2015), openness to experience (Chory & Goodboy, 2011; Ventura, Shute, & Kim, 2012; Witt, Massman, & Jackson, 2011), college grades (Skoric, Teo, & Neo, 2009; Ventura Shute, & Kim, 2012), persistence (Ventura, Shute, & Zhao, 2012), creativity (Jackson et al., 2012), and civic engagement (Ferguson & Garza, 2011). Digital games can also motivate students to learn valuable academic content and skills (e.g., Coller & Scott, 2009; DeRouin-Jessen, 2008; for recent reviews, see Clark, Tanner-Smith, & Killingsworth, 2015; Tobias & Fletcher, 2011; Wilson et al., 2009; Young et al., 2012). However, peer-reviewed literature published on the design and evaluation of game-based learning for science is still limited (National Research Council [NRC], 2011; Young et al., 2012).

We are working to expand the research on game-based learning of science through our ongoing enhancements to a physics game we developed called *Physics Playground* (*PP*) (Shute & Ventura, 2013). *PP* is a computer game that dynamically assesses and supports students' understanding of qualitative physics (the nonverbal understanding of Newton's three laws of motion, potential and kinetic energy, balance, mass, and gravity; see Ploetzner & VanLehn, 1997). We believe that *PP* can leverage the popularity of digital games to capture and sustain students' attention and teach physics to a broader audience than traditional physics classrooms, making it an attractive tool for teaching physics to diverse gender, ethnic, or economic groups. Next we will review the theoretical foundation of learning and motivation on which we base our research.

Motivation and Learning Support Via Games

There is a convergence between the core elements of a good game and the characteristics of productive learning (Shute, Rieber, & Van Eck, 2011). Our proposition is that (a) learning is at its best when it is active, goal-oriented, contextualized, and interesting (e.g., Bransford, Brown, & Cocking, 2000); and (b) learning environments should be interactive, provide ongoing feedback, grab and hold attention, and have appropriate and adaptive levels of challenge—all features of good games. Gee (2003) has argued that the secret of a good game is not its 3D graphics and other bells and whistles, but its underlying architecture in which each level dances around the outer limits of the player's abilities (see also Csikszentmihalyi, 1990, on flow theory). Along the same line, psychologists (e.g., Vygotsky, 1987) have long argued that the best instruction hovers at the boundary of a student's competence. Finally, both well-designed games and productive learning processes employ ongoing feedback as a major mechanism of play or learning support.

Motivation Support via Games

Well-designed games are highly engaging (e.g., Desurvire, Caplan, & Toth, 2004; Fullerton, Swain, & Hoffman, 2008). Play is voluntary, intrinsically motivating, and involves active cognitive and/or physical engagement that allows for the freedom to fail (and recover) and to experiment freely (Klopfer, Osterweil, & Salen, 2009; Pellegrini, 1995; Rieber, 1996). Unlike "free play," a game is usually a contest of physical or mental skills and strengths, requiring the player to follow a specific set of rules to attain a goal (Hogle, 1996). The logic model of the *PP* design uses core game actions and aesthetics (e.g., puzzle solving, drawing-based creative play, adaptive challenges, and dynamic feedback) to engender motivation, which, in turn, will support game-task engagement and ultimately learning. Specifically, puzzle solving and drawing-based creative play are particularly appealing to female gamers and are gender inclusive (Kinzie & Joseph, 2008; Steiner, Kickmeier-Rust, & Albert, 2009). Adaptive challenges and dynamic performance feedback in a game help to create a sense of competence and an optimal environment for diverse players, which will foster the sense of flow and potentially cultivate the growth mindset that engenders effort-driven, challenge-centered competency development (Dweck, 2006).

Learning Support via Games

Well-designed games can be seen as vehicles for engaging players in iterative intellectual activities. People who want to excel at something—from surgeons to artists—spend countless hours of intellectual effort while practicing their craft. There is considerable evidence in the literature, going back more than 100 years, supporting that practice substantially improves knowledge and skills (e.g., Ericsson, Krampe, & Tesch-Römer, 1993; Newell & Rosenbloom, 1981; Schneider & Shiffrin, 1977; Thorndike, 1898). But practice can be tedious and frustrating, causing some learners to abandon their practice and, hence, expertise development. However, good games can provide an engaging and authentic environment designed to keep practice meaningful and personally relevant. With simulated visualization, authentic problem solving, and instant feedback, computer games can afford a realistic framework for experimentation and situated understanding, and thus act as rich primers for active learning (Barab, Thomas, Dodge, Carteaux, & Tuzun, 2005; Gee, 2003; NRC, 2011; Squire, 2006). Furthermore, within-game learning support enables learners to do more advanced intellectual activities and to engage in more advanced thinking than they could without such help (Vygotsky, 1987). The complicated part about including learning support in games is to not disrupt engagement while reinforcing the construction and application of cognitive generalizations that deepen learning and engender transfer to other contexts.

Types of Learning Supports in Games

Educational game researchers (e.g., Wouters & van Oostendorp, 2013) have concluded that to keep novice players engaged with and learning from the game, it must include purposively designed learning supports. That is, digital games are complex and challenging environments that demand a lot of cognitive effort, and learners will likely get frustrated, disengaged, or distracted by play without being involved in learning (Wouters, van Nimwegen, van Oostendorp, & van Der Spek, 2013). In that case, learning outcomes may be in jeopardy. Including supports in educational games increases the odds of improving game-based learning engagement and knowledge development.

Wouters and van Oostendorp (2013) conducted a meta-analysis on the effectiveness of various learning supports in educational games. They selected 29 studies (with 3,675 participants) and computed 107 pairwise comparisons to investigate the effectiveness of learning supports in educational games. They found a positive and moderately-weighted effect size of $d = .34$ ($z = 7.26$, $p < .001$) which suggests that the use of learning supports in games can, in fact, improve learning. Furthermore, Wouters and van Oostendorp identified 24 different types of learning supports.

According to Wouters and van Oostendorp (2013), there are eight different types of supports that are most commonly used in educational games: reflection, modeling, advice, collaboration, interactivity, narrative elements, feedback, and modality. The first type of support is *reflection*, which aims to stimulate learners' thinking about their performance and learning in the game. Research has shown that knowledge retention is improved if students are required to reflect on what they learned (e.g., Leemkuil, 2006). Some of the learning supports in games categorized under reflection include (1) self-explanation (asking learners to explain to themselves—verbally or written—as they study a lesson or concept; Johnson & Mayer, 2010), (2) elaboration (extra task-related cognitive activities; Shebilske, Goettl, Corrington, & Day, 1999), and (3) reflective inquiries (e.g., queries to find relationships between two or more variables; Leemkuil, 2006). This group of supports helps learners pause gameplay for a moment, analyze their gaming answers or solutions, and use organizational and integrational cognitive processes to learn the underlying concepts within the game.

The second type of support is *modeling*. This type of support provides an explication or illustration of how to solve a problem or perform a task in the game. The two most common supports categorized under the modeling category are: (1) scaffolding (Barzilai & Blau, 2014), and (2) worked examples (or expert solutions; Lang & O'Neil, 2008). Modeling can be provided either inside or outside of the game, by a peer, an expert, or the game itself; and it can be delivered verbally, graphically, or via animated form. One possible criticism regarding the inclusion of worked examples in a game is that learners can see a solution and then replicate it without actually thinking about the underlying concepts being used to solve the problem. However, with a good reward and penalty system in place, negative effects of using worked examples can be minimized. Also, providing partially worked examples can reduce the potential negative effect of fully worked examples. This is described in more detail later in this chapter where we present an example of integrating such worked examples in *PP*.

The third type of support is *advice* (e.g., Leutner, 1993), intended to guide the learner in the right direction without revealing the solution. Varied types of pre- or post-action advice (contextualized, adaptive or not) that are game-generated can be grouped under this category. For example, a hint can provide the learner with suggestions about what to do next in the game or provide an elaborated explanation about possible consequences of his or her action. Advice can consist of a short message asking the player to focus on a particular aspect of the task or give a cue about where to start.

The fourth type of support is *collaboration* (van der Meij, Albers, & Leemkuil, 2011), which may involve game talk with other players on a particular level or a gameplay strategy. Collaboration can help novice players figure out ambiguities in the game and better understand the knowledge and skills they need to learn. Many games allow for live chat and exchange of information among players. Alternatively, collaborative gameplay may be done with learners playing the game in dyads or small groups, then they can get involved in after-game discussions in online forums or in physical environments (e.g., a classroom).

The fifth learning support type is *interactivity*. This type of support focuses on soliciting active input from the learners when they process a learning support. Any type of learning support that is responsive to learners' actions can be categorized under this group. For example, Moreno and

Mayer (2005) designed their agent-based multimedia game with interactivity where students had to select roots, stems, and leaves that best helped plants survive on the planet. Another group of students used a different version of the game (with no interactivity). They interacted with a pedagogical agent who simply showed them pertinent information regarding the plants. The authors found that interactivity helped students learn and retain knowledge.

Narrative elements comprise the sixth type of learning support, where content can be integrated into the story line of a game via narratives that contain surprises, foreshadowing, and fantasies. The narrative of a game provides a cognitive framework for the learners with which they can better learn and remember the underlying concepts in the game (e.g., Adams, Mayer, MacNamara, Koenig, & Wainess, 2012). This type of support can be seen, as Prensky (2001) pointed out, in genres such as adventure games or role-playing games.

The seventh type of learning support—and likely the most frequently used one—is *feedback*, especially formative feedback, which is essential for learning (Shute, 2008). Given the high degree of interactivity existing in most games, feedback becomes critically important. As Shute (2008) notes, there are many types of feedback, but the two most common types used in educational games are corrective feedback (e.g., showing if an answer or solution is correct or not), and explanatory feedback (e.g., describing why the answer or solution was right or wrong). Cameron and Dwyer (2005) found statistically significant differences on all learning outcomes when feedback was included in the game versus when it was not.

Finally, *modality* (Ginns, 2005; Moreno & Mayer, 2002; Ritterfeld, Shen, Wang, Nocera, & Wong, 2009) refers to the representation of the support (e.g., auditory, visual, textual), and each type of modality can positively or negatively affect learning. For example, Moreno and Mayer (2002) found that learners remembered more of the materials, achieved better transfer, and rated more favorably virtual reality environments that used speech rather than on-screen text to deliver learning materials. Also, Ritterfeld and colleagues (2009) point out that multimodality is one of the most important facets of educational game success—providing learners with materials via different channels. Results of their study showed that multimodality positively affects knowledge gains for both short-term (at the posttest) and long-term (follow-up test) outcomes.

After conducting a moderator analysis, Wouters and van Oostendorp (2013) found out that among the 29 studies they examined, reflection, modeling, collaboration, modality, and feedback enhanced learning, but advice, interactivity, and narrative did not. Thus, the first group of support types is where we focus our attention. It should be noted, though, that the effectiveness of learning supports depends on how they are integrated into educational games.

GAME-BASED STEALTH ASSESSMENT FOR ADAPTIVE SUPPORT OF LEARNING

The underlying mechanism of adaptive learning support is real-time assessment and tracking of learners' competency development during gameplay. Again, the challenge is validly and reliably measuring learning in games without disrupting engagement and leveraging that information to bolster learning. Our solution involves using stealth assessment (Shute, 2011) for crafting valid game-based assessments and dynamically linking those assessments to various learning supports. This methodology can contribute to the design of next-generation learning games that successfully blur the distinction between assessment and learning.

Stealth Assessment

For the past decade, we have been researching various ways to embed valid assessments directly into games with a technology called stealth assessment (see Shute, 2011; Shute & Ke, 2012; Shute & Ventura, 2013; Shute, Ventura, Bauer, & Zapata-Rivera, 2009). In 2011, we received funding from the Bill & Melinda Gates Foundation to build and test the stealth assessment technology in a game we developed called *Physics Playground (PP)*. Stealth assessment is based on an assessment design framework called evidence-centered design (ECD; Mislevy, Steinberg, & Almond, 2003). In general, the main purpose of any assessment is to collect information that will allow the assessor to make valid inferences about what people know, can do, and to what degree (collectively referred to as "competencies" in this chapter). ECD defines a framework that consists of several conceptual and computational models that work in concert. The framework requires an assessor to: (a) define the claims to be made about learners' competencies, (b) establish what constitutes valid evidence of a claim, (c) determine the nature and form of tasks that will elicit that evidence, and (d) determine how much evidence is required to support each claim.

Stealth assessment complements ECD by determining specific gameplay behaviors (specified in the evidence model) and linking them to the competency model (Shute & Ventura, 2013). As students interact with tasks or problems in a game during the solution process, they are providing a continuous stream of data (captured in a log file) that is analyzed by the evidence identification (EI) process. The results of this analysis are data (e.g., scores, tallies) that are passed to the evidence accumulation (EA) process, which statistically updates the claims about relevant competencies in the student model—the student's individual copy of the competency model. The ECD approach combined with stealth assessment provides a framework for developing assessment tasks that are explicitly linked to claims about personal competencies via an evidentiary chain (i.e., valid arguments that serve to connect task performance to competency estimates) and are thus valid for their intended purposes. The estimates of competency levels can also be used diagnostically and formatively to provide adaptively selected levels, feedback, and other forms of learning support to students as they continue to engage in gameplay. *PP* uses these tools as the basis for developing adaptive learning supports. Again, the tricky part is embedding learning supports deeply in the game and not disrupting engagement.

The Original Version of *Physics Playground—PPv1*

Since its inception, *PP* has gone through various improvements regarding game design and embedding learning supports in the game. To clarify which version of *PP* we are referring to, we call the first version of *PP* without learning supports as *PPv1*, and the current version of *PP* with learning supports as *PPv2*. Also, we will use *PPv2.1*, *2.2*, and *2.3* to refer to the usability studies we conducted using *PPv2*. Note that when the specifications we refer to are included in both versions, we simply use *PP*.

PPv1 is nonlinear: players can choose any level in the game to play or replay. There is only one level type in *PPv1*—sketching levels. The goal of all levels (or problems) in *PP* is to guide a green ball to hit a red balloon. Using the mouse or stylus, players draw objects on the screen that "come to life" as physical objects when the mouse button or stylus is released. These objects interact with the game environment according to Newtonian mechanics and can be used to move the ball. When objects interact within the game environment, they act as "agents of force and motion" or just "agents"—simple machines in formal physics: ramp, lever, pendulum, and springboard. Figures 12.1 and 12.2 show screenshots from *PP* illustrating solutions using different agents and their associated physics concepts.

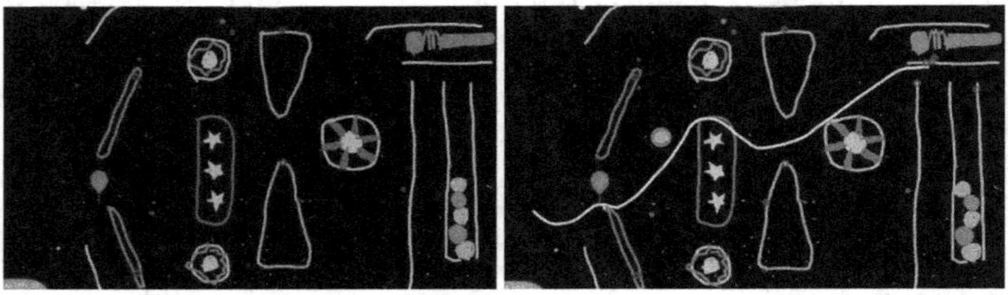

FIGURE 12.1 Screen captures of a "ramp" solution level from *PP* informing Newton's first law.

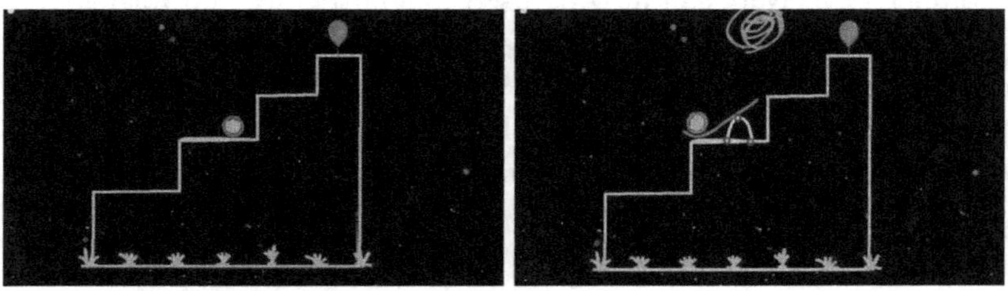

FIGURE 12.2 Screen capture of a "lever" solution level from PP informing energy can transfer.

We used ECD to design *PPv1* (Shute & Ventura, 2013). That is, we first established a simple physics competency model that included Newton's laws of force and motion with two main facets, angular momentum and energy, that were associated with various agents (e.g., understanding potential and kinetic energy was statistically linked to ramp and springboard solutions). Second, evidence was defined as the behaviors demonstrated by a player in the game that would provide information about particular competency levels. For instance, the degree of understanding angular momentum is partly informed by evidence relating to the number of successful solutions involving pendulums. Third, task models provided a blueprint for creating all of the levels in *PPv1*, where each level focused on eliciting different agents (related to different physics principles) for solution. Levels also varied by difficulty. The difficulty of a problem was based on a number of factors, including relative location of the ball to the balloon, number of obstacles present, number of agents required to solve the problem, and novelty of the problem. Difficult problems provide greater weight of evidence to the estimate of a competency level than easy problems. Also, "elegant" solutions (i.e., those using a minimal number of objects in the solution, suggesting mastery) give greater weight to competency level inferences than regular solutions.

Advancing Understanding of Game-Based Learning

Preliminary Empirical Findings

We've now tested *PPv1* in several studies to (a) validate the in-game (stealth assessment) measures, and (b) examine any learning of qualitative physics that may have occurred from playing the game, and the results are consistent. For instance, in Shute, Ventura, and Kim (2013), we found that performance data in *PP* as captured in the log files (e.g., use of a particular agent) significantly correlated with our external test scores, serving to validate the stealth assessment measures. In addition, we found that students (Grades 8 and 9, $n = 168$) do improve in their qualitative physics understanding ($t\ (154) = 2.12, p < .05$) after 4 hours of gameplay with no content instruction or any other learning support. The pretest and posttest each consisted of 12 matched multiple-choice items related to relevant physics principles, similar to those in the Force Concept Inventory (Hestenes, Wells, & Swackhamer, 1992), which is a multiple-choice test designed to monitor students' understanding of force and related kinematics. Finally, males and females demonstrated comparable learning gains and equally enjoyed playing *PPv1* after controlling for pretest knowledge. The findings have been replicated (e.g., Shute et al., 2015), suggesting that this game has potential to foster motivation and learning in physics for diverse learners.

Fostering Conceptual Physics Understanding

Given these preliminary results, we wanted to substantially bolster learning in *PP*—from qualitative construal of physics to a deeper, more conceptual and formal understanding—via engaging and effective in-game learning supports that foster conceptual processing during physics-governed puzzle solving. In support of this approach, Hatano asserts that conceptual knowledge gives "meaning to each step of the skill and provide[s] criteria for selection among alternative possibilities for each step within the procedures" (1982, p. 15). Without this pairing between concepts and procedures, children develop only routine expertise: the ability to solve narrowly defined, predictable, and often artificial (school-based) problems. Routine expertise is not very helpful outside of the school setting because it cannot be adjusted for and/or applied to real-life or unexpected situations.

Another reason to lay a solid conceptual physics foundation in *PP* is because even college students with acceptable grades in one or more physics courses have limited understanding of conceptual physics and hold erroneous views about the basic physical principles that govern the motion of objects in the world (Halloun, 1996; Reiner, Proffit, & Salthouse, 2005; Swann, 1950). Recognition of this problem has led to interest in the mechanisms by which physics students make the transition from informal (or naive) physics to more formal physics understanding (diSessa, 1982) and to the possibility of using video games to assist in the learning process (Masson, Bub, & Lalonde, 2011; White, 1994). One way to help remove misconceptions in physics is to illustrate physics principles with physical machines—including simple machines like ramps, levers, and pendulums (devices designed to change either the magnitude or the direction of a force in *PP*), which are widely used to introduce physics concepts (Hewitt, 2009). Research on science education also indicates that learners' hands-on experience with such machines (virtually and physically) supports understanding of physics concepts (Hake, 1998).

The enhanced game helps players lay the conceptual foundation of physics, before adding formalizations. In other words, we want *PP* players to learn physics at a deep and meaningful level before being introduced to formal physics terms and equations. For example, in *PPv2*, players first *experience* the relationship between force, mass, and acceleration when solving problems in the game (e.g., creating successful pendulum solutions) and then are introduced to relevant formalizations (e.g., $F = ma$, or Newton's second law) via embedded learning supports.

Core Physics Concepts to Be Assessed and Supported

PP behaves according to Newtonian (real-world) physics principles and dynamically responds to players' interactions with the environment. To accomplish this responsiveness, *PP* performs a detailed formal simulation of a virtual physics "world" using actual, accurate physics formulas and calculations to account for mass, gravity, friction, momentum, and other physics concepts. Some of the physics concepts that we are assessing and supporting in the current research include Newton's three laws of force and motion; potential and kinetic energy; torque; collisions and conservation of linear momentum; and energy and dissipative forces.

Challenges for Games as Formal Learning Tools

Well-designed games typically possess the following game features: interactivity, ongoing feedback, and adaptive challenges. What good game designers have been doing intuitively for decades (applying these features within games as embedded learning support) is what we want to identify, codify, apply, and test in *PP* with the goal of creating a methodology that can be used in the design of next-generation learning games. Clark and his colleagues (e.g., Clark et al., 2011; Martinez-Garza, Clark, Nelson, Slack, & D'Angelo, 2013) have been tackling a similar problem of how to combine gameplay activities (in a game called *Surge*) with formal physics representations and terminology to support the learning of Newtonian mechanics. However, Clark and his colleagues (2011) found no significant gains for US students on physics concepts after gameplay. They also reported that the in-game performance measures (e.g., number of replays, scores) were not related to students' performance on physics tests. They concluded that more research is needed that provides "supports for students to help them articulate their intuitive understandings from gameplay with the explicit formal concepts and representations of the discipline" (p. 2192). Developing and testing these types of supports comprises our current research; specifically, technology innovations that include coupling stealth assessment processes with adaptive sequencing of levels along with just-in-time feedback—the latter via multiple representations, such as text, overlays, and animations.

IN-GAME LEARNING SUPPORTS IN PHYSICS PLAYGROUND

While different types of learning supports tend to promote learning across educational games (Wouters & van Oostendorp, 2013), details about particular features and their associated effectiveness of different types of learning supports are lacking in the literature (Johnson, Bailey, & Van Buskirk, 2017; Ke, 2016). Ke and Shute (2015) pointed out that the next generation of educational games will likely embody two related functions: (1) game-based stealth assessment, and (2) adaptive learning supports, which are based on the results of the in-game assessment. Effectively integrating the assessment and associated supports must rely on an iterative design and testing process.

In this section, we describe some of our processes related to iteratively developing, implementing, and testing various learning supports in *PPv2*.

New Version of *Physics Playground—PPv2*

Over the past two years, we have been designing and testing the effectiveness of a variety of learning supports in *PPv1* to foster deep, more formal understanding of Newtonian physics without disrupting flow. We are finalizing the cognitive supports and working toward developing an adaptive, stealth assessment–based level selection algorithm. In this section, we describe the steps we took to design and develop the supports.

Expanded Competency Model

To expand the content to be measured and supported in the game, our first step was to revise *PPv1* to extend the physics competency model. Using the Next Generation Science Standards (NGSS) as our guidepost, we worked with our two physics experts to select primary physics competencies and subcompetencies to be assessed in *PPv2*. We also identified all salient game behaviors (or observables) that can provide evidence of the proficiency status of each variable in the competency model. After many revisions (Almond, Tingir, Lu, Sun, & Rahimi, 2017), we finally came up with the competency model shown in Figure 12.3. The model involves four primary competencies: force and motion, linear momentum, energy, and torque. The model serves as the foundation for subsequent design phases.

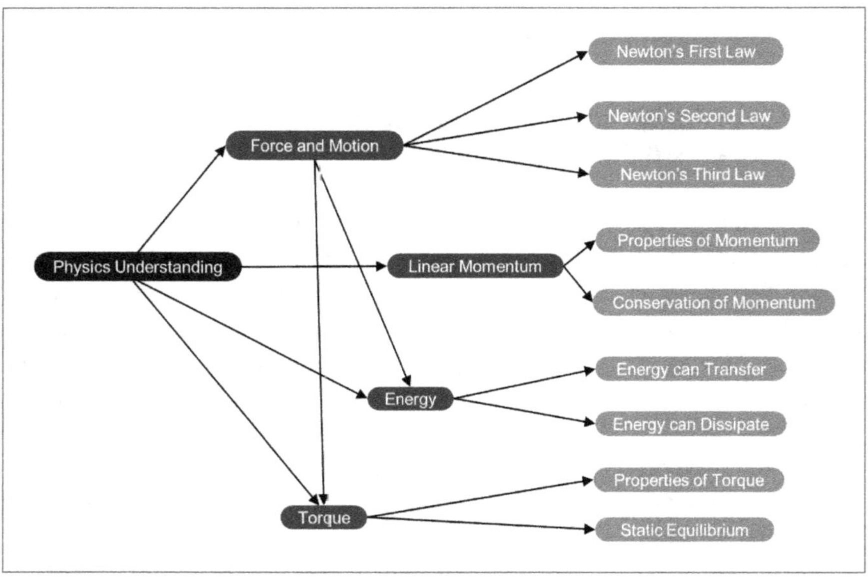

FIGURE 12.3 Competency model for *Physics Playground*

The model also serves as a foundation for the psychometric model driving the stealth assessment and adaptivity. To that end, the model must capture both hierarchical dependencies among the concepts and correlations in their acquisition in the target community. To ensure that the final model captured these, multiple models were created by the psychometric team and presented to the physics experts, allowing them to weigh in on design alternatives (Almond, et al., 2017).

New Task Types and Levels

The next step involved designing new task types that can elicit evidence of this more elaborated set of physics concepts. This resulted in the design of our new manipulation task type. Manipulation tasks require players to move three sliders (i.e., gravity, mass, and air resistance) and/or add external forces (i.e., static or dynamic blowers and puffers) to solve a level without drawing new objects. For instance, solving the *Whale* level (see Figure 12.4) requires players to adjust air resistance. In gameplay, increasing air resistance will slow down the falling of the ball and allow it to hit the balloon inside the whale's mouth.

FIGURE 12.4. *Whale* level in *PPv2*

New Learning Supports

Across the past two years, we developed eight different learning supports for *PPv2*: (1) worked examples, (2) animations, (3) interactive definitions, (4) formulas, (5) Hewitt videos, (6) glossary, (7) hints, and (8) interactive tutorials.

In line with Wouters and van Oostendorp's (2013) categorization, our worked examples serve the function of *modeling*; our hints focus on *advice*; and our animations, formulas, Hewitt videos, and glossary promote conceptual understanding via dynamic *modalities* (i.e., each physics concept in the game can be presented across multimodal representations of the targeted physics knowledge). We selected *modeling*, *modality*, and *hints* as the main types of support to include in the game because they are found as the most effective supports to elevate student learning relative to other learning supports (Wouters & van Oostendorp, 2013).

USABILITY STUDIES OF LEARNING SUPPORTS

Three usability studies were conducted over the course of development of *PPv2*. The first version of *PPv2* that we piloted—*PPv2.1*—consisted of 30 sketching levels and 30 manipulation levels, and the learning supports included worked examples, physics facts, advice, and Hewitt videos. The first usability study focused on gathering qualitative data on student opinions of both the task types and learning supports.

Usability Study 1—PPv2.1

Based on our observations and interviews, students enjoyed playing both sketching and manipulation levels. For the sketching levels, students enjoyed drawing on the screen and inventing creative solutions. However, sketching levels were reported as more difficult than manipulation levels by students. For the manipulation levels, students liked the direct maneuvering of the physics variables and the ability to see immediate results of the change in variables. They also liked that they were not limited by their ability to draw accurately and could focus more on controlling the movement of the ball.

Of all the learning supports included in the game, students preferred the worked examples. Worked examples are videos of expert solutions. All worked examples are less than a minute long with the majority being less than 30 seconds. The worked examples, created for 130+ game levels, can be viewed on our YouTube channel (https://www.youtube.com/channel/UCJpWi45D51ITxaj_NaClqJQ). Physics Facts was the least favorite support. It was a document containing definitions and examples of the relevant physics terms. Students reported it as an intensive reading, that it lacked visuals and/or interactions, and that it was not gamelike. Another support feature (called Advice) consisted of level-specific suggestions on problem-solving thinking. However, the advice support was not available until after five minutes of playing a level. Due to this delay, many students did not access this support. The majority of students who did see the advice support reported it as nonhelpful, vague, or confusing. Hewitt videos are an engaging series of cartoon videos explaining various physics concepts, developed by Paul Hewitt. The physics experts helped us select the most relevant videos for the game. With the permission of the author (Paul Hewitt), the team edited the length of each video to make it illustrate a targeted competency. Most students reported Hewitt videos as helpful.

Another major finding of the first usability study is that students never accessed the supports voluntarily even though the learning support is ever-present and accessible at players' control. The learning supports were housed in a sidebar that opened from the left side of the screen. The green triangular tab remained on the screen throughout every level, so students could click to open the supports any time during gameplay.

Usability Study 2—*PPv2.2*

The results of the first usability study led to revisions and additions to the learning supports in the game. In the second version of the learning supports, students access support through a help button in the lower-right corner of the screen (note: currently accessing supports is controlled by the player, but in upcoming studies, we will examine the effects of player- vs. game-control of the supports). Clicking the help button triggered a pop-up window showing two options: "Show me the Physics" and "Show me a Solution." The two options provide students two paths: learning support or gameplay support. "Show me the Physics" comprises the Modality-related, content-rich learning supports—where students can learn about physics phenomena via multiple representations (i.e., physics animations, interactive definitions, formulas, Hewitt videos, and a glossary). "Show me a Solution" focuses on game action–oriented problem solution modeling (i.e., worked examples). The only revision made to the worked examples after the first usability study was to remove the audio track containing the physics explanations.

"Show me the Physics" leads the student to the physics support page showing the following options: "Animation," "Definition," "Formula," "Hewitt video," and "Glossary" (note that the formula option is not present if the concept doesn't have an associated formula or equation).

- ***Animations.*** We developed short (5–15 seconds) animations to illustrate the targeted physics concepts (e.g., gravity) in the game context. The team storyboarded all the animations, which were reviewed by the physics experts. The animations can be viewed on our YouTube channel (https://www.youtube.com/channel/UCJpWi45D51ITxaj_NaClqJQ).

- ***Interactive definitions.*** Given findings from the first usability study about the physics facts support, we turned this static element into an interactive, drag-and-drop quiz. Clicking on the definition option opens a window showing an incomplete definition with five blanks to fill, five phrases to use, and relevant animation of the term or concept. Students watch the animation and drag each of the five phrases to the correct blanks within the definition. If the dragged phrase is not correct, it snaps back to its original place. When the blanks are correctly filled, a congratulation message pops up and displays the complete definition.

- ***Formulas.*** In collaboration with the physics experts, we created annotated mathematical formulas for the physics terms. Clicking on the formula option reveals the formula, along with a short explanation of each component or variable.

- ***Hewitt videos.*** This is the same support used in the first version discussed earlier.

- ***Glossary.*** The glossary provides brief explanations of 28 physics terms. The terms have been selected, edited, and revised by the physics experts.

The second usability study focused on testing the effectiveness of the updated learning supports and the overall learning gains from gameplay and supports. Forty-four eighth-grade science students (23 males and 21 females) participated in a 4-day quasi-experimental study. Half of the participants were selected to play the with-support version of the game, while the others played the no-support version of the game. Students were provided with 60 levels in total (i.e., 30 sketching levels and 30 manipulation levels targeting nine physics concepts). Their conceptual physics understanding was measured by two parallel 18-item far transfer physics tests. Participants' experiences and attitudes were also collected through a poststudy survey.

Although previous empirical studies have shown playing *PP* improves students' conceptual physics understanding (Shute, Ventura, & Kim, 2013), this specific usability study failed to detect any learning gains ($t(43) = .96$, $p = .37$, $d = 0.14$). In addition, the group playing without supports had higher posttest scores when holding pretest scores constant ($F(1,43) = 4.06$, $p = 0.05$, $d = 0.61$). Potential reasons for the results are that the gameplay time was insufficient, the incentives for support usage were not implemented, and the supports were not all effective. In spite of a 4-day study, the actual gameplay time was less than 2 hours due to technical and logistical issues. Again, students favored worked examples. Viewing solutions might have helped students solve the game levels but not assisted the development of physics understanding. Adding an incentive system for learning support usage will help to limit the abuse of worked examples and direct more attention to the other supports that are intended to enhance physics understanding. Finally, the usability of certain in-game supports is not fully aligned with the gameplay flow. For example, tutorial levels were too long to be processed and internalized. Players had to replay the tutorial levels, which broke their flow of gameplay.

The implications of the second usability study led to further revisions of the learning supports. In the third version of the learning supports, when students click on the help button, the pop-up window shows three options: "Show me the Physics," "Show me a Solution or a Hint," and "Show me Game Tips." The three options still provide two different kinds of supports: learning and gameplay. "Show me the Physics" stayed the same and contains animations, interactive definitions, formulas, Hewitt videos, and a glossary to aid in students' development of conceptual physics. "Show me a Solution or a Hint" and "Show me Game Tips" are revised or new additions with a focus on game actions, solution modeling, and level-specific advice. Within these options students can access tutorial and game mechanic reminders and learn about "My Backpack," which depicts their gameplay progress and allows them to customize the game environment.

We purposefully designed an incentive system for *PPv2* to motivate usage of the physics supports. Now, clicking on "Show me a Solution or a Hint" activates a pop-up window with two buttons: "Show me a hint $0" and "Show me a solution $60." If a student selects the former, a hint message pops up. Again, hints are free, partially worked examples. Research shows that a partially worked example or level-specific hint can facilitate learning (ter Vrugte, de Jong, Vandercruysse, Wouters, & van Oostendorp, 2017). Also, based on feedback from the previous two usability studies, we designed hints to help those who are struggling but are reluctant to watch full solutions. For instance, if a sketching level can only be solved by a springboard, the level-specific hint may be "Try drawing a springboard." The worked examples did not change. If a student elects to view a worked example, he or she will watch one of our video-recorded expert solutions after paying $60 as a disincentive. If students do not have enough money, a message pops up telling them they have insufficient funds to access the solution and need to collect some gold or silver coins by completing more game levels and come back again.

Finally, "Show me Game Tips" is where students can review game mechanics, a visualized game tutorial, and learn about "My Backpack." Clicking on the button leads to a page containing several navigation tabs. "Controls," "Simple Machines," and "My Backpack" tabs appear in sketching levels, and "Tools" and "My Backpack" appear in manipulation levels.

- ***Controls.*** When a student clicks this tab, a scrollable page appears showing game mechanics (e.g., nudge, draw an object, and delete an object) for sketching levels. The page shows the rules and explanations along with associated static images.

- ***Simple Machines.*** When a student clicks this tab, images of the four simple machines (lever, pendulum, ramp, and springboard) show up. This helps students remember how the agents work without having to go through the full tutorials again.

- ***Tools.*** Clicking on this tab provides a review of the rules for the sliders in manipulation tasks and a short explanation about other tools available (puffers and blowers). For example, students see the images of mass sliders and the bounciness function on the left-hand side of the page, and the corresponding text on the right-hand side (e.g., "Mass and bounciness only affect the ball").

- ***My Backpack.*** This tab appears in both sketching and manipulation levels. See Figure 12.5. On the left the physics tab is open. Here students can see their progress in the game as well as estimates of their current level of physics understanding (soon to be linked with the real-time stealth assessment). On the right, the store tab is open. Here, they can change the type of the ball, background music, and background image. This is an additional component of the incentive system, as the customizations must be purchased by the students.

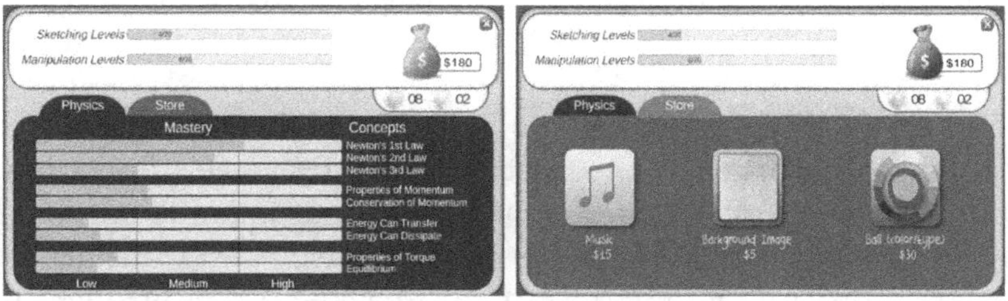

FIGURE 12.5. My Backpack views—Physics estimates and Store

Another major revision coming out of the usability study using *PPv2.2* was the redesign of the game tutorials as sandbox game levels. In the first two usability studies, the tutorials were interactive videos. Students watched how to do something and then got the opportunity to try it. Observational data revealed that students were not retaining the information in the tutorial videos, and students reported the tutorials were too long. Therefore, the tutorials in *PPv2.2* were changed to interactive levels with on-screen instructions and were used in *PPv2.3*—explained next. Sketching tutorial levels show how to draw simple machines. Manipulation tutorial levels show how to use the puffer or blower (that can exert a one-time and small force or a constant force, respectively), sliders (i.e., that control the values of mass, gravity, and air resistance), and the bounciness function. Students can either access them from the playgrounds or view static images of the tutorial levels in the "Show me Game Tips" button.

A final revision coming from the usability studies was the decision to develop a new type of learning support. The new support better integrates the support for learning and gameplay. We reviewed all the game levels, both sketching and manipulation, focusing on how the level was solved and the competencies with which it was linked. For each intersection of solution agent and competency, a video has been (or is being) developed. The videos illustrate the physics concepts through a worked example of the solution agent's tutorial level (e.g., ramp, lever, pendulum). Narration and on-screen text with video pauses provide an overlay of the physics involved in the solution. These physics-related videos follow the same structure: (1) introduce the concept that will be presented in the video (e.g., "Here you are going to see how energy is transferred to a ball using a pendulum"), (2) state the concept (e.g., "gravitational potential energy is the energy of height . . ."), (3) demonstrate a failed attempt to solve a level in the *PP* environment (e.g., the pendulum does not have enough angular height), and then (4) show a successful attempt to solve that level.

Usability Study 3—*PPv2.3*

The third usability study was conducted to investigate the effectiveness of the *new learning supports* (seven animations explaining the underlying physics concepts with text overlays and narration) when combined with gameplay—using *PPv2.3*. For the study, we chose two of the nine competencies with less overlap in our competency model: energy can transfer (ECT) and properties of torque (POT). Then, we selected a mixture of 30 sketching levels ranging from easy to hard with POT or ECT as their primary underlying physics concept. We also included the new set of sketching tutorial levels. So, in total, students had 35 levels to complete.

Our sample included 14 students (6 seventh graders, 8 eighth graders; 6 females, 8 males) from a small charter school in Florida. The study took place on one day for 2 hours. In the first 20 minutes, students completed a demographic questionnaire and pretest. Then, all the students played the game for 75 minutes in two stages: (1) the first 20 minutes: getting familiar with the game through the tutorials and freely accessing all the learning supports, and (2) the next 45 minutes: playing the game and accessing only the "physics supports" (in this stage the researchers prompted the students to access the "physics supports" after playing three levels or approximately every 8 minutes). At the end of the gameplay, students completed the posttest and the game and learning support satisfaction questionnaires (all the tests were administered online using Qualtrics).

Despite the limitations of this usability study (small sample size and short gameplay time), we obtained some useful findings that can help us improve the game for future studies. Examining pretest and posttest scores, students scored significantly higher on the posttest compared to the pretest ($M_{pre} = 0.57$, $M_{post} = 0.63$, $t\ (13) = -2.20$, $p < 0.05$, Cohen's $d = 0.60$). Also, the analysis of students' overall game and learning supports satisfaction (ranging from 1—Strongly Disagree, to 5—Strongly Agree) showed that students enjoyed playing the game ($M = 4.24$, $SD = 0.62$), and they saw the learning supports as useful and easy to use

($M = 3.99$, $SD = 0.51$). Moreover, males and females equally enjoyed the game and the supports. These findings suggest that we are on the right path, and we will continue to improve the game for the future studies. The reflection on students' learning experience also prepares us for the next phase of the project—implementing an adaptive algorithm into the game.

MEASUREMENT OF COMPETENCIES IN PHYSICS PLAYGROUND

To make real-time estimates of students' competency states, our evidence model has two processes: (a) evidence identification (EI)—the scoring of student actions, called "observables," recorded in the log file, and (b) evidence accumulation (EA)—i.e., making inferences about competency states given the observables. The EA process for *PPv2* is implemented using Bayesian networks based on an evidence-centered assessment design framework (Almond, Mislevy, Steinberg, Yan, & Williamson, 2015). At the hub is a central Bayesian network representing the competency model, and the spokes are evidence models—Bayesian network fragments associated with each game level. As the player interacts with the game, the game engine logs key events to an event database.

The scoring engine works as follows: (1) Each user is given a student model—an individual copy of the competency model—in which information about that student is stored. (2) When information comes from the game engine that a student has completed a particular level, the evidence identification (EI) engine is run to extract the key observable features from that student's performance according to the specifications in the evidence model. (3) The evidence accumulation (EA) engine attaches Bayesian network fragments for the evidence model to the student model and updates the competency estimates for that student.

If *PPv2* is being run in an adaptive mode, the activity selection process runs on top of the EA code. The adaptive algorithm consists of an outer loop and an inner loop. The outer loop follows the critiquing strategy (Barr & Feigenbaum, 1982) where a series of target competencies are chosen in sequence. In each case, tasks and activities related to the target competency are presented to the student until the probability of mastery exceeds either a high or low threshold. If students pass the high threshold, they are passed on to the next competency in sequence. If they fall below the low threshold, they are routed to remedial activities. In the inner loop, the expected weight of evidence (EWOE; Madigan & Almond, 1996) algorithm is used to select the task that provides the highest EWOE for the currently targeted proficiency. Shute, Hansen and Almond (2008) speculate that tasks with high EWOE are in the center of the zone of proximal development (Vygotsky, 1978) of the student.

Because the Bayesian network scoring model is closely tied to the evidence-centered design (ECD) models, it is necessary to be able to quickly update the Bayesian networks when the ECD models change, and vice versa. The R package Peanut (Almond, 2018) automates this translation process, providing both network and tabular views of the assessment. It also uses the DiBello parameterization for the Bayesian networks, allowing cognitive scientists to specify relationships in terms of difficulties and discriminations instead of conditional probabilities. The probabilities used in the network are initially specified by experts and then revised as data become available to calibrate the network (Kim, Almond, & Shute, 2016).

The use of learning supports could be treated as additional game levels, with their own evidence models. Accessing a learning support would provide a small amount of positive evidence that the player has mastered the associated competency. We do not think that the availability of the learning supports will influence the measurement. That is, Shute, Hansen, and Almond (2008) found that (a) students assigned to an elaborated feedback condition showed significantly greater learning gains than students who received accuracy-only feedback, and (b) those students in the elaborated feedback condition showed a higher (although not significantly so) correlation with posttest scores than the accuracy-only feedback condition. Evidence models for learning supports have not yet been implemented but are a possibility for future versions.

DISCUSSION

In this chapter we described the general effectiveness of educational games with embedded learning supports, discussed various types of learning supports identified in the literature, and illustrated how we designed, developed, and have begun testing different learning supports in our educational game—*PP*. After conducting the first two usability studies, we found that students were not adequately motivated to access the more helpful learning supports (i.e., physics-related supports) given the absence of an appropriate in-game reward system. Therefore, we revised the game and supports to (a) further clarify and enhance the appearance and interactivity of the learning supports, (b) provide easier, more direct access to the supports, and (c) set up a compelling and functional reward system.

Moving forward, there are a number of potential avenues for research in this area, such as determining the degree to which a reward system actually influences students' play experience and motivation to access learning supports in the game. Toward that end, we are optimizing the learning supports and the game reward system. As the third usability study demonstrated, students had positive opinions of the new learning supports and showed significant learning gains in an abbreviated gameplay experience. We will continue developing the new support videos, following these results.

We are also developing affective supports to complement the cognitive supports that we have developed (not focused on in this chapter). Moreover, we have created a new "near transfer" physics test (where items have the look and feel of the game) to accompany our current "far transfer" test (where items are more formal and inspired by the Force Concept Inventory; Hestenes, Wells, & Swackhamer, 1992) to see the degree to which intuitive physics conceptualizations vs. formalizations are acquired from gameplay. Finally, we are using stealth assessment technology with an in-game adaptive algorithm to select the best next level for a person—one that is not too difficult nor too easy and related to the targeted physics concept.

This sampler of ongoing research will help us and other researchers in the field figure out ways to optimize the design and delivery of learning supports that may be unobtrusively incorporated into games. The process should be iterative and provide research-backed evidence on: (1) the effects of different types of cognitive and affective supports that promote formal learning and enjoyment in educational games; (2) the timing and control of such supports (e.g., when should they be available, and who—computer or player—controls the delivery; and (3) the factors that mediate the influence of supports on learning and gameplay.

On a broader note, this ongoing research involves developing and testing a specific methodology for crafting valid game-based assessments and dynamically linking those assessments to various learning supports. This methodology will contribute to the design of next-generation learning games that successfully blur the distinction between assessment and learning. There are four major contributions to the fields of learning science from this research: (a) cumulative evidence of the instructional effectiveness of an educational game designed using principles of instructional, game, and assessment design; (b) advancement of understanding of the influences of different kinds of learning supports (e.g., visualizations and explanations) and adaptivity to game-based learning; (c) informing the design of next-generation learning games that successfully blur the distinction between assessment and learning; and (d) generation of research findings that can be immediately incorporated into other types of STEM learning games and linked with the Common Core Standards and Next Generation Science Standards.

REFERENCES

Adams, D. M., Mayer, R. E., MacNamara, A., Koenig, A., & Wainess, R. (2012). Narrative games for learning: Testing the discovery and narrative hypotheses. *Journal of Educational Psychology, 104*(1), 235.

Almond, R. G. (2018). *Peanut* [R Package]. Retrieved from https://pluto.coe.fsu.edu/RNetica/Peanut.html

Almond, R. G., Mislevy, R. J., Steinberg, L. S., Yan, D., & Williamson, D. M. (2015). *Bayesian networks in educational assessment*. New York, NY: Springer-Verlag.

Almond, R. G., Tingir, S., Lu, X., Sun, C., & Rahimi, S. (presented 2017, August). A validation tool for conditional probability tables (CPT) for Physics Playground. In J-M. Agosta & T. Singlair (Chair), *Bayesian Modeling Application Workshop 2017*. Symposium conducted at the meeting of Association for Uncertainty in Artificial Intelligence, Sydney, Australia. (International). Retrieved from http://bmaw2017.azurewebsites.net/

Barab, S. A., Thomas, M., Dodge, T., Carteaux, R., & Tuzun, H. (2005). Making learning fun: Quest Atlantis, a game without guns. *Educational Technology Research and Development, 53*(1), 86–108.

Barr, A., & Feigenbaum, E. (1982). *The handbook of artificial intelligence* (Vol. II). London: Pittman Books Ltd.

Barzilai, S., & Blau, I. (2014). Scaffolding game-based learning: Impact on learning achievements, perceived learning, and game experiences. *Computers & Education, 70*, 65–79.

Bransford, J., Brown, A., & Cocking, R. (2000). *How people learn: Brain, mind, and experience & school*. Washington, DC: National Academies Press.

Cameron, B., & Dwyer, F. (2005). The effect of online gaming, cognition and feedback type in facilitating delayed achievement of different learning objectives. *Journal of Interactive Learning Research, 16*(3), 243–258.

Chory, R. M., & Goodboy, A. K. (2011). Is basic personality related to violent and non-violent video game play and preferences? *Cyberpsychology, Behavior, and Social Networking, 14*(4), 191–198.

Clark, D. B., Nelson, B., Chang, H., D'Angelo, C. M., Slack, K., & Martinez-Garza, M. (2011). Exploring Newtonian mechanics in a conceptually-integrated digital game: Comparison of learning and affective outcomes for students in Taiwan and the United States. *Computers and Education, 57*(3), 2178–2195.

Clark, D. B., Tanner-Smith, E. E., & Killingsworth, S. S. (2015). Digital games, design, and learning A systematic review and meta-Analysis. *Review of Educational Research*. doi:10.3102/0034654315582065

Coller, B. D., & Scott, M. J. (2009). Effectiveness of using a video game to teach a course in mechanical engineering. *Computers and Education, 53*(3), 900–912. http://dx.doi.org/10.1016/j.compedu.2009.05.012

Csikszentmihalyi, M. (1990). *Flow: The psychology of optimal experience.* New York: Harper & Row.

DeRouin-Jessen, R. (2008). *Game on: The impact of game features in computer-based training* [Unpublished doctoral dissertation]. University of Central Florida, Orlando.

Desurvire, H., Caplan, M., & Toth, J. A. (2004). Using heuristics to evaluate the playability of games. In *Extended Abstracts of the 2004 Conference on Human Factors in Computing Systems* (pp. 1509–1512). New York: ACM Press.

diSessa, A. A. (1982). Unlearning Aristotelian physics: A study of knowledge-based learning. *Cognitive Science, 6*, 37–75.

Dweck, C. (2006). *Mindset: The new psychology of success.* New York: Random House.

Ericsson, K. A., Krampe, R. T., & Tesch-Römer, C. (1993). The role of deliberate practice in the acquisition of expert performance. *Psychological Review, 100*(3), 363–406.

Ferguson, C. J., & Garza, A. (2011). Call of (civic) duty: Action games and civic behavior in a large sample of youth. *Computers in Human Behavior, 27*, 770–775.

Fullerton, T., Swain, C., & Hoffman, S. (2008). *Game design workshop: A playcentric approach to creating innovative games* (2nd ed.). Burlington, MA: Morgan Kaufmann.

Gee, J. P. (2003). *What digital games have to teach us about learning and literacy.* New York: Palgrave Macmillan.

Ginns, P. (2005). Meta-analysis of the modality effect. *Learning and instruction, 15*(4), 313–331.

Green, C. S., & Bavelier, D. (2007). Action-video-game experience alters the spatial resolution of vision. *Psychological Science, 18*(1), 88–94.

Green, C. S., & Bavelier, D. (2012). Learning, attentional control, and action video games. *Current Biology, 22*(6), 197–206.

Hake, R. R. (1998). Interactive-engagement versus traditional methods: A six-thousand-student survey of mechanics test data for introductory physics courses. *American Journal of Physics, 66*(1), 64–74.

Halloun, I. (1996). Views about science and physics achievement. The VASS story. In E. F. Rediss & J. S. Rigden (Eds.), *Proceedings of the International Conference on Undergraduate Physics Education (1996)* (pp. 605–613). Washington, DC: American Institute of Physics.

Hanushek, E. A., Peterson, P. E., & Woessmann, L. (2012). Achievement growth: International and U.S. state trends in student performance (PEPG Report No.12-03). Cambridge, MA: Harvard's Program on Education Policy and Governance & Education Next. Retrieved from http://www.hks.harvard.edu/pepg/PDF/Papers/PEPG12-03_CatchingUp.pdf

Hatano, G. (1982). Cognitive consequences of practice in culture specific procedural skills. *The Quarterly Newsletter of the Laboratory of Comparative Human Cognition, 4*, 15–18.

Hestenes, D., Wells, M., & Swackhamer, G. (1992). Force Concept Inventory. *Physics Teacher, 30*, 141–158.

Hewitt, P. G. (2009). *Conceptual physics* (11th ed.). San Francisco, CA: Pearson Education.

Hogle, J. G. (1996). *Considering games as cognitive tools: In search of effective "edutainment."* University of Georgia Department of Instructional Technology (ERIC Document ED 425 737).

Jackson, L. A., Witt, E. A., Games, A. I., Fitzgerald, H. E., von Eye, A., & Zhao, Y. (2012). Information technology use and creativity: Findings from the children and technology project. *Computers in Human Behavior, 28*, 370–376.

Johnson, C., Bailey, S., & Van Buskirk, W. (2017). Designing effective feedback messages in serious games and simulations: A research review. In P. Wouters & H. van Oostendorp (Eds.), *Instructional techniques to facilitate learning and motivation of serious games* (pp.119–140). New York, NY: Springer.

Johnson, C. I., & Mayer, R. E. (2010). Applying the self-explanation principle to multimedia learning in a computer-based game-like environment. *Computers in Human Behavior, 26*(6), 1246–1252.

Ke, F. (2016). Designing and integrating purposeful learning in game play: A systematic review. *Educational Technology Research and Development, 64*(2), 219–244.

Ke, F. F., & Shute, V. J. (2015). Design of game-based stealth assessment and learning support. In C. Loh, Y. Sheng, & D. Ifenthaler (Eds.), *Serious games analytics* (pp. 301–318). New York, NY: Springer.

Kim, Y. J., Almond, R. G., & Shute, V. J. (2016). Applying evidence-centered design for the development of game-based assessments in Physics Playground. *International Journal of Testing, 16*(2), 142–163.

Kinzie, M. B., & Joseph, D. R. (2008). Gender differences in game activity preferences of middle school children: Implications for educational game design. *Educational Technology Research and Development, 56*(5–6), 643–663.

Klopfer, E., Osterweil, S., & Salen, K. (2009). *Moving learning games forward: Obstacles, opportunities and openness.* Cambridge, MA: The Education Arcade.

Lang, J., & O'Neil, H. (2008). *The effect of presenting just-in-time worked examples for problem solving in a computer game.* Paper presented at the American Educational Research Association, New York.

Leemkuil, H. H. (2006). *Is it all in the game? Learner support in an educational knowledge management simulation game* [Unpublished doctoral dissertation]. Universiteit Twente, The Netherlands.

Leutner, D. (1993). Guided discovery learning with computer-based simulation games: Effects of adaptive and non-adaptive instructional support. *Learning and Instruction, 3*(2), 113–132.

Madigan, D., & Almond, R. G. (1996). On test selection strategies for belief networks. In D. Fisher & H.-J. Lenz (Eds.) *Learning from data: AI and statistics IV* (pp. 89–98). New York: Springer-Verlag.

Martinez-Garza, M., Clark, D. B., Nelson, B., Slack, K., & D'Angelo, C. (2013). Advances in assessment of students' intuitive understanding of physics through gameplay data. *International Journal of Gaming and Computer-Mediated Simulations, 5*(4), 1–16.

Masson, M. E. J., Bub, D. N., & Lalonde, C. E. (2011). Video-game training and naïve reasoning about object motion. *Applied Cognitive Psychology, 25*, 166–173.

Mislevy, R. J., Steinberg, L. S., & Almond, R. G. (2003). On the structure of educational assessments. *Measurement: Interdisciplinary Research and Perspectives, 1*(1), 3–62.

Moreno, R., & Mayer, R. E. (2002). Learning science in virtual reality multimedia environments: Role of methods and media. *Journal of Educational Psychology, 94*(3), 598.

Moreno, R., & Mayer, R. E. (2005). Role of guidance, reflection, and interactivity in an agent-based multimedia game. *Journal of Educational Psychology, 97*(1), 117.

NGSS Lead States (2013). *Next generation science standards: For states, by states.* Washington, DC: The National Academies Press.

National Research Council (NRC). (2011). Learning science through computer games and simulations. Washington, DC: National Academies Press.

Newell, A., & Rosenbloom, P. S. (1981). Mechanism of skill acquisition and the law of practice. In J. R, Anderson (Ed.), *Cognitive skills and their acquisition* (pp. 1–51). Hillsdale, NJ: Lawrence Erlbaum Associates, Inc.

Pellegrini, A. D. (1995). *The future of play theory: A multidisciplinary inquiry into the contributions of Brian Sutton-Smith.* Albany, NY: State University of New York Press.

Ploetzner, R., & VanLehn, K. (1997). The acquisition of informal physics knowledge during formal physics training. *Cognition and Instruction, 15*(2), 169–206.

Prensky, M. (2001). Digital natives, digital immigrants part 1. *On the Horizon*, *9*(5), 1–6.
President's Council of Advisors on Science and Technology. (2012). *Engage to excel: Producing one million additional college graduates with degrees in science, technology, engineering, and mathematics.* Retrieved from http://www.whitehouse.gov/sites/default/files/microsites/ostp/pcast- executive-report-final_2-13-12.pdf
Programme for International Student Assessment (PISA). (2012). Retrieved from: https://nces.ed.gov/surveys/pisa/pisa2012/pisa2012highlights_2e.asp
Reiner, C., Proffit, D. R., & Salthouse, T. (2005). A psychometric approach to intuitive physics. *Psychonomic Bulletin and Review*, *12*, 740–745.
Rieber, L. P. (1996). Seriously considering play: Designing interactive learning environments based on the blending of microworlds, simulations, and games. *Educational Technology Research and Development*, *44*(1), 43–58.
Ritterfeld, U., Shen, C., Wang, H., Nocera, L., & Wong, W. L. (2009). Multimodality and interactivity: Connecting properties of serious games with educational outcomes. *Cyberpsychology & Behavior*, *12*(6), 691–697.
Schneider, W., & Shiffrin, R. M. (1977). Controlled and automatic human information processing: Detection, search, and attention. *Psychological Review*, *84*(1), 1–66.
Shebilske, W. L., Goettl, B. P., Corrington, K., & Day, E. A. (1999). Interlesson spacing and task-related processing during complex skill acquisition. *Journal of Experimental Psychology: Applied*, *5*(4), 413.
Shute, V. J. (2008). Focus on formative feedback. *Review of Educational Research*, *78*(1), 153–189.
Shute, V. J. (2011). Stealth assessment in computer-based games to support learning. In S. Tobias & J. D. Fletcher (Eds.), *Computer games and instruction* (pp. 503–524). Charlotte, NC: Information Age Publishers.
Shute, V. J., D'Mello, S. K., Baker, R., Bosch, N., Ocumpaugh, J., Ventura, M., & Almeda, V. (2015). Modeling how incoming knowledge, persistence, affective states, and in-game progress influence student learning from an educational game. *Computers & Education, 86*, 224–235.
Shute, V. J., Hansen, E. G., & Almond, R. G. (2008). You can't fatten a hog by weighing it—Or can you? Evaluating an assessment for learning system called ACED. *International Journal of Artificial Intelligence and Education*, *18*(4), 289–316.
Shute, V. J., & Ke, F. (2012). Games, learning, and assessment. In D. Ifenthaler, D. Eseryel, & S. Ge (Eds.), *Assessment in game-based learning: Foundations, innovations, and perspectives* (pp. 43–58). New York: Springer.
Shute, V. J., Rieber, L., & Van Eck, R. (2011). Games . . . and . . . learning. In R. Reiser & J. Dempsey (Eds.), *Trends and issues in instructional design and technology* (3rd ed.) (pp. 321–332). Upper Saddle River, NJ: Pearson Education.
Shute, V. J., & Ventura, M. (2013). *Measuring and supporting learning in games: Stealth assessment.* Cambridge, MA: The MIT Press.
Shute, V. J., Ventura, M., Bauer, M. I., & Zapata-Rivera, D. (2009). Melding the power of serious games and embedded assessment to monitor and foster learning: Flow and grow. In U. Ritterfeld, M. Cody, & P. Vorderer (Eds.), *Serious games: Mechanisms and effects* (pp. 295–321). Mahwah, NJ: Routledge, Taylor and Francis.
Shute, V. J., Ventura, M., & Ke, F. (2015). The power of play: The effects of Portal 2 and Lumosity on cognitive and noncognitive skills. *Computers & Education, 80*, 58–67.
Shute, V. J., Ventura, M., & Kim, Y. J. (2013). Assessment and learning of qualitative physics in Newton's Playground. *The Journal of Educational Research*, *106*, 423–430.
Skoric, M. M., Teo, L. L. C., & Neo, R. L. (2009). Children and video games: addiction, engagement, and scholastic achievement. *CyberPsychology & Behavior*, *12*(5), 567–572.

Squire, K. (2006). From content to context: Videogames as designed experience. *Educational Researcher, 35*(8), 19–29.
Steiner, C. M., Kickmeier-Rust, M. D., & Albert, D. (2009). Little big difference: Gender aspects and gender-based adaptation in educational games. *Proceedings of the 4th International Conference on E-Learning and Games* (EDUTAINMENT 2009), August 9–11, 2009, Banff, Canada. *Lecture Notes in Computer Science, 5670*, 150–161. Berlin: Springer.
Swann, W. F. G. (1950). The teaching of physics. *American Journal of Physics, 19*(2), 182–187.
ter Vrugte, J., de Jong, T., Vandercruysse, S., Wouters, P., & van Oostendorp, H. (2017). Computer game-based mathematics education: Embedded faded worked examples facilitate knowledge acquisition. *Learning and instruction, 50*, 44–53.
Thorndike, E. L. (1898). Animal intelligence: An experimental study of the associative processes in animals. *Psychological Monographs: General and Applied, 2*(4), 1–109.
Tobias, S., & Fletcher, J. D. (Eds.). (2011). *Computer games and instruction.* Charlotte, NC: Information Age Publishers.
Trends in International Mathematics and Science Study (TIMSS). (2011). Retrieved from: https://timssandpirls.bc.edu/timss2011/frameworks.html
US Department of Education (USDOE). (2015). Science, technology, engineering and math: Education for global leadership. Retrieved from http://www.ed.gov/stem
van der Meij, H., Albers, E., & Leemkuil, H. (2011). Learning from games: does collaboration help? *British Journal of Educational Technology, 42*(4), 655–664.
Ventura, M., Shute, V. J., & Kim, Y. J. (2012). Video gameplay, personality and academic performance. *Computers & Education, 58*, 1260–1266.
Ventura, M., Shute, V., & Zhao, W. (2012). The relationship between video game use and a performance-based measure of persistence. *Computers & Education, 60*, 52–58.
Vygotsky, L. (1978). *Mind in society: The development of higher psychological process.* Cambridge, MA: Harvard University Press.
Vygotsky, L. S. (1987). *The collected works of L. S. Vygotsky.* New York: Plenum.
White, B. Y. (1994). Designing computer games to help physics students understand Newton's laws of motion. *Cognition and Instruction, 1*(1), 69–108.
Wilson, K. A., Bedwell, W., Lazzara, E. H., Salas, E., Burke, C. S., Estock, Orvis, K. L., Conkey, C. (2009). Relationships between game attributes and learning outcomes: Review and research proposals. *Simulation and Gaming, 40*(2), 217–266.
Witt, E. A., Massman, A. J., & Jackson, L. A. (2011). Trends in youth's videogame playing, overall computer use, and communication technology use: The impact of self-esteem and the big five personality factors. *Computers in Human Behavior, 27*(2), 763–769.
Wouters, P., & van Oostendorp, H. (2013). A meta-analytic review of the role of instructional support in game-based learning. *Computers & Education, 60*(1), 412–425.
Wouters, P., van Nimwegen, C., van Oostendorp, H., & van Der Spek, E. D. (2013). A meta-analysis of the cognitive and motivational effects of serious games. *Journal of Educational Psychology, 105*(2), 249.
Young, M. F., Slota, S., Cutter, A. B., Jalette, G., Mullin, G., Lai, B., Simeoni, Z., Tran, M., & Yukhymenko, M. (2012). Our princess is in another castle: A review of trends in serious gaming for education. *Review of Educational Research, 82*(61), 61–89. doi:10.3102/0034654312436980

ABOUT THE AUTHORS

Valerie Shute is the Campbell Tyner Endowed Professor in Education at Florida State University. Her general research relates to the design, development, and evaluation of advanced systems to support learning, and current research involves using games with stealth assessment to support learning of cognitive and noncognitive knowledge, skills, and dispositions.

Fengfeng Ke is a professor in the Department of Educational Psychology and Learning Systems at Florida State University. Her current research focuses on digital game-based learning, inclusive design of computer supported collaborative learning, mixed-reality integrated immersive learning, and adaptive e-learning.

Russell Almond is an associate professor in the Department of Educational Psychology and Learning Systems at Florida State University. He received his undergraduate degree from the California Institute of Technology and received his PhD in statistics from Harvard University.

Seyedahmad Rahimi is a doctoral candidate at Florida State University in the Instructional Systems and Learning Technologies program at Florida State University. His general research interests include game-based stealth assessment and enhancement of 21st-century competencies (e.g., creativity and problem-solving skills).

Ginny Smith is a doctoral candidate, research assistant, and instructor in the Instructional Systems and Learning Technologies program at Florida State University. Her research interests center around the design, development, and evaluation of learning games and interactive learning experiences in secondary and higher education.

Xi Lu is a doctoral candidate in the Instructional Systems and Learning Technologies program at Florida State University. Her current research interest focuses on designing and developing optimal learning supports to facilitate STEM learning in digital interactive environments.

ACKNOWLEDGMENTS

We wish to express our gratitude for the funding by the US National Science Foundation (NSF #037988) and the US Department of Education (IES #039019) for generously supporting this research.

INDEX

Page numbers followed by *f* and *t* refer to figures and tables, respectively.

CPSIA information can be obtained
at www.ICGtesting.com
Printed in the USA
LVHW081629011121
702129LV00002B/45

9 781260 457995